U0685155

国际视角下的理财规划

Financial Planning
– An International Perspective

【美】约翰·格拉布尔（John E. Grable）
姚　　睿（Rui Yao）
雷　　闪（Shan Lei）　　　　著

中国金融出版社

责任编辑：董　飞
责任校对：李俊英
责任印制：丁淮宾

图书在版编目（CIP）数据

国际视角下的理财规划（Guoji Shijiao Xia de Licai Guihua）/［美］约翰·格拉布尔（John E. Grable），姚睿，雷闪著．—北京：中国金融出版社，2017.6
ISBN 978－7－5049－8997－0

Ⅰ．①国…　Ⅱ．①约…②姚…③雷…　Ⅲ．①投资—基本知识　Ⅳ．①F830.59

中国版本图书馆 CIP 数据核字（2017）第 095328 号

出版发行　中国金融出版社
社址　北京市丰台区益泽路 2 号
市场开发部　(010)63266347，63805472，63439533（传真）
网上书店　http://www.chinafph.com
(010)63286832，63365686（传真）
读者服务部　(010)66070833，62568380
邮编　100071
经销　新华书店
印刷　北京市松源印刷有限公司
尺寸　185 毫米×260 毫米
印张　24.75
字数　450 千
版次　2017 年 6 月第 1 版
印次　2017 年 6 月第 1 次印刷
定价　70.00 元
ISBN 978－7－5049－8997－0

前　　言

在过去的 20 年，理财规划行业呈现了蓬勃发展的景象。以美国为例，大型理财规划公司年收益额达到将近 600 亿美元。如果算上一些区域性和小型的理财规划公司，全美金融理财师每年共创造将近1 000亿美元的收益。当这些关于美国理财行业的统计数据给我们带来小小震撼的同时，我们希望大家意识到整个世界的理财规划行业正在崛起。以中国为例，随着消费者对于理财规划行业需求的不断扩大，每年的新晋理财师正在以两位数的速度增长。

作为一个专业职业，理财规划的独特之处在于其定位于帮助客户解决复杂的理财问题。国际理财规划标准委员会（Financial Planning Standards Board，FPSB）指出理财规划师在为客户提供规划方案和实施计划时，运用以下 6 个步骤对客户的财务状况进行全方位的考量。

1. 确立和界定与客户的关系；
2. 收集客户的相关信息；
3. 分析及评估客户提供的信息；
4. 根据客户的实际情况，为客户制定和演示适合的理财规划；
5. 执行理财规划方案；
6. 持续监督理财规划方案的执行情况。

理财规划师站在全局角度审视客户的财务状况，而非售卖金融产品或提供简单孤立的理财建议。理财规划师在制定理财规划时，往往与客户一起商定如何实现他们人生中的多个理财目标。

整个理财规划过程旨在建立长期的合作关系。这种合作关系是建立在信任、良好沟通以及共同制定目标的基础上的。理财规划师和客户这种良好的合作关系可以帮助客户和理财规划师获得各自的人生及财务成功。

本书希望帮助中国的理财规划师以及今后可能从事理财规划职业的人们更好地了解理财规划行业以及为理财规划执业提供指导。本书介绍的理财规划执业模式在相对成熟的理财规划市场（比如美国）已经经历了验证。但是，我们希望读者们在了解这些理财规划执业模式时，抱有“取其精华，弃其糟粕”的态度，针对中国消费者的特殊需求和文化特点加以吸收和改进，切勿生搬硬套。

本书共包括四个主要章节。第一章介绍了理财规划执业的历史发展。在这一章，读者可以了解到理财规划是如何在北美、欧洲以及亚洲萌芽并发展，世界范围内还有哪些理财规划的契机。

第二章着重介绍了理财规划服务的经营模式。具体介绍了保险业、银行业、证券行业、综合理财规划及独立第三方理财规划的经营模式。此外，本章还介绍了理财规划服务的收费模式。在介绍以费用模式为主的报酬模式时，本书结合了信托责任标准及适用性标准对其进行了深入探讨。同时也简单介绍了与理财规划相关的法律法规。

第三章结合案例重点并详细介绍了理财规划的实务操作，包括理财规划的流程、要点以及理财规划的内容（包括财务管理、风险管理、资产管理、退休规划、税务筹划，以及遗产规划）。本章最后还概述了理财规划方案的实施。

第四章向读者介绍了打造成功理财规划师职业生涯的一些战略。本章开篇介绍了理财规划国际执业标准以及道德标准，紧接着与读者详细探讨了成为优秀理财规划师应有的素质，包括个人性格、沟通能力以及客户关系管理等。

最后的附录主要向读者介绍了理财规划工具的应用，特别是如何应用金融计算器及 Excel 进行理财规划。

作为本书的作者，我们真心希望这本书能够为广大读者的理财规划实践提供些许帮助。理财规划市场正迅速扩张和壮大。这更加需要知识和能力兼备的理财规划师投入到这个事业中去。我们真心希望那些想成为世界一流理财规划师的人们梦想成真，并为帮助消费者提高他们的财务能力贡献力量。

我们希望借此机会向支持本书写作和出版的中国以及美国的广大同仁们致谢。正因为有了他们对本书的意见、建议、批评和鼓励，才有了本书的出版。我们还特别感谢中国金融出版社的编辑们。此外，我们还要对我们的家人在本书的写作过程中给予的支持表示感谢。最后我们真心感谢开创并支持中国理财规划事业发展的元老们。希望本书能为中国理财师事业的发展尽绵薄之力。

John Grable，姚睿，雷闪
2017 年夏

Preface

The development of financial planning as a profession over the past 20 years has been phenomenal. In the United States alone, large financial planning firms generate close to $60 billion dollars in annual revenue. When local and boutique financial planning firms are included, revenues are close to $100 billion annually. While these statistics are impressive, it is even more noteworthy to consider that the real growth in financial planning has been, and will continue to be, outside the United States. The Chinese market for financial planning services is particularly strong. The number of individuals entering the financial planning profession continues to increase at double digit rates as the demand for advice from consumers continues to grow.

Financial planning, as a profession, is uniquely positioned to help consumers navigate the increasingly complex world of finance. The Financial Planning Standards Board defines financial planning as:

A process that consists of six steps that financial planning professionals use to consider all aspects of a client's financial situation when formulating financial planning strategies and making recommendations.

The six – step process is shown in Figure 1.

As the definition implies, financial planners take a comprehensive view of their clients' situation. Rather than focus on the sale of one product or the implementation of a few service recommendations, financial planners engage with their clients to craft plans to meet multiple lifetime financial goals. The process of financial planning tends to be based on long – lasting client – planner relationships that are built on trust, open dialog, and mutually defined objectives. When practiced appropriately, both client and financial planner achieve personal and financial success.

The purpose of this book is to help financial planners working in the Chinese market, and those who are considering a career in the profession, effectively practice the financial planning process. This book summarizes and builds upon models that have been developed in markets

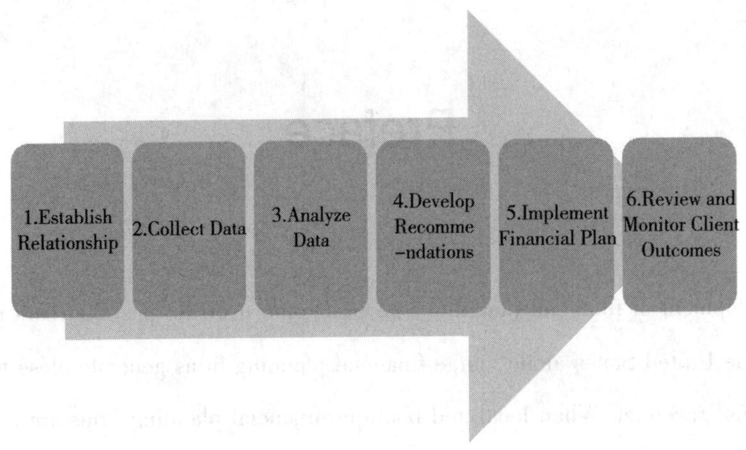

where financial planning has been proven successful. One unique contribution of this book is its focus on presenting this information in the unique context of the Chinese marketplace. Rather than simply reporting what is being done in the United States, and then recommending that Chinese practitioners replicate this approach, this book argues that Chinese financial planners should adopt the best practices from the around the world but only to the extent that these practices match the special needs of Chinese consumers.

This book is divided into four core chapters. The first chapter provides a definitional and historical review of the financial planning profession. You will learn how financial planning emerged during the 1960s in North America, Europe, and Asia and what opportunities exist for financial planners worldwide.

The second chapter focuses on the delivery of financial planning services by reviewing the most common planning models and approaches. Special attention is devoted to insurance, banking, investment, comprehensive, and independent service platforms. The chapter also introduces the multiple ways in which financial planners are most often paid. Fee structures are framed within a discussion of fiduciary and suitability standards. A review of compliance and regulatory issues is also presented.

The third chapter provides a comprehensive overview of financial planning practice with a case illustration. The process of financial planning is discussed in detail. This is followed by a review of the elements of the financial planning process. The core content of this chapter involves a detailed discussion about financial planning components, including cash flow and net worth planning, risk management, asset management, retirement planning, tax planning, and estate planning. The chapter concludes with an overview of the intricacies involved with implementing and monitoring financial planning recommendations.

The fourth chapter describes strategies that can be used to build a successful financial planning practice. The discussion begins by reviewing international standards of practice, as well as common ethical considerations. A special emphasis of the chapter involves a summary of the personal characteristics, institutional support, communication skills, and relationship management attributes that are necessary to achieve long – term success as a financial planning professional.

The tools and techniques that can be used in the development of financial planning recommendations are presented in the appendix.

As authors, it is our sincere hope that this book provides useful insights and innovative approaches to help readers elevate their practice of financial planning. The market for financial planning services continues to expand at a remarkable rate. More well – educated and competent financial planners are needed to meet this need. Our goal in writing this book is to help those who have a heartfelt desire to become world – class financial planners reach their goals. In the end, this is the best way to ensure that consumer financial well – being is improved and enhanced.

This book would not have come to fruition without the support and guidance of numerous people. We are particularly grateful to our colleagues in China and the United States who provided encouragement, critiques, and suggestions that helped make this book what it is today. We are also very appreciative of our editors at China Financial Publishing House. We also want to thank our families for their support and flexibility during the writing process. Finally, our sincere thanks go out to the pioneers of the financial planning profession in China who have blazed a path for this profession to grow and flourish. Our hope is that this book will help this growth continue into the future.

John Grable

Rui Yao

Shan Lei

目　　录

Table of Contents

第一章　理财规划的含义及历史沿革

本书旨在向不熟悉理财规划这一新兴行业的人们介绍理财规划的理论、流程及发展。基于这个目标，我们首先需要了解理财规划的基本含义。从字面上看，理财规划比较通俗易懂。然而，随着这个行业的发展，学术界、媒体及行业本身对它有了不同的诠释。理财规划对于不同人群也往往有着不同的含义。

在过去40年中，理财规划被赋予了各种解释。如ISO/TC222 2004中对理财规划的解释是：能够帮助客户达到个人理财目标的互动过程。Financial Planning Standards Board（FPSB）将理财规划定义为通过适当的财务策划达到个人生活目标的过程。有些学者在研究理财规划时将个人的自我规划也包含在内（Lusardi 和 Mitchell，2011）。但是目前广为接受的含义为：理财规划是指通过恰当的金融资源的调配，从而帮助个人达到生活目标的过程。这个含义最初是由美国理财规划标准委员会（Certified Financial Planner Board of Standards）提出的，而后成为美国大多数理财规划执业者广为接受并且使用的标准定义。这个定义对于理财规划的理解，区别于其他定义的独特之处在于向客户描述理财服务的具体过程。

- 确立和界定与客户的关系。
- 收集客户的相关信息。
- 分析及评估收集到的客户信息并测算客户的财务状况。
- 根据客户的实际情况，为客户制定和演示适合的理财规划。
- 执行理财规划方案。
- 持续监督理财规划方案的执行情况。

从技术层面上讲，理财规划方案是伴随理财规划过程所产生的结果或者产品。有些理财规划师撰写综合理财规划方案，有些则提供的是目标型，单一或者模块理财规划方案。为了理解两种理财规划方案的区别，我们需要重点了解理财规划师向客户提供的核心理财服务的内容。

在中文翻译上，中国香港财务策划师协会将“financial planning”翻译为“财务策划”，台湾理财顾问认证协会将“financial planning”翻译为“理财规划”。本书参照台湾理财顾问认证协会的翻译，将“financial planning”翻译为“理财规划”。

理财规划的类型

确定理财规划师在向客户提供服务时所涉及的专业领域，这是最好也是最简单地理解综合理财规划含义的方法。一般来讲，理财规划师帮助客户确定及解决以下领域的问题：

- 财务管理，包括现金流及净资产规划，债务管理。
- 资产管理或投资规划。
- 风险管理或保险规划，包括人寿保险、残疾保险、财产险、长期护理险及特殊需求保险。
- 税务规划。
- 退休规划。
- 遗产规划。
- 教育规划。
- 特殊情况时的规划。

从定义上讲，综合理财规划需要包含以上每一领域的部分或者全部内容。然而，单一/模块理财规划方案则只需包含客户感兴趣的某一领域的内容。[①] 比如，一个客户也许只关心退休规划的相关问题，而不关心或者不需要有关遗产规划的内容（如遗嘱分析，信托及遗产税等问题），那么在这种情况下，理财规划师只需向客户提供单一/模块理财规划服务。但是，无论理财规划师向客户提供综合理财规划还是单一/模块理财规划服务，他都将遵循理财规划的六个步骤。据统计，在美国，提供综合理财规划服务的理财规划师占总体理财规划师的比重不到50%，由此看来，市场对于可提供综合理财规划的理财规划师的需求相当大。[②]

---

① Lytton，Grable 及 Klock（2013）是这样定义综合理财规划的：通过对个人理财策略的整合和应用帮助客户达成多个理财规划目标的过程（p. 13）。

② 理财规划学院，2011。

第一节　北美、欧洲及亚洲理财规划发展的历史

理财规划，作为描述协助客户达成财务目标的过程的专业词汇，已经成为现代经济术语的一部分。在了解了理财规划的理论和概念之后，人们更加感兴趣的是理财规划师已经成为当今世界最为年轻的专业职业。①

在美国，可以在一些顶尖的学术机构和大学学习理财规划专业，但是这仍旧是一门较新的学科。目前全世界仅有不到 10 所大学设有理财规划的博士学位。大约超过 100 家大学或学院设有理财规划的本科学位，但我们相信这一学科的未来发展前景是相当乐观的。需要重点指明的是，没有一个理财规划学位是在 20 世纪 80 年代以前设立的。② 为了达到中期和长期目标，美国消费者开始要求更加复杂、综合的产品及服务。伴随着这一现象，对于理财规划培训的需求也随之增加。在此之前，在美国，主要的"理财规划"产品是指寿险及年金产品。

寿险产业对于现代理财规划职业的发展起着至关重要的作用。不同于当代社会，直到 20 世纪 60 年代，寿险是大多数美国家庭的主要的长期储蓄产品，少有家庭投资股票、债券或者期货。人们偏好投资保险产品的原因非常简单。在 20 世纪初，平均寿命大约为 49 岁③。对于大多数的家庭来说，人们考虑最多的不是为退休做储蓄准备，而是在家庭成员死亡的情况下如何保障收入的稳定性。相比其他金融产品，寿险产品是帮助家庭达到收入替代需求的最理想工具。另外，投资寿险产品的成本很低，而投资如股票或者债券则需要相对较多的初始投入。

20 世纪，有一个寿险产品脱颖而出：带有现金价值的终身人寿保险。这类产品有两种用途：首先，它可以在投保人（一般是家庭的主要收入来源提供者）最终死亡时为家庭提供一笔免税的资金，另外它还可以作为一种退休安排。我们在理解终身寿险的第二种用途之前，大家需要明确，在 20 世纪初至 20 世纪 40 年代，美国几乎没有家庭有任何的退休规划。美国社会保障产品在 20 世纪 30 年代建立，然而它所提供的保障微乎其微。终身人寿保险的死亡收益显然为大部分美国家庭提供了重要的资产和

---

① Magali 在 1978 年所著的书中这样描述专业职业：从事的专业活动需要专业训练，执行人隶属某专业团体，遵循公开认可的道德准则，接受正规机构的继续教育。

② 一些博士项目是从其他专业领域，如资源管理或消费者经济学转型而来。

③ 精算协会，2005。

收入来源。

20 世纪，保险行业发展十分迅速。人寿保险与当时的美国制造业、消费品的分销方式完美地结合。寿险的经营模式是基于大众营销，统一承销及规模经济的理念。终身人寿保险产品被视为大众营销产品，并进行了合理定价。市场也充分认可保险行业的财务能力。几乎所有的寿险公司都参与了产品价格和客户服务的竞争。20 世纪 60 年代早期的口号是，“如果你有终身寿险产品，客户就会买”。

金融服务从 20 世纪 60 年代开始发生变化，整个寿险产品市场已经趋于饱和，市场份额增长呈下降趋势。这引发了从生产及产品营销的经营手段到市场定位及产品细分的变革。在早期，每家公司销售的寿险产品的保单都十分类似，而今，公司开始意识到客户的态度、品位及期望是在不断变化的。事实上，整个市场激发一些保险公司、经纪人和中介开始重新思考他们该如何提供金融服务。

然而，寿险公司在市场突飞猛进的黄金增长时代，并没有对它们的核心产品进行过多的改进。市场在 20 世纪六七十年代发生了巨大的变化，为了解决销售额持续低迷的状况，公司开始雇佣更多的产品销售人员。产品的销售和供应从一开始的办讲座销售到后来的挨家挨户进行推广。到 20 世纪 70 年代，任何规模的城镇都至少拥有一个寿险办公地点。与此同时，保险行业和监管机构基于最新的死亡率统计表合作，对承销要求进行了标准化管理，创造了更多复杂的产品定价结构并且同意执行统一的风险分类。从表面上看，一切都风平浪静，然而，整个行业实际上已经遭到了文化及经济变化带来的冲击。

如前所述，在寿险产业中，终身寿险的市场占有量已经达到了一个较高的水平，美国社会的两大重要变化永久并彻底改变了美国的寿险产业，并且最终推动了理财规划师这一新职业的诞生。第一个变化是消费者运动的萌芽和发展。消费者运动的倡导者，比如 Ralph Nader，领导消费者抵制高价格低质量的商品和服务。有关产品及佣金的披露问题成了消费者最为关注的话题。几乎一夜之间，保险公司成为众矢之的，被指责欺骗消费者，产品可选范围狭窄以此牟取不正当利益。同时，美国的股票和房地产市场蓬勃发展。消费者的收入和财富不断增长，达到了历史最高点。

在这样的社会背景下：消费者运动蓬勃发展，不断增长的财富及寿险市场占有饱和使得寿险行业面临岌岌可危的境地。为了使寿险行业走出困境，1969 年的一天，包括一些人寿保险的精英销售人员、公司高层管理人员及一位金融记者在内的 13 人相聚在芝加哥，他们对如何向消费者提供多样的产品和服务进行了探讨。大家一致认为整齐划一的产品，比如终身人寿保险和固定收益年金，是不能解决所有消费者的需求的。这些行业的领导者预见到将来消费者需要与顾问讨论各种各样的财务问题并需要顾问提供产品和建议。换言之，消费者需要保险销售人员转变为理财规划师。

寿险公司并没有在一夜之间完全接受理财规划的概念。有些人可能会说，即使是在今天的北美市场上，一些寿险公司仍然没有完全接受理财规划的概念。但这并没有阻挡那些在芝加哥开启“理财规划”理念的先行者们继续改革和探索的脚步。虽然没有公司的大力支持和宣传，他们成立了国际理财规划师协会（International Association of Financial Planners，之后更名为国际理财规划协会，International Association of Financial Planning，IAFP）和国际理财规划学院（之后更名为理财规划学院，后来改名为 College for Financial Planning）。如今，国际理财规划师协会，即为现在的理财规划协会（the Financial Planning Association）仍然为理财规划在美国的发展发挥着重要的作用。理财规划学院不断发展和壮大，并且为美国理财规划行业输送完成认证的理财规划师，即注册理财规划师（Certified Financial Planner，CFP®）。

1973 年，理财规划学院迎来了他们的第一批 42 名毕业生。虽然寿险行业从来没有将理财规划占为己有，但是理财规划，作为一个新兴职业发展极为迅速。早期，人们对理财规划有颇多疑虑。他们认为，理财规划协会、理财学院及 CFP 认证都只不过是为了将保险销售隐藏在所谓复杂的理财规划之后的把戏。保险行业自身同样也不愿意接受一些本身并不是“正宗的保险理念”来改变他们的销售模式。比如高级保险销售人员不赞同初级理财规划师打理客户的税务及投资事务，因为他们认为初级理财规划师在事业初期应该把精力放在寿险和年金保单的销售上。

那些将理财规划作为一生要追求的事业的理财规划师在那个时代被视为异类，受到客户的质疑及行业的反对。一些理财规划师在这样的困境中没有生存下去，然而另一些理财规划师却成功了。慢慢地，大家发现消费者非常渴望不掺杂保险产品销售的单纯的建议和指导。消费者对于这样战略性规划建议的需求不断增加，可以说，理财需求是通过改变消费者的偏好及规划一生的理念而产生的，这种需求不仅需要而且必要。

理财规划的执业者强烈需要道德准则和执业标准为他们的实际业务提供指导。在 1985 年，之前主要专注于教授课程和颁发 CFP 认证的理财规划学院分解为两个实体。一个机构负责教学，另一个机构负责管理 CFP 资格认证考试，并将其命名为 CFP 委员会（the Certified Financial Planner Board of Standards，Inc. CFP Board）。CFP 委员会主要负责管理 CFP 资格认证考试，保证理财规划师的竞争力，包括对理财规划师进行充分的培训，使其理财规划行为符合道德标准，并且为客户的利益服务。1987 年，第一所大学引进了

CFP 认证项目。不到50年的时间里，美国的CFP持证人数从最初的42人增长为2017年的76 724人[①]。全美共有超过150家学术机构提供CFP认证项目的培训。

理财规划全球发展趋势

全球理财规划的发展是美国理财规划发展历史的折射，理财规划的概念首先在美国形成，理财规划行业在美国初步稳定发展后的十年逐步传播到世界其他地方。在2004年，国际理财规划标准委员会（Financial Planning Standards Board Ltd.，FPSB）成立，这成为理财规划行业发展的重要里程碑。国际理财规划标准委员会的成立旨在管理和推广资格认证、培训及关注美国以外地区有关理财规划的问题。国际理财规划标准委员会拥有美国以外地区CFP商标并建立了国际竞争力、道德及执业标准和准则。国际理财规划标准委员会还有一项重要的职能，即与世界各国或地区建立授权和会员协议，管理和推广CFP资格认证项目。

截至2014年年底，全世界共有157 586位CFP执业人士。虽然大部分的CFP执业人士都集中在美国，但是CFP持证人数增长率最高的国家却不是美国。

表1－1　　CFP持证人全球分布一览

国家	人数（人）	国家	人数（人）
美国	71 296	印度尼西亚	1 019
日本	19 776	英国	1 010
加拿大	16 738	新加坡	9 08
中国	16 653	中国台北	673
澳大利亚	5 450	新西兰	333
中国香港	4 784	爱尔兰	315
南非	4 524	奥地利	311
韩国	4 011	瑞士	293
马来西亚	2 484	以色列	133
印度	1 820	荷兰	132
巴西	1 741	泰国	129
法国	1 604	哥伦比亚	0
德国	1 449	土耳其	0

数据来源：FPSB（http：//www. fpsb. org/about/64. html），更新至2014年12月31日。

① http：//www. cfp. net/news－events/research－facts－figures/cfp－professional－demographics.

第二节　理财规划职业发展现状

理财规划是由一些理财机构或者理财规划师个人，为个人、家庭或其他公司提供金融服务、建议和管理服务的过程。[①] 这个定义被全世界广为使用。理财规划公司的主要收入来源包括理财规划书费用、资产管理费用及产品佣金。我们需要清楚地界定理财规划师与以下相关职业的区别。

虽然理财规划师经常与资产组合管理经理有业务往来，但是理财规划师绝不是资产组合管理经理（资产组合管理经理是指那些管理客户共同基金、浮动年金、对冲基金、交易所交易基金及其他类似产品的个人或者企业）。

理财规划师不是共同基金经理、经纪人、对冲基金经理或者其他在金融服务领域提供直接操作业务的专业人士。

此外，理财规划师的收费方式因公司或者地域不同而有所不同。

虽然这样的区别方式过于简单，但是我们可以这么认为，理财规划师与资产组合管理经理的区别在于与客户沟通交流的层面不同。理财规划师直接与客户交流，与客户共同明确财务目标，他们为客户设定合理的理财假设和投资区间，测算风险容忍度和风险能力[②]并制定理财规划，最终能够帮助客户提高他们的财务幸福感。理财规划师分析、选择及推荐适合客户的投资产品，比如共同基金作为实现财务目标的工具。在实践中，理财规划师选择什么样的资产组合管理经理是理财规划的一部分。理财规划的内容包括整个资金及资产管理，而资产组合管理经理的服务内容只涉及买卖个别股票资产。[③]

部分金融服务专业人士可能是理财规划师，但并不是所有的金融服务专业人士都是理财规划师。以寿险销售为例，如果一个销售人员遵循之前提及的理财规划流程，收集综合的信息进行分析判断并且提供完整的、具有广度和深度的建议和意见，那么他们有能力提供理财规划服务并被人们称为理财规划师。但是，如果一个销售人员向几乎所有的客户，不论任何情况，都推荐同一个保险产品，那么这个销售人员就绝不是理财规划师。同样地，不是所有的股票经纪人都可以被视为理财规划师。在美国，股票经纪人很

---

① Schmidt, 2012.

② 风险容忍是指一个人承担财务风险的意愿，而风险能力是指一个客户承担风险损失的能力。

③ 从理论上说，理财规划师可以是客户的资产组合经理，但在实践中这种情况较少。

少使用理财规划六步法向客户提供建议。此外，他们也很少向客户提供与投资规划无关的建议。

一、市场占有率

我们很难统计有关全世界理财规划职业情况的数据，但是我们可以通过评估美国理财规划行业的市场占有及业务情况来达到窥一斑而见全豹的目的。在2012—2013年间，全美理财规划师共创造超过500亿美元的总收益，利润总额超过80亿美元，利润率超过16%（考虑到行业的性质，员工工资是成本的主要内容，共约240亿美元）[①]。

目前，全美共有约136 000家理财规划机构。但是这个数字不能反映行业的实际情况，因为四家大型金融机构占到市场份额的45%。最大的为摩根士丹利（Morgan Stanley Smith Barney LLC），其他三家分别为富国银行（Wells Fargo & Company）、美国银行（Bank of America Corporation[②]）以及阿默普莱斯金融公司（Amerprise Financial Incorporated）。大家可能感到有些困惑，为什么这些金融机构被划分为理财规划公司而不是中介经纪公司。虽然这些机构的理财规划师也为客户提供买卖交易的服务，但是他们遵循理财规划流程并向客户提供书面的理财规划报告（通常都是单一/模块理财规划书）。富国银行和阿默普莱斯金融公司积极鼓励他们的理财规划师参加CFP资格认证考试。美国大部分的理财规划机构都是不超过5个人的公司，并且大部分是只有一名理财规划师的私人企业。

相比美国的人口来讲，美国理财规划机构及理财规划师的数量还是相对较少（一个理财公司要为大约2 200人服务），因此，竞争不是十分激烈。实际上，根据Schimidt在2012年的研究，美国仍然存在未被开发的金融服务市场。这就使得理财规划公司可以将主要的营销精力放在高净值客户的身上。高净值客户是指：

在管资产超过750 000美元。

净资产达到1 500 000美元。

可投资金融资产达到1 000 000美元。

换句话说，很少有理财规划公司为所谓的中间市场服务。年收入大约在50 000美元的家庭，其中仅有不到1/4的家庭寻求理财规划师服务。原因之一就是鲜有公司为这些收入相对较低或者可投资资产较少的家庭提供服务。通常，理财规划公司都会设定客户

---

① 数据来源于美国劳动部及IBISWorld. com。参见Schmidt，2012。

② 美国银行的理财规划服务来自其收购的美林证券。美林证券拥有近17 000名理财师。

的进入门槛。比如，一些小的理财规划机构通常要求客户至少有500 000 美元的可投资资产。另一个原因是理财规划公司更愿意与高净值的客户合作，因为他们能带来更高的收益。为一个资产仅有 100 000 美元的客户提供服务需要做的工作与为一个资产为1 000 000美元的客户提供服务需要做的工作是完全一样的。考虑到美国理财规划服务的收费方式，向高净值客户提供服务，对于理财规划机构来讲显然更加符合收益成本原则。

二、关于理财规划师业务收费的相关问题

有关理财规划师的收费问题一直是行业中广泛争论的话题。在美国，理财规划师一般有两种收费方式，一是收取佣金，二是收取费用。收取佣金是最古老也是最常用的收费方式。几乎所有的寿险及投资产品都会基于产品售价收取一定的佣金。例如，一些共同基金会按照产品售价收取高达8.25%的佣金费用。一些理财规划师也会收取售后佣金，即在产品销售完毕后付给理财规划师佣金。售后佣金在客户拥有投资或保险产品期间一直都会收取。

费用是理财规划师收取报酬的另一种方式。最常见的费用收取标准是基于在管资产。几乎所有的理财规划师除就非投资领域提供建议外，都会提供资产管理服务。理财规划师一般会收取资产 0.5% ~2.5% 不等的资产管理费。通常情况下，在管资产越多，年费越低。一些拥有 1 000 000 美元资产的客户通常需要缴纳约 1%（10 000 美元）的年费。

然而，20 年前，佣金还是理财规划师收取报酬的主要手段，如今，更多的理财规划师采取收取费用或者以费用为主的报酬收取方式。在这种情况下，他们对理财规划书收取统一费用，对为了达到理财目的而推荐的产品则收取佣金。另外一种叫做费用补偿机制。理财规划师让客户支付相对昂贵的理财规划费和免收规划费但要对所销售产品收取佣金的两种情况作出选择。在这种方式下，佣金实际上是对面授理财规划费的一种补偿，即费用补偿机制。还有一种是仅收取费用的报酬收取方式。这种收费方式法律规定不允许收取任何形式的佣金。采用这种收费方式的理财规划师并不多，他们通常只收取制作和帮助实施理财规划的费用，有时是按照小时收费。2012—2013 年的费用标准大概是 1 小时 200 美元。那些只收取费用的理财规划师，通常都会收取资产管理费用作为其收入的主要来源。①

① 在美林证券工作的理财师之前主要收取佣金。而如今在大型全国性理财规划公司工作的理财师收入主要来源于独立投资账户的管理费。独立投资账户管理费用与资产管理费用类似。但是独立投资账户的年费较高并提供除资金管理以外的其他服务。

美国关于理财规划师的监管情况有些复杂。总体上讲，任何提供理财规划服务收取佣金的个人或者机构都需要获取相应执照才可以销售金融产品。比如，销售证券产品（股票、债券和共同基金），理财规划师需要获得由金融监管局（FINRA）颁发的系列7① 和系列63② 号执照。美国金融监管局是一个自律组织。销售保险产品以获取佣金的理财规划师则需要得到业务经营所在州的执照许可。收取费用的理财规划师则必须在美国证券监管委员会或者业务经营所在州的证券监管委员会登记注册。证券监管委员会要求理财规划师必须持有金融监管局监管的系列65③ 或66号④注册投资顾问法律执照。另外，在管资产超过1亿美元的理财规划师需要在美国证券监管委员会注册投资顾问资格，其他理财规划师则必须在州证券监管委员会注册。实际上，理财规划师一方面需要拥有系列7号执照以拥有合法销售证券的资格，另一方面还要在相应的证券监管委员会注册投资顾问资格以合法收取费用。

虽然美国是理财规划流程和实践的发源地，但是其他一些国家和地区由此发展出了更加清晰的报酬收取方式。比如澳大利亚证券和投资委员会规定，澳洲的理财规划师可以采取以下3种收费方式之一：(1) 以向客户售卖的产品收取佣金；(2) 以在管金融资产的一部分收取费用；(3) 按小时收费。在英国，理财规划师的收费方式更加简化。理财规划师不允许收取佣金而只能按小时或者一笔手续费以覆盖理财规划及监督实施的成本。

第三节　理财规划行业展望

理财规划行业的前景是十分光明的，虽然这种趋势在目前看来并不是十分明显。整个世界目前正面临着老龄化的趋势，尤其以欧洲最为严重，许多亚洲国家也有这样的问题。虽然老龄化不能对一些国家整体的财务金融能力产生正面的影响，但却创造了对于理财规划职业的需求。一般来说，老年人掌握着一个国家的大部分财富。但是老龄化带来的主要问题就是医疗及健康方面的花费增多，老年人如何分配自己的资源以达到保全资产的目标是全球理财规划行业发展的主要原因。

全球财富繁荣是促进理财规划行业发展的另一个重要因素。高净值个人和家庭的数

① 美国证券经纪人执照。

② 此执照授权持证者在本州内进行交易。

③ 提供金融类建议或提供无佣金基础服务的理财规划师需持有此执照。

④ 此执照是系列63和系列65的结合。

量增多意味着今后对理财规划服务需求的增加。可以预见，大部分的需求将来自欧洲和美国外的其他国家和地区。另外，对于那些针对女性市场提供理财服务的公司将会获得另外的收益。

作为一个正在发展的专业职业，理财规划行业的前景是颇为乐观的，但是我们也必须意识到一些潜在的风险。正如上文所提及，如果理财业务的收费方式遵循英国和澳大利亚的收费模式，一些大公司的利益空间将被挤压。这是因为在世界上的大部分国家和地区，客户在购买理财产品时并没有为理财服务付费，并且他们并不了解理财服务的成本。在绝大多数情况下，佣金构成了产品的成本。一旦佣金收费模式被取消，消费者则需要为服务买单。虽然净成本是相同的，但是我们却需要花费时间引导消费者缴纳费用而非佣金。在这种情况下，理财规划行业也将面临额外的监管。2010 年在美国推行实施的《多德—弗兰克华尔街改革和消费者保护法案》旨在保护消费者免受金融市场的欺诈、错误引导及不实金融交易。虽然大部分的金融监管改革都是针对较大的公司，但是增加的监管压力势必影响中小理财规划公司的发展。

一、理财规划需求的驱动力

全世界理财规划行业①创造了仅 10 亿美元的总收入。② IBISWorld 预测未来十年理财

---

① 此书中理财规划是指通过恰当的金融资源的调配，能够帮助个人达到生活目标的过程，包含理财规划过程及内容两个方面的内容。理财规划六步骤：

(1) 确立和界定与客户的关系；

(2) 收集客户的相关信息；

(3) 分析及评估收集到的客户信息并测算客户的财务状况；

(4) 根据客户的实际情况，为客户制定和演示适合的理财规划；

(5) 执行理财规划方案；

(6) 持续监督理财规划方案的执行情况。

理财规划的内容包含但不限于以下几个方面：

- 现金流及净资产规划；
- 税务规划；
- 保险规划，包括人寿保险、残疾保险、财产险、长期护理险及特殊需求保险；
- 退休规划；
- 投资规划；
- 教育规划；
- 特殊情况时的规划；
- 遗产规划。

更多内容请参看：http：//www.cfp.net/for-cfp-professionals/professional-standards-enforcement/compliance-resources/frequently-asked-questions/financial-planning#sthash.5oPzc5Dj.dpuf.

② Schmidt, D. (2012, March). *IBISWorld Industry Report* 52393: *Financial Planning and Advice in the US.* Los Angeles: IBISWorld.

规划收入增长率将超过4%。七大因素促进理财规划行业的发展，分别是：（1）不断增长的可支配收入及财富；（2）人口老龄化；（3）储蓄率的提高；（4）投资者不确定性；（5）企业需求；（6）女性消费者的增长；（7）资产配置的多元化。

二、不断增长的可支配收入及财富

理财规划服务需要客户拥有足够的可支配的现金流①供理财规划师管理及向理财规划师支付服务费用。这就是为什么大多数的金融机构及理财规划师会把营销和服务的重点定位在高净值个人及家庭上。如图1－1所示，高净值人群占总人口的10%，但却消费70%的理财规划服务。根据美国证券监督管理委员会的规定，至少拥有75万美元可投资资产或者拥有至少150万美元净资产②的个人或家庭才可被视作高净值人群。还有些机构规定拥有100万美元金融资产（扣除个人资产及房产）的个人或家庭才可视作高净值人群。③

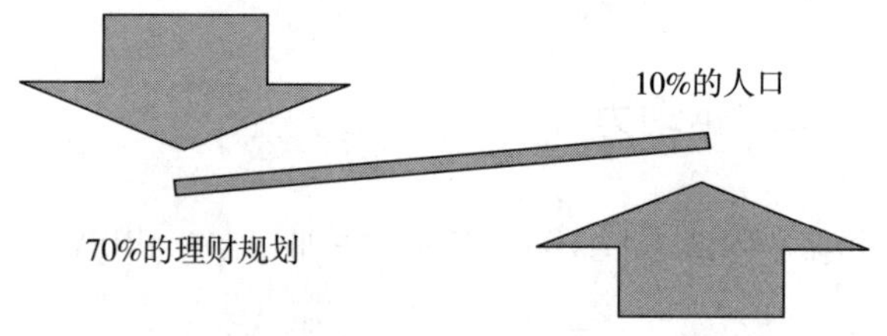

图1－1　高净值人群及理财规划服务

从世界范围内看，高净值客户拥有将近450亿美元的资产。根据凯捷美林全球财务管理报告统计，全世界共有将近110万高净值家庭④。其中，北美的高净值家庭数量最多，亚洲其次，拥有超过300万的高净值家庭。欧洲的高净值家庭拥有超过100亿美元的财富。拉丁美洲、中国及印度的高净值家庭也越来越多，虽然目前美国、日本及德国的高净值家庭占据世界高净值人群的50%以上。

这些有关高净值人群的统计数据映射出未来对于理财规划的需求。亚洲高净值家庭人数正以每年10%的速度增长。中东及亚太地区的净财富增长最快。以下这些地区无论是在高净值家庭的数量方面，还是在相应的可投资资产的数量的增长方面都位居世界前

① 可支配现金流是指家庭总收入减去固定及可变费用后的净值。

② 净值＝资产－负债。

③ 参见Schmidt，D.（2012）。

④ Capgemini and Merrill Lynch Wealth Management（2011）.

茅：(1) 中国香港；(2) 越南；(3) 斯里兰卡；(4) 印度尼西亚；(5) 新加坡；(6) 印度。澳大利亚的高净值家庭数量也悄然上升。这些表明了对于理财规划的需求也将随着这些地区财富的增长持续稳步地扩大。

三、人口老龄化

低出生率导致全国人口年龄的中位数不断增加，老龄人口在适龄工作人群中的比例不断扩大。由此，两大问题引起大家的广泛关注，一是退休金的融资问题，二是健康风险的防范问题。这两大问题都增加了对理财规划服务的需求。

再者，另一个有关反映世界范围的老龄化趋势的因素是理财规划目标从财富的增值转向财富的保值及分配。将近半个世纪以来，人们理财的重点都是如何使财富增长。那些出生在20世纪50年代和60年代（美国及西欧的婴儿潮时代出生的人群）的人们催生了对理财规划服务的需求。理财规划行业的主要竞争来源于证券经纪及保险公司。老龄化人口的庞大数量使得对理财规划服务的需求将持续出现大于供给的局面。

与此相关的一个重要问题就是老龄家庭的资产配置问题。美国家庭偏好投资股票，而大部分亚洲地区的家庭则更偏好投资房地产。① 不同地区的资产偏好的差异可以成为理财规划的一个关注点。高净值客户不仅要求在本国内对资产进行多样化的配置，更要求理财规划师进行全球的资产配置。因此，那些能够提供综合的（包括如期货、货币、股票、固定收益及房地产投资）、世界范围的理财规划机构，将逐渐赢得高净值客户的青睐，从而占据更多的市场份额。②

四、储蓄率的提高

2007—2008年的经济危机带来的一个正面影响就是使得全世界家庭的储蓄率提高。消费者主动或被动开始审视自己的收入和支出。很多家庭不再依赖借债提前消费，而是开始储蓄。在大危机时期，利率水平跌至历史最低水平，这导致很多家庭陷入两难境地。一方面，他们有很多闲钱可以储蓄；另一方面，可投资的机构又少之又少。在这种情况下，许多家庭都需要理财规划师的帮助。虽然这种需求是短暂的，但是一个国家的储蓄率水平却可以用来衡量家庭对理财规划服务的需求。

---

① 凯捷及美林2011财富管理报告显示，亚洲投资者投资资产中有31%是在房地产，而美国人投资资产的40%则投资在证券。日本投资者更偏向固定收益类产品。日本高净值客户资产组合中有超过50%的债券类投资。

② 高净值客户需要的理财规划服务还包括运动投资、收藏品及珠宝等。

五、投资的不确定性

2007—2009 年金融危机期间，美国最重要的股票指数——标普 500 指数下跌了近 40%，利率也跌至历史最低水平。与此同时，房地产价值在全美大幅缩水，失业率快速上升，人们的收入不断下降。这些情况使消费者信心受到了严重的打击。世界其他国家和地区也遭受了相似的状况。比如，欧洲的债务危机导致南欧国家的失业率严重增长，政府支出大幅缩水。投资及储蓄的不确定性使人们更加需要理财规划师的帮助。只要金融及财务问题一直是复杂并且不确定的，那么世界范围内对理财规划服务的需求就会不断增加。

从某种意义上讲，理财规划是一个经济中性活动。一些产业是周期行业或反周期行业，而理财规划却可以在市场低迷和高潮的情况下都获益。当经济情况好转，人们的收入增加，财富的增加促进了人们对于财富分配服务的需求。当经济情况恶化，市场的不确定性增加，次优的财务战略仍然可以发挥积极作用。这都使得人们对于理财规划服务的需求增加。

理财规划市场在这场经济危机中获得前所未有的发展。根据美国政府责任办公室（GAO）① 的报告，2000—2008 年，美国理财规划师的人数翻倍。经济危机不仅没有降低对于理财规划服务需求，反而促进了对于理财规划服务的需求。GAO 预测，到 2018 年，全美将会有近 271 000 名理财规划师。并且，对于理财规划的需求将大大超过理财规划服务的供给。

美国被认为是理财规划发展较为成熟的市场，但是目前，全美仅有 22% 的人口享受理财规划服务。理财规划服务供给可翻 4 倍，但仍不能满足潜在的理财需求。

六、企业需求

活跃的经济活动，如公司的兼并、收购及跨国经营对理财规划服务产生了积极影响。对于会计、资本管理及承销服务的需求将会由于经济低迷而降低，与之不同的是，经济的周期变化将会促进对于理财规划行业管理者及服务人员的需求。

七、女性消费者的增长

以往，对于理财规划服务的需求多数是由于男性的金融服务要求。男性在几个世纪

① GAO（2011）.

以来都是家庭收入的主要提供者，但是这种情况正在不断改变。女权运动发展得十分迅速。以美国为例，在过去20年，女性掌握了家庭的主要财富。但如今，女性理财规划师在数量上和比例上仍然较少。女性理财规划师仅占全美理财规划师的10%。女性客户期望更多个性化的服务并且愿意与能够提供多样化服务及多元文化的理财公司合作。可以预见，在未来几十年，那些能够为女性客户提供更多新产品和服务的理财规划公司将受到这些女性客户的欣赏和青睐。

八、资产配置走向多元化

20世纪八九十年代：存款时代；2000年以后：地产时代；2014年以后：金融时代。以前居民去银行，通常只是存钱，或者找银行贷款买房。现在去银行，可以发现银行什么都在卖，除了卖存款，还卖理财、卖保险、卖信托、卖基金，等等，不一而足。据统计，2014年居民新增财富的17%来自银行理财、16%来自存款、12%来自股票，其他还包括信托、基金、保险等，这意味着居民财富配置多元化的时代已经来临，对金融资产的需求正在急剧上升。

如前所述，由于世界财富的不断增长，人们对于理财规划服务的需求也将不断增长。目前，将近75%的高净值人群是男性。然而，凯捷美林的财富管理报告①显示，世界财富在未来将会转移到年轻女性的手中，并且，从某种意义上讲，这种转变已经发生了。在东亚（除日本以外），将近25%的高净值人群是女性。这是促进理财规划服务的一个重要因素，因为财富的代际转移为新的理财规划公司提供了占据市场的机会。

参考文献

［1］Capgemini and Merrill Lynch Wealth Management.（2011）. World wealth report. New York：Author.

［2］College for Financial Planning.（2011）. Survey of Trends. Denver，CO：College for Financial Planning.

［3］GAO. 2011. "Report to Congressional Addressees：Consumer Finance." www. gao. gov/new. items/d11235. pdf.

［4］Lytton，R. H.，Grable，J. E.，& Klock，D. D.（2013）. The process of financial

① Capgemini and Merrill Lynch Wealth Management（2011）.

planning: Developing a financial plan (2nd ed.). Erlanger, KY: National Underwriter.

[5] Lusardi, A., & Mitchell, O. S. (2011). Financial literacy and planning: Implications for retirement wellbeing (Working Paper No. 2005 - 108). Cambridge, MA: National Bureau of Economic Research. Retrieved from http://papers.ssrn.com/sol3/papers.cfm?abstract_id=881847.

[6] Magali, S. L. (1978). The rise of professionalism: a sociological analysis. Berkeley, CA: University of California Press.

[7] Schmidt, D. (2012, March). IBISWorld industry report 52393: Financial planning & advice in the US. Santa Monica, CA: IBISWorld.

[8] Society of Actuaries. (2005). A strategic analysis of the U.S. life insurance industry Part I: Customers. The Actuary. http://www.soa.org/library/newsletters/the-actuary-magazine/2005/april/str2005april.aspx.

第二章　理财规划全球实践经验

如第一章所述，在过去20年，市场对理财规划服务的需求在全球范围内迅速增长。大多数的需求来源于消费者的构成及需求的不断变化。金融机构对于这些变化也积极采取应对措施。本章主要阐述大型金融机构理财规划业务的发展。

美国理财规划的发展历史可以为金融机构理财规划业务的发展提供了很好的借鉴。在美国，理财规划起源于寿险及年金销售，而作为单独的行业发展则开始于20世纪60年代末70年代初。理财规划行业兴起的时间并不是一个巧合。如图2－1所示，寿险行业的发展及金融服务业的发展经历了7个主要的历史阶段。理财规划在这个发展阶段的成熟期才崭露头角。

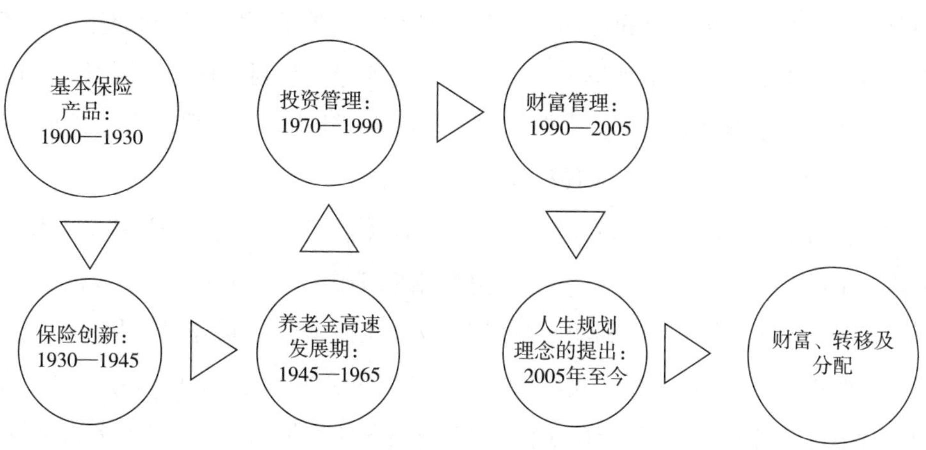

图2－1　行业发展的主要阶段

图2－1所示的金融服务的发展阶段适合于各个工业化国家。但是，每个国家从一个阶段过渡到另一个阶段的速度并不完全一致。有些国家，特别是东亚的一些国家，从萌芽阶段到成熟阶段的过渡是相当迅速的。许多东亚国家，如中国，目前处于理财规划发展的萌芽阶段，而韩国，则大概处于萌芽到成熟阶段的过渡阶段。下面就逐一阐述每一个发展阶段的特点。

阶段一

处于萌芽阶段的金融市场的主要特点：公司主要通过大型的销售网络销售定期及两全险。在几乎所有处于萌芽阶段的市场，保险产品的分销都是通过领取佣金的销售人员完成的①。一般情况下，这些销售人员缺乏家庭及个人金融知识的培训，而更多接受的是有关销售方面的技巧和技能的训练②。此外，这些销售人员受聘的原因大多是基于他们的销售技能而非专业知识。

阶段二

随着一个国家工业化的发展，金融机构不断进行产品创新以满足消费者不断变化的需求。在美国，工业化导致人口的城市化。目前中国也正经历着这一变化。城市化的一个重要的副产品是家庭经济来源不再仅仅依赖于家庭成员提供的单一收入或家庭储蓄。因此，为了适应这一变化，市场亟待开发新的金融产品以弥补家庭主要收入提供者死亡或者伤残造成的家庭收入损失。于是，意外险、伤残险及集体寿险在这一阶段发展起来。

阶段三

工业化及城市化促进了国家的经济繁荣及家庭的财务稳定。处在这一阶段的消费者更多地将注意力集中在未来经济保障，而非眼前的财务需求。另外，企业希望获得训练有素及高效率的员工，因而公司之间，在某种程度上，展开了员工福利的竞争。其中一个主要的福利是向员工提供某种形式的，有保障的养老金计划。在这一阶段，寿险及年金产品主要用于养老金计划的供款。保险公司及相关行业在这一阶段获得了长足的发展。消费者及企业对于保险产品的需求使得保险公司的盈利十分丰厚。

金融机构希望市场在这一阶段稳定下来，然而他们并不能决定经济环境的变化。截至这一阶段，市场上的金融产品都是统一的，并且相当有限。两全险是这一阶段的主要产品。虽然这一产品对于保险公司来说利润回报相当可观，但是许多公司并没有利用这一阶段消费者需求的变化来拓展新的业务。我们将看到，在第四阶段，消费者的偏好发生了大的转变。消费者不再仅仅满足于与银行存款利率相持平的投资回报率，他们开始涉猎风险更高，回报率更高的产品，比如股票、共同基金及房地产投资。在这一阶段，市场的监管更加严

---

① 有现金价值的人寿保险要求一定比例的存款数额。每笔佣金的一部分都用来抵偿定期寿险的成本。剩下的部分用于保险公司的承销费用、保单费用及现金价值账户的利息。保单持有人可以用现金价值及利息支付未来的保费或者作为借款抵押。传统的人寿保险保单提供一笔固定偿付及投资回报。有现金价值的人寿保险保费通常是定期寿险保费的10～20倍。

② 定期寿险是保险公司提供的一种纯保障险种。例如，投保人可购买期限为10年，保额为100 000美元的定期寿险。如果投保人在10年内身亡，受益人则可获得全部保额。如果投保人10年后身亡，受益人将不能获得任何收益。

格，但是争取消费者可支配资金进行其他投资的市场准入门槛却并不高。

阶段四

正是在这一阶段，理财规划成为为客户与理财规划师关系增值的工具。由于客户要求更大的风险及更高的收益，对于投资管理服务的需求也相应增加。金融机构开始要求其销售人员不再单一地向客户提供固定收费的保险产品及年金产品。事实上，销售团队也向金融机构提出进行更多的创新，以抗衡他们的竞争对手，如投资顾问公司、经纪公司及其他提供综合投资管理服务的公司。保险公司自身也开始提供可变收益的产品，如变额人寿保险及年金。

在这一阶段，还发生了另一个重要的变化：理财规划师收取报酬的方式不再仅限于收取佣金，还收取费用。这是理财规划行业发展史上具有里程碑意义的一步。

阶段五

当两全险不再占据市场主导地位时，整个行业开始从第四阶段发展到第五阶段。在美国，这种转变发生在大约 20 世纪 90 年代，这时变额年金产品的保费收入超过了寿险产品的保费收入，通过市场上活跃的金融机构的行为可以总结出这一阶段的特点。在这一时期，金融机构不仅提供简单的投资建议，同时也更加强调财富管理。消费者则更加关心家庭整体的财富水平而不是某个单一产品的回报。能够在财富积累和管理上提供全面建议和服务的公司在市场上表现出竞争力。换句话说，能够尽早实施理财规划理念经营业务的公司在这一阶段成为市场上的领导者。

阶段六

在这一发展阶段，经济繁荣，人口增长。每个国家和地区都面临不同的经济发展情况、利率水平及人口寿命增长的情况。消费者对遗产问题越来越关注。遗产是指死者留下的财产。对许多人来说，遗产不仅仅是给后人留有金钱财富，也是人们纪念逝者的方式。因此，慈善开始成为留有遗产的源动力。理财规划和人生规划，这两个概念在这一阶段的运用交织在了一起。理财规划师不仅打理客户的金钱财富，并且开始为客户的梦想、理想及抱负掌舵。理财规划专业人士不再专注于售卖金融产品，而是全面关注客户的财务及情感各方面的问题。

社会对于理财规划师的理解在这一阶段也发生了变化。消费者不再认为他们的金融服务人员是单纯的销售人员，而是可以信任的咨询师。消费者希望他们的理财规划师提供无偏和全面的建议，帮助他们提升自身及家庭的幸福度。从各方面衡量，这一阶段是理财规划发展阶段的顶峰。理财规划师首次获得了与会计师及律师一样的地位和认可。

在这一阶段，仅有一小部分的理财规划师是百分百依赖佣金作为报酬方式。大部分的理财规划师依靠费用作为主要的收入来源，或者采取费用和佣金并行的报酬收取方式。要想成为理财规划师需要具备一定的资质，拥有大学本科学位几乎是必要条件。消费者希望理财规划师拥有过硬的资格及高水准的教育水平，这成为该阶段一个显著的特点。

阶段七

第六阶段和第七阶段的发展在某种程度上讲是交织在一起同步进行的。这是理财规划发展的成熟阶段，在美国，理财规划成为帮助客户积累、管理及分配财富的手段。理财规划不再仅是书本上的概念，而是在实践中的一个综合理财行为。消费者希望披露更多的信息，如收费、支出及利益冲突。虽然有些机构仍然以销售金融产品为主，那些专注于为客户提供人生及梦想规划①的金融机构则更受市场的欢迎。消费者更愿意为咨询建议付费，而不愿意仅仅购买金融产品。

一、市场细分

美国的金融市场是相对比较成熟的。消费者逐渐接受从产品推荐服务到可以满足个性需求的广泛的金融服务。理财规划作为以提供全面金融服务为导向的服务模式是适应这一发展趋势的。但是，每个国家和地区金融市场发展所处的阶段不尽相同。有些国家目前仍然是以基本的保险产品占据主要市场，有些国家则以投资管理服务为主，因此，金融机构对于理财规划服务的发展和推广取决于当地市场的具体情况。

如图 2 -2 所示，产品销售占据了金融行业发展的前三个阶段。在这些发展阶段，金融机构主要通过建立销售网络向消费者售卖产品，也有少数机构在进入市场时是以提供综合理财规划服务为特色。阶段四是一个转折点。随着消费者的需求从产品转为服务，一些金融机构也随之对自己的业务范围进行了调整，但也有一些机构坚持产品销售导向并采取更为激进的销售手段。

对于金融机构自身发展而言，阶段四也是一个重要的阶段。一些行业领导者接受了理财规划服务模式，而有些机构则拒绝接受他们的销售力量只不过是连接消费者和公司的纽带的这一说法。例如，在美国，经营财产保险和意外险的保险公司鲜有采用理财规划的经营模式。大型财产和汽车保险公司一直秉承销售统一产品的经营策略。他们认为在这一细分市场，消费者不要求量身订制的产品，而只关心产品和服务本身，对于建立

① 更多有关保险行业发展的内容，请参看：National Association of Insurance Commissioners 及 the Center for Insurance Policy and Research 发布的 *CIPR Study WPS* 2013：*State of the Life Insurance Industry*.

以高质量服务为基础的理财规划师—消费者关系并不感兴趣，因此，为消费者提供其他的理财规划建议对于公司和销售团队来说只是一种负担。

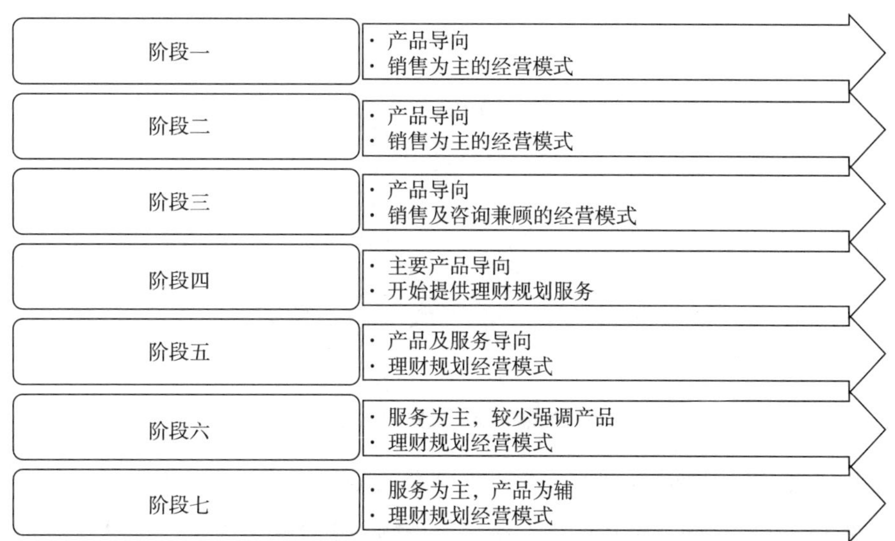

图 2－2　理财规划各发展阶段的产品及服务提供情况

不管金融机构是否提供理财规划服务，随着行业的发展，消费者对于理财规划的需求是不断增长的。在以财富管理为主的发展阶段，服务类型从产品导向发展为服务导向。如果金融机构不及时调整他们的经营方式，采用理财规划服务模式，他们的市场份额将大幅下降。而那些在早期就投资培训他们的销售团队从单纯售卖金融产品转向投资咨询方式经营的金融机构，获得了显著的发展。随着市场逐渐成熟，金融机构之间的经营方式发生了显著的分化。到了阶段六，领先的金融机构已经在经营的各个方面采用理财规划服务和产品售卖共同发展的经营模式。

如图 2－3 所示，当金融服务市场发展到成熟阶段，四种主要的金融机构占据市场。在这一阶段，消费者需求已经明显转向寻求关于财富积累、管理和分配的服务和建议上来。而财富涵盖的内容也十分宽泛，包括家庭财务及如人力资本、遗产规划等的内容。

如图 2－3 所示，虽然当市场发展到成熟阶段，消费者需求会转为寻求理财规划建议为主，但是仍然有三类金融机构没有完全采用理财规划的经营模式。第一类机构主要服务于“独立客户”。任何市场都有愿意 DIY 的投资者。这些客户只需要找寻一家公司帮助管理他们的资产，然后自己进行理财规划的相关决定。换句话说，“独立客户”不需要也不愿意接受理财规划师的服务。第二种类型的公司主要帮助客户处理日常交易事务。虽不多见，但这种公司多为大型金融机构，他们的销售团队继续使用以佣金为主的收费

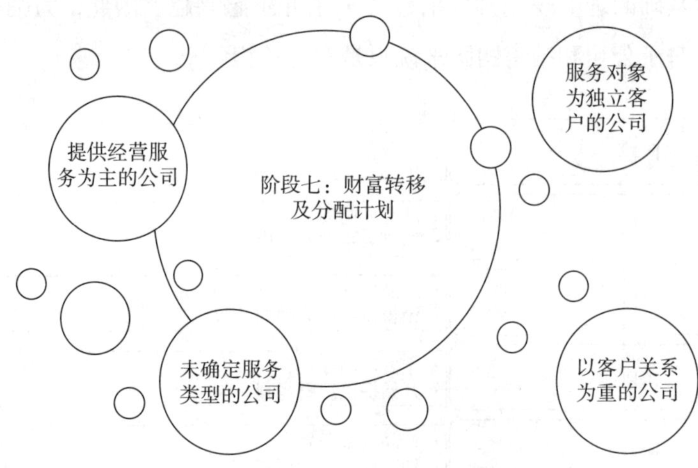

图 2－3　成熟市场中理财规划服务的发展

方式。这些“交易”型金融机构在早期的发展阶段是市场的中坚力量，然而随着市场发展到成熟阶段，这类金融公司在市场上所占的份额是少之又少。第三类公司则为“不确定型”，他们尚未决定是否采取理财规划的经营模式，或者没有决定到底将理财规划的经营模式推广到何种程度。大多数情况下，市场的竞争压力会推动这些公司从严格的“交易”导向转为以理财服务为主的经营模式。

第四类金融机构完全采用理财规划作为与客户沟通的工具。这些机构被称为“客户关系导向型公司”。虽然这些机构仍然会向客户售卖金融产品，但是收入的主要来源是服务费用。此外，图 2－3 中最大的气泡图形代表着数目众多的小型公司，构成除上述四种类型金融机构之外的第五种美国公司。在美国，这第五类公司被划分为投资咨询公司、资产管理公司及理财规划公司。围绕着大气泡图形周围的小气泡图形代表那些向客户提供非传统意义上服务的金融服务的公司。①

从以上金融机构的分类，我们可以总结出金融机构应该继续将理财规划的理念融入经营模式中的原因。市场发展的最后一个阶段是以消费者的偏好和期望为发展动力的，因此，能够满足消费者需求的公司才能获得长远的利益。

二、理财规划在成熟市场的主导地位

在本章的开篇，我们介绍了美国理财规划市场的发展历史可以作为其他国家或地区

① 例如，典当行、现金垫款、抵押贷款业务和其他消费者贷款公司。

推广和采用理财规划模式的一个参考案例。美国理财规划市场创造了将近470亿美元的年收益。在这个市场上，共有超过135 000家机构，但有4家机构[①]占据市场的主要份额。需求的主要动力源于老龄人口可支配收入的增加、相对增加的储蓄率及有关市场利率和股票价格的投资不确定性。

值得一提的是，这些市场领先机构都是近年才采用理财规划经营模式的。以全美第三大理财规划服务机构——美国银行为例，它从传统商业银行向理财规划市场领先公司的转变十分迅速。在2008年，美国银行收购了美林公司，美林公司是经营证券及经纪业务的老牌公司，虽然美林公司是最先在经纪行业推广收取费用模式的公司之一，但是他们也是近期才从佣金为主的收费模式转向收费为主。这种转变，从一定意义上讲，标示着他们对理财规划模式的重视，同时为他们赢得了很大的市场份额。

其他金融机构也注意到了这一市场变化。那些经营传统交易业务的公司鼓励他们的销售人员考取理财规划的相关证照。利用这一方法，LPL Financial[②]和Raymond James[③]公司分别实现了接近4%和3%的市场份额增长。

第一节 理财规划服务模式在各行业的发展和运用

一、保险行业

最初，理财规划业务与传统人寿保险行业紧密相连。如第一章所述，理财规划模式的发起和推广是从保险行业开始的。鉴于保险行业在理财规划发展的重要历史地位，我们应该了解人寿保险行业的发展情况。

人寿保险行业在美国有着悠长而丰富的历史。第一份人寿保险保单在1759年由长老会牧师基金售出。从这样渺小的起步到现在，人寿保险已经发展得十分壮大。例如，2012年，人寿保险公司拥有全美55亿美元的金融资产[④]。人寿保险凭借两种经营模式获

① 这四家公司分别是：摩根士丹利公司，富国银行，美国银行及Ameriprise金融公司。

② 全美第一大的独立经纪公司。

③ 美国著名的多元化控股金融服务公司。

④ National Association of Insurance Commissioners and the Center for Insurance Policy and Research.（2013）. *State of the life insurance industry*：*Implications of industry trends*. http：//www. naic. org/documents/cipr_ home_ 130823_ implications_ industry_ trends_ final. pdf.

得这样的成就，了解这两种经营模式有利于我们理解美国寿险行业的发展趋势。

最初，寿险公司的经营模式与股票公司十分类似，公司成立并向公众发行股票，利用筹集的资金投资到股票市场以赚取回报支付保险偿付。随着保单售出的越来越多，保费也成为股票投资的资金来源，在市场繁荣的时候，股票不仅可以赚得股息，还可以享受股票升值获得的资本利得。19 世纪早期至中期，市场遭受了严重的经济波动。在美国内战前期，寿险公司很难再利用股票市场募集资金。这种变化促使了另一种经营模式的产生。

投保人希望自己拥有保险公司的所有权，在这样的前提下，相互保险公司便应运而生了。由于股票不再向公众发行，寿险公司必须积极销售他们的全部产品，这对公司的发展变得尤为重要。唯一可以使保险公司增加市场份额，殷实股本的方法就是多多发行保单。这就要求保险公司雇用和培训大量的销售力量渗透到全国各地的城市和乡镇，如果相互保险公司财务状况良好，那么投保人便可以获得股息分红以抵减保费。①

由于这种公司存在较多的欺诈和管理不善等潜在问题，不久，美国各州开始监管人寿保险产品的销售。1849 年，纽约州首先出台关于保险公司最低的留存资金金额的规定，以保证已发行保单的偿付。新罕布什尔州设立名为保险专员的新的管理职位。到 19 世纪 70 年代，全美几乎都实施了某种形式的寿险监管政策。为了施行统一的保险监管，全国保险监管委员会在 1871 年正式成立。

19 世纪晚期到 20 世纪早期是寿险行业蓬勃发展的时期。在这期间，虽然市场上也开始出现一些其他的保险产品②，但定期寿险和终身人寿保险仍是主要的产品。第二次世界大战之后，消费者的偏好发生了戏剧性的变化。这一阶段即是婴儿潮时期的开始。大量新生儿的诞生，使得人们对于寿险产品的需求大大增加。但是与此同时，消费者对于终身寿险产品的需求也变得日趋复杂化，人们希望有其他新产品既能保护当前收益，又能保障未来收益。1952 年，教授保险及年金协会——大学退休股票基金（TIAA - CREF）发行了第一款可变年金产品。在这之前，所有的年金产品都是基于固定利率，而这个固定利率是根据保险行业剔除收费后的投资收益计算的。③

现在我们可以回顾在这个历史时期，理财规划是如何产生的。20 世纪 60 年代早期，寿险行业的精英们集聚一堂，发展并创立了第一个理财规划资格。这一资格涵盖金融服

① 值得一提的一个很有趣的逆转现象，大多数的共同保险公司都重新成为公开上市的股份公司。在 2013 年，前十位的上市公司占据了整个寿险市场 40% 的保费收入。共同保险公司在市场中的地位越来越小。

② 20 世纪 20 年代和 30 年代的典型产品包括重要人物保险，团体人寿及医疗险，残疾保障及现金价值保单中的双重赔偿条款。

③ 这些产品仍然以固定年金的形式存在。

务的各个方面。美国人寿保险学院创立、发展并监管特许人寿保险师资格。这一时期大约在 1969 年，这标志着理财规划的诞生。

消费者运动在 20 世纪六七十年代轰轰烈烈地展开。保险行业在这种情况下得到了严格的监管，发展举步维艰。销售技能，如上门推销产品、销售隐性的佣金产品、进行无退还保证或高价的销售行为，被披露曝光，成为媒体的头条。消费者开始要求提供与投资及财富管理相关的服务，而不仅仅是产品销售。消费者需求的转变和对服务的强烈要求促使保险行业内部创建了第一个理财规划经营模式。这些企业家采用新的经营模式的目的有二：（1）他们希望扩大保险产品和服务的市场；（2）他们希望帮助消费者积累和管理财富，并提供遗产规划的服务。在此之前，保险产品只不过是遗产管理及财富转移的工具罢了。顷刻之间，寿险及其他保险产品，在理财规划的理念之下，开始成为消费者达成综合理财目标并有效节税的方法。

寿险行业内部推广和学习理财规划经营模式的风潮转瞬即逝。20 世纪 80 年代，保险行业不断推出寿险及年金的创新产品，但是在开发综合投资及财富管理服务业务上却止步不前。从各个角度分析，由于寿险及年金产品是销售人员能够帮助客户进行理财规划的唯一产品，因此寿险产品阻碍了寿险行业理财规划模式的发展。

20 世纪 80 年代和 90 年代，市场的竞争局势发生了很大的变化。保险行业为了满足消费者的需求创新了各种人寿保险产品，如可变保险、万能寿险及可变或万能寿险。为了积聚财富，保险公司仍旧售卖固定及可变年金产品。如前所述，这些产品的最大特点是投保人可以通过这些产品累积财富，延期缴税。可变万能寿险产品的发展代表了保险行业与其他金融机构竞争的历史。

可变万能寿险产品应消费者希望运用延期税务工具参与股票市场的需求而产生。最简单的可变万能寿险产品允许消费者利用传统的具有现金价值的产品为股票产品的账户注资。与可变寿险产品不同，可变万能寿险产品的保费是浮动的，同时，现金价值也是浮动的。20 世纪 90 年代，世界股票市场的回报率都十分可观，那些购买可变万能寿险产品的投资者获得了较高的延期缴税收益。在这一时期，较为常见的退休规划是大多投资于可变万能寿险产品，利用其现金价值执行较为激进的投资策略。假设现金账户的增长足够快，投保人便可以利用现金价值贷款。只要股票市场持续利好，保费及保单贷款都可以用收益偿付。理论上，我们可以将资金存放于延期缴税的账户，然后再从免税的退休账户中取出[①]。在亡故后，保单的全部面值及剩余的现金价值可以免税转移给继承人。

① 从美国税法角度上讲，保单借款不被认定为一种收入来源。

可变万能寿险产品从理论角度上分析，似乎是金融市场上最具有竞争力的产品。

但实际上，可变万能寿险产品在市场上仅风靡了几年而已。第一，保险公司定位可变万能寿险产品为高端产品，持续收费很高。虽然在股票市场繁荣时，投保人不会介意多支付费用，然而当股票市场开始低迷，现金价值跳水的时候，投保人还要为不断贬值的保单支付昂贵的费用。第二，如前所述，利用可变万能寿险产品的退休规划策略仅适用于股票价格持续高涨的情形。20 世纪 90 年代末期，一直到 21 世纪前十年，股票价格持续走低。大部分的可变万能寿险产品都失效了，导致投保人损失惨重或要支付大笔税款。

如今，寿险行业是保险行业收入的第二支柱。20 世纪 90 年代中期，年金产品①的销量超过了寿险产品的销量。年金产品对于那些无法使用传统退休计划或者个人退休账户的消费者提供了一个积累退休资金的好途径。保险行业在金融市场中仍旧占据重要地位，然而，这个理财规划的创造者无力引领理财规划继续发展，进而满足消费者的需求。从许多方面讲，理财规划当前的发展已经远远超过了之前保险行业设计的初衷，为理财规划师—消费者关系增加了价值。

图 2 –4 展示了当今保险公司主要的理财规划目标市场及销售渠道。目前活跃在市场上的主要是大型全国或地区性的保险公司。几乎所有的这些公司都利用专属销售团队售卖自己公司的产品和服务，尤其在普通消费者市场、中产阶级市场及富有阶级市场特别突出。这些公司无独有偶为高净值客户量身订做专门的产品和服务。这些产品通常由独

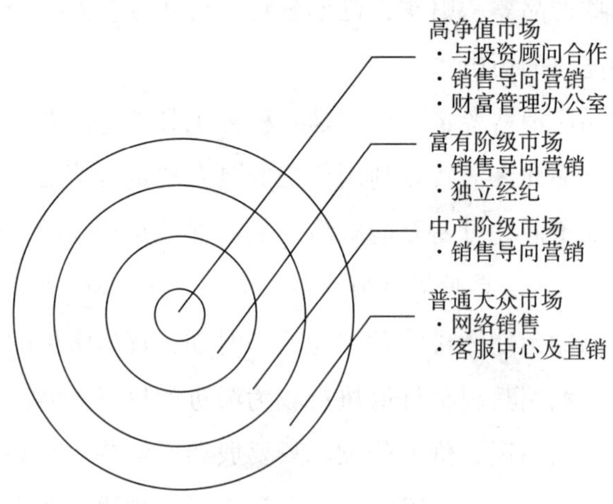

图 2 –4　保险公司目标市场及销售渠道

① National Association of Insurance Commissioners and the Center for Insurance Policy and Research (2013).

立的理财规划师及非专属保险经纪进行销售。几乎所有的保险公司都会雇用理财规划师或者创立财富管理机构为高净值客户提供服务。这些客户不仅可以购买传统的保险产品和服务，而且可以享受一对一的财富管理服务，而通常这样的财富管理服务仅提供给机构客户。

二、银行业

20 世纪 80 年代之前，银行的存贷款业务与理财规划服务是严格分开经营的。银行通过私人银行部门及信托部门为他们的高净值客户提供专属的税务、遗产及投资服务。在 1984 年，这一情况得到了扭转。波士顿银行的理财服务向所有的客户开放，客户不仅可以办理有关存贷款业务，也可以向他们的客户经理咨询理财规划建议。实际上，波士顿银行是将理财服务外包给其他公司经营。但这也是银行业的一个重要转变。波士顿银行不再将理财服务的范围局限于信托客户，这表明他们接受了理财规划应服务于更多人群的理念。

其他银行也纷纷效仿波士顿银行的做法，将理财规划业务外包给第三方公司。一些大银行表示这种方法可以最大程度地降低准入门槛，也有利于促进私人银行及信托业务的发展。这种状况一直持续到 1999 年。1999 年 11 月，美国国会废除了 1933 年《格拉斯—斯蒂格尔法案》中有关银行不可以拥有其他银行、投资银行及提供多样综合的投资产品的规定。

银行控股公司如雨后春笋般成长起来。以富国银行为例来介绍银行如何将理财规划纳入其产品和服务当中。银行控股公司一般有四个不同的业务单位。第一个称为社区银行，这是人们通常说起银行时所指的概念。社区银行管理当地支行，并且为客户提供存款、信用卡、公司银行业务、其他个人及商业贷款服务。在社区银行辖下还提供抵押贷款业务。第二个称为企业银行（批发银行）。这个业务部门为其他公司提供共同基金、资产抵押贷款、房地产、信托及商业贷款服务。第三个业务单位为富国证券，这实际上是银行的投资银行部门。理财规划服务隶属第四个业务单位，称为富国理财。这个部门提供财富管理、经纪业务及退休规划。私人银行部门及高净值客户服务也隶属这个业务单位。与其他银行控股公司类似，富国银行通过并购其他金融机构（美联银行），进入理财规划市场。①

① 美国银行收购了美林证券，从而为银行在理财规划市场上赢得一席之地。

大型银行机构的目标市场和销售渠道与保险行业类似。图 2－5 展示了这些市场及银行满足客户需求的不同途径。值得一提的是，一些地区性银行和乡镇银行也积极推行理财规划服务。通常，这些理财规划服务是外包给其他公司，但有些情况下，大型银行、地区性银行和乡镇银行也设立自己的投资管理和理财服务团队。

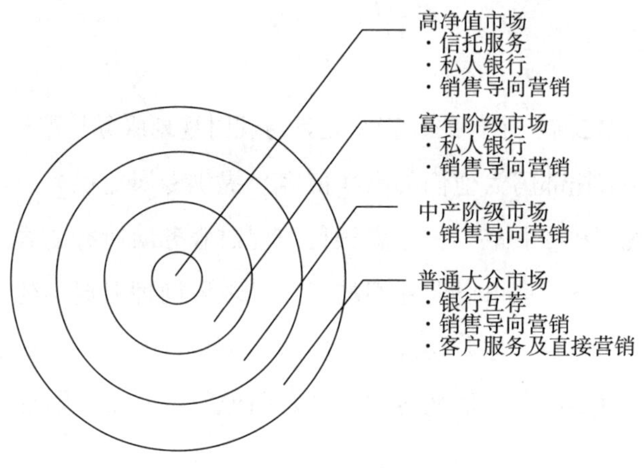

图 2－5　银行目标市场及营销渠道

三、投资机构

在投资机构中理财规划服务的推广是通过经纪—代理公司进行的。对于普通大众来讲，理财规划的概念很容易与经纪代理服务混淆。实际上，这两者是不同的。经纪人和代理人提供以推荐及交易股票、债券、年金产品、共同基金、保险和资产管理产品为主的服务。典型的报酬方式是收费。这就意味着经纪—代理人提供的理财服务收费是基于产品推荐的佣金。他们亦会对规划服务或推荐投资产品收取费用。

在 2000 年末的经济大危机爆发之前，美国大部分的咨询服务是由经纪—代理公司提供的。大危机之后，这些公司大多与银行控股公司合并或收购。如今，这种模式的理财服务是通过一些小的当地机构实现的，如 LPL Financial ，Raymond James 公司。与保险公司和银行控股公司类似，这些投资机构把营销的重点放在普通消费者市场、中产阶级市场、富有阶级市场及高净值阶层。与保险公司类似，几乎所有的产品和服务都是通过专属代表销售。公司的销售人员被称作经纪人、金融服务代表、注册代表或者理财规划师。

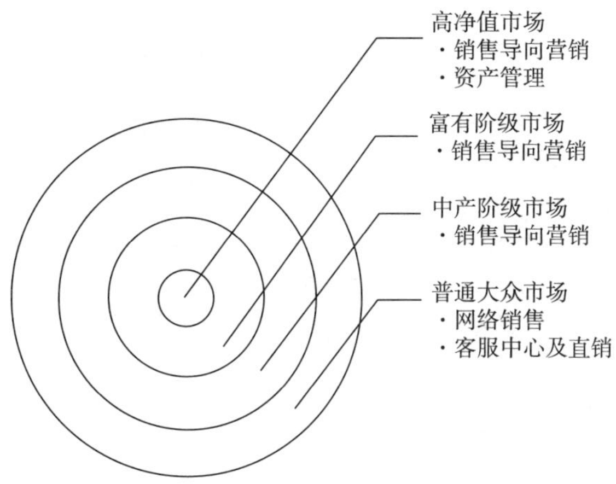

图 2－6　投资公司的目标市场及营销渠道

四、综合理财规划服务机构

在美国，真正意义的综合理财规划服务机构是非常少的。下面的章节将会讲到，大部分这种类型的公司都属于独立第三方理财公司。然而，仍有几家大型的全国性公司向普通消费者、中产阶级、富有阶级及高净值阶层提供综合理财规划服务。

其中最大的两家理财服务公司是 Ameriprise Financial 和 Waddell & Reed。目前 Ameriprise Financial 是规模最大的公司，他们在向客户提供服务时充分地运用理财规划程序。2012 年，Ameriprise 拥有 12 000 名理财规划师，客户资产总计近 1 200 万美元。Ameriprise 是全美拥有 CFP 持证人最多的公司。相比之下，Waddell & Reed 规模较小，主要经营投资管理及保险规划业务。

以 Ameriprise 经营模式为例来介绍这类公司市场营销及服务提供的情况。Ameriprise 通常运用两种方式服务客户。公司拥有自己的理财规划师，在全国各分支机构向客户提供理财规划服务。从很多方面讲，这种经营模式与传统的销售模式是类似的。理财规划师很少通过产品佣金的方式获得报酬，服务的运营成本也相对较低。最大的服务提供方式就是通过加盟 Ameriprise，利用其品牌、公司网络、市场销售力量吸引和维持客户群。Ameriprise 有 60% 的理财规划师是这种独立理财规划师。

类似 Ameriprise 的这种综合理财规划服务机构可以很大程度地服务于普通大众消费市场及中产阶级市场，虽然通常加盟的理财规划师更愿意服务富有人群。图 2－7 展示了综合理财规划服务机构大多运用的服务渠道。

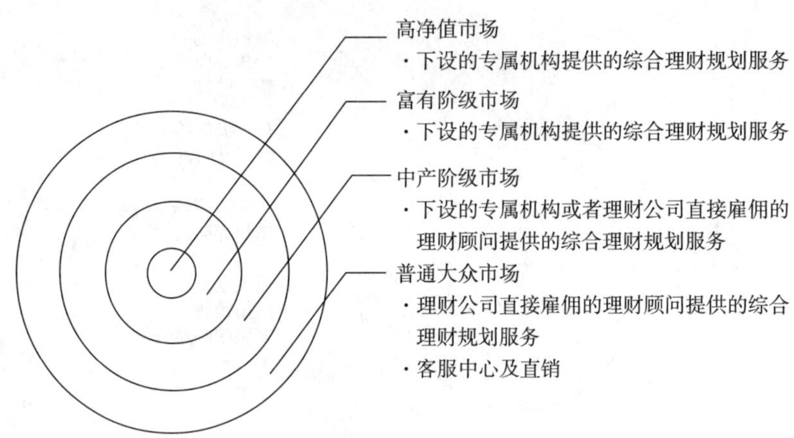

图 2－7　综合理财服务公司的目标市场及营销渠道

五、独立理财规划师

虽然少数几家大型金融机构在员工数量和收益上占据市场主导地位，但是几乎美国所有的理财规划公司都是以独立理财公司的形式存在。超过 12 000 位理财规划师在联邦证券交易委员会注册在案，还有很多是在州级委员会注册。虽然不是所有的理财公司都提供综合的理财规划，但是他们都会或多或少提供理财规划服务，他们更多地是提供投资规划方面的建议。这些独立理财公司共管理近 45 亿美元的资产，但是大部分公司管理的客户可投资资产均在 100 万美元以下。

独立理财公司的一个独有特点是它的规模。少于 5 人以下的公司规模在这一经营模式下并不罕见。许多独立理财公司只有 1 名或 2 名主要的经营者而没有雇员。根据证券交易委员会的记录，2/3 的独立理财公司的雇员不到 10 名。这些记录还表明，这些公司所提供的产品和服务分散但多样。

总体来讲，目前，大部分的独立理财公司都借助第三方托管的形式托管客户资产。也就是说，客户的资产是由一家大型的券商保管，如 Charles Schwab，Fidelity 或者 TDAmeritrade。理财规划师拥有对客户资产自由支配的权力，这保证了理财规划师可以在任何时间对客户持有的证券进行交易，对客户的资产组合进行调整。但是理财规划师不能直接支取客户资产。产品和服务的提供也是借由第三方机构。少有独立理财规划师公司是专门代理某一家公司的产品的。换而言之，这些理财规划师可以在市场上挑选适合的产品推荐给自己的客户。

与保险公司、投资公司相比，独立理财规划师通常只服务于较少的客户。2012 年，独立理财规划师服务的客户数量平均值不到150名。正因为如此，独立理财规划师一般服务于富有阶层和高净值客户，他们之所以选择这样的客户群体源于他们的收费方式。费用与佣金相结合的收费方式对于独立理财规划师十分常见。1%的资产管理费是十分普遍的，即独立理财规划师的收入等于他们在管客户资产的1%。考虑到服务一个拥有10万美元资产的客户与服务一个拥有100万美元资产的客户所花费的时间和精力是几乎等同的，大多数的独立理财规划师倾向于服务高净值客户。如图2－8所示，在所有提供理财规划服务的机构当中，独立理财机构最有可能选择高净值客户市场，同时，他们也积极活跃在富裕阶层市场。如果有普通大众客户或者中产阶级客户，独立理财公司的经营者通常会让他们的雇员提供服务。

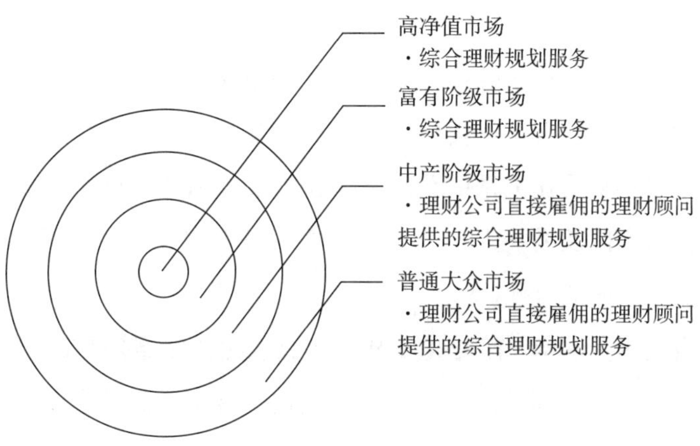

图2－8　独立理财服务公司的目标市场及营销渠道

第二节　理财规划服务的收费模式

研究表明，在美国，理财规划师共有8种不同形式的收费方式①，但没有一个理财规划师是仅采用一种收费方式的，他们通常会将几种收费方式相结合。接下来，我们将介绍在信托及适用性标准下，美国理财规划行业现行的主要费用及收入补偿方式。

① Lytton, R. H., Grable, J. E., & Klock, D. D. (2013). The Process of Financial Planning: Developing a Financial Plan (2nd ed.). Erlanger, KY: National Underwriter.

一、关于信托责任及适用性标准的讨论

在美国，关于理财规划师在客户关系中应当扮演什么样的角色的争论一直十分激烈，在某些情况下，甚至达到白热化的境地。在实践中，存在两种截然不同的操作模式。一方面，理财规划师被视为客户的信托代理人，意味着他们在向客户提供建议时必须完全遵循客户利益至上的原则。另一方面，一些理财规划师认为他们只是服务和产品的提供者，因此所提供的建议只要适合客户当前的状况即可。在实际工作中，理财规划师自己很难决定到底运用哪个标准。这是因为理财规划师就职的公司或者消费者金融法律会规定理财规划师应该遵循哪个标准。为了理解和区分这两个标准，我们首先从他们各自的定义出发进行探讨。

根据康奈尔大学法律信息学院关于“信托”的定义，“信托”是指完全保护另一方利益和行为的法律责任。负有这一责任的一方称为受托人。将责任进行托付的一方称为委托人。受托人一般不从受托关系中获利除非获得委托人明确的意思表示。受托人还负有避免他们与委托人之间及委托人与其他客户之间发生利益冲突的责任。受托责任是美国法律体系中规定最严格的责任。

另一定义来自美国劳动部①有关《雇员退休收入保障法案》中的规定。法案中界定受托人须谨慎并完全从客户利益出发从事活动。这一规定避免了个人交易，并为消费者提供了法律保护。

从广泛的定义上讲，受托人包括任何收费给予投资建议的人，这些人负有按照委托方利益行为的责任。1975 年，劳动部发布了关于投资建议的 5 项规定，对于受托责任给予了严格的规定。根据此规定，受托人必须满足如下条件：（1）对于投资、购买、售出股票或其他资产做出投资建议，或者就他们的价值提供建议；（2）咨询建议服务是经常性的行为；（3）基于共同谅解的原则；（4）投资意见的主要决策方；（5）给予的意见是针对个人的投资计划的特定需求。因此，根据联邦法律的规定，投资顾问，或者理财规划师，除非满足以上 5 个条件，才可以被称为受托人。但在最近，劳动部对此定义进行了修改，新规定指出受托人是针对以下服务收费的个人或团体：

对于股票或其他资产的价值作出评估或给予公允意见；

对于投资、购买、售出股票或其他资产作出投资建议；

---

① 参见 http：//www. dol. gov/ebsa/newsroom/fsfiduciary. html.

对于股票或其他资产的管理提出建议。

并满足如下条件：

按照 ERISA 中有关受托责任的规定代表某项投资计划、个人或受托人从事活动；

对于投资计划财产的管理及处置拥有决定权，并可以自己决定投资计划的日常管理，因而在实质上称为 ERISA 受托人；

是《1940 年投资顾问法案》中规定的投资顾问；

提供有关计划资产特殊需求的投资及管理的意见。

美国 CFP 委员会在某种程度上也规定了有关受托责任的范围，只是有关定义稍显宽泛。“准则要求所有提供理财规划服务的 CFP 专业人士必须遵循委员会规定的有关受托责任的规定，即 CFP 专业人士在任何时候都要将客户利益置于自己的个人利益之上。”委员会规定所有的 CFP 专业人士，无论其采用何种收费方式，都要遵循这一基本原则。①

美国最大的仅收取咨询费的理财规划师协会——全美个人理财咨询顾问协会同样遵循信托标准。该协会规定：遵循信托标准的个人理财顾问在向客户提供服务时，与客户拥有特殊的信托及信任关系。这包括须向客户披露理财顾问的报酬收取方式及任何相关利益冲突。少有保险公司、银行或投资公司要求他们管理的理财规划师遵循信托责任标准。

全部或部分收取佣金的理财规划师则遵循适用性标准。如果一个理财规划师拥有售卖保险或证券产品的资格，他们大部分情况下遵循适用性标准。金融业监管局（FINRA）② 对适用性标准的规定如下：

会员及相关人员须依据充分的理由来判断为客户提供的股票、与股票相关的交易或投资策略是否适合，他们需要收集信息以便对客户的投资情况、评估情况进行详细且尽职的调查。客户的投资情况评估包括但不限于客户的年龄、其他投资情况、财务状况及需求、税务情况、投资目标、投资经验、投资期限、流动性需求及客户向会员及相关人在进行交易或投资策略推荐时所披露的有关信息。

会员及相关人员在向机构客户提供服务时，在以下 2111 准则中规定的情况被视为遵循适用性准则。准则内容包括：（1）会员及相关人员依据充分的理由认为机构客户对于一般及某类交易和投资策略都具备独立评估自身投资风险的能力；（2）机构客户明确表示自身能够独立判断会员及相关人员所作出的推荐是否适合。

---

① 参见规定 1.4：http：//www. cfp. net/for - cfp - professionals/professional - standards - enforcement/compliance - resources/frequently - asked - questions/fiduciary - duty#sthash. D2egdxxY. dpuf.

② 参见 http：//finra. complinet. com/en/display/display_ main. html？ rbid = 2403&element_ id = 9859.

若机构客户委托代理机构进行投资抉择，如投资顾问或者银行的信托部门，则以上规定适用于代理机构。

信托标准的支持者认为理财规划师在向客户提供建议和产品时，需要最大程度减少利益冲突，收费合理并充分给予披露，并始终将客户的利益置于首位。适用性标准则要求理财规划师基于客户、市场及雇主条件进行合理判断向客户提供适合的产品和服务。

案例：堪萨斯州的一名理财规划师有一个客户。该客户需要筹集退休资金，投资期限较长，中等风险容忍度，应对市场波动的财务能力适中。理财规划师经过市场调查，发现有两款共同基金的产品可以满足客户的投资目标。第一只基金无前端收费，收费比率0.5%；第二只基金收取4.5%的佣金，收费比率较第一只基金略高，0.6%。这只基金还提供一个销售激励政策，即向售出100 000美元的理财规划师提供一周双人夏威夷旅游资助。如果两只基金的3年、5年及10年的年化收益率几乎相同，理财规划师应该向客户提供哪只基金?

若该名理财规划师遵循信托标准，那么问题的答案很简单。理财规划师需要选择年收费比率较低的基金产品，因为这对客户来说是最好的选择。然而，如果理财规划师遵循适用性标准，可选择任一基金。因为这两只基金都能满足客户的需求。理财规划师很有可能向客户推荐收取佣金的基金。虽然这只基金的年收费比率较高，但是理财规划师会认为与第一只基金的区别甚微，并且推荐这只基金还有额外的益处，即夏威夷旅游。另外，需注意的是，根据证券法规，有些理财规划师是不允许售卖无前端收费的基金产品的。经纪代理人推荐的产品都需要经过事先审核，如果无前端收费的产品不在其列，即使这只产品再好，也不允许推荐给消费者。遵循信托标准的理财规划师基于此声称其他理财规划师误导和欺骗客户。①

现实操作中，如果支付方式不需要披露，理财规划师的支付方式只是推荐产品和服务时的一个考虑因素。所有的理财规划师都会收取报酬，报酬收取方式不应成为一个问题，除非存在隐瞒利益冲突和收费结构的情况。如果理财规划师充分向客户披露其收费方式，客户可自行判断收费是否合理合适。

---

① 关于这个问题有很多争议。仅收取费用，遵循信托标准的理财师同样面临不能充分披露的利益冲突。设想一位客户咨询他/她的理财师是否应该付清该名理财师正在帮助其打理的房产的贷款。如果理财师说“不”，客户如何确定这个建议是基于诚信的。有可能，这位理财师推荐客户不要偿清所有贷款是因为这会降低他/她的资产管理费用。因此问题的关键又回到了要充分披露利益冲突及报酬补偿。

二、美国理财规划师常用的收费方式

以下介绍美国理财规划师常用的5种收费方式：

（一）仅收取费用

仅收取费用的理财规划师的报酬100%依靠收取资产管理费、计划书制作费及咨询费①，绝不收取事前或事后佣金。虽然这个解释简单直接，但是多年以来，人们对此的理解都存在偏差。一些理财规划师对外宣称自己仅收取费用，但仍然同时收取佣金。这在概念层面上是不对的，也是不合适的。但是，因为有时理财规划师认为如果他们有提供咨询服务的能力，他们就可以称为收取费用的理财规划师。然而，最清晰的理解仍然是我们一开始介绍的，仅收取费用的理财规划师是不包括那些从除客户以外的第三方收取佣金的理财规划师。仅收取费用的收费模式包括资产管理费、理财计划制作费、聘用费及按小时计算的咨询费。

大多数仅收取费用的理财规划师都会收取资产管理费，通常是在管资产金额的0.5%~2.5%。资产规模越大，收费越低。50%以上的理财规划师都会对制作和执行理财计划收取一个固定的费用，250~5 000美元不等。有些理财规划师会收取年服务费。缴纳这笔一次性费用可以使消费者整年随时咨询有关理财方面的问题。这与律师收取的年费类似。现在，越来越多的仅收取费用的理财规划师都会增加小时收费项目以方便消费者按小时咨询一些特殊的问题，该费用从100美元至500美元1小时不等。通常，资历越深的理财规划师收取的年费越高。某位理财规划师或某家理财公司可能会采取以上介绍的一种或多种收费形式。

（二）以收取费用为主的收费方式

采用该收费形式的理财规划师通常会同时收取费用和佣金，因此这种收费方式又被称为“费用加佣金”。例如，理财规划师可能对制作理财计划收取较低廉的费用，250美元。但是理财规划师会对推荐的产品收取标价的佣金费用。理财规划师在推荐保险产品时，通常会采用这种做法。与这种形式比较类似的收费方法是，理财规划师虽然对制作理财计划收取费用，但是允许客户使用在购买推荐产品时支付的佣金抵销这笔费用。

（三）佣金

本章前面章节已经讲述过佣金的用途。佣金是从产品销售时提取。通常，佣金的提

① 美国最大的独立理财师协会允许其会员最多收取占其年收入2%的佣金及其他除费用之外形式的补偿。

取是基于销售金额的一定比率。比如，如果佣金比率是销售的5%，一个理财规划师销售100 000美元的产品，就可以获得5 000美元的佣金提成。一般情况下，理财规划师都需要将佣金与所在机构分享，分享比率从三七开到八二开不等。当今从业的理财规划师大多都会从销售产品中赚取佣金①。

（四）资产管理费

资产管理费被视为仅收取费用的收费方式。一些大型的投资公司或者银行提供类似的服务，称为打包账户。打包账户为那些可能会为购买的产品支付佣金的客户提供基于资产金额的资产管理服务。资产管理费及打包账户是当今市场上为富裕客户及高净值客户提供服务的两种主要的收费方式。通常情况下，只要在管资产金额足够覆盖预期费用，理财规划师通常会为这些客户提供免费的基本理财规划服务。

（五）综合收费方式

许多公司开始采用综合的收费方式，这在理财规划行业里变得越来越普遍，费用收取不仅基于在管资产而且还要结合客户的总资产或者收入水平。收取费用与收取佣金相结合是另外一种综合收费方式。理财规划师和理财机构偏向使用多种收费方式相结合的综合收费方式。如果仅收取资产管理费，在市场经济环境不良的情况下，理财规划师的收入就会下降。同样地，如果仅收取佣金，那么理财规划师的收入就会随着销售额的变化而变化（没有哪个客户每年都会购买100万美元的人寿保险）。采用综合的收费方式可以避免理财规划师收入的波动。

第三节　法律法规

有关理财规划师及理财公司的法律和法规问题相当复杂。以下关于这方面的讨论仅起到抛砖引玉的作用，希望对中国及其他亚洲地区的监管问题有所裨益。

一、主要的法律法规体系

理财规划师与客户合作的方式受到道德标准的约束。这些道德标准是行业内部的执业者、监管者及消费者达成共识的结果。对于理财规划、投资及金融咨询服务行业，道

① 需要指出的是，所谓以收取佣金为主的产品通常都是事前佣金。只要客户继续持有某个产品，销售人员就可以获得0.25%～1%的佣金提成。这样做的目的是为了给理财师向客户提供持续服务的激励。

德标准在本质上是一个规范问题。这意味着法律、法规及行为准则的制定是基于理财规划师在为客户提供服务时应该如何做的问题。换而言之，道德标准是理财规划师行为表现的标尺。

尽管道德标准的定义表面上看简单易懂，但在实际运用时却不是那么容易的。回顾我们在这章开始介绍的关于信托标准时的案例。堪萨斯州的那位理财规划师面临如何向客户推荐产品的难题。两种基金产品都可以满足客户的投资需要，税后收益也近似。第一只基金产品没有前端收费，总体费用比率为0.5%。第二只基金产品延迟收费，总体费用比率为0.6%。但是第二只基金为销售金额达到100 000美元的理财规划师提供夏威夷一周双人游的销售激励。

遵循信托标准的理财规划师总是会选择无前端收费的基金。因为这符合理财规划师的价值观并且也是信托标准中要求的理财规划师应该做的。理财规划师面临一个非常清晰的选择，这称为伦理道德的选择。遵循信托标准的理财规划师必须为客户选择最好的产品和服务，而不能考虑其选择对自己造成的利益影响。

不遵循信托标准的理财规划师则从技术层面判断基金产品的选择。所谓技术判断的道德标准是基于相对结果及对结果的评价。那些选择更高费用比率的基金产品，但能给出合理解释的理财规划师，他们面临的是一个情境道德的选择。这是人们每天都要面临的选择问题。人们经常开车超速，在杂货店拿水果当零食或者编造一些善意的谎言。也就是说，人们每天都在破坏法律和社会规范，但是人们之所以这么做是因为这些行为不会造成什么重大的影响。

尽管一些理财规划师在制定理财计划和与客户沟通时往往遵循技术判断的道德标准，但是政府机构、监管机构及标准设定机构则是运用伦理道德标准。没有人受到损失或伤害的托词不能让理财规划师免责。所有法律、法规及行为准则的制定都是基于规范。监管者在制定和解释准则时都是非常细化的，因此理财规划师的行为要么在准则规定之内，要么违反准则的规定。对于那些违反准则规定的理财规划师，则要缴纳罚款或接受其他惩罚。

二、政府监管机构

1933年以前，美国、欧洲及澳大利亚的监管政策是非常疏松的。任何人或机构都可以在法律规定范围内推广投资证券或提供金融服务。这段期间被称为买方警惕期。因为这段时期有关金融资询方面的误导、欺诈行为都没有被很好地纠正，也鲜有资料可以查询。

1929 年爆发的经济危机着实改变了政府对理财规划师和咨询师的监管方式。三条重要的法规约束了理财规划师对客户提供服务的方式，首先是 1938 年美国国会通过的《马洛尼法案》。该法案帮助设立了全国证券经纪委员会，这是第一个证券行业的自律组织。1940 年，美国国会通过了《投资咨询师法案》。该法案对于理财规划行业的影响最为深远。

《投资咨询师法案》规定，所有对投资服务和建议直接向客户收取报酬的理财规划师必须在证券交易委员会注册①。2007 年金融危机之后，美国国会通过了《多德—弗兰克法案》，该法案对于自 1930 年以来证券和投资顾问的法规做了较大的更改。最主要的更改是将金融顾问公司分为两类，一类是管理资产多于 1 亿美元，另一类是管理资产少于 1 亿美元。实际上，任何在管资产超过 1 亿美元的公司都需要在联邦证券委员会登记注册。管理资产少于 1 亿美元的理财规划师和公司则需要在他们经营的所在州证券委员会登记注册。

这样，几乎所有对投资咨询服务收取报酬的公司或个人都在联邦或州证券委员会登记在案。公众可通过查询 ADV 表格（该表格是投资顾问服务统一的注册申请表格）查看这些公司或个人理财规划师的注册信息。② ADV 表格包括两部分的内容，需要理财规划师提供有关他们经营、雇员及监管相关的信息，还需要提供理财规划师教育经历、经营背景、资格认证、收费、服务客户的类型、运用的投资方法、投资建议的类型、利益冲突、遵循的道德准则及投资服务程序。根据法律规定，这些详细的信息必须提供给客户。一些公司会直接把 ADV 表格提供给客户，而有些则将 ADV 表格上的内容进行整理，变成宣传小册发给客户。除了要在规定的监管机构注册备案，所有州都规定投资顾问需要参加并通过系列 65 考试。美国 50 个州中的 48 个州对于持有 CFP®资格、ChFC®资格、PFS®资格或者 CFA®资格的理财规划师豁免参加系列 65 考试。

理财规划师有可能还需要受到全国保险专员协会的监管。该协会并不是联邦级别的，但是却由各州保险监管办公室的代表组成。③ 全国保险专员协会成立于 1871 年，旨在监管保险产品的销售。任何销售保险产品的个人必须在经营所在州获得许可。因此，理财

① 1940 年法案提出可以偶尔提供投资服务 4 个例外情况。（1）银行及银行控股公司；（2）律师、会计师、工程师及教师，他们所提供的投资建议相对他们的核心业务来说是微乎其微的；（3）报纸、杂志、金融出版物及一般的出版商；（4）为美国政府债券提供咨询服务的理财师。

② 消费者可以向证券交易委员会索取这些资料。

③ 在美国，保险行业受各州机构而非联邦机构监管。

规划师需要获得保险许可及投资顾问许可。

三、自律机构

1938 年的《马洛尼法案》创造了一个新的监管概念——自律监管。意指经纪代理及其他金融服务公司成立机构进行自我监督和约束。如前所述，全国证券经纪委员会即是经纪公司及他们的雇员的自律组织。全国证券经纪委员会后来更名为金融行业监管局，负责监管将近 4 500 家金融机构和近 630 000 个雇员的服务行为活动。金融行业监管局的主要任务是对经纪行业的公司进行认证许可和监管。特别重要的是，金融行业监管局对注册经纪人进行认证许可。注册经纪人是在投资银行或证券公司工作并将收取佣金为主要收入来源的咨询师。

所有注册的经纪人必须持有相关的证券许可。虽然证券许可的种类五花八门，但是有一种最为常见，即一般证券代表许可，又称为系列 7 许可。金融行业监管局认证的这一许可考试共有 250 道题目，涉及投资相关的各种问题。考试时间为 6 个小时，难度很大。任何需要向客户推荐投资证券产品的专业人员都需要考取系列 7 许可。另一个非常受欢迎的证照是投资公司产品/可变合同专业代表许可（系列 6 许可）。获得该许可的专业人士可以向客户推荐共同基金及年金产品，但现在其受欢迎程度不如以往。①

四、市场及消费者披露

根据联邦证券交易委员会及州投资顾问条款的规定，理财规划师需要向当前及潜在客户详细披露以下信息。这些披露的信息是最基本的要求：

以往违纪行为

以往破产文件

报酬收取表格（不必披露收入总额）

其他经营所得

所有违纪相关信息

背景资料

以往经验

相关财务信息

① 这个考试时长 2 小时，共有 100 道题目。

有关对客户资产自由支配的相关事项

托管披露及程序

账户审核程序

市场分析程序

利益冲突

隐私条款

风险及资产配置多样化策略

其他客户的总体情况（不要求披露客户姓名）

所提供服务清单

认证情况

理财规划师个人情况介绍

有关投资顾问的披露条款与经纪代表的披露条款不同，需要披露的内容更多。政策制定者认为之所以制定不同的披露规定，是因为与客户关系不同。他们认为收取费用的理财规划师应遵循信托标准，须向客户提供最好的服务和产品，因此，需要更高要求的披露标准。收取佣金的理财规划师是交易导向的，而经纪人只需针对客户的某种情况推荐某种合理的产品或服务。因此所需要披露的信息比较有限，保险销售人员需要遵循的披露准则与经纪人类似。

目前我们讨论的监管及披露政策分为联邦层面、州一级及自律组织。但实际上理财规划师有可能同时受到这三个层级的监管机构的监督，虽然这种情况很少发生，但是如果是这样的，理财规划师需要花费大量的时间和精力处理与之相关的合规要求。

如上提及的披露准则若仍显不足，持有专业证照的理财规划师还要受到所在协会的约束。在美国，最受欢迎的是 CFP 资格认证。完成 CFP 教育并通过资格认证考试的理财规划师必须遵守美国 CFP 委员会[①]发布的道德准则和实践标准。截至目前，有近 70 000 人持有 CFP 资格并向客户提供理财规划服务。不管这些理财规划师是否受到联邦、州一级或自律组织的监管都需要按照美国 CFP 委员会的要求向客户进行广泛而详细的披露。[②]

所有的 CFP 专业人士都需要遵循以下七大道德准则和行为标准：

正直诚信

① CFP 委员会（CFP Board of Standards，Inc. ）拥有 CFP® 商标。

② 与联邦及州立监管机构不同，CFP Board 仅拥有限制 CFP 商标使用的权力。而联邦、州及自律组织拥有取消理财师向客户提供服务的法律权力。

客观公正

专业胜任

公平公正

保守秘密

专业精神

恪尽职守

以上每一个准则都有细则进行解释说明。总体来讲，CFP 持证人必须向现有及潜在客户进行有关利益冲突的信息披露。披露内容必须完整、易懂，并进行一定的解释说明。最为重要的是有关报酬的披露。与金融监管局的规定不同，所有的 CFP 持证人必须披露支付方式及来源。

图 2 –9 展示了目前为止，美国理财规划行业有关不同层级的披露规定。最底层为自律组织及州级保险代理人的标准，披露的内容相对有限。遵循证券交易委员会或者州投资代理人标准的理财规划师必须遵守更高一级的披露标准。一般来说，对服务收取费用的投资顾问遵循信托标准，他们需要遵循的披露标准也更高一级。遵循最高披露标准的是由美国 CFP 委员会认证的 CFP 专业人士。这些理财规划师需要遵循许可准则，有时还需要遵循证券交易委员会的规定，同时需要遵循 CFP 委员会发布的有关披露及行为标准。

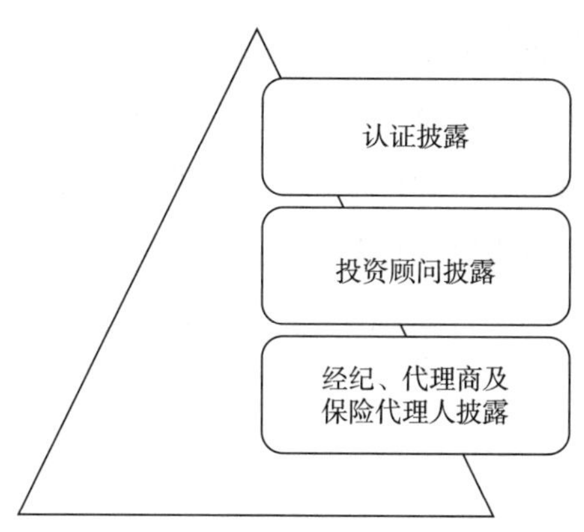

图 2 –9　披露层级金字塔

第三章　理财规划实务操作

第一节　理财规划服务流程

根据理财规划的基本定义，理财规划是以流程为导向的。理财规划与战略管理的发展携手并进。提供理财规划服务，首先要和客户建立联系，包括界定服务范围、披露收费和报酬标准及明确进行理财计划的假设前提。第二步是收集相关客户信息，在这一流程，要求理财规划师确定客户的个人和家庭理财目标、财务需求及财务状况。除了收集这些定量信息以外，理财规划师还应搜集一些定性信息，如客户的风险容忍程度、目标期望及其他可能影响数据分析的信息。

理财规划流程的第三步是十分重要的，包括分析及评估客户当前的财务状况。一般来说，这一步骤的分析是相当综合和广泛的，但是理财规划师也可以就客户的某一个理财目标进行分析评估。通常分为以下几个方面：

现金流及净资产状况

所得税情况

风险管理包括：

寿险

残障险

健康险

长期护理险

财产及意外险

投资相关情况

退休相关情况

遗产管理

特殊需求包括：

教育

老年护理

慈善及遗产

孩子的特殊需求

接下来就需要制作及报告理财规划建议。这一步需要发挥理财规划师的创造力及专业能力。下一步的关键是激发客户积极实施理财规划中的建议。对于许多理财规划师来说，这一步是产生利润的重要步骤，尤其是对于那些收取佣金的理财规划师而言。在这一步骤，理财规划师会选择最能满足客户需求的产品。但理财规划并不止步于理财规划的实施。理财规划流程要求理财规划师跟踪客户的后续情况，及时对理财建议进行调整。

图 3－1 展示了六步理财规划流程。整个过程是圆形的，而非线性的。理财流程在理财规划师与客户解除业务关系时才宣告终止。理财流程连续性的特点可以从监督客户执行理财计划和建立与客户的关系中总结出来。有时，理财服务完全是交易性质的。在这种情况下，产品或服务一经提供给消费者，理财关系即终止。大多数情况下，监督流程，包括持续的资产组合审核、年度目标评估及其他形式的执行监督，可以加深理财规划师与客户之间的关系，建立新的服务内容并创造新的服务机会。新的理财计划仍遵循六步骤理财流程。

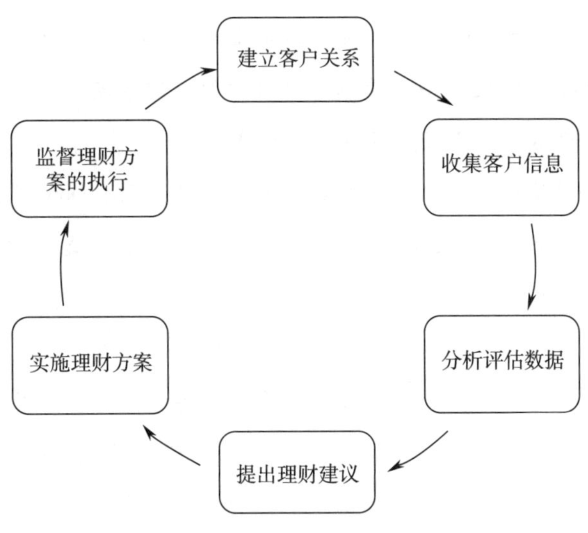

图 3－1　理财规划流程

案例

本书中，我们将运用 Smith 夫妇理财规划案例展示如何将理财流程运用到实际理财规划中。首先，作为理财规划的第一步，我们需要建立客户关系并收集客户的相关信息以了解我们的客户。

Don Smith 和 Rachel Smith 是一对夫妇，他们最近刚搬家到 S 市，并都有稳定的工作。他们正在考虑聘请一位理财规划师帮助管理自己的资产以实现未来的理财目标。在向亲朋好友打听有实力的理财规划师，并上网查询了相关信息之后，他们决定和你面谈，以决定是否聘请你担任他们的理财规划师。在第一次面谈会议中，你发现 Don 和 Rachel 都提出了非常好的问题，并且仔细聆听你对于问题的回答。一小时的面谈结束后，他们决定聘请你担任他们的理财规划师。

现在 Smith 夫妇正坐在你的办公室里，虽然在第一次面谈中，你已经对他们有了初步的了解，不过你还是需要收集一些必要的信息以开展理财规划服务。在这次会议之前，你让他们配合填写客户资料收集表。虽然 Smith 夫妇尽最大努力完成了表格的大部分内容，但是，和大多数客户一样，对于有些问题的回答，他们不是十分确定。以下是你收集到的有关 Smith 夫妇的信息：

一、个人资料

Don Smith

年龄：47 岁

工作情况：S 大学市场营销系副教授。这是 Don 的第二份工作。之前他在 A 大学供职 4 年。Don 最近开始向学校提供的退休账户里缴费，但学校并不为其缴费。

健康状况：Don 身体状况良好。预期寿命为 90 岁。

遗产继承：Don 的父母曾表示他和妹妹是遗产的受益人。Don 将获得大约 $300 000。Don 的父母目前身体状况良好。Don 预期在 10 年内不会获得这笔遗产。

Rachel Smith

年龄：37 岁

工作情况：Rachel 是一名会计。她曾从事多个财务管理工作。为了支持 Don 的工作，她放弃了在 A 市的工作而随 Don 一同搬到 S 市。很幸运，她也很快在 S 市找到了一份工作。Rachel 和她的工作单位每月分别向其退休账户缴纳工资收入的 3%。对于超过工资收入 3% 但不到 5% 的部分，Rachel 的工作单位为她配套缴纳其缴费部分的 50%。

健康状况：Rachel 总体健康状况良好。但是因为受到颈椎问题的困扰，每两周，

Rachel都需要进行理疗。预期寿命为 85 岁。

遗产继承：Rachel 预期将从母亲那里继承 $ 100 000。Rachel 的母亲目前身体状况良好，Rachel 预期在 10 年内不会获得这笔遗产。

Jackie Smith

Smith 夫妇有一个女儿，叫 Jackie，今年 9 岁，正在读小学，身体状况良好。

二、Smith 夫妇的理财目标及财务状况

Smith 夫妇希望你对他们的退休规划提供建议。他们本以为你只是推荐一个单一的理财产品或者退休规划建议。当了解到你可以进行综合理财规划时，他们决定和你共同商讨一个综合的理财规划。

Smith 夫妇的风险容忍程度相同。Don 在家中负责执行所有的投资计划并管理他们的个人和共同账户。Rachel 负责家中各项账单缴费并整理家庭理财报表和报税。

Smith 夫妇搬到 S 市时向银行贷款购置了一幢价值 $ 300 000 的公寓。贷款利率为固定利率 4%，贷款期限为 30 年。

三、理财规划目标（折算为当今价值）

Don 的目标（重要）

1. 退休前每年花费 $ 12 000 携 Rachel 和 Jackie 旅游及每年花费 $ 3 000 进行跳伞运动。

2. 储备足够的资金保证舒适的退休生活。

Rachel 的目标（重要）

1. 增加具有税收优惠的储蓄。

2. 在未来两年内准备充足的紧急备用金。

家庭理财目标（重要）

1. 为 Jackie 准备足够的四年大学的费用。他们预期每年的大学学费为 $ 15 000。

2. 15 年后偿清所有债务。

3. 明年将一间客房改为书房，费用约为 $ 18 000。

4. 改建厨房，费用约为 $ 15 000。

5. 在 2035 年共同退休。退休后预期每年花费为 $ 120 000。Don 去世后，Rachel 每年花费为 $ 75 000。如果 Rachel 先去世，Don 每年花费为 $ 80 000。

四、相关经济假设

1. 通货膨胀率：每年 4.35%。

2. 教育金增长：每年 8.0%。

3. 房产增值：每年 3.5%。

4. 当前的 30 年抵押贷款利率：3.125%；当前的 15 年抵押贷款利率：2.500%。

五、保险

1. 车险：100/300/300 renewed every six months on 08/15 每半年续保一次。

2. 寿险：$240 000 定期寿险，受益人为 Rachel，投保人为 Don。$50 000 万能寿险，投保人为 Rachel，年增长率为 4.8%，Jackie 为受益人。保险金额没有设定任何特定理财目标。

3. 健康险：免赔额为 $2 000；共保比率为 90/10；止损金额为 $5 000；终身保险限额为 $300 万。

4. 伤残险：Don100% 自己支付一份长期职业伤残险的保费。保费支付可使用税后资金，领取赔付时免税。保险收益包含 60% 疾病和意外，并有 180 天的等待期。保险赔付至受益人伤残恢复或 65 岁时终止。

六、投资方面

1. 没有特别的投资计划。

2. Rachel 辞职时，将所有的养老金余额转至个人退休账户。

3. 除特别说明，所有的金融资产都用于理财目标的实现。

4. 他们不打算变卖资产来实现目标。

七、税务方面

尽可能减少个人所得税。

八、退休方面

1. Smith 夫妇二人都有社会保障。他们打算仅用社保账户的资金支持退休生活。

2. Don 的大学提供确定收益型退休计划。Don 每年缴费为工资收入的 2.2% 。目前该退休计划的年收益率为 5.7%。到 70 岁时，Don 可获得的年退休金为 $203 845（以未来现金价值计算）。给付开始时，该退休金将随通货膨胀调整。

3. 他们计划每年向 Don 和 Rachel 的个人退休账户缴纳最高限额。

九、遗产方面

Smith 夫妇在 8 年前设立了遗嘱，并规定将所有资产留给对方，并在所有的退休账户将对方设定为受益人（Don 的受益人是 Rachel；Rachel 的受益人是 Don）。除个人资产外，所有的资产都登记为共同所有。

第二节　理财规划流程的组成部分

理财规划流程的复杂程度取决于单个理财规划师在实践中的决定。接下来我们将探讨现金流分析在大多数家庭理财规划中的重要作用，理财规划目标的建立和分析，理财规划财务报表在流程规划中的运用（包括现金流量表和资产负债表）及理财规划中的宏观经济因素假设。

一、理财规划的重要组成部分：现金流量规划

在实践中，理财规划师实施理财规划时，通常有两种方式。第一种是称为目标导向的资产规划，第二种是客户导向的现金流规划。这两种规划方法最大的不同点在于规划建议形成的方式。目标导向的规划方法是将企业资金管理的方法运用到个人和家庭的财务规划中。对企业进行理财规划，特别是为非营利机构进行财务规划，理财规划师在为客户构建资产组合时，通常是基于客户当前和未来的债务需求。因此当理财规划师把这套方法运用到个人或家庭的财务规划时，往往会先确定客户的某项融资需求。例如，某客户希望自己在67岁退休，退休后余寿为25年，退休后经通货膨胀调整后的年收入为90 000美元。理财规划师会将客户的所有理财目标进行排序，然后分析客户的资产负债表，而不是现金流量表。如果分析结果显示基于客户当前的资产负债状况及合理假设，理财目标不能实现，理财规划的重点将在于如何弥补资金缺口以满足客户一个或多个财务需求。例如，理财规划师可能建议客户适当增加资产组合的风险以达成目标。

这是目标理财规划方法的特别之处。通过比较当前财务状况和未来特定目标，理财规划师可以判断客户理财目标成功的概率。资金缺口可估算为未来资产现金价值与期望目标成本之间的差值。这种方法在资产配置上也相当灵活。由于可以构建多种资产组合，因此每一个理财目标都可以搭配各自的资产配置。这也是目标理财规划方法与客户导向的理财规划方法的最大分歧所在。运用目标规划法的理财规划师在进行分析规划时的重点并不是客户的个人风险态度、投资态度、以往投资经验及其他定性的数据，他们更加关注客户的风险承受能力而非客户承担投资失败结果的主观意愿。风险承受能力是指客户能够承担财务损失的能力，通常与客户的净资产状况相关。几乎所有的财务能力因素都体现在客户的资产负债表及他们的税务和风险评价表中。理财规划师在运用目标规划

法分析时竭力剔除非定量因素的影响。

从理财规划师实践经验角度看，目标规划法似乎既考虑了主观因素，又具有可操作性。每个客户的目标都是可以分别定价的，关键是如何定价。考虑到很少有客户投入足够的资金来实现自己的目标，因此资产组合都可以通过动态及税务调整的战略进行改进，这样通过一段时间的调整，资金缺口就会补足。

目标规划法简单易用，但同样也是它的缺点。由于它固定了理财规划中的定量数据，导致了理财目标的失败。我们可以这样来看待目标理财规划法：理财规划建议是基于客户的态度、情绪及心理等因素而做出的满足客户最低要求的建议，因此往往导致未来理财目标的失败。我们需要知道客户大多数是风险厌恶的。当遇到长期或者没有料想到的资产损失时，客户会对自己的理财战略产生犹豫并且会重新评估自己的选择。而目标规划法有时会迫使客户承担自己不愿意承担的风险。这在资产增值的时候不会发生问题，然而，一旦资产发生损失，规划执行就会受到阻碍和质疑。简而言之，目标规划法较适用于有足够风险承受能力的客户。对于那些因现金流不足而需要在资产配置抉择时犹豫不决并且十分纠结的客户，目标规划法则不是十分适用。

理财规划师利用以客户为中心的现金流规划法帮助客户以最大的可能性实现对客户来说最有价值的理财目标。该方法迫使客户理性斟酌自己的理财目标，理财规划师继而根据这个理财目标对客户的理财规划周期、遗产遗愿、生命周期、风险态度及其他重要因素进行全面分析后做出理财建议，其重点在于通过现金流的分配来为未来理财目标的实现筹集资金。虽然理财规划师也会考虑客户当前的资产状况，但是理财规划的重点在于最大化可支配现金流。

可支配现金流 = 总收入 - 固定支出 - 可变支出 - 储蓄

理财规划师认为，客户态度因素，如风险态度和情绪的运用对于利用现金流规划引导客户未来行为起着非常重要的作用。回顾之前关于退休规划的例子。采用现金流规划的理财规划师会预测若采用目标规划法，客户的退休目标可能不会实现。有哪些证据支持这个论断呢？答案源于客户的风险容忍度及未来行为的关系。实证分析表明风险容忍度与财富水平正相关①，并且随着时间的推移，客户不断平衡风险承受意愿及风险承受能力。没有几个人会承受高于自己意愿水平的风险。

如果纯粹从技术角度进行分析，理财规划师就需要对每位当前及潜在客户的现金流

① Finke, Michael S., and Sandra J. Huston. 2003. "The Brighter Side of Financial Risk: Financial Risk Tolerance and Wealth." *Journal of Family and Economic Issues* 24 (3): 233 - 256.

进行分析。原因有二：首先，理财规划师需要分析客户现在和将来是否有足够的资金为理财目标投入资金。有些客户可以利用当前拥有的资产来为理财目标投资，但是这样的客户并不多见。大多数客户是依赖当前的现金流来投资的。其次，客户的现金流是支付理财规划师报酬的基础。换而言之，客户必须有充沛的可支配现金流投资自己的理财目标并支付理财规划师的服务费用。

接下来的章节会详细阐述现金流分析的方法。

二、理财目标及需求分析

不论理财规划师在实践中采用哪种方法进行理财规划分析，都需要先确立客户的理财目标。理财目标可以视为理财规划最终希望达到的终点。例如，一个客户的理财目标可能是在小孩满 18 岁时筹集足够的大学费用。具体内容可能包括四年大学的学费以及食宿、书本等杂费。为了最终达成理财目标，理财规划师有必要帮助客户制定清晰的、可实施的、具体的阶段性理财目标。在这个例子中，一个阶段性目标就是每月定期在享有税收优惠的大学存款计划中存入一定的资金。理财目标和阶段性理财目标是紧密相连的，如果客户不能循序渐进地完成每一个阶段性目标，那么最终理财目标的实现也只是空中楼阁。

理财目标和阶段性理财目标在理财规划的第一阶段就应明确设立。如果我们把理财计划过程当作一次旅行，理财规划书就是地图。显然，理财目标和阶段性理财目标就是在旅行中需要确立的完成进度及衡量理财成功与否的标准。

许多理财规划师和理财规划研究学者使用称为“SMART”的方法来帮助客户确立他们的理财目标。如图 3－2 所示，S 代表具体的，M 代表可衡量的，A 代表可行的，R 代表可实现的，T 代表可跟踪的。

S	·具体
M	·可衡量的
A	·可行的
R	·可实现的
T	·可跟踪的

图 3－2　SMART 理财目标的组成部分

通过运用 SMART 方法帮助客户确立行程目标和阶段目标对于帮助客户理解他们的财务情况是十分重要的。这个方法对于跟踪理财目标的达成是十分有效的。例如，如果一个客户希望她能够在有生之年做一次环游世界的旅行，并且希望在退休后两年内完成。该客户让理财规划师帮助她设计一个理财计划来帮助她实现梦想。显然，客户提供的信息是不足的。如果没有清晰的目标，理财规划师很难为客户提供最大的帮助。

理财规划师不应被动接受客户有关目标设定的陈述，而应当运用 SMART 方法帮助客户重新确立和完善目标。目前，该客户提供了有关理财目标的部分具体信息，即她希望在退休两年内完成环球旅行的梦想。紧接着，理财规划师想到的问题应该是，目标达成是在 5 年后，10 年后，15 年后还是 20 年后。这样看来，客户陈述的目标是不可测量的。理财规划师需要计算出旅行花费的现值。因为完成一个 10 000 美元的目标和完成一个 100 000 美元的目标所提出的理财建议是完全不同的。这引发我们思考另一个问题，即目标的可行性。每个人都有梦想和愿望。没有哪个人会拒绝豪华的世界环游计划。现实的问题是，拥有这个愿望的人是否能支付得起这笔费用？换句话讲，理财规划师需要评估客户是否拥有达成理财目标的财务能力。财务能力由流动资产、可支配现金流及未来财富所得等因素决定。因此，目标设定应该充分考虑它的可实现性。例如，该客户希望完成一个价值 100 000 美元的世界旅行，但却只能支付 25 000 美元，那么她的目标就是不可实现的。试图完成一个根本无法达成的愿望，结果往往是不尽如人意的。在实践中，如果一个理财规划师在与客户合作的初期就判断出客户的目标是不可实现的，那么在理财计划实施的过程中，理财规划师与客户关系就会中止。最后，理财目标必须是可以跟踪的。理财规划师和客户都需要随时监测理财计划的实施是否在实现理财目标的轨道上稳步发展。在这个案例中，可跟踪性包括计算为世界旅行所投资的年回报率及未达成目标的储蓄率。

在实践中，理财规划师很少只考虑客户的单一理财目标。理财规划师是一个综合的过程，需要综合考虑客户方方面面的财务状况，各种目标也是交织在一起的。通常，实现一个目标可能会影响另一个目标的完成。理财规划师在帮助客户设立目标时，需要清楚地设定各个目标完成的时间进度表。如表 3－1 所示，目标期限可以分为短期、长期或介于两者之间的中期。如果客户的理财目标较短，理财建议一般趋向于保守。

表 3－1　目标达成时间

目标期限	目标时间
超短期	≤9 个月
短期	9 个月至 2.5 年
中短期	2.5～5 年
中长期	5～10 年
长期	10 年以上

运用SMART方法设定目标是十分容易的。客户会觉得目标设定没有那么复杂，甚至还是很有乐趣的。但这可能导致客户目标设定得特别冗余。虽然客户参与理财目标的设定对于理财规划计划的制定是十分重要的，但有时也会给理财规划师带来操作的不便。除非客户拥有不计其数的财产，否则所有的理财目标都必须按照一定标准的优先顺序进行排序。这个过程说起来容易，做起来难。回顾刚才环球旅行的案例。虽然客户的理财目标是世界旅行，但理财规划师应该能够判断这不应该也不可以是她的主要理财目标。其他诸如退休计划、支付日常费用及其他目标都需要被优先考虑。以下问题可以帮助理财规划师厘清思路，以便对客户的理财目标进行排序。①

该目标对于客户来说有多重要？

在整个理财计划中，该目标的实现有多重要？

该目标是客户的需求还是愿望？

是否有其他方法可以解决？

这个目标需要一次性投入资金完成吗？

目标实现的概率有多大？

目标实现的资金何时需要？

是否可以延期完成目标？

筹集完成目标所需的资金需要多长时间？

如果目标不能完成，是否会对客户产生严重的影响？

对于以上的问题并没有一个统一的标准答案。例如之前的案例。环球旅行不能完成对于客户能产生多么严重的影响，只有客户自己可以回答。如果她说，“如果可以实现当然很好，实现不了也没什么要紧”，这就表示，理财规划师可以把该理财目标排在所有需要实现的目标中较次级的位置。但是如果客户说，“如果不能实现，我的人生就不完整了，我的余生都会为此感到遗憾。”那么理财规划师就需要重新调整这个目标实现的优先级别了。通常情况下，优先级别高的理财目标是那些如果不实现，就会产生严重影响的目标。平衡短期和长期目标可以帮助客户了解他们的财务目标实现的情况。

---

① 这个清单是根据以下资料来源整理：Slade，Stephen. 1994. “Goal - Based Decision Making：An Interpersonal Model. ” Hillsdale，NJ：Lawrence Erlbaum Associates.

三、财务诊断及财务报表分析

客户理财目标的确立是整个理财过程的基础。理财规划师在确立了客户的理财目标并完成目标的优先级排序后，接下来就要对客户的财务能力进行评估，以保证理财目标最终实现。制作理财计划时需要用到两个重要的报表：现金流量表[①]和资产负债表。

在介绍有关如何运用这两个报表的详细内容之前，我们有必要先明确几个重要的概念。本章所提及现金流量表是记录客户在一段时间内的所得和所花费的金额的记录。这与预算的概念完全不同。预算是理财规划师和财务咨询师帮助客户确定未来花费的工具。有时，预算也被称为花费计划。理财规划师可以借助现金流量表判断客户的理财目标是否按照既定的计划顺利达成。当客户的存储计划执行不力或者收入遇到波动时，理财规划师可以采用预算技术帮助客户进行规划。

（一）现金流量表

如前章所述，可支配现金流在理财规划流程中起着至关重要的作用。判断客户是否能够达成部分或全部理财目标的一个重要因素是客户从现金流中获得资金达成储蓄目标的能力[②]。表3－2展示了一个典型的现金流量表。

收入列在现金流量表的顶部。把收入分为既得收入、未得收入和免税收入，对今后理财规划师进行税务筹划十分有用。例如，既得收入比起未得收入，可能会征收不同的税率。

支出通常被分为固定支出（不可支配支出）和可变支出（可支配支出）。固定支出存在很强的规律性。例如房屋支出（房屋贷款或者租金）必须按期缴付，因此这种支出被视为固定支出。需要重点强调的是，如果客户定期进行存款，那么存款也可以划分在固定支出类。例如与客户工资收入相挂钩的退休存款就可以视为固定支出。再投资的股息、利息及资本利得也可以划分为固定支出。收入费用化不当可能造成高估收入，或者收入计算不准确，因而影响可支配现金流的计算。可变支出是指那些客户可以自由支配的花费，例如食品。几乎所有的客户都可以在食物支配上进行调整。这样的调整并不是出于客户的喜好，而是一个增加现金流的方法。

确定客户的可支配现金流的方法相对直接。收入减去固定支出和可变支出的结果可以判断客户是否有多余的现金流用以理财目标的资金投入。

---

① 有时，现金流量表又被称作收入费用表。

② 简单起见，现金流分析以年为单位。

表 3－2　　现金流量表

收入	客户 A	客户 A－附属	总计
既得收入 工资薪金 奖金 其他			
未得收入 利息 股息 经营收入 年金 租金 版税 其他			
免税收入 赠予 借款 奖学金 其他			
收入总计			
固定支出	客户 A	客户 A－附属	总计
税务支出 个人所得税 其他			
工资收入抵减项 健康医疗保险 退休金 其他			
债务偿还 房屋（本金及利息）或者租金 房屋净值贷款 汽车贷款 学生贷款 抵押贷款 无抵押贷款 信用卡 其他			

续表

收入	客户 A	客户 A－附属	总计
保险			
汽车			
房屋或租屋			
寿险（非工资收入抵减部分）			
残障险（非工资收入抵减部分）			
健康险（非工资收入抵减部分）			
长期护理险			
其他			
固定的储蓄和投资			
一般存款			
为退休生活的存款			
为子女教育的存款			
为特殊需要的存款			
为特定目的的存款			
再投资的股息、红利及资本利得			
固定支出总计			
可变支出	客户 A	客户 A－附属	总计
房屋及公共事业费			
房屋修理及维护费			
草坪、院子整理维护费用			
公共事业费			
其他			
家庭支出			
衣服鞋帽支出			
洗衣、干洗费			
个人护理			
家具			
钟点工			
补贴			
子女幼托费用			
其他			
食品			
杂货			
外出就餐			

续表

可变支出	客户 A	客户 A－附属	总计
娱乐 网络、电视 个人爱好 娱乐设施 旅游 俱乐部会费 其他			
医疗 个人自付款 处方药 一般医疗费用 未报销的医疗费用 其他			
交通 汽油及汽车维护费 牌照及手续费 停车拖车费 公共交通 其他			
杂费 订阅 电话 礼品 慈善捐助 烟酒等 子女补助 赡养费 宠物 邮费 银行手续费 投资手续费 律师费 其他			
可变支出总计			

续表

收入	客户 A	客户 A - 附属	总计
总收入			
固定支出总计			
可变支出总计			
= 可支配现金流			

案例

还记得在本章第一节介绍的 Smith 夫妇吗？作为理财师，在第一次面谈时，你搜集了关于 Smith 家庭生活方式、理财目标及总体财务状况的相关信息。在收集客户信息这一理财规划阶段，要尽可能收集有关客户收入及支出所有来源的相关信息。以下的现金流量表囊括了有关客户年（月）现金流情况。这个现金流量表与之前展示的现金流量表范例（表 3－2）有所不同，这是因为现金流量表的具体科目设置需要根据客户的实际情况进行调整。估算现金流量是理财规划中至关重要的一步。当你已经掌握了客户的现金流量情况后，就可以对客户的财务状况进行分析。如下表所示，Smith 一家对于自身的财务管理还是相当不错的。他们每月（年）都有储蓄。对于这样的客户，理财规划师提出的理财建议有资金保证实施。

现金流量表

January 1，20XX to December 31，20XX

收入	年度数据	月度数据
工资薪金（H）	$150 000	$12 500
工资薪金（W）	65 000	5 417
利息股息收入	1 326	111
资本利得	5 787	482
总计	$222 113	$18 509
支出		
403b 退休计划（H）	$17 000	$1 417
401k 退休计划（W）	$17 000	$1 417
个人退休投资账户（H）	5 000	417
个人退休投资账户（W）	5 000	417
灵活消费账户（H）	3 000	250
灵活消费账户（W）	1 000	83
定期储蓄账户（JT）	1 000	83
联邦个人所得税代扣代缴	33 617	2 801

续表

收入	年度数据	月度数据
州个人所得税代扣代缴	9 511	793
社会保险账户	10 472	873
抵押贷款	12 780	1 194
财产税	6 319	527
车辆贷款	8 625	719
公共事业缴费：电	1 350	113
天然气	1 560	130
水	660	55
电话	1 440	120
有线电视	480	40
网络	720	60
保险：车辆	1 250	104
健康	4 200	350
残障	220	18
保险伞	260	22
内陆水上运输	60	5
定期寿险	90	8
两全险	250	21
房屋	620	52
医疗/牙齿/眼睛护理费用	3 000	250
孩子托儿所/幼儿园费用	5 760	480
硬件/软件	5 200	433
清洁服务	960	80
草坪维护	1 580	132
汽油及汽车维护费用	2 600	217
食品	10 800	900
个人护理/置装费用	7 260	605
协会会员费	1 050	88
跳伞运动	3 000	250
度假旅游	12 000	1 000
捐赠	18 000	1 500
总计	$205 314	$17 238
盈余＝可自由支配的现金流	$16 799	$1 271

（二）资产负债表

理财规划中用到的第二张重要的报表是资产负债表。资产负债表提供了客户拥有的资产和所欠的债务情况。表3－3为一张资产负债表。在实际运用中，理财规划师需要针对客户的具体情况更改表格中的具体项目，但是资产负债科目的顺序是不变的。通常，资产是按照其流动性排列的。很容易在市场中转换为现金的资产列在资产类的开始部分，例如，支票及储蓄资产一般都列在资产负债表的第一项。流动性差的资产，例如收藏品、家具及船只通常列在资产类的最底端。

同样地，负债科目是按照他们的偿付期列示在资产负债表中。在负债科目中首先列示的是短期债务，包括信用卡余额。短期负债是指当前尚未偿付但会在一年内付清的所有债券、负债及消费。如果客户延期缴付公共事业费及其他短期未偿付消费，需要列示在负债科目中。

理财规划师在帮助客户估算资产负债价值时，需要向客户阐明以下原则。首先，资产需要以公允价值估算。公允价值是在公开市场中资产的现金价值。有时，客户会使用资产当时购买时的价值记账，但这种处理是不对的，因为资产负债表中客户和理财规划师对资产的评估衡量了资产流动性。对货币及投资资产进行估值比对个人及使用资产进行估值要容易得多。在美国和加拿大，理财规划师可以通过查询例如 Edmunds. com 及 KBB. com 网站估算使用过的汽车的价值。对于船只及家具的价值，则可以通过查询二手店的价格来进行估算。其次，债务的价值须等于付清债务所需的全部资金。例如，一个客户拥有一辆汽车，并附有三年的汽车贷款尚未还清，资产负债表中的债务价值须等于客户每月账单中应偿付的资金。

资产负债表中最后列示的数据是客户的净资产。

$$净资产 = 资产 - 负债$$

在某一阶段，客户应当持有多少金额的净资产，是没有固定的标准的。总体上，客户的净资产应当随着客户生命周期的推移不断增长，每一个客户的净资产绝对数额会因客户年龄、投资态度（债务厌恶水平）、可支配现金流及财务意外所得这些因素的不同而不同。

有时，客户对于资产负债表和现金流量表的用途感到困惑。这两个报表是所有理财计划的基础，因此，理财规划师会认为客户理所当然懂得区分出这两种报表用途的不同。而实际不然，这有时会造成理财规划师和客户的分歧。所以，理财规划师需要向客户，特别是新客户，解释两种报表的不同。现金流量表是用来记录收入所得、存储及支出情况。资产负债表仅用以记录客户的资产和负债。客户经常对储蓄在两张报表中的含义感到不解。现金流科目，例如在享有税务延期的退休账户中的存款体现为资产负债表资产的增加。同样地，用资产偿付债务会增加客户的现金流但不会改变净资产的数值。理财规划师可以一步步演示这些过程，以帮助客户清晰地理解这两张报表之间的关系。理财规划师不应想当然认为客户会理解现金流科目（例如每月的退休储蓄）、资产及负债科目之间的不同，而应通过现实或假设的数据向客户演示这两张报表的钩稽关系。

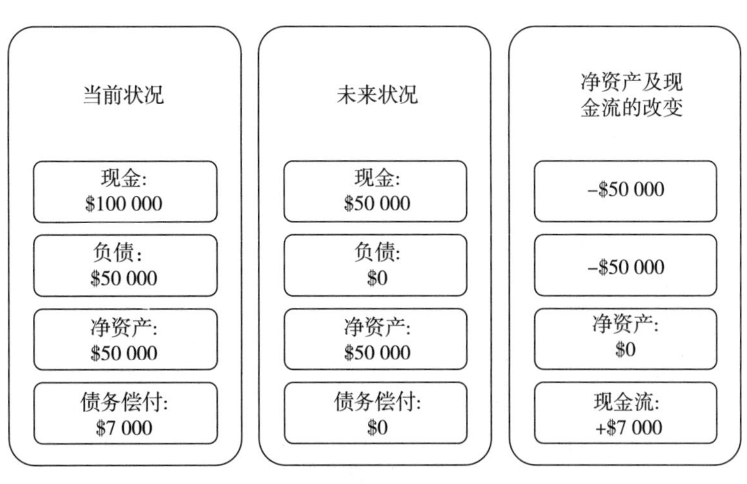

图 3－3　净资产及现金流举例

理财规划师可以利用如图 3－3 所示的内容向客户解释资产负债表和现金流量表的不同。图 3－3 清晰地说明了利用资产减少负债对客户的净资产并不产生影响，但可以增加可支配现金流。这个简单的道理正是理财规划及咨询的基础。在理财规划流程中，重要的一步就是确定可以用以实现理财规划目标的现金流。其他常用的增加现金流的方法有：再融资当前债务、减少当前可支配的支出、增加增产的投资回报及平衡各种债务的运用以增加客户的财务灵活度。

表 3－3　　　　资产负债表

资产	客户 A	客户 A－附属	总计
货币性资产			
支票账户			
储蓄账户			
货币基金			
存单			
其他			

续表

资产	客户 A	客户 A－附属	总计
投资资产 股票 债券 共同基金 期货 其他			
房地产 自住房屋 第二套房屋 度假房屋 其他			
投资资产 税务递延型退休计划 免税资产 其他			
保险资产 雇主提供的寿险保单 有现金价值保单 其他			
为教育准备的资产 有税收优势的资产 储蓄债券 其他			
个人资产 汽车 船只 收藏品 其他			
使用资产 家具 电器 其他			

续表

总负债	客户 A	客户 A－附属	总计
短期债务 信用卡 短期的分期付款的债务 其他			
长期债务 抵押贷款 汽车贷款 消费性贷款 其他			
总资产			
总负债			
净值			

案例

以下为 Smith 家庭的资产负债表。正如 Smith 家庭的现金流量表与样本现金流量表的科目设置有所不同，Smith 家庭的资产负债表也与样本资产负债表不同。Smith 家庭的资产负债管理情况良好。对于他们这个年龄阶段而言，他们目前的资产净值相对较高。之后我们将利用财务指标对 Smith 家庭的整体财务状况作出分析。

资产负债表

截至 1 月 1 日，20××年

资产	所有权	余额	历史价值		负债	所有权	余额	
现金及现金等价物					汽车贷款余额	JT	$10 513	
支票账户	JT	$5 200			抵押贷款	JT	231 284	
货币基金	JT	16 800						
经纪账户	W	5 032						
人寿保险的现金价值	W	3 647						
		总计		$30 679				
投资								
股票 1	H	$10 518	$6 000		总负债			$241 797
股票 2	H	33 839	18 000					
股票 3	W	30 849	15 000					
股票 4	W	27 678	20 000					

续表

资产	所有权	余额	历史价值		负债	所有权	余额	
共同基金	JT	84 782	65 000					
		总计		$ 187 666				
退休账户资产								
不可行权支取的确定收益	H	$ 38 463						
403b	H	70 263			净值			$ 862 577
401（k）1	W	73 776						
401（k）2	H	135 837						
IRA1	H	53 814						
IRA2	H	9 460						
IRA3	W	82 435						
IRA4	W	5 524						
		总计		$ 431 109				
使用性资产								
住房	JT	$ 315 920						
车辆	JT	61 000						
家具	JT	30 000						
计算机（硬件，软件及网络）	H	5 000						
珠宝	W	20 000						
收藏品	W	23 000						
		总计		$ 454 920				
总资产				$ 1 104 374	总负债及净值			$1 104 374

注：H ＝ 丈夫的资产；W ＝ 妻子的资产；JT ＝ 共同所有。

（三）运用财务指标评估当前财务状况

理财规划师及他们的客户需要了解，根据资产累积、债务结构及现金流管理的情况，我们可以预测理财目标是否能按照原定计划实现。然而在30年或40年前，我们一般认为资产和收入越高的客户更加有可能实现财务计划中的推荐目标，现在，理财规划师了解到起决定作用的是资产与债务、资产与可支配现金流之间的比率。根据目标分析，拥有最多财富的家庭或个人通常杠杆比率较高，流动性较差。

当今，理财规划师利用多种财务比率衡量客户实现理财方案的能力及目标实现的进度。表3－4列示了最常用的财务比率（这里没有列示衡量房屋贷款可能性的比率，在本书后面的部分会详细介绍）。对于熟悉证券分析的人来讲，这些比率与财务经理所使用的比率十分类似。事实上，理财规划师采用了公司财务的这些比率并把它们运用到家庭理财中。表3－4还列示了每个比率的标准。这些标准比率是得到理财规划行业公认，并一致同意的。例如，一些理财规划师认为客户只需要2个月的紧急储备金就足够了，而一些理财规划师则认为客户需要9个月以上的储备金，这些储备金必须能从存款或者能够兑换成现金价值的寿险中得到。这些标准比率给理财规划师执行理财计划提供了参考依据。

表3－4　　　　财务比率

比率	计算公式	衡量标准
流动比率	货币资产／流动负债	>1.0
紧急储备金比率	货币资产/月生活支出	3~6个月
储蓄比率	总存款/ 总收入	>10%
债务比率	总负债/ 总资产	< 40%
长期债务负债比率	年总收入/总负债	>2.5
债务收入比	消费负债/ 税后收入	< 15%

需要注意的是，财务比率只是衡量财务健康状况的客观指标。正因为如此，比率的绝对数值取决于每一个客户特定的生命周期所处的阶段。例如，刚毕业踏入工作岗位的职员可能没有或刚达到流动比率或债务比率标准。他们的学生贷款和消费贷款的金额可能超过了他们的全部资产。如果他们使用的债务是投资于人力资本（为以后的收入增长能力的投资），那么这个比率就是完全可以接受的。随着今后资产金额的提高，债务水平会逐渐下降。在这种情况下，财务比率变成了财务目标。另外，接近退休的客户的财务比率大部分都超过标准比率。如果这类客户的财务比率严重不达标，则需要立刻采取措施进行弥补。

案例

在对客户进行综合理财规划时，我们通常首先通过估算财务指标来分析和评估客户的财务状况。Smith一家的财务指标如下表所示。总体来说，Smith夫妇能够有效管理自己的资产。我们无法计算Smith家庭的流动比率和债务收入比率，因为他们并没有短期消费性债务。这意味着他们拥有更多的现金流用来满足储蓄及其他目标。紧急备用金比率介于1个月至3个半月之间。这个比率之所以有这么大的波动范围，是因为我们使用的数据不同。如果我们使用月支出计算，则该比率将低于标准值，如果我们剔除退休账户支出及税务支出，紧急备用金的数量将足够大。Smith家庭的储蓄率大于10%，这表明他们在储蓄这方面做得很好。在计算储蓄时，我们将可自由支配的现金流、其他形式的储蓄及退休账户的扣缴都包含在内。22%的负债比率表明Smith家庭的债务在其可控范围内。Smith家庭理财比率分析：

比率	参考比率	实际比率
流动比率	大于1.0	n. a.
紧急储备金比率	3~6个月	1.78~3.53
储蓄比率	大于10%	28%
债务比率	少于40%	22%
长期债务负债比率	大于2.5	10.38
债务收入比	少于15%	n. a.

在理财规划的这一阶段，理财师需要归纳总结客户财务情况的优势及劣势。我们结合这个案例总结了Smith夫妇家庭的财务状况。

优势：

- 资产净值较高；
- 年收入较高，现金流较充分；
- 夫妇二人每月都向自己的退休账户内供款；
- Don拥有残障险保障；
- 所有的家庭成员都有健康保险；
- 收藏品有保险保障。

劣势：

- Smith家庭需要考虑有关遗产规划的相关问题。目前他们的遗嘱没有关于生存条款及医疗照护事前指示的条款。目前的遗嘱为8年前拟定，需要根据当前的家庭情况进行相应更新和调整。
- Smith家庭没有对其珠宝购买保险保障。
- Smith家庭需要对其寿险保单的保单持有人情况进行梳理和确认。按照目前的情况，如果一方发生亡故，将会增加遗产税的负担。
- 抵押贷款利息水平高于当前市场水平。
- 教育金准备不足。
- Rachel的残障险保障不足。
- 双方都没有长期护理险。

四、理财规划的宏观经济环境及基本假设

与其他行业不同，理财规划需要大量依赖对经济变量的假设。Lytton，Grable 和 Klock 2013 年[①]出版的《理财规划流程：制作理财规划》一书中将理财规划假设定义为“基于影响客户理财规划需求及实现理财目标的相关数据的前提、合理推论、事实或相关依据的参考”（第 265 页）。在理财规划中经常出现的假设有收益回报率、利率、生命周期、健康状况、幸福度及经济假设等。经济指标是帮助理财规划师进行合理假设的工具。这些假设从理财规划开始阶段就要确立，直到理财规划的实施阶段仍旧使用。接下来，介绍几乎所有的理财规划师在日常理财实践中都要使用的主要宏观经济指标。

理解和预测未来经济通货膨胀水平是十分重要的。实际和预测的通货膨胀水平是资产价格的主要决定因素之一。总体来说，增长的物价水平会反映到金融资产价格水平的跌落上，特别是固定收益类的股票产品。理财规划师如果判断未来通货膨胀水平的上涨，那么就会将这一假设运用到理财规划的所有计算中。例如，上涨的通货膨胀水平会增加退休资产的需求、教育储蓄的需求并需要进行保护资产价格下降的资产配置。另外，如果通货膨胀水平下降，理财规划师则会考虑更加激进的投资战略。理财规划师实时关注和预测以下指标以发现通货膨胀率。一般来说，增长的物价、产品供应、工资、就业水平、房产、进口及 GDP 价格被认为是未来通货膨胀的预警。

消费价格指数：某一时期城镇居民一揽子日常消费商品的价格。

生产价格指数：某一时期已经完成的商品的价格。

劳动力价格指数：城镇居民的工资福利指数。

就业指数：城镇居民失业率水平。

房产价格指数：房地产市场的季度价格变化。

进出口价格指数：进出口商品和服务的价格。

国内生产总值价格指数：一定时期国内生产总值的价格变化。

除预测通货膨胀水平外，理财规划师还经常追踪主要投资和资产市场的情况。这些市场的变化是理财规划中投资回报率假设的基础。几乎所有的专业理财软件都包含投资回报率、价格相关系数及价格波动率假设。然而，这些设定的假设只能作为理财规划师对于个别理财规划方案设定假设的参考，因为软件中的假设都是由专业人士或专业小组

---

① Lytton, R. H., Grable, J. E., & Klock, D. D.（2013）. *The process of financial planning: Developing a financial plan*（2nd ed.）. Erlanger, KY: National Underwriter.

根据整体市场趋势设定的。无论这些假设是如何计算的，以下这些市场指数都会作为投资回报率假设的历史参考。

股票市场

澳洲普通股票指数

美国 AMEX 综合指数

巴西 Bovespa 指数

法国 CAC40 指数

德国 DAX 指数

道琼斯欧洲 50 股票指数

道琼斯工业指数

道琼斯 5000 指数

金融时报英国 100 指数

金融时报富时 100 指数

金融时报新兴市场指数

泛欧 300 指数

恒生指数

西班牙 IBEX 35 指数

墨西哥指数

爱尔兰 ISEQ 20 指数

印度尼西亚 JSX 指数

韩国 KOSPI 指数

MSCI 全球指数

纳斯达克指数

日经 225 指数

新西兰 NZX50 指数

俄罗斯 RTS 指数

罗素 3000 指数

S&P500 指数

S&P 亚洲 50 指数

印度指数

S&P 欧洲 350 指数

S&P 意大利 MIB 指数

中国上证指数

新加坡 ST 指数

瑞士市场指数

伊拉克 TA－25 指数

中国台湾 TSEC

货币市场

加拿大元

欧元

日元

英镑

美元

商品期货

黄金

轻质原油

天然气

谷物

股票

3 个月美国短期国库券

10 年期美国长期国债

30 年期美国长期国债

3 个月 LIBOR

总体来说，理财规划假设可以分为与客户情况相关的假设和基本假设。例如，与客户情况相关的假设包括客户的寿命，这个假设与客户的健康情况、家庭组织情况及可能的发展、未来的收入所得税税率及风险调整后的收益率有关。大部分情况下，与客户情况相关的假设是通过与客户的面谈和沟通得来。例如，在客户投资理财目标期间，是否需要增加存款需要理财规划师与客户沟通共同商定。基本假设适用于各种客户的总体理财计划。基本假设的举例如下，有些与之前介绍的市场指数类似：

平均通货膨胀率

平均养老院费用

平均固定收益产品回报率

平均房产收益率

平均股票价格回报率

基准安全取款率

大学学费增长率

当前和未来遗产及赠予税率

当前和未来普通收入税率

五、生命周期及现金流生涯仿真

生命周期是指一个人由于经济环境、自身态度及心理因素的变化而随之发生变化的过程。本章的开始部分展示了一个基本的现金流报表。现金流报表是所有理财规划工作的重点。实际上，一个年度的现金流量表记录了一个客户所有的收入及支出情况。

对客户的整个生命周期进行现金流模拟能够增加理财规划流程的价值。理财规划师和他们的客户都需要检验理财建议是否一直合理有效。简单的现金流量表或者资产负债表是不能提供充分依据的。现金流模拟可以展示综合理财规划计划的实施是如何改变客户一生的财务状况的。需要理财规划师注意的是，当我们对客户的现金流进行生涯仿真时，这里生命周期的概念相对广义，会因客户具体情况而异。分析的长度可以很短，又可以很长，甚至计算到客户生命终止。

表3－5展示了一个简单的现金流生涯仿真的例子。生涯仿真分析向大家说明了对四年大学费用的融资是如何影响一个客户现金流状况的。这个分析的主旨是探讨该客户是否有能力负担子女就读一个学费相对昂贵的大学，或即使自身现金流不能负担也要举债负担或选择另一所大学。分析结果表明供子女完成四年大学学业使家庭现金流下降。该客户需要借债以平衡收支。然而，借债部分与客户的年收入相比，并不庞大。利用现金流生涯仿真，理财规划师可以向客户展示，当完成了子女教育费用的支出后，客户的现金流状况会迅速改善。

通常来讲，整个生命周期的生涯仿真要比我们在表3－5展示的例子复杂得多。所有的理财建议的影响都会反映在一个综合理财规划中。关于历史情况的分析对客户来说十分有用，因为几乎所有的客户都会担心自己目前的现金流状况。平衡收支是十分重要的，然而，理财规划师需要提醒客户专注于长期的目标达成计划，因此，现金流生涯仿真分析在此时就十分重要。

现金流生涯仿真还可以帮助理财规划师监控理财计划的实施情况。例如，如果所有的理财计划实施将导致负现金流的出现，那么理财规划师可以判定该理财计划几乎是不可能实现的。基于这个模拟结果，理财规划师可以帮助客户重新调整理财方案，以保证收支平衡。

表 3－5　　　　现金流生涯仿真举例

	第1年	第2年	第3年	第4年	第5年	第6年	第7年	第8年	第9年	第10年
年收入										
工资收入－客户1	$152 000	$158 080	$164 403	$170 979	$177 819	$184 931	$192 328	$200 022	$208 022	$216 343
工资收入－客户2	$65 000	$67 275	$69 630	$72 067	$74 589	$77 200	$79 902	$82 698	$85 593	$88 588
利息收入	$3 600	$3 744	$3 894	$4 050	$4 211	$4 380	$4 555	$4 737	$4 927	$5 124
公司福利收入	$475	$494	$514	$535	$556	$578	$601	$625	$650	$676
收入总计	$221 075	$229 593	$238 441	$247 630	$257 175	$267 089	$277 387	$288 082	$299 192	$310 732
年度固定支出										
房屋贷款本金和利息支出	$18 037	$18 037	$18 037	$18 037	$18 037	$18 037	$18 037	$18 037	$18 037	$18 037
教育金支出	$13 000	$13 000	$13 000	$13 000	$2 400	$2 400	$2 400	$2 400	$2 400	$2 400
孩子学费	$9 600	$10 080	$10 584	$11 113	$11 669	$12 252	$12 865	$13 508	$14 184	$14 893
信用卡	$3 800	$3 914	$4 031	$4 152	$4 277	$4 405	$4 537	$4 674	$4 814	$4 958
固定支出总计	$44 437	$45 031	$45 653	$46 303	$36 383	$37 095	$37 840	$38 619	$39 435	$40 288
人寿保险保费支出	$7 344	$7 564	$7 791	$8 025	$8 266	$8 514	$8 769	$9 032	$9 303	$9 582
伤残险支出*	$748	$770	$794	$817	$842	$867	$893	$920	$948	$976
医疗保险支出*	$9 600	$9 888	$10 185	$10 490	$10 805	$11 129	$11 463	$11 807	$12 161	$12 526
房屋险支出	$2 265	$2 333	$2 403	$2 475	$2 549	$2 625	$2 704	$2 785	$2 869	$2 955
机动车辆险支出	$3 600	$3 708	$3 819	$3 934	$4 052	$4 173	$4 299	$4 428	$4 560	$4 697
集体保险支出	$475	$489	$504	$519	$535	$551	$567	$584	$602	$620
其他保费支出	$588	$606	$624	$643	$662	$682	$702	$723	$745	$767
保险支出小计	$24 620	$25 359	$26 119	$26 903	$27 710	$28 541	$29 398	$30 279	$31 188	$32 123
联邦税收支出	$30 573	$31 643	$32 750	$33 896	$35 083	$36 311	$37 582	$38 897	$40 258	$41 667
税支出	$8 632	$8 934	$9 247	$9 570	$9 905	$10 252	$10 611	$10 982	$11 367	$11 764
社保保险支出	$14 226	$14 724	$15 239	$15 773	$16 325	$16 896	$17 487	$18 099	$18 733	$19 388
税支出	$4 800	$4 968	$5 142	$5 322	$5 508	$5 701	$5 900	$6 107	$6 321	$6 542

续表

	第1年	第2年	第3年	第4年	第5年	第6年	第7年	第8年	第9年	第10年
个人财产税支出	$3 200	$3 312	$3 428	$3 548	$3 672	$3 801	$3 934	$4 071	$4 214	$4 361
其他税收支出	$1 900	$1 967	$2 035	$2 107	$2 180	$2 257	$2 336	$2 417	$2 502	$2 590
税收小计	$63 331	$65 547	$67 841	$70 216	$72 673	$75 217	$77 849	$80 574	$83 394	$86 313
有特定目的的存款	$4 200	$4 368	$4 543	$4 724	$4 913	$5 110	$5 314	$5 527	$5 748	$5 978
无特定目的的存款	$3 750	$3 900	$4 056	$4 218	$4 387	$4 562	$4 745	$4 935	$5 132	$5 337
再投资股息、资产增值及利息	$3 600	$3 744	$3 894	$4 050	$4 211	$4 380	$4 555	$4 737	$4 927	$5 124
退休计划*	$17 350	$18 044	$18 766	$19 516	$20 297	$21 109	$21 953	$22 831	$23 745	$24 694
税后退休存款	$10 000	$10 400	$10 816	$11 249	$11 699	$12 167	$12 653	$13 159	$13 686	$14 233
存款小计	$38 900	$40 456	$42 074	$43 757	$45 507	$47 328	$49 221	$51 190	$53 237	$55 367
年度可变支出										
公共事业费	$6 900	$7 142	$7 391	$7 650	$7 918	$8 195	$8 482	$8 779	$9 086	$9 404
电话费	$1 500	$1 553	$1 607	$1 663	$1 721	$1 782	$1 844	$1 908	$1 975	$2 044
公共事业费小计	$8 400	$8 694	$8 998	$9 313	$9 639	$9 977	$10 326	$10 687	$11 061	$11 448
房屋修缮费	$3 000	$3 105	$3 214	$3 326	$3 443	$3 563	$3 688	$3 817	$3 950	$4 089
房屋费用小计	$3 000	$3 105	$3 214	$3 326	$3 443	$3 563	$3 688	$3 817	$3 950	$4 089
伙食费	$9 000	$9 315	$9 641	$9 978	$10 328	$10 689	$11 063	$11 451	$11 851	$12 266
置装费	$3 600	$3 726	$3 856	$3 991	$4 131	$4 276	$4 425	$4 580	$4 741	$4 906
车辆修理费	$5 200	$5 382	$5 570	$5 765	$5 967	$6 176	$6 392	$6 616	$6 847	$7 087
日常支出小计	$17 800	$18 423	$19 068	$19 735	$20 426	$21 141	$21 881	$22 647	$23 439	$24 260
娱乐休闲费用	$6 000	$6 210	$6 427	$6 652	$6 885	$7 126	$7 376	$7 634	$7 901	$8 177
礼物及捐赠	$12 000	$12 420	$12 855	$13 305	$13 770	$14 252	$14 751	$15 267	$15 802	$16 355
其他支出小计	$18 000	$18 630	$19 282	$19 957	$20 655	$21 378	$22 127	$22 901	$23 703	$24 532
未报销医疗费用	$3 000	$3 105	$3 214	$3 326	$3 443	$3 563	$3 688	$3 817	$3 950	$4 089
杂费	$5 400	$5 589	$5 785	$5 987	$6 197	$6 414	$6 638	$6 870	$7 111	$7 360
杂费小计	$8 400	$8 694	$8 998	$9 313	$9 639	$9 977	$10 326	$10 687	$11 061	$11 448
可支配现金流										
总收入	$221 075	$229 593	$238 441	$247 630	$257 175	$267 089	$277 387	$288 082	$299 192	$310 732

续表

	第 1 年	第 2 年	第 3 年	第 4 年	第 5 年	第 6 年	第 7 年	第 8 年	第 9 年	第 10 年
总固定支出	$ 171 288	$ 176 393	$ 181 687	$ 187 179	$ 182 274	$ 188 181	$ 194 307	$ 200 662	$ 207 254	$ 214 091
总可变支出	$ 55 600	$ 57 546	$ 59 560	$ 61 645	$ 63 802	$ 66 035	$ 68 347	$ 70 739	$ 73 215	$ 75 777
可支配现金流	($ 5 813)	($ 4 346)	($ 2 807)	($ 1 193)	$ 11 099	$ 12 873	$ 14 733	$ 16 681	$ 18 724	$ 20 863

* 税前列支项目

第三节　理财规划内容

理财规划是用来帮助个人或家庭设定他们的财务目标，制定和实施理财计划并使其实现的过程。在理财规划的整个实施过程中，理财规划师需要考虑适合家庭和个人实际情况的所有理财规划方案，保证计划的实施并进行定期跟踪监督。一般来说，理财规划的内容包括投资、存储计划、保险、退休计划、税务筹划、风险管理及遗产规划。理财规划应被视为一个整体的过程。应从何处开始呢？爱丽丝漫游记中的国王说“从开始的地方开始，走到尽头然后停下”。然而，即使已经完成了全部理财目标，理财规划仍需要不时检视理财实施的效果。

1. 风险管理。风险管理需要考虑对以下事项的保护：（1）早逝；（2）伤残；（3）医疗费用；（4）财产及第三方责任；（5）失业。

早逝。人固有一死，这是不可抗拒的规律，在风险管理和遗产规划中将详细讨论。在这里，我们重点探讨早逝，即死亡发生时理财计划还未完成。家庭收入主要来源者的死亡会造成家庭收入能力的大大降低。如果家庭主妇早逝，那么会增加预算外的家庭儿童保育费用。家庭生活的各种责任的履行，包括财务上的或者其他方面的，都和时间节点有关，因此完成的时间节点一旦发生改变，理财计划也应相应改变。房贷和其他债务，孩子的培养及退休收入的累积都需要时间，在这些目标尚未实现前的家庭成员的死亡会对这些目标的实现产生巨大的影响。此外，任何死亡都需要支付丧葬费用及进行其他身后安排。因此为了降低早逝带来的财务影响，其中的一个解决方法是通过购买终身寿险将风险转移给保险公司。购买终身寿险的消费者需要向保险公司提供可保的证据（例如健康体检证明）及缴纳一定的保费。当然，寿险不能代替逝去的生命，但是却可以避免死亡带来的财务损失。人寿保险通常会根据投保金额向受益人一次性支付 100 000 美元或 1 000 000 美元的赔付。消费者可以个人从保险公司购买寿险，也可以通过雇主的员工福利计划购买。但是如果参加雇主的员工福利计划购买寿险，需要注意更换工作保险可以中止的情况。

伤残。伤残是指人们的行动能力受损或者受限，这会影响人们的生活质量及通过正常的途径获取收入的能力，例如，雇佣工作。残疾风险可以通过购买伤残险将风险转嫁给保险公司。众所周知，在有劳动能力阶段发生的伤残，对受雇产生影响的可能性远远大于死亡。即使如此，伤残险也经常被人们忽视，购买人寿保险的消费者远高于购买伤残险的消费者。伤残险可以弥补不能工作带来的经济损失，甚至有些还会根据伤残者的具体情况提供额外的保健服务。伤残险通常需要定期缴纳保费，以获得在约定时间提供伤残人士月收入的权利。消费者可以个人名义在保险公司购买也可以通过受雇单位购买团体险。因保费支付方式的不同，消费者在兑付赔付收益时可能需要缴纳不同的税费。例如，在美国，如果消费者使用税后收入支付保费，则在领取赔付时不用缴税；如果使用税前收入支付保费，则在领取赔付时就需要付税。消费者需要向雇主核实，如果更换工作，集体伤残险是否继续有效。在美国，社会保险也提供有关残疾险的内容。例如，如果保险人发生伤残，可以每月领取 1 000 美元直到 65 岁。

医疗费用。疾病、受伤及相关的医疗花费对个人的生活及财务都会产生影响。最多的个人破产原因之一就是医疗费用。人们可以通过购买保险来支付医疗费用。这是非常复杂的理财规划内容。医疗费用是非常昂贵的，人们购买医疗保险不仅可以用来帮助支付医疗费用，还可以避免因医疗费用负担过重而对自己的生活在财务上产生影响。消费者需要详细了解有关医疗保险的相关费用及承保范围。一般来说，投保人定期向保险公司支付一定的保费，保险公司会在约定的承保范围内向投保人支付医疗费用。即使保险公司可以负担一定的医疗费用，未保部分的费用及一些必要的个人支出加起来，数目也是相当大的。消费者需要特别关注健康保险承包范围的细节，并且随时检查投保的费用和承保范围。有些人可能可以申报政府的医疗保险，如 Medicare 或 Medicaid。理财规划师需要帮助消费者对已知和未知的费用作出合理的预算。

财产及第三方责任。如果个人拥有财产或负有第三方责任风险，例如，房产、其他商业地产、汽车等，那么就有可能发生财产及第三方责任风险损失。如果商业地产投资失利，投资者会遭受资本价值及收入的损失。第三方责任风险敞口或者损失来源于其他人的法律敞口。投资者可以考虑通过保险转移这部分风险。第三方责任保险责任范围可能包括与投保财产有关的人身安全。例如，某参观者因投保房产倒塌受伤，如果房产所有者没有投保财产险，房产所有者需要个人承担受伤人员的所有相关费用。财产及第三方责任保险通常需要投保人定期支付保费。保险公司为财产损失进行赔付，有时可以赔偿与该财产相关的收入损失。这类保险的保单合同可能会相当复杂，投保人应当注意投保责任范围及限制的细节。几乎所有的投资活动都可能发生第三方责任损失，例如拥有房产、汽车、商业地产及租赁活动等。

失业。失业造成人们的收入损失。大多数情况下，人们的财富积累来源于受雇的收入或工资。正因为如此，失业将使个人和家庭陷入财务困境。人们可以通过以下几种方式避免失业带来的风险。首先，人们可以通过储蓄一定的备用金进行自保，用以支付失业期间的生活费用。备用金储蓄要求人们对其财务来源进行分配或占用，但却可以保证自己在失业期间的生活免受影响。通常，在美国，失业保险是由政府提供赔付。员工在受雇期间，雇主向失业保险计划缴纳一定的保费，用以支付失业者的赔付。保费支付金额因适用税率及员工的工作时间长短不同而不同。另外，如果一个雇主总是有相当一部分的失业员工领取失业金，那么相比其他雇主，这个雇主缴纳的保费就更高。失业人员可以在一段时间领取政府提供的一定金额的失业金。如果失业保险资金池余额不足，政府会进行注资。如有必要，也会延长支付失业金的时间。鲜有个人购买失业保险，有些保单会支付特定的费用，如房贷。有时人们可能可以从雇主那里领取一些收入，但大多数情况下是包含在伤残补助中。

2. 资产管理。个人和家庭积累财富存在多种用途，包括：（1）为紧急情况提供备用金；（2）为日常家庭花费提供资金；（3）构建一般投资组合；（4）管理投资和财产。紧急备用金在任何情况下都是十分必要的。生活总是充满无法预期的财务突发情况。紧急备用金可以在失业时支付各种账单而且可以用来支付计划外的支出，例如医疗保险没有赔付的医疗费用。以上这些用途有助于个人和家庭积累资金。人们希望拥有自己喜欢的房子和汽车，拥有足够的资金支付每月日常开销及度假和娱乐费用，同样希望有资金教育子女及享受退休生活。一般投资组合在构建和管理时没有给予特定目的，在投资中途也没有其他用途，因此会构成个人的遗产，留给继承人。投资和财产的管理对于获得期望的投资和其他财产是十分重要的。

3. 退休规划。退休规划对于个人和家庭累积足够的资源保证退休生活是十分必要的。退休时不用工作就可以保证日常生活是大多数人的目标。如果没有合理的规划，要想实现这个目标是十分困难的，但这个目标存在很多不确定因素，因为退休规划是一个长期规划，相比短期目标有较多不稳定因素。例如，市场环境的改变，利率及通货膨胀率的变化都会对退休规划的结果产生重大影响。

4. 税务筹划。税务筹划包括减少、转移及延迟税负从而利用现有资源完成其他目标。人们的生活涉及各种税收，在留有遗产时也会发生税负。利用非法手段达到节税的目的是不可取的。然而，人们却没有必要缴纳本不应该承担的税费，税务筹划就是帮助人们解决这一问题。税费占用了人们实现其他目标的财务资源，因此节税有利于人们其他目标的实现。

5. 遗产规划。为了保证最终遗产继承有效且低成本的完成，在有生之年，人们需要对遗产及资产的分配和转移进行规划。设计周到的遗产规划除了有效和低成本两个特点之外，还可以保证财产按照所有人的意愿得以继承。但是人们出于多种原因缺乏遗产规划，这会导致遗产走向不能完全如所有者所愿。俗话说，没有计划就是失败的计划，这在遗产规划领域是十分正确的。如果没有详细的遗产规划，那么遗产分配就会按照资产所有人所在地的法律进行。遗产规划的内容包括生前和死后财产的处置问题。虽然当前的规划费用是已知的，但是不进行规划可能造成的成本和损失却是未知，并且巨大的。家庭成员可能没有留有足够的遗产去完成各种财务目标及支付遗产继承带来的额外税负。

一、理财规划流程

个人理财规划过程是将个人目标转化为特定计划，进而利用各种财务手段实施这些计划的过程。因此需要遵循严格的步骤。本章第一节已经对此进行了详细的阐述，在这里我们进行简单的回顾和总结。

收集信息是理财规划过程的第一步。首先需要制定个人财务报表，包括资产负债表、收入表及现金流量表。理财规划师可以通过查阅客户的一些对账单来收集需要的信息，如银行、投资账户对账单及退休计划对账单。资产负债表中还需要列示债务情况。与债务相关的财务报表，如房屋贷款、车辆贷款及信用卡对账单都可以提供这些信息。理财规划师还可以利用银行及信用卡对账单收集有关制作收入表、现金流量表及遗产规划的相关信息。保险保单，特别是寿险保单，也可以提供一些有用的信息，例如亡故收益及现金价值。遗嘱及信托文件可以为理财规划师提供客户有关过去理财目标的资料。银行、共同基金、公司雇员福利对账单、保险公司、律师、会计师等相关机构都可以为理财规划师和客户提供个人财务信息。银行或投资公司提供财务数据整理单样张，理财规划师可以此作为参考。收集这些基本的财务信息是理财规划的起点，在之后理财规划过程中，可能还需要补充相关数据。阶段性信息收集清单是十分有用的，不仅可以帮助整理这些信息，还可以供日后查询使用。

理财规划过程的第二步是设定理财目标。俗话说“如果你无所谓你的目标，那么任何道路都可以实现你的目标”。这句话从某种角度分析是有道理的。个人理财规划的过程是将你从起点带领到你希望的终点。如果你对你的财务目标毫不在乎，那么也就没有任何理由进行理财规划。

所谓理财目标，必须是经过深思熟虑且希望能够实现的。当然，我们应当知道事情总是在改变的，理财目标也会改变。小孩出生，长大，建立自己的家庭，随之改变的教育目标，婚姻状况的改变，死亡，残疾，生病，遗产继承，市场投资风险，职业的改变等，这些事情的发生都会改变我们的理财目标。因此我们需要保存这些规划文件，在必要的时候予以更新。

在理财报表制作完毕，目标设定完成之后，理财规划师需要帮助客户制定完成这些目标的途径和战略。达成理财目标的战略和方法有很多。因此理财规划师可以通过制作战略对比表来比较这些方法。虽然信息的收集很容易条理化，但是目标在客户的各个生命周期都会发生变化，因此严谨的理财规划师和客户会定期审查理财计划，如果有任何情况发生变化，理财规划也要随之更改。

理财规划目标的表述越清晰越好。通过设定理财目标，人们强迫自己仔细思考自己的目标到底是什么，因此可以避免顾此失彼。有时，理财计划还没有完全完成，然而在梳理理财目标时，理财方案也会随之生成。

需要重点指出的是，通货膨胀在长期会有很大的影响。虽然价格每年只上涨 1% 或 2%，不会对现有情况产生明显的影响，但如果在长期来看，影响是十分巨大的。无论在进行大学教育金，退休后住房或退休收入的规划，通货膨胀因素都应该予以充分的考虑。例如，某人的退休收入的预算是每月 3 000 美元，在现在看来还是十分充足的。即使名义通货膨胀率的增长也会使他/她的退休需求翻一倍。通货紧缩是通货膨胀的反面情形，发生的概率很小，在进行理财规划时也很少考虑。

在理财规划的最后，理财规划师和客户都应当牢记“人”是理财规划的一部分。所有的目标都应当符合个人或家庭的理财目标。即使理财方案在逻辑上再合理准确，但是如果让客户离他们自己的目标越来越远，就是错误的。如果理财规划师为一个没有子女的家庭进行子女教育金规划，而挪用了他们的退休资源，这种规划方案是不可取的。理财规划师和客户都应将规划的重点放在目标的设定上，然后据此制定理财规划方案并加以实施。

二、风险管理

人们每天都必须面对风险。问题是我们该如何应对这些无法避免的事情。有些人选择忽略它，而有些人则是默默祈祷，更理性的选择应该是试着理解和管理风险。

管理风险的策略有多种。最简单的方法是维持现有的风险敞口，不采取任何主动行动直到死亡或者其他灾难发生再进行处理。例如，如果一个人的房屋被烧毁，利用自有存款或借钱修复是一种策略。很多情况下，自我保险或风险自留可以采取缺省的战略或者通过一定的计划进行安排。例如，设置紧急储备金。如果通过数学计算比较风险发生的概率和投保成本，人们可能不愿意通过自我保险或者存储本来可以用来消费的资金来规避风险。其他人则选择将风险转嫁。购买保险是风险转嫁的一种常规方法，其目的是识别和控制风险。

识别和分析风险是风险管理的第一步。一旦风险敞口确认，人们可以评估风险来源和控制方法，这个过程可以通过对风险进行分类进行进一步优化。对每一个分类，评估风险发生的概率，发生损失的成本及如何应对风险的细节。一旦这些问题都考虑清楚，就可以进一步分析适合的风险管理策略。风险有时是可以避免的。风险避免是通过避免风险来源达成的。如果没有汽车或者不开车，那么发生车祸的风险就大大降低。在房子的后院挖一个泳池会增加风险，如果没有泳池或者移除现有的泳池就避免了风险的发生。当然，这并不一定是避免风险最有效的途径。如果需要开车或者必须开车去工作，那么不开车就是不现实的。需要指出的是，有些情况下，风险和潜在损失是很小的，没有必要花费精力去避免风险。

风险降低（或减损）与风险避免在某种程度上类似。例如，如果你的后院有一个游泳池，在周围安装上栅栏防止人进入导致受伤就是一种风险降低的手段。安装好的轮胎、刹车、安全气囊等安全措施可以有效避免或降低受伤的程度。在屋内安装烟雾探测器、自动喷水灭火系统及安置灭火器可以降低房屋着火带来的损失。安置防盗系统可以避免偷盗的风险。

风险保留是有意识的保留风险而不是采取措施避免、减少或者转移风险暴露。其前提是风险已经经过识别、评估并决定保留。通常时间风险会进行保留因为风险不能确认和识别，但这并不是一个好的规划。有时风险不可以避免、减少或者转移的，我们只能选择保留。但对风险进行确认还是有价值的。

风险管理的另一个重要手段即把风险从一方转移到另一方，通常是通过向保险公司购买保险产品来实现。另外，转移风险的手段可能涉及某些法律程序。例如，人们有时会需要在接受某项服务时签署潜在风险免责协议。例如，在进行医疗程序前，医生或者其他医疗工作人员会让患者签署免责声明，通过这种方式，风险从服务提供者转移到服务接受者。保险是最常见的将风险从个人或企业转移到保险公司的手段。售后服务保证书是将风险转移给厂商的方式。例如，某人为自己购买的家用电器，如洗衣机，增加了延保功能以防机器出现故障时可以更换和维修。保险公司是评估和认定风险的专业机构，收取保费作为承担投保人转移风险的补偿。换言之，站在投保人的角度，保险是通过支付保费将风险转移给第三方（保险公司）的方法。

并不是所有的风险都可以投保或者转移给第三方或保险公司。转移小风险既不经济也不现实。

如前所述，保险是最常见的转移风险的方式。但是很多风险不会产生重大的财务后果。例如，人们可以对事故发生造成的车辆损失购买保险，但是保修合同就可以提供例如引擎或者制动装置失灵的维修和更换，因此对车辆的常用配件投保是非常昂贵和不值得的。造成可能产生重大经济损失、伤残或死亡的事件需要进行详细评估并制定相应策略。这种风险是风险管理中较为关心的内容。

保险从本质上说，是利用保险公司与他人分担风险的方法。例如，假设有 1 000 个人希望购买保额为 10 000 美元的人身保险。他们的性别、年龄、健康状况等都相似，并且死亡概率是千分之二。没有人知道具体哪两个人会在具体哪一年身故，因此每个人都愿意出资 20 美元建立资金池，总计为 20 000 美元。因此最后可能的结果是 1 000 个投保人中有两位身故，获得来自资金池各自 10 000 美元的赔付。通过这个案例，我们可以看出，个人通过付出确定的 20 美元的保费换取对潜在死亡风险的经济保障。当然，那些没有身故的人如果不支付 20 美元的保费，生活水平可能会更高一点。保险公司会向投保人提供一系列的服务获得利润，例如管理保险过程中的各种细节，建立保险储备及保证赔付等。以上有关人寿保险的案例可以拓展至车险、火险或其他险种。在实务操作中的保险是十分复杂的。人们需要详细比较各家保险公司的保单细则、投保范围及保险责任等。

一旦人们认为某项风险可能对他们造成困扰和损失，就需要确定应对风险的方式。是自保？降低？或者转移？评估的过程需要确立风险，潜在损失的金额及发生的概率。一旦这些细节确立，就可以进一步确定是否需要通过购买保险转移风险和支付保费。损失的严重程度将影响投保的决策。如果从财务角度分析，潜在损失很小，我们可以决定进行风险自留，如果损失很大，我们将可能选择投保。

投保时需要考虑很多细节。免赔额部分要求投保人在保险公司履行赔付义务之前自己承担一部分损失。附有免赔额条款的保险通常费率也相应降低，因为保险公司相对承担较小的财务风险和易变的管理工作。健康保险和财产保险都有免赔额的规定。通过接受免赔额条款，投保人可以节约一部分保费开支。健康保险通常还伴有针对每项索赔要求的共保条款。

并不是所有保险公司都是相同的。需要考虑的问题包括保单中提及的管理细节及公司的财务偿还能力。一般来说，信用度低的公司保费也相对较低。由于保单涉及方方面面的内容，所以在比较不同公司的服务时会非常复杂。正因为如此，很多情况下，消费者会选择自留风险或者聘请保险经纪代为购买保险。获取保险公司的信息来源有很多，人们在投保前需要收集充分的信息进行比较。

寿险的种类很多，特点各异，包括贷款额度、雇主投保的团体寿险、定期寿险、终身寿险、可变寿险及两全险。有时投保人可以将其他人添加到保单作为额外保险责任范围或附加责任。例如，父亲投保寿险时可以将配偶或子女作为附加责任。定期寿险是用来提供一段时间的保险保障，例如10年或20年。定期寿险可能伴有其他收益，例如保险保证或可转换条款。定期保险的保险责任随合同到期终止。定期保险的附加责任人可以对保单做出重大修改。可以续约的定期保险的保费相对比较昂贵。终身寿险、可变寿险和两全险通常伴有现金价值部分。终身寿险的保费在首次购买后相对固定，其现金价值部分通常投资在固定收益类产品。可变寿险和两全险的现金价值部分通常可以投资在其他产品中，如类似共同基金的产品。另外，可变寿险和两全险的身故偿付也会比较灵活。终身寿险的费用是固定和已知的，而可变寿险和两全险的费用和其他细节在保单中会详细说明。

大多数人购买人身保险的目的是补偿投保人身故带来的经济损失。有些人则为了增加死后的遗产，因为他们发现生前可能无法达到的财务目标可以通过终身寿险进行弥补。例如，某人可能希望向毕业母校捐赠奖学金，但是在生存期间无法达成，但是通过购买终身寿险，可以达成这个心愿。有时，人们在身故后仍有需要照顾的子女，例如有特殊需要或残障的孩子，通过购买寿险可以利用赔付支付子女在其身故后昂贵的医疗及生活费用。

一般情况下，除被保险人外，大部分寿险保单在购买后可以对其内容进行重大调整。因此，在购买时，消费者应当与保险公司进行确认。可以更改的内容包括投保人和受益人。投保人可以分配收益，抵押保单贷款或者利用现金价值直接从保险公司借款。如果保单负有债务，则在保险给付时会扣除这部分债务进行偿付。寿险保单持有人有时可以享受一定时期的宽限期，自动恢复保险金额条款及对于自杀等行为发生后的保险给付限制条款等。寿险保单是保单持有人与保险公司的法律合同。正如其他法律合同一样，寿险保单的内容会很复杂，消费者在购买和签署前需要自己阅读其细节。保单持有人拥有在保单购买后审核保单的权利，如不满意可以要求退款。报告期通常为 10 天，但不同保险公司的规定会有所不同。

健康险旨在提高人们的总体生活质量。健康不仅能提高人们的日常生活质量，还能在经济上带来益处。因为拥有健康的身体可以避免人们在保健治疗方面的花费，从而带来其他的经济利益，例如就业。

和其他风险一样，健康风险管理也存在多种方式。大多数人都意识到生活方式对健康的影响。例如人们了解健康饮食，锻炼及其他保持健康的方式。但是只了解怎么做是不够的。即使人们做到了以上提及的所有保持健康的注意事项，但仍然有可能生病，发生事故，或存在需要健康保健和医疗照顾的其他原因。正因如此，购买健康保险将风险转嫁给保险公司是常见的风险管理的方式。

目前，在美国，存在两种基本的健康保险：残障险和医疗险。任何一种风险都会导致人们财务上的巨大压力，因此需要理财规划的协助。

健康保险不仅可以保护投保人因疾病或受伤的财务损失，而且可以享受保险特定覆盖的医疗服务。投保健康保险可以保证人们能够继续稳定长久地工作，对其财务满意度也有很大帮助。

此外，人们也可以通过提高自身的健康意识减少疾病的产生和相应的医疗费用，例如参加体育锻炼和健康的饮食。

在美国，大部分人都享受政府支持的医疗保险项目，如社会保险的残障险、Medicare 、Medicaid 及员工补助。还有一些人会享受雇主提供的医疗保险项目。团体健康险可以投保在同一工作地点工作的人群，包括健康保险、残障险及人寿保险。通常，雇主会与保险公司签订合同，雇员就可以参保了。

人们可以自己购买健康保险。与团体险不同，个人购买的健康保险是被保人与保险公司直接签订合同。

关于残障险，需要考虑几个细节。首先，对于大部分残障险都有一个最高赔付期，通常每月支付一定金额。例如每月 1 000 美元。偿付时间可能为 10 年或者固定的一段时间，但通常给付至正常的退休年龄，在美国是 65 岁。另外，残障险还有一个等待期。等待期要求残疾的被保险人等待一段时间开始领取赔偿金。例如，一旦赔付条件确立，被保险人可能需要等待 90 天左右才可以收到第一笔赔付。

最高赔付期和等待期的长短影响投保成本。通常情况下，赔付期越长，等待期越短，保费越高。

残障的含义对于确定残障险的保险责任范围有重要的影响。残障的定义范围直接影响某被保人是否能够获得赔付。有两种残疾类型可以获得保险赔付，从事“任何职业”或“特定职业”。“任何职业”下的残疾一般是指完全残疾。“特定职业”下的残疾要求被保险人从事“特定职业”而不是“任何职业”。“任何职业”是指被保险人可以从事任何工作。从事特定职业或高新职业的被保险人希望选择“特定职业”保险保障。例如一个成功的眼科医生可能希望投保“特定职业”残障险。该眼科医生可能一年的收入为 300 000 美元，显然不会满意一份年薪只有 25 000 美元的零售店员的工作。但是，一名年收入 40 000 美元的劳工可能愿意投保“任何职业”残障险。

消费者可以自己向保险公司购买残障险或通过所在单位购买。雇主集体残障险的残障收入条款可能包含短期残疾或长期残疾。短期残疾保险计划在某种程度上类似长期“病假赔偿”。团体短期残疾保险通常等待期较短，大约比长期残疾保险少几天或者几个月。然而，短期残疾险的赔付期较短，可能只有 30 天或 60 天。团体长期残疾保险与个人购买的残障险类似。同时购买短期和长期残疾险以获得较完整的保险赔付责任是没有必要的。保险提供的赔付收益越多，保费也越昂贵。能够获得短期、长期及政府这三者的共同保险保障当然很好，但是所花费的成本也是三者之和。

大部分都有权享受社会保险伤残补助，其特点如下。雇员福利提供部分补助和伤残补贴。受雇员工可以享受员工福利。雇主支付员工伤残保险的保费。如果某位员工因公受伤或者生病，就可以享受伤残补助。员工福利中的伤残补助包括受伤或生病的诊疗费及误工费。

医疗保险是人们保险保障的重要组成部分。医疗费用有时会十分昂贵，如果没有保险保障，将严重影响人们的财务状况。但是医疗保险的保险责任范围十分复杂，而且随着医疗保健体系的改变将会更加复杂。人们考虑购买医疗保险时，需要仔细阅读保单的相关条款，并与其他类似保单内容进行比较。医疗保险保障涉及医疗保健的任何费用，包括医生处方、药物、预防治疗、住院费、急诊费及其他杂费。有些医疗保险责任范围对投保人一生支付的保额有上限。例如某保险公司的医疗保险的保额上限为 1 000 000 美元。

Medicare 是美国针对 65 岁以上人群的健康保险，包含的内容覆盖人们保险需求的各个方面。个人可以享受个人投保的保险保障，如作为某人的配偶享受的医疗保险保障，或者可以通过雇主参加医疗保险。通常情况下，某人享受的保险赔付不可以超过实际发生的医疗费用。正因如此，拥有多份保单并不一定能带来更多益处。保险公司之间会相互沟通以减少他们的成本。如果投保人已经知道自己的健康状况，在阅读保单保险责任范围时要注意留意这些已知的健康状况所带来的任何会影响保险赔付及相关保费的问题。

拥有财产同时带来收益和风险。财产保险可以将风险转嫁给保险公司。像大多数风险一样，消费者可以选择自留、减少或者转移风险。如果某人拥有的用于租赁的建筑被火灾摧毁，他们可以选择承担这个风险，在建筑倒塌后利用其他资源重建。他们也可以通过安装自动灭火装置减少风险，还可以通过购买保险提供保障。大部分的财产拥有者都面临类似的选择，自保？减小？或者转移风险？因个人愿意缴纳的保费多寡，所有的潜在损失的赔付程度会有所不同。

消费者可以通过收益—成本分析对保单及保险承保责任范围进行判断。消费者可以首先假设没有保险的情况下的风险及损失承担额度，然后不断增加保险承保责任范围，结合自己可以承担的保费成本判断不同方法优劣。

在查看财产保险承保范围时，消费者应当关注被保险的对象。虽然所有的保单都会赔付一定的损失，但是消费者还是需要仔细阅读细节。例如有些保单承保水淹损失，但不承担洪水造成的损失。有些保单会区分偷窃和抢劫。因此消费者要理解承保范围及保费成本。另外，大部分财产保险都不会承保自然损耗及折旧，如果消费者希望投保这些损失，就要考虑提供重修成本补偿的保险品种。

租赁主要居住房产的消费者也将会面临同样的保险选择问题，市场上也有保险产品覆盖这些风险。

此外，存在第三方责任风险的消费者也面临同样的风险管理问题。人们可以选择自保、消除或转移第三方责任风险。第三方责任风险来自个人对他人可能造成的损失。如果某人拥有汽车、房屋或其他资产，如果牵扯到其他人，那么就有可能产生第三方责任风险。例如，某人的狗将行人咬伤，或者撞车造成他人人身或财务的损失。

人们通过购买第三方责任保险对这类风险进行保障。例如消费者可以通过购买第三方责任险保障用于普通交通事故造成的损失赔付。第三方责任风险可以覆盖一般和特殊领域责任。综合保单可以用来保障除商业活动以外的大多数风险损失。其他第三方责任保险用以保障商业投资行为，例如董事及高级管理人员责任保险。

风险管理应当包含以下步骤：

发现风险；

判断可能发生的后果；

评估每种风险及潜在损失；

决定采取何种风险管理策略：自留、减少还是转移；

如果选择转移风险，那么需要评估潜在的保险范围和成本并作出决定；

风险管理策略确定后，要定期检视其效果。

三、资产管理

为了达到家庭财务目标，人们需要累积财富，并保证这些资产能够满足自己的最大利益。家庭获得资产的主要来源是个人净收入，一般是指在剔除必要费用和花销后的工资。其他累积资产的来源包括继承、馈赠、商业经营的销售和增长及来自养老金或退休计划的收益。一旦资产累积到一定程度，家庭和个人需要决定如何投资使其增长。

家庭最主要的投资目标是在限制条件范围内使资产获得最高收益。可能的限制条件包括家庭财务目标，风险容忍程度及投资时间范围等。当前，投资者面临多种投资选择。没有一个完整的清单列举所有的投资产品。即使存在这样的清单，投资选择变化很快，谨慎的投资者和理财规划师也应当实时关注金融创新。一个主要的原则是尽量浏览较全面和详细的投资渠道。

投资选择分类存在很多划分标准，最主要的分类为所有权和债权。所有权有时被认为是权益，而债务有时被定义为固定收益。权益投资包括股票、股票基金、可变收益保险产品、房产其他商业投资。债权投资包括公司或政府债券、固定收益保险产品及银行存单。

在选择不同的投资工具时，理财规划师和消费者需要考虑有关投资的特点及其他因素。例如本金安全性、回报、回报率、流动性、分散性、税务情况、需要投入的精力等。每种因素的重要程度因人而异。

没有任何一项投资是在所有方面都优于其他投资选择的。例如，某项投资可能有好的增长空间但是安全性较差。消费者应当牢记个人的需求和目标远比投资工具的特点重要得多。理财规划师和消费者需要了解风险和收益是高度相关的。

对大多数投资者而言，本金安全是第一位的。拥有较高安全目标的投资者经常被形容为“总是要保证投资全部收回”或“不愿意损失一分钱”。实际上，投资者在如此表述自己的投资目标时忽略了随之相伴的风险，因为当这些投资者希望“将所有的资金投入全部收回”时忽略了通货膨胀因素，这只是名义货币的表达。具有较高概率保证本金收回的投资是一回事，而将资金投入全部一分不差收回，并能够购买相同的产品和服务的投资是另一回事。通货膨胀风险是人们容易忽视却无法避免的风险。随着时间的流逝，通货膨胀将会削减资金的实际价值。当我们在考虑风险时，与之相关的因素包括本金回报率、经通货膨胀调整后的真实本金金额、财务风险、市场风险、利率风险及其他。

财务风险是指一项投资能够保证其债务清偿的能力。例如，当购买某公司股票时，该公司能够负担其日常运营费用的能力即为财务风险。股票和债券投资者依赖发行人发放利息，股息及股票或债券的增值。市场风险是指当投资者愿意转让投资时的销售可能性。流动性与可销售性有关，并且两者经常会被混淆。流动性是指投资者将投资转换为等值现金的能力，而不仅是售卖成功。而可销售性仅仅与是否存在销售市场有关。利率风险是指利率的变化对已发行债务或债券的影响。如果市场利率上升，债券持有人会发现他们的收益率低于票面利率。固定收益债券的价格与市场利率存在数理关系。当市场利率上升，债券价格下降；反之，债券价格上升。有关债券投资的其他细节将在本节后面的内容进行详细介绍。

投资者和理财规划师总是根据投资增值情况或收入情况判断投资方向。的确，从有些投资历史上看更适合获得增值或收入。收入是指投资者拥有某项投资获得的现金流。收入投资是通过现金给付的方式回报给投资者。例如债券（或债券基金）的付息及股票分红。收入投资者倾向于关注那些有较高现金流回报的投资。

现金流收益通常以收益率的形式计算。债券通过利息收益率计算，股票通过股息收益率计算。如果一笔 1 000 美元的债券或股票投资每年能获得 50 美元的现金流收入，那么其收益率即为 5%。通常，给付较高现金流收入的投资，增值空间较为有限。有些投资者会选择股息或利息再投资以获得复利收益。价值投资者不太关心现金流，而更关注投资在一段时期的增长情况。一般情况下，价值投资者会获得较少的现金流收入，有时甚至没有现金流入。

以价值增值为目标的公司股票（或股票基金）投资，不论期间赚取多少收益都会将收益再投资以获得长时间价值的增长。一笔 20 美元的初始投资所获得 5 美元的收入进行再投资，可能可以获得 25% 的价值增长。投资者和理财规划师总是认为与以增值为目的的价值相比，获得现金流的投资更加稳定且风险较低。但事实并不总是如此，两者风险的差异并不单单来自现金。高收益低信用度的股票显然比经营良好公司的股票风险更高。

另外，需要注意的是，投资者在获得股息和利息收入时需要缴税。

通常，人们都不会将所有资金都投入到单一的投资产品上，而是选择多种投资以分散风险，即多样化投资。多样化投资可以通过多种方式实现。例如投资者可以通过同时购买股票和债券进行多样化投资，或者通过持有不同种类的股票或债券进行多样化投资。持有来自不同行业，不同公司甚至不同国家的股票或债券可以更好地分散风险。

个人本身的特点可能会影响其风险容忍度，包括家庭收入及收入的稳定性，人们的年龄，健康程度，家庭负担，财务状况（包括资产和负债），可能的遗产继承，投资目的（获得现金流收入还是资产增值），对通货膨胀的期望，流动性需求，税务及接受资产价值波动的个人情绪等。

人们经常会谈论投资目标，包括收入、收入增长、如何增长及快速增长的情况。

很多投资者认为制作投资政策说明书非常有帮助。因为它不仅对投资具有指导意义，而且在投资发生困扰的时候还可以翻阅它进行查询，并且投资者可以和理财规划师共同讨论说明书上的内容以达成共识。投资政策说明书随着时间可以更改，但需要相对稳定，只有在情况发生变化时才可以对其做出修正。

普通股及股票基金是人们持有的资产的一部分。普通股投资有如下特点：（1）它代表公司的所有权；（2）股票有私募和公募两种；（3）通常可以在网络和财经报纸上获得公募股票的信息，而私募股票的信息一般在公开渠道不易取得。当人们考虑普通股票投资时，通常会参考每股收益、市盈率、每股账面价值、股息率及分红比率等指标。

另外，根据公司是如何管理收益及分红比率还可以将股票分为收入型股票或成长型股票。股票分红比率是指以现金形式向股东发放的股利占公司收益的百分比。

有时，房产投资对投资者具有很大的吸引力。投资房产存在多种方式。例如投资者可以购买没有开发的土地或可耕种的农田。或者投资者可以选择投资商业或住宅地产进行出租。另外，投资者还可以通过投资房地产信托产品的方式投资房地产。房地产信托类似基金，所不同的是其标的物是房产而非股票。

共同基金目前成为个人投资者和机构投资者的主要投资对象。共同基金投资的基本原理是它可以聚集小资本成为大资本，聘请专业基金经理管理并且可以从规模效应中获益。仅拥有 1 000 美元甚至 1 000 000 美元的投资者无法单独投资某个项目，但是将这些小型投资聚集起来就可以获得数百万美元甚至上亿美元资金，进而投资之前不能涉猎的项目。雇佣专业人士投资，并监管和报告投资组合的情况同样需要每年上万美元的成本，只拥有几千美元资金的投资者没有能力承担，即使拥有数百万美元资金的投资者单独聘请这样的团队也是没有意义的。如果有很多人共同承担管理成本，单位成本会大大降低。

共同基金的费用包括管理费、手续费及其他费用等，并且按照共同基金的资产额进行收取。如果在计算收益时将费用也考虑在内，则会对共同基金的收益有直接的影响。共同基金的费用比率幅度较大。例如，某项 100 000 美元的投资，费用比率是 0.25%，即每年 250 美元。如果同样的投资，费用比率是 2%，则费用为 2 000 美元，是之前成本的 8 倍。

基金的类型在很大程度上决定了费用比率的大小。以美国为例，短期债券基金及货币市场基金通常的费用比率较低，从 0.10% ~0.50% 不等。长期基金或者特殊的证券基金费用比率从 0.25% ~1.00% 不等。基于非托管指数，以股票为投资标的的共同基金的费率是从 0.10% ~0.50% 不等。

主动管理型等较复杂的基金，费用比率相对较高。主动管理型基金或新兴市场国际基金的费用比率可达到每年 1% ~2%，甚至更多。查看这些费用比率时，一定要特别仔细。费用越高的基金就要创造更高的利润以弥补费用对收益的影响。费用比率通常以基点和年化的形式表示。1 个基点等于 0.01%，50 个基点就等于 0.5%，依此类推。

共同基金有几种常见的结构类型。大部分共同基金都是开放式基金而非封闭式。当投资者增加投资，开放式基金通过发行新份额的形式吸纳，对基金池大小几乎没有上限，并且接受投资者回购和赎回份额，但只以每天的收盘价接受这些份额。然而，封闭式基金只发行固定的份额，不再增发。封闭式基金在投资者之间的交易类似公开市场的股票交易。

共同基金市场的一大创新是交易所交易基金（ETF 或 ETN）。ETF 和 ETN 的功能大体类似。ETF 的交易类似每天的股票交易，因此相比开放式基金，对投资者而言具有更高的流动性和交易机会。ETF 通常以接近其基础资产价值进行交易，而共同基金通常以净资产价值定价。净资产价值是资金投资的总价值与在外发行股票份额的比值。

封闭式基金通常在市场上的买卖双方之间按照不同于净资产价值的价格进行交易。有些共同基金会收取佣金或手续费，用来支付给销售人员或者公司。这个手续费被称为负担基金。不收取这笔费用的基金称为无佣基金。

除此之外，市场上还存在其他投资类型，统称为衍生品。衍生品的标的可以是股票、股票指数或者其他投资类型。常见的衍生品有期权和期货合约。

期权的标的物可以是股票、股票指数、债券、利率、农产品或其他实物期货（如黄金或原油）、货币等。期权分为看涨期权和看跌期权。期货合约允许投资者买空或买多。

买多意味着投资者拥有标的物，买空意味着投资者出售标的物，但最终会将其买回。

所有的期货期权合约都较为复杂。与之相关的有两个价格，一个价格是投资者需要支付的购买合约的价格或收取售卖合同的价格。另一个是标的物的价格，例如股票的价格或者一桶原油的价格。另外，投资者还需要考虑合约数量。例如，合约是基于多少桶原油或多少股股票（股票期权通常是基于100股，但不是绝对的）。期货合约几乎都要使用保证金账户，因此会牵涉到杠杆的使用。期权合约不一定要使用保证金账户。

使用保证金或者债务都会增加投资的风险，因此投资者在考虑使用时应当清楚地了解相关细节。拥有看涨期权意味着投资者拥有“买”的权力或者标的股票的所有权。反之，售出看涨期权意味着投资者承担在合约履行时售出标的股票的义务。拥有看跌期权意味着投资者拥有让对方“卖出”股票的权力；反之，售出看跌期权意味着投资者负有合约履行时买回股票的义务。大家可以看出，衍生品的投资相对复杂，因此大大提高了投资的难度。

债券是许多投资组合的重要组成部分。市场上有很多债券投资类型。债券投资有时被称为固定收益投资。“固定收益”是指债券的收益回报通常比较固定。债券通常有确定的到期日期，因发行主体及购买主体不同，有效期从30天至30年不等。债券通常半年付息一次，但也有不同付息期的债券，例如按月付息或仅到期时一次性付息。债券可以由公司、市政府或者联邦政府发行。债券通常以年利率表示其收益率，如投资者拥有10 000美元年收益率6%的债券，那么可以在约定日期获得每年600美元的利息收入。到期一次付息或者无利息给付的债券被称为零息债券。之所以称为息票是因为债券持有人在向发行人索取利息时，需要持有一个纸质的票据进行兑付。

投资者在考虑购买债券时需要考虑债券的到期日，利息收入、付息频率，债券的安全性及相关税负等。有些付息债券享有税收优惠，例如当地政府、州政府或者联邦政府的税收减免。由于债券存在最后到期日，因此债券存在到期日前赎回的日期，这个日期被称为“提前赎回日”。此外，债券的安全性与债券的种类有关，如抵押贷款、普通债务或其他类型的债务。了解债券的安全等级是十分重要的。很多专业的公司对债券进行排名，为投资者提供参考。投资者一旦认购证券，只有等到到期日才可以赎回，除非债券伴有看跌期权。除此之外，投资者只能按照类似股票转让的方式在二级市场出售债券，但是价格波动很大。影响债券价格的因素主要有两个：（1）市场利率；（2）债券发行后债券安全性的变化。在其他因素不变的情况下，如果发行人的风险等级增加，债券价格就会下降。如果市场利率上升，现有债券的吸引力下降，价格也随之下降。需要注意的是，债券价格和市场利率呈反向变化：利率上升，债券价格下降；反之，债券价格上升。

资产负债表和债务管理对于家庭的财务情况有重要的影响。在考虑如何最大化家庭财务总量时，家庭的债务情况也必须予以考虑。如果缺乏对债务的考量，那么理财过程就是不完整的。

家庭面临投资债务或者削减债务的选择。相关的考虑因素包括债务的利息率，其他投资的潜在收益，投资的回报率等。另外，税务因素也不能忽视。利息给付是否可以抵税？投资收入如何纳税？这些都应在投资者的考虑范围之内。

债务对家庭财务的影响表现在多个方面。家庭可以举债购买当前无力承担的物品，一般是能提高家庭财务满意度的大宗物品，否则会对家庭财务产生不利影响。此外，家庭最主要举债购买的就是住房。购买住房能够带来以下积极影响：首先，它可以将房屋租赁的费用转为所有权；其次，可以锁定未来的与房产有关的费用，例如房屋继承等；此外，因房产本身特点不同，可能还有某些投资机会。例如如果购置的房屋较大，并且打算出售，消费者可以换一个小房，那么出售大房的净收入即是一笔投资收入。或者将大房改为两个小房，一个作为自用，另一个出租或者售卖。这样相当于购买房产的一半资金就是用以投资的。

债务还有杠杆作用。一个家庭可以用自己的资金作为抵押，借贷更多的资金进行投资。例如，某家庭拥有投资资金 10 000 美元，以此作为抵押另外借款 5 000 美元，这样就有 15 000 美元进行投资。如果投资收益超过债务成本，那么投资回报就得到了提高。但需要指出的是，投资不会总是按照自己的期望实现。因此杠杆具有同时放大收益和损失的作用。

人们要么消费，要么投资自己拥有的资源。有时，人们错误地认为投资是可以延迟的。人们可以将钱存入银行或者自己保存现金，但必须进行投资。因此，人们需要决定如何及该投资什么以最大化自己的收益。怀疑的态度和探索的精神是投资的良好品质，投资者要善于利用这两个工具实现自己的财务目标。

四、退休规划

人们都希望有一天结束工作，依靠自己的周密计划享受退休生活。为了保证退休生活水平，有一些必要的步骤需要考虑。家庭和他们的理财规划师总是会考虑人寿保险以对冲在理财计划达成前的死亡风险，如早逝。但是如果家庭成员能够正常生存呢？人们有必要对所有的经济状况进行安排，包括退休规划，这要求我们评估当前状况，设定目标及按计划完成。退休规划还需要考虑目前的生活方式，力图保证退休后的生活方式不受影响。

很多情况下，人们认为退休后的预算计划应该与退休之前不同。但实际并非如此，退休后家庭开支会大大减少的假设并没有得到确切的证实。

人们可能会考虑退休前后的开支哪个更多。经过周密思考，人们会发现退休后的开支也许更多些。虽然与工作相关的开支在退休后大大减少，然而，大部分购买的物品都是在退休前不会考虑的。度假会增大开支。一些退休人员会将退休比喻成永久的放假，如果这样的话，那么退休后的家庭开支是增加还是减少呢？在实践中，应当具体分析退休前后的预算，以更好地进行退休规划。

供退休后使用的收入包括无特定使用目的的资金及退休账户的资金等。虽然无特定使用目的的资金看上去是一个缺省分类，但实际上是一个重要的资源。对于大多数家庭来说，退休收入是家庭的最后一个财务需求，因此无特定使用目的的资金往往用来填补这一需求的资金空白。有些家庭的储蓄过多，造成退休时有很多闲置资金，虽然数据表明这样的情况很少见。

合格的退休计划中“合格”是指满足美国国税局的相关规定。在美国，共有几种类型的合格的退休计划，可以分为雇主提供的和个人提供的；还可以根据退休收益的定义分类，分为“收益确定型”（DB）和“支出确定型”（DC）。

收益确定型计划通常被称为养老金计划。收益确定型计划，是指收益是固定的，而需要的资金投入是不确定的。例如，该计划可能向20年服务期满的员工提供退休后每月1 000美元的退休金。虽然具体计划的计算公司略有不同，但是收益是确定的。收益确定型计划的风险主要由项目管理者或出资者通常是雇主承担。参加计划的个人可以使用计划中的收益而不必担心资金注入的问题。2000年时，收益确定型计划稍有改变，要求员工也参与计划的供款。

支出确定型计划，是指供款是固定的，而收益是不确定的。这种退休计划在近些年十分普遍和流行，因为雇主饱尝因提供收益确定型退休计划而承担的不确定负债的风险，并且这些负债还会影响他们的财务报表。

退休收入主要来源于三个部分：个人积累，所在公司提供的退休金收入及政府的退休计划。对于个人来说，明智之举是不可以仅依赖一个来源，而要试图管理好每一个收入来源，这样可以保证收入来源的多样化，退休收入也更有保障。

综观历史发展，退休收入的来源主要依靠个人及家庭的积累。如今，考虑到人们退休之后的各种挑战，建议利用可以利用的所有资源，因为仅凭一种资源是很难积累足够的资源的。长寿、通货膨胀及退休资源的不确定性使理财规划及多样化退休资源变得尤为重要。

政府通过社会保险向大部分的美国居民提供退休收入。1935 年颁布的《社会安全法案》为所有符合要求的老年居民提供保障。社会保险可以视为一个基本的保证收入。大多数人认为社会保险不能成为退休收入的唯一来源，而是安全网。

雇主为员工积累退休收入提供了一种选择。政府向雇主授权并列示了退休储蓄的多种方法。员工应充分利用雇主提供的退休计划。人们可以或正式或非正式地制定自己的退休规划。正式和有目的的规划更有可能帮助人们实现退休规划中的目标。个人或者雇主提供的正式退休计划虽然稍显复杂，但是却可以明确各种不确定性及退休规划中产生的问题，使人们获益更多。

雇主提供的退休计划可以是专项或非专项的。非专项计划类似“即付制”安排，没有专门的资产支持允诺给员工的收益。这种非专项计划在雇主提供退休计划刚兴起之时非常普遍。大多数情况下，雇主只是简单承诺在员工退休时付给员工一笔退休金，要么是一次性给付，要么是分批给付。非专项计划在很多方面都不能保证员工退休收入的资金投入。这种不确定性没有给员工参加非专项计划提供足够的动力和信心，因此并没有推广，只是提供给少部分员工。以上关于非专项计划和专项计划的讨论又引出合格退休计划和不合格退休计划的讨论。可以判断，非专项计划属于不合格退休计划。

合格退休计划几乎都是专项计划。是否合格的标准来自美国国税局及劳动局的相关规定。相关细节可以参阅国税局的税务代码及劳动局的相关法律规定。大部分劳动局的规定都可以参阅 1974 年颁布的《员工退休收入安全法案》的条款。

合格的退休计划对于雇主和员工都带来了很多的益处。员工可以针对明确的规定制定自己的退休计划。确定性首先来自于计划是专项拨款的。资金存入一个合法的专项账户，并且所有权不归雇主或雇主的债权人所有。由于资金与公司本身的账目分开，因此退休计划本身可以建立会计体系和财务报表。在过去，财务和会计系统设计没有那么复杂和高级，单独的报表和余额是无法提取的。由于系统不是十分完善，因此许多退休计划都是简单将资金混在一起，一起投资，并且信息的获取也不是经常性的。

目前，几乎所有的退休计划都是按个人账户设立，只有收益确定型养老金计划仍然保留统一资金池的运作方式。大部分员工目前都必须定期收到账单并可以在线查看账户余额。这激发和鼓励员工参加雇主提供的退休计划。合格的退休计划对于雇主的益处大部分与税收有关。直至员工需要领取时为止，员工退休计划账户中的余额是不用交税的，可以全额随退休计划增长。当员工可以从退休账户领取退休金时，员工可以自己办理有关税收优惠的手续。其中一个可以利用的税收优惠是，员工可以将雇主提供的退休账户中的资金滚动或转移到个人退休账户中。

一般来说，在满足特定条件下，雇主向合格的退休计划中的注资都是可以享受税收减免的。对于雇主提供的非专项或非合格退休计划，雇主在注资或者员工收到雇主打款时，可享受为员工注资部分的税收减免。换言之，当资金的所有权从雇主转移到雇员时，税负也随之转移，美国国税局将其称为“推定收入”。员工可以要求雇主将退休收入余额直接转入或者“滚动”到他们的个人退休账户中，从而避免推定收入产生的税负。

在满足一定的条件下，员工可以利用税前收入缴纳或者提取合格退休计划中的资金。例如退休计划必须以合法的书面形式起草，并通知员工；并且退休计划仅能使员工或其受益人受益；退休计划资产必须与公司其他资产分开管理且退休计划必须使大部分员工受益，管理人员、股东或高薪员工不得额外受惠。

依资金来源不同，员工保留退休金领取的权利不尽相同。保留退休金权利是指员工实际可以拥有的退休金比例。延迟领取退休金的员工几乎可以享受100%的保留退休金权利。但雇主都会制订一份保留退休金权利计划。一般来说，参加计划一年的员工可享受领取20%的退休金，第二年可以享受40%，第三年可以享受60%，第四年可以享受80%，之后便可以享受100%。

因此，在第五年时，参加计划的员工可享受100%保留退休金权利，同样，雇主的供款也是100%到位。如果员工在此时离职，他/她仍然享受100%保留退休金权利，不过可以选择将资金余额转入到自己的个人退休计划账户中。

正常的退休年龄会在合格的退休计划中规定和界定。虽然对于支出确定型退休计划，是否在计划中明确规定退休年龄不是那么重要，但是一般来讲，在实务中也都会规定。而对于收益确定型退休计划，界定退休年龄就显得非常重要，首先，退休年龄与收益和供款直接相关。如果计划规定在员工退休后每月给付1 000美元退休收入，雇主必须清楚了解这笔资金何时需要付出并制定相应供款计划。另外，无论参与计划时间长短，达到规定退休年龄的员工都可以开始使用保留退休金权利。

可以利用详细的公式计算收益确定型退休计划的退休收入何时开始给付及给付金额的大小。人们在进行自己的退休规划时可以利用这个公式进行计算。例如，服务期每增加1年，退休资金需增加工资的1%。如果某员工服务满25年，那么他/她可以享受最后一年收入 25% 的退休金。雇主和员工都会向退休账户中供款。由于雇主还需要为员工社会保险的退休账户供款，因此美国国税局和劳动局允许两项供款合并。可以使雇主减少向退休计划中缴纳与社会保险供款等值的金额。

支出确定型退休计划的供款同样可以和社会保险供款合并。

收益确定型退休计划由美国政府机构养老金收益保证公司（PBGC）提供保障。养老金收益保证公司收取养老金收益保证供款公司的付款，并且由美国联邦政府的后备支持。不是所有的收益确定型退休计划都由养老金收益保证公司提供保障。例如极个别的政府、州、郡及市级的宗教机构的退休计划就不在其保障范围之内。

当员工从合格退休计划账户中提取资金时需要缴纳相应的收入所得税。与前面提及的美国国税局规定的“推定收入”的情况类似，当人们收到合格退休计划退休金时，就需要缴税。退休金可以一次性提取，或者分几次提取或以月收入的形式长期提取。有些退休金可以通过转入其他退休计划而延迟缴税。例如收益确定型退休计划或支出确定型退休计划可以转入、再存入或者投资到其他的退休计划中，例如支出确定型退休或个人退休账户。退休账户分为雇主提供的退休计划及个人退休计划。个人退休计划账户是个人为自己退休收入开设的账户。其他个人退休账户或合格退休计划账户中的余额可以转入其中。

在这里，大部分的税收相关问题都与美国联邦一般的收入税有关，当然还会有其他税种牵扯其中。基于退休金领取的方式、时间和年龄的差异，可能会产生罚金。各州级收入税法也会有相关退休金领取时征税的规定。此外，退休账户中的资金可能还会牵扯到遗产税。

当退休账户的持有人身故，但退休账户仍有余额时，受益人可以享受这些收益。有关受益人如何管理从合格退休计划或个人退休计划继承的退休金是相当复杂的。但人们在决定继承前最好研究到所有的继承方式。大多数情况下，配偶继承人有权将继承的退休金转入自己的退休计划。非配偶继承人没有这项特权，但也可以进行相应的规划。

在之前的内容中，我们反复强调了通货膨胀率的重要作用，在退休规划中，也是不能忽视的。随着人们寿命的延长，时间的推移会对价格的增长产生重要的影响。即使只有 2% 的通货膨胀率，也会使人们的生活成本在 18 年内翻一番。随着人们希望退休的年龄越来越早，并且退休后的生存时间越来越长，18 年甚至更长，延长的投资期限必须要予以考虑。一个每月 2 500 美元的退休收入预算计划，如果从 60 岁开始算起，在他/她 78 岁时就变为 7 800 美元，才可以满足相当的生活水平。通货膨胀率在历史上可能高于或低于2%，在实践中，消费者和理财规划师在进行退休规划时，都应当对通货膨胀率的影响引起足够的重视。很多年前，在退休规划概念刚刚兴起之时，大部分情况下，人们退休后仅会有几年的生存时间。一个人可能在退休时拥有足够的收入满足每月的开支，但是2%的通货膨胀率就会使他第二年的预算下降为原来的98%，到第三年，可能下降为96%，到生命终结时可能下降更多。如果将退休后预算降低几个百分点是可行的，但如果降低50%可能就比较困难。之前讨论的社会保险就已经考虑了生活成本的增加问题。

常见的可以提供退休收入的其他资产中还包括年金产品。年金是一种人寿保险合同，通常按月向投保人支付资金，直至生命终结。年金通常被定义为一系列的付款，有多种形式，有些会比较复杂。在考虑购买年金产品时，投资者需要仔细研究各项细节。年金可能是退休资产的重要形式之一。最大的吸引力在于它可以将退休资产进行投资，从而为投资者提供确定的收入。有时，年金产品不仅可以在投资者生命终结前提供赔付，还可以向其配偶在一段时间内提供赔付。

五、税务筹划

人们在构建财务目标时，会考虑任何占用资源的形式。收入所得税不仅影响财务资源的积累，还会影响财务资源的使用。每一分用以缴税的资金不能用作他途。因此，人们需要进行有关税负的筹划和管理。税务不仅对人们的经济生活产生影响，还会影响人们生活的其他方面。

美国联邦法官 Learned Hand 有一句名言：“任何人总希望使自己的缴税越低越好，他们没有义务选择对财政部有利的行为。增加税负甚至并不是一种爱国责任的体现。”“因此，法院一遍遍重申，税务筹划并不是一种有罪的行为。”

本节重点阐述有关税务筹划的有关内容。在美国，税收由美国国税局征收，有关税收的法律可以在国税局官网查阅 http：//www. irs. gov/。

美国的联邦收入税是十分复杂的，有很多上千页的书介绍和解释收入税。联邦收入税代码也是要数千页。1913 年国税局用来申报个人所得税的 1040 表格刚开始启用时，收入税代码的小册子只有 1 页纸而已，如今已经有 200 页之长。个人纳税人适用的报税表格有很多，每一种都附有介绍说明，介绍确定个人纳税人应缴税额的基本公式和方法，但不包括规则、细则和一些例外情况的说明。

本节主要介绍与收入所得税有关的内容。为了清楚了解有关税收的情况，我们必须先搞清楚什么是收入。国税局关于收入分类有详细的定义解释，我们需要详细了解每一种分类，及之间的相互关系以便更好地进行税务筹划和管理。

计算收入所得税的基本思路如下：

总收入－调整项＝调整后总收入－抵免项

据此计算出的税额与其他具体税额的总和即为应纳税额。税额需要每年进行计算，并且许多纳税人都会从工资收入中代扣代缴，或者在最后缴税日估算应纳税额。确立了应纳税额后，从中扣除代扣代缴部分，即得到最终的应纳税额，可能会需要补交税款，也可能得到国税局的退款。

（一）总收入

第一个需要了解的收入是总收入，有时也称为收入，是最宽泛的一个含义，包括所有来源的收入所得。如果在报税时不是十分清楚某个收入来源是否应该包括在内，那么建议先将其包含在内，然后再具体查询。只有国税局明确规定不用包含的收入来源才可以不申报，因此我们最好先申报所有的收入来源，之后再根据情况剔除。收入来源可能包括工作补偿、商业收入、利息、房租、红利及售卖资产所得。国税局甚至明确要求纳税人申报非法所得，如贪污、毒品买卖所得等。总收入是确定其他收入及税负的起点。

除非法所得外，收入应包含：工资收入及小费；免税和应税的利息收入；普通股及绩优股红利所得；税收退款及其他免税优惠；抚养费；商业收入（或损失）；资本利得或损失；个人退休账户及其他养老金和年金账户的收入；租金收入，版税收入，合伙人所得，经营合资公司所得及来自信托及类似情况所得；农场收入；失业补助；社会保险收益。另外，国税局还要求列示所有的“其他收入”，以免漏报。

调整后总收入：

国税局允许从总收入中扣减某些抵扣项和减免项。包括但不限于如下内容：教育费用；某些类型的经营费用；健康储蓄账户供款；搬家费；个体经营税额抵减项；IRA，SEP，SIMPLE IRAs或其他合格退休计划的抵减项；个体经营健康保险抵减项；因提早提取某些存款的罚金；支付的赡养费；学费、教育费用、学生贷款利息等；某些国内生产费用的抵减项。

将所有调整项从总收入中扣减即得到调整后总收入。用调整后总收入计算的税额经其他缴税额和税务优惠调整，即得到应纳税额。将应纳税额与代扣代缴所得税额比较，就可以得知是需要缴税还是会得到退款。

（二）税率及税率分级

在进行税务筹划时，需要了解几个有关税率的概念，平均税率和边际税率。美国所得税体系属于累进制，收入越高，所对应的税率也越高。因此这种税率制度对于纳税人应该对应哪个税率会有两个不同的答案。随着收入的增加，每1美元的收入承担更高阶的税率。例如，第一个10 000美元收入不纳税，接下来的第二个10 000美元承担10%的税率，再接下来的10 000美元承担20%的税率。收入为30 000美元的纳税人的边际税率即为20%。边际税率是指最后1美元收入承担的税率水平。该纳税人的平均税率为10%，而非20%。平均税率是这样计算出来的：第一个10 000美元收入不纳税，接下来的第二个10 000美元须缴纳1 000美元的税额，再接下来的10 000美元须缴纳2 000美元的税额，总计为3 000美元的税额，因此平均税率为10%。

税率等级表是边际税率的分级表格，在每一栏列示每高一级应税收入和相对应的税率。以上这些概念之所以重要，是因为当计算纳税人实际承担的税负时，我们应当使用平均税率。但是当考虑不同收入选择时，就应当考虑纳税人的边际税率。

为了更好地了解税率计税率分级表，可以浏览美国国税局的网站。记住这些税率是毫无用处的，因为税率表几乎至少每年都要变更一次，但是迅速浏览这些概念对于税务筹划是有一定帮助的。

（三）资本利得

国税局不仅对一般的收入来源征税，如工资收入、利息及红利所得，售卖资产的利得同样需要缴税。当纳税人购买了一项资产，售卖获取利润，即被称为资本利得。简而言之，资本利得是因资本出售而获得的利润。例如，某纳税人购买了一项价值10 000美元的资产，售出时价格为20 000美元，资本利得即为10 000美元。如果这笔利润是应税收入，那么国税局就要求纳税人在申报纳税时将其列入收入总额中。

国税局将资本利得分为长期和短期。想获得最准确的分类标准，要咨询国税局的相关部门。表面上看，决定资本利得长短期分类的因素是持有资产的长短。国税局规定短期利得为持有资产少于一年而长期利得为持有资产多于一年。持有是国税局描述纳税人拥有某项资产的术语。

了解有关如何处理资本利得的细节是十分重要的。当购买和持有资产时，纳税人当然希望获得利润，有时会心想事成，但有时会事与愿违。因此我们有必要了解税务上如何加总利得和损失。通常，纳税人将短期利得和短期损失进行轧差，然后再与长期利得和长期损失的净额轧差，最后得到净应税所得。有时，净应税损失可以抵减一般收入的税额。但仅限于名义总额，而且需要与国税局进行核实。

纳税人都希望利用损失来抵减应税收入，但是在操作时，应当注意不要故意出现亏损。相同的投资在短期内又赎回可以认定为故意亏损，那么这样的亏损是不允许抵减收入的。国税局将这种发生在30天以内的回购定义为“虚卖”。

以往，资本利得通常以优惠于普通收入如工资或利息收入的税率征税。有时，税率征收设有上限，而不是以百分比方式征收。随时查看国税局的相关规定是非常必要的，因为有时因纳税人总收入的不同，对资本利得的税率也有所不同。

当售卖资产时，需要考虑不同购买批次的影响。如果纳税人购买了几批同一只股票，之后希望售卖部分持有股票，那么选择哪个批次售卖对税负会有不同影响。如果出售的这批股票的购买价较低，那么就会产生资本利得；相反，就会产生资本损失。一个聪明的纳税人在售卖自己的不同批次的资产时，需要将这些问题都考虑在内。

如果纳税人有做慈善的想法，那么可以通过将升值的资产捐助给符合条件的机构来避免税负。通过捐赠升值的资产，纳税人可以以当前市场价格申报捐助，而不必申报资本利得。符合捐助条件的机构可以以升值的价格售卖该资产而不必纳税，因为他们一般享受资本利得的税收优惠。这样，纳税人和获得捐助的机构都获得好处，只是国税局将损失这一部分的税收。

纳税人还可以考虑将税负转移给另一个税率等级较低的纳税人。例如，边际税率较高的父母可以通过赠送升值的股票给上大学的子女，让子女出售该股票，因为他们可能享受较低的税率甚至没有税收义务。

有做慈善想法的纳税人不仅可以捐赠升值的证券，而且可以通过捐赠现金的方式减少税收负担。

（四）税务筹划战略

市政债券利息收入享有联邦收入所得税减免。债券在发行时就已经决定了债券购买人的纳税义务。大部分的州政府及下属机构发行的债券，其利息都是不用缴纳联邦收入所得税。这种“免税”证券的利息通常也不用缴纳州税和地方税。但是纳税人需要查询相关州税务局和地方税务局的规定。一般来说，纳税人购买所在州内发行的债券产生的利息不用缴纳联邦和州所得税。

不管哪种情况，市政债券利息都是免税的。这个免税的特点对纳税人来说是非常有益的。纳税人所在的税率等级越高，利息免税给他们带来的好处越大。但是由于某些特定的免税市政债券的发行目的不同，有些利息支付是需要缴税的。免税的市政债券通常会有发行额的限制，如果他们发行金额过多，就需要缴税。纳税人最好与发行机构进行确认。美国政府债券也享受州收入所得税减免的权力。联邦收入所得税税率通常高于州收入所得税税率，正因如此，纳税人应先策划如何获得联邦收入所得税的减免，其次再考虑州收入所得税的减免问题。因为有些州或地方根本不征收收入所得税。

如果纳税人希望借款购买免税债券，就需要查阅国税局的相关规定，因为一不小心就可能违反法律规定。

美国政府储蓄债券在计算累积利息时也是免税的。另外，美国国债的利息同样享有州及地方免税的权力。

寿险和年金本身积累的现金价值不需要享受当期税负，但是从这些产品中支取现金可能涉及缴税，纳税人需要及时查阅相关信息。一般来说，人寿保险的身故赔付是免税的。有些投资同样享受税收优惠，例如纳税人可以利用投资品的折旧、摊销和损耗避免纳税，或者将应税收入转为非应税收入。

征税是政府的一项重要职能，最终解释权归政府税务机关所有。因此纳税人和他们的理财规划师应当视政府为某项税负的最高权威机构。美国国税局是美国联邦收入所得税的最高权威机构，并且有官方网站帮助大家理解各项规定，甚至还有小测试测验读者的理解程度。州及地方税务机关同样也有相关网站供纳税人查询。

（五）遗产规划

大多数情况下，遗产规划是对一个人身故后的财产的安排。但实际上，这些财产在生前就是存在的，因此也需要在生前进行规划和管理。理财规划的大部分内容与人生前的财产有关。

因此，遗产实际上是一个人或家庭的全部财产。简而言之，遗产可能包括经营所得（包括公共和私人的）、房产（包括个人住房）、其他投资性资产（例如股票、债券、基金及退休计划）、个人资产及其他资产。

本节所介绍的遗产规划的重点在于现有资产的转移和管理，尽管所有权将转移给他人。他人包括资产的继承人或受益人。大多数情况下，资产的下一代主人是家庭的下一代成员。受益人或继承人所继承的财产称为遗产。

遗产的现有主人应当对资产设立相应目标。有关遗产规划的问题包括：决定谁将是资产的下一任主人，及他/她将继承多少；如果现任主人有抚养对象或者有向他们提供财务支持的目标，该如何完成该目标？及目标的完成程度如何？需要指出的是，除了通常列举的遗产范围之外，人寿保险也是我们在遗产规划时应当考虑的内容。

遗产转移时是否会产生相关费用？费用可能包括管理费和税费。遗产规划可以帮助我们减免这些费用。减免遗产继承中的相关费用是遗产规划的重要内容。

很多客户和理财规划师在考虑遗产时会考虑它的总值和净值。遗产总值是税费前的资产价值，遗产净值则是扣除税费之后的资产价值，即受益人或继承人可以继承的部分。

税法允许部分资产通过遗产继承方式进行转移，并且这种方式是免税的。因此我们需要了解这种节税方式的相关公式、规则、税务优惠政策等。

遗产规划中的另一个重要内容即要保证遗产所有人及继承人的财务的流动性。在规划过程中，我们需要考虑支付的成本及可以用以支付的资金的流动性。如果遗产包含非流动资产，如一个农场或者私人企业，流动性问题就是一个需要重点考虑的问题。如果没有足够的流动性来支付遗产继承的费用，就需要尽快变卖遗产，这可能导致资产会以低于期望价格出售，或者被迫出售本不愿意出售的遗产。

如果遗产是私人企业，所有权将如何传承，是否有可行的计划保证其实施。缺乏详细的规划可能导致资产受损甚至无法继续经营，从而损害它的价值。

遗产规划还包括谁负责遗产管理。这个负责人被称为个人代表，之前称为执行者，有时是某些资产的信托的受托人。这个负责人的主要职责是使遗产规划的执行尽可能完美。

如何将遗产转移给继承人是一个重要的话题。遗产转移有多种方式。遗产可以在所有人生前或逝世后转移。在所有人身故后，遗产的所有权仍然可以变更。可以利用所有人生前和身故馈赠及遗产转移的方式进行遗产规划。

在所有人一生中，遗产有哪些其他的表现形式？这些不同的形式该如何转移？

财产的所有表现为多种形式：（1）独占；（2）与另一主体的共同拥有；（3）共同所有权；（4）合有所有权；（5）信托。

个人独有的所有权是通常所指的“拥有”。这可以称为所有权的最高形式。独占的所有者以他们的名义拥有资产，并且可以一生依自己的意愿管理资产。财产归该个人所有并且财产所产生的所有利润，如租金或其他收入也全部归该所有人所有。他们可以售卖、抵押，重新注册，在身故后按照自己的意愿处置资产。

附有幸存权力的共有是一个分享所有权的结构。主要特点是所有人其中一人亡故，所有权将自动转移给幸存者。因此如果两人拥有100股“XYZ”的股票的附有幸存权力的共有所有权，如果其中一人亡故，另外一人将自动获得全部100股的所有权。所有权的转移不需要经过认证。另外，这种附有幸存权力的共有所有权并不仅适用于两个人之间。

共同所有权与附有幸存权力的共有所有权类似。共同所有权存在于配偶之间，如要更改所有权的任何形式，都需双方的同意。有些州允许除配偶以外的人之间享有共同所有权。

合有所有权是指两个人（或更多人）共同拥有不可分割的所有权。所有人不享有幸存权力，即一人亡故，所有权不会自动转移给幸存者。一般来说这些所有人拥有平等的权力，但也不完全如此。合有所有权也可能是一方拥有75%的所有权，另一方拥有25%的所有权。资产产生的收入会按比例在所有人之间分摊。

有些州在配偶之间会存在共同资产所有权。每个配偶都拥有资产一半的所有权，不管这项资产的署名权或对资产的贡献度多寡。在这些州进行遗产规划时，需要考虑共同资产所有权的情况。允许共同资产所有权的州被称为“共同法律州”。

基于资产所有权的方式，有些资产可能存在受益人。

谈及受益人，人们最容易想到的是保险保单或退休账户，但实际上很多账户都会用到受益人的概念。这些账户会注册TOD或POD。TOD是指身故后转移，POD只是身故后给付。TOD和POD在将账户转移给受益人时十分有用，但是多用于不同类型的财产上。

TOD账户通常用来处理个人和实物资产，通常很难直接给付给受益人。例如，很难想象如何将一辆汽车“付”给某人。相比之下，将银行储蓄账户中的资金付给某人是很自然的事情。因此存款账户、银行账户通常使用POD注册而其他资产则使用TOD注册。房地产可以使用“受益人契约”，与TOD的运作方式基本相同。

资产可以以多种方式转移给下一个继承人。资产可以通过正常的法律继承的方式进行转移。如共有或附有幸存者权利的共有。

资产还可以通过遗嘱的形式转移。负责遗产处理的人称为遗嘱执行者、遗产代理人或者遗产管理人（无遗嘱情形下）。

如果某人死后留有遗嘱或最后遗言和见证文件，那么遗产代理人就可以依据这份法律文件作为指导处理遗产。如果某人死后没有遗嘱或见证文件，那么遗产就视为未留有遗嘱的遗产。在法庭上，见证人将陈述或递交声明描述他们所知道的有关遗产处理的情况备案。最后遗言和见证文件是对遗嘱主人遗愿的描述。

如果某人死后没有遗嘱，或者任何指导遗产分配的文件，那么各州会有相关法律程序对死者的财产进行分配。虽然处理方式各不相同，但一定存在明确的指导文件，尽管不一定与死者的个人意愿相一致。这实际上为遗产规划提供了另一个机会。

遗产规划通常是指对资产从上一代转移给下一代的安排。对此，最重要的两个需要考虑的问题是财产转移的效率和准确性。效率是指尽量减少财产转移的税务成本和管理程序。准确是指财产转移尽量实现财产所有者的意愿。

遗嘱认证是管理遗产，解决索取要求及按遗嘱处理遗产的法律程序。遗嘱认证法庭是对遗产有司法权的法庭。遗嘱认证法庭通常从两个渠道获取信息和指导。遗产代理人与法庭共同合作保证遗产处理的顺利进行。遗嘱认证法庭和遗产代理人寻找的第一个线索是最后遗嘱及遗产处理的认证文件。之所以称之为最后遗言，是因为死者有可能写有多份遗嘱。通常情况下，最后的遗嘱会取代之前的所有遗嘱。遗产代理人负责执行具体事务，遗嘱认证法庭保证其正确执行。遗产代理人需要向法庭进行汇报，当整个取证程序结束后，整理成文，递交给法庭。

遗嘱认证是一个公共事件，对每一个相关人员都起到保护作用。遗产代理人须发布公众通知，表明遗产处理是公开进行的，并且已经在处理之中。在这期间，相关人员可以提出对遗产的索取，受益人也清楚了解自己的立场。当所有这些程序结束之后，遗产处理人会发出通告，报告所有的相关处理事件，因此，所有的遗产索取必须在此之前完成。

对于没有遗嘱的遗产，遗嘱认证法庭会指派相关人员监管遗产的处理。这名人员仍然需要向法庭回报并呈交报告。

美国的遗嘱认证在每个州是不同的。有时，遗产创造是遗产规划应考虑的内容。大多数遗产规划都是围绕着所有人生前的遗产管理及身故后的遗产处理进行。但有时，人们在生前的财务目标无法实现，可能利用人寿保险来帮助他们完成心愿。例如，某人可能希望向自己毕业的母校捐助一笔奖学金，但是在生前无法完成，但是可以通过人寿保险的赔付在死后完成这个目标。人们可能有在亡故后仍需要照顾的、有特殊需要和存在残障的子女，他们需要花费大量的金钱和精力，因此通过购买人寿保险，可以满足这一需要。

如果没有什么财产，是否需要进行遗产规划？答案是肯定的。之前，我们已经讨论了有关遗产代理人的选择及无遗嘱情况下的遗产处理问题。当然，如果某人没有明确的遗产分配的意愿，州法院可以按照相关法律程序进行处理。如果没有什么财产，遗产规划的重点可能与金钱和有形财产无关。即使没有财产，很多人都有一些遗物需要处理，例如珠宝首饰、汽车、保险赔偿金等。

其他与遗产规划相关的问题还包括：如果家庭中负责照顾子女的人亡故，谁来接替这个职责？谁负有法律能力管理子女的生活直至他们成长的法定年龄？

即使父母双方亡故时没有留下任何资产，未成年子女仍然会收到一些福利。如果法定监护人在亡故前能够留有谁及如何照看未成年子女的线索，他们的遗愿可以很好地执行。有特殊需要的子女即使成长到法定年龄，仍然需要一定的照顾。有时他们仍不能管理自己的财务事务，在这种情形下，关于财务处理方面的规定和程序几乎是永久性的。

谁负责管理你的财务事务，包括处理现金、支付账单、接收没有到期的收入等。

未婚夫妻或者同性伴侣可能需要了解其他相关法律来进行遗产规划。

如果某人患有严重的疾病，谁可以替他/她处理有关遗产的问题?

详细的遗产规划还应包含有关律师的财务权限、健康管理的权限及有关临终关怀的法律文件。

案例

Smith 夫妇的理财规划制作

界定理财目标

根据 Smith 夫妇理财目标实现的优先顺序，重新整理理财目标如下：

Don：年家庭旅行费用：$20 000。

Rachel：增加税收优惠的存款。

双方：准备女儿 Jackie 的大学学费，预计每年学费为 $15 000，共 4 年。

双方：于 2035 年共同退休，并保证退休后每年 $150 000 的消费水平。

Don 死后财务状况分析

当前 Smith 家庭财务情况的一个明显弱点是缺乏紧急备用金。较为稳妥的策略是准备相当于 3 ~6 个月的日常消费支出的紧急备用金，将其存入活期账户。当前 Smith 家庭的流动资产为，尚有的缺口。

Smith 夫妇债务管理情况良好。年房产相关支出仅占年总收入的 9%，年房产相关支出及其他债务支出占年总收入的 12.9%。

Smith 夫妇年储蓄占其可支配收入的 26.7%，远高于全国平均水平①。投资资产占总资产的 71.7%。

夫妻双方每年向弹性消费账户存入 $4 000，但仅消费 $3 550 用于医疗费用。

风险管理分析

人寿保险：我们将分析如果 Smith 夫妇中一方亡故，Smith 家庭是否有足够的投资资产或其他财务资源保证整个家庭今后的生活不受影响。目前，Rachel 两全险的年保费为

① 根据经济分析局的数据，2015 年美国全国平均储蓄率占可支配收入的 5.6%。

250 美元。现金价值为 $3 467，增长率约为 4.8%，远低于整个投资组合 9.9% 的回报率。如果 Don 今年亡故，为保证 Rachel 活至 85 岁的费用为 $912 751。这些费用包含 $10 000 的丧葬费，偿付所有债务，以及无须变卖房产、车辆或者任何家庭财产能保证 Rachel至 85 岁的生活费。目前，Don 的人寿保险保额为 $290 000，资金缺口为 $622 751。如果 Rachel 今年亡故，为保证 Don 活至 90 岁的费用为 $ 241 590。这些费用包含 $10 000 的丧葬费，偿付所有债务，以及无须变卖房产、车辆或者任何家庭财产能保证 Rachel 至 85 岁的生活费。目前，Rachel 的人寿保险保额为 $50 000，资金缺口为 $191 590。

残障险：如果 Don 不幸残疾，终身都不能工作。那么在 Don 残疾的第一年，整个家庭将损失 $23 907，准备的紧急备用金可以用来弥补这个资金缺口。从第二年至第十七年，整个家庭一直都有收入盈余，直至第十八年，收入开始出现缺口，大约为 $86 565。但是通过早年对收入盈余的存储，可以解决这个收入缺口的问题。但前提是，Don 能够领取社保残疾金及团体残障保险金。如果 Rachel 不幸残疾，终身都不能工作。那么整个家庭一直都存在收入缺口，Rachel 残疾的第一年，家庭收入缺口为 $50 357，最后一年为 $129 724。整个计算也是以 Rachel 能够领取社保残疾金为前提的。

长期护理险：虽然目前看来 Smith 夫妻双方都没有重大疾病，但是研究表明，长期护理需求成为年过 50 岁的人财富健康一个最大潜在威胁。下面我们就来分析长期护理需求对于家庭投资组合的负面影响及如何运用长期护理险的保障化解这一潜在危机。

如果 Don 在 80 岁时搬入护理中心，计划入住的时间为 3 年。以目前价格计算，年费用为 $58 400。假设通货膨胀率为 6%，长期护理费用总计为 $1 131 913。如果 Rachel 在 80 岁时搬入护理中心，计划入住的时间为 3 年。以目前价格计算，年费用为 $58 400。假设通货膨胀率为 6%，长期护理费用总计为 $2 027 084。因此，如果家庭成员中发生过长期护理需求，购买长期护理险覆盖这一潜在风险是十分必要的。

房屋险：目前 Smith 夫妇家庭财产保险的一个最大缺陷是仅购买了标准房屋保险，没有对房屋不同需求的单独保障。

<u>风险容忍度分析</u>

根据风险容忍度评分表，Smith 夫妇家庭的风险容忍度评分为 72，而其他年龄相仿的投资者平均得分为 54。因此 Smith 夫妇的风险容忍度高于平均水平。

<u>资产组合配置分析</u>

Smith 夫妇的资产总额当前的市场价值为 $1 104 374。Smith 夫妇的负债总额为

$241.797。因此，Smith 夫妇的总净资产（总资产 - 总负债）为 $ 862 577。

Smith 夫妇当前的投资组合配置是：

2% 的现金及现金等价物；

3% 的中期债券；

3% 的长期债券；

30% 的大盘价值股票；

40% 的大盘成长型股票；

9% 的中盘股；

4% 的小盘股；

7% 的在国际市场开发的股票；

9% 的国际新兴股市股票。

在所有可投资资产中，股票占比为 17.73%。

投资组合业绩

目前，Smith 夫妇的可投资组合的加权平均收益率为 9.91%，比 Smith 夫妇要求的回报率的 10% 略低。当前无风险利率为 0.25%。投资组合的标准差为 15.82%。投资组合的夏普比率为 0.611。这意味着对于 Smith 夫妇所能承受的每 1% 的标准差，Smith 夫妇的投资组合可获得超过无风险利率 0.611% 的回报。

女儿 Jackie 的教育基金需求分析

Jackie 在上大学期间，Don 和 Rachel 仍然会工作。预计大学学费为每年 $15 000（以当今成本计算），以每年 8% 的速度增加。如果以 9.91% 的投资组合回报率进行估算，Smith 夫妇现在需要预留 $69 835 或每月存储 $675 以备 Jackie 今后上大学所需。

个人所得税分析

假设 Smith 夫妇以已婚共同申报个人所得税，估计 Smith 夫妇的联邦平均税率为 18%，州（密苏里州）税为 6%。

Smith 夫妇每年向 Don 的 403B 退休计划缴纳 $17 000，Rachel 的 401K 退休计划缴纳 $17 000，各自的个人退休账户 $5 000。今年确定缴费型年金的限额为 $17 500。个人退休账户的最大缴费额为 $ 5 500。Don 的雇主 S 大学，为所有员工提供 457 计划，而 Don 目前并未向该计划缴费。

退休准备分析

社会保障收入

如果Don70岁退休，他将每年从社会保障获得$41 372。如果Rachel与Don同时退休，她在退休时将是60岁。她将在从2038年，即她满62岁（美国可以从社会保障领取退休金的最早年龄）时每年从社会保障获得$17 528。这些数据已根据通货膨胀率进行了调整。

Don的收益确定型养老金计划可获得的退休收入

Don从S大学退休后，每年可获得$190 940直至终老。这个数额是不考虑通货膨胀因素的。

Don和Rachel退休需求分析

Don和Rachel都期望在2035年退休。Don的预期寿命为90岁，Rachel的预期寿命为85岁。据估算，以当前货币价值计算，退休后整个家庭每年需要$150 000。如果其中一方亡故，每年的退休收入将下降。若Don先于Rachel亡故，Rachel每年需要10万美元。若Rachel先于Don亡故，则Don每年需要$110 000。根据测算，退休后，Smith夫妇将不会遇到退休收入不足的情况。

遗产规划分析

根据2014年现行税法规定，遗产税免税额为每人不超过500万美元。这可能会在未来几年大幅度减少。意味着今后遗产税负的增加。

Don的遗嘱管理遗产，遗产总额及遗产税负

如果Don和Rachel今天同时去世，并且Don先于Rachel亡故，Don的总遗产将是$854 582。假设第一次遗嘱继承的管理费为2%，遗嘱认证费用为$987。假设丧葬费为$10 000。配偶遗产税扣除额为$843 595。遗产税的应税总额为$0。

如果Don和Rachel今天同时去世，并且Rachel先于Don亡故，Don的遗产是$854 582，Don从Rachel继承的总遗产是$49 7082。因此，Don的总遗产将是$ 1 351.664。假设第二次遗嘱继承的管理费为5%，遗嘱认证费用为$987。需要偿还的债务为$241 797。假设丧葬费为$10 000。应税遗产将是$1 068 340。Don的团体人寿保险死亡给付是$50 000，这是不征税的。最终的遗产税的应税额为$0。

Rachel的遗嘱管理遗产，遗产总额及遗产税负

如果Don和Rachel今天同时去世，并且Rachel先于Don亡故，Rachel的总遗产将是$ 559 113。假设第一次遗嘱继承的管理费为2%，遗嘱认证费用为$2 031。假设丧葬费为$10 000。配偶遗产税扣除额为$497 082。Rachel的团体人寿保险死亡给付是$50 000，这是不征税的。遗产税的应税总额为$ 0。

如果Don和Rachel今天同时去世，并且Don先于Rachel亡故，Rachel的遗产是

$ 559 113，Rachel 从 Don 继承的总遗产是 $ 843 595。因此，Rachel 的总遗产将是 $1 402. 708。假设第二次遗嘱继承的管理费为 5%，遗嘱认证费用为 $ 31 580。需要偿还的债务为 $241 797。假设丧葬费为 $10 000。应税遗产将是 $ 1 119 331。最终的遗产税的应税额为 $0。

第四节　理财规划方案的制作和设计

理财规划流程中最重要的一步即制作和设计理财规划方案。这是理财规划师向客户展现自己专业实力的时刻。理财规划的类型和质量表明了理财规划师的专业技巧和能力，包括收集数据、分析数据及最终整合理财规划。设计周密的理财规划实施起来也较为容易，并更能帮助客户达成理财目标。反之，设计粗糙的理财规划不仅在实施中较为困难，而且会影响客户理财目标的实现。

理财规划建议分为两种类型。一种是服务性和流程性建议。Lytton，Grable 和 Klock 2013 年[①]出版的《理财规划流程：制作理财规划》一书中定义流程性建议是指客户的理财规划方案中强调某一过程或服务的建议。常见的流程性建议包括改变理财计划假设、重新安排某项资产的所有权及提醒或鼓励客户实施某项计划。第二种理财建议是产品导向的。产品建议，主要在于帮助客户选择合适的产品实现理财目标。这使很多新晋理财规划师误认为理财规划只是促进销售的一种手段和技能。流程性建议和产品建议共同构成了理财规划建议，但实际上，理财规划方案中大部分建议在本质上都是流程性的。表 3－6 分别举例介绍了流程性战略和产品战略。

表 3－6　　　　流程建议和产品建议举例

理财规划内容	流程建议	产品建议
人寿保险规划	在已有的寿险保单上增加一个受益人	用不可撤销寿险信托产品替代有现金价值的寿险保单
教育规划	为享受联邦资助，将年终奖挪至下一年领取	将定期存款中的 34 000 美元转入 UTMA 托管账户
投资规划	资产重新配置，使年化收益率增加 200 个百分点	购买 100 只 XYZ 股票，500 只 ABC 基金和 600 只 MNO ETF
普通保险规划	考虑增加免赔额以降低保费	将赔偿责任限额从 25 000 美元增加至 100 000 美元

① Lytton, R. H., Grable, J. E., & Klock, D. D. (2013). *The process of financial planning: Developing a financial plan* (2nd ed.). Erlanger, KY: National Underwriter.

理财规划方案的设计从很多方面来说是整个理财规划流程中最有趣的环节。这一环节要求理财规划师发挥他们的创造力并挖掘自身潜力。新晋理财规划师往往急于进行理财建议。这种焦躁的情绪应当尽量避免。考虑这个理财建议：“你应当进行资产重组以在未来获得更高的收益率。”虽然这个建议本身没有错，但对客户来讲是毫无用处的。因为这个建议太粗糙并且含义模糊，根本无法实施。许多理财规划师会担心，如果他们的建议太详细，那么客户就可以摆脱他们自己实施。这实际上是过分担忧。客户的信心随着理财建议的实施增长。理财规划师模棱两可的态度不会增强客户的信心。如果理财流程的终极目标是实施理财方案，那么理财规划建议就必须流畅、一致而且准确。

国际理财规划标准委员会（Financial Planning Standards Board）在《理财规划执业标准》中将理财规划方案的实施总结为三大步骤：

第一，拟定并评估理财规划策略。理财规划师应拟定一个或几个符合客户当前状况的理财策略，并对每个备选策略在实现客户目标、需求及优先顺序等方面进行可行性评估。评估工作可能包含与客户沟通其目标、需求的重要性，目标实现的优先顺序及时间要求，考虑各种假设条件，进行调查或咨询其他专业人士等。最终理财规划师会确定一个或多个策略。

第二，拟定理财规划建议。在对各种理财策略及客户当前理财状况进行辨识和评估后，理财规划师应提出详细可行的理财建议。理财建议可以是一个或者一系列需同时展开的行动。

第三，向客户提交理财规划方案。理财规划师应向客户提交理财规划方案并提供其依据，以便客户能够在充分知情的情况下做出决策。

Lytton, Grable 和 Klock 在 2013 年出版的《理财规划流程：制作理财规划》一书中总结了理财规划方案制作问题清单供理财规划师在实际工作中参考。该问题清单帮助理财规划师及其客户理解理财规划的具体步骤及在理财规划方案实施过程中可能需要承担的成本。问题清单共包含七大问题：

谁负责理财规划建议的实施？客户？理财规划师？第三方？或者理财规划师和客户合作？例如，客户资产重组计划的实施可能是由理财规划师针对其管理的客户资产实施，也可能是针对退休账户中的资产提出的建议，那么就由客户自己实施。

需要具体做些什么？这个问题的答案越详细越好。理财规划师不可以简单说“资产组合重组”，而是需要详细提出如何进行资产组合的重新分配。理财规划师可以制作行动清单，向客户具体说明该做些什么。

何时实施理财建议？虽然这是理财规划师无论如何都会回答的问题。但是我们还是需要反复说明理财规划师需要考虑每个客户理财建议实施的时间周期。例如某项理财建议是需要在一周内，一个月内，一年内，还是未来某个时期实施？理财建议越详尽，实施起来就越容易。

理财建议在何地实施？在客户的理财规划方案中，每个具体实施措施可能会大有不同。有些理财建议是由理财规划师完成，有些可能只能通过雇主或者其他专业人士，如保险经纪人或者政府机构实施。

为什么实施理财建议？向客户表明实施理财建议的原因与表明如何实施理财建议同样重要。

如何实施理财建议？虽然许多理财建议的实施都是在理财规划师的帮助下完成，但是有些理财建议，特别是流程性的，需要客户独立完成。基于此，理财规划师需要为客户准备一张“行动地图”，帮助客户更便捷和更有效地实施理财建议。例如，某理财建议要求客户利用现有的存款增加退休账户中的投入。完成“如何实施理财建议”，理财规划师需要回答如下具体步骤：

约见公司的福利负责人，要求领取表格 T；

填写表格 T，把退休账户的投入从现在的 4% 增加到 7%；

将表格 T 交还公司的薪酬部门。

需要花费多少钱？有些理财规划师不太愿意估计理财建议的花费。与其回避这个问题，理财规划师应当充分把握理财规划方案制作这一环节，向客户披露理财建议实施的成本及其益处。有些理财建议有直接的实施成本。例如，增加保险赔偿责任限额会使保费增加。有些理财建议的成本则不那么直接、透明。总体来讲，几乎所有的产品推荐建议都会影响客户的现金流或者净资产金额。有些时候这种影响是正面的，有时，则是负面的。例如一个典型的涉及现金流和净资产建议：再融资房屋贷款。通常这个理财建议的初衷是为了增加月现金流，却会由于动用现金资产偿付解约费用而使净资产下降。实施再融资房屋贷款理财建议还可以获得相应的税收优惠，从而增加年现金流。理财规划师充分披露理财建议实施对客户带来的各方面影响，这可以增强客户的信心。另外，跟踪所有的理财规划成本及收益也可以更好地跟踪现金流变化。

以上分析表明，实施理财计划中的理财建议并不像单纯向客户提出某个建议那样简单。在理财规划行业内部，当实施理财规划方案时，大家对理财规划师的作用展开了激烈的讨论。以上分析是假设理财规划师的主要职能是收集和分析客户的数据，并向客户提出一个或多个理财建议以帮助客户理财目标的实现。这表明提出的理财建议是理财规划师站在专业角度提出的对客户在当前最有利的方案。但也有一些理财规划师辩驳让客户“执行”理财建议并不是理财规划师的职责。他们认为理财规划师应该给客户提供多个理财方案，让客户从中选择对实现理财目标最有利的方案。

以上讨论的两种提供理财规划方案的方法的差异是很大的。传统方法将理财规划师的角色定位在有信托责任的咨询师上，与会计师、律师和医生的角色十分相似。赞成传统方法的理财规划师认为如果每次就医都是让医生提供3~4种解决病症的方法，然后让患者自己选择其中一种感觉不错的治疗方案，无疑是不妥的。但是持反对观点的人认为客户或者患者总是最了解自己的需求、需要及愿望。理财规划师组织要根据客户的实际情况提供多种选择就可以了。在实际工作中，每个理财规划师都要面临到底该选择哪种方法向客户展示理财规划方案。目前，大部分执业的理财规划师都选择“专家模式”，即他们向客户提供站在自己专业角度认为最好的理财建议，但也提供他们认为可以接受的其他次优选择。例如，一名理财规划师可能建议他/她的客户融资房贷。如果理财建议旨在增加客户的现金流，那么理财规划师会建议使用30年贷款，但也会提供15年和20年贷款的选择。理财规划师建议选择30年贷款的理财建议的原因十分清楚，那就是用30年房屋贷款进行再融资可增加客户的可支配现金流。但是如果客户不愿意持有长期债务，那么就会选择提供的其他方案。

案例

基于Smith家庭的财务情况，可以考虑为其提供一份综合理财规划。在这里，列示一些可能的理财建议以满足Smith家庭的短期、中期及长期的财务目标。在提供理财建议之前，理财师有必要再次审核客户的理财目标及在分析中运用的假设前提。这会帮助理财师进行进一步的分析及建议。理财师在向客户提出理财建议前可认真考虑以下问题：

残障险是否符合生病及意外的情况？具体的赔付条款是怎样的？

自上次遗嘱订立至今，家庭都发生了哪些重要的变化？

遗嘱中是否包含在健康及财务危机情况下的律师权力条款？

家庭所有投资产品的购买日期和购买价值如何？

在过去5年，家庭收入的稳定性如何？

假定理财师可以获得以上问题的答案，那么我们就可以起草理财建议。

基本建议

紧急备用金

从每月的收入盈余中拿出 $160 存入货币市场基金账户。24 个月即可完成紧急备用金储蓄目标。

抵押贷款再融资

将目前贷款余额为 $231 284 的 30 年期的抵押贷款换成 15 年期固定利率抵押贷款，以达到在 15 年内还清所有债务的目标。假设初始费用和其他费用（包括鉴定费、信用报告、水灾认证、产权保险等）为 $4 000，我们将其包含在再融资金额中进行估算，那么新的月还款额将是 $1 596.69，比目前的月还款额多出 $410，可通过每月的收入盈余进行支付。

弹性消费账户

建议用完弹性消费账户中到期日为 3 月 31 日的 $450 并可以考虑减少弹性消费账户每年的缴费。

请与 S 大学人力资源部确认他们是否提供托儿弹性消费账户。如果有，建议每年向该账户缴费 $5 000 用于支付托儿费用。

车辆相关费用

Smith 夫妇的汽车贷款是 15 个月还清，继续现在每月 $ 720 的存款以支付未来换车消费。

<u>风险管理</u>

Don 和 Rachel 的人寿保险

建议为 Don 增加购买保额为 $ 625 000 的 20 年定期寿险。

建议为 Rachel 增加购买保额为 $20 万的 20 年定期寿险。

残障险

建议为 Rachel 购买长期伤残保险，直到她退休。这种长期伤残保险有 3 个月的等待期和每月 $4 000 补助金。每月收入盈余的其余部分可覆盖每月保费。有了这个保险，如果 Rachel 现在丧失工作能力，整个家庭在第一年有 $ 2 989 的收入缺口。但这可以用紧急备用金进行弥补。从第二年开始至 Rachel 49 岁，整个家庭都会有一个收入盈余，但之后会出现收入缺口。前几年的盈余可以保存抵消晚年收入不足的情况。这种计算是基于 Smith 夫妇将收到社会保障残疾福利金的假设。

Medicare 的长期护理保险

Don 和 Rachel 或许可以利用 Medicare 的长期护理保障。Medicare 覆盖养老院和家庭医疗保健，但它仅限于熟练的护理康复的性质，并且只覆盖 100 天的高级护理，其中只有前 20 天负担 100% 的费用。建议购买商业长期护理保险。

房屋保险

Smith 夫妇的个人财产赔付是基于实际现金值（AVC）。建议购买一个基于更换成本的保单。

考虑额外购买覆盖 Smith 夫妇价值大约 $20 000 珠宝的保单。

投资

除非 Smith 夫妇愿意自己频繁监控个股的表现，Smith 夫妇应该考虑更换这些股票，转而购买中型或大型股票的共同基金或交易所买卖基金（ETF）。

个人所得税

Smith 夫妇目前还没有专门为 Jackie 设立一个教育储蓄账户。Smith 夫妇可考虑购买 MOST 529 计划（密苏里州的 529 大学储蓄计划），Smith 夫妇的一个目标是增加税务优惠的储蓄。该账户将帮助 Smith 夫妇实现这一目标：

1. Smith 夫妇不会支付收入所得税。在 529 账户的资金的增长可享受联邦及州所得税递延。

2. Smith 夫妇可以免税取款。如果这些款项是用于支付符合条件的高等教育费用，Smith 夫妇将不必缴纳联邦或州所得税。然而，对于不符合条件的高等教育费用，Smith 夫妇将需要支付联邦所得税和 10% 的联邦税务罚款，及州税和地方税。

3. Smith 夫妇可以节省更多的州所得税。考虑到 Smith 夫妇拥有教育储蓄账户并且长住在密苏里州，Smith 夫妇可以享受高达 $16 000 的税务抵扣。

4. Smith 夫妇可以享受联邦赠予税的优惠。如果 Smith 夫妇以已婚联合报税人身份报税，那么 Smith 夫妇可以获得每年 $28 000 的免赠予税税额。而不会触发联邦赠予税。如果 Smith 夫妇有大笔的一次性赠予，Smith 夫妇的赠予额为最高每位受益人 $140 000（已婚联合申报），然后 Smith 夫妇可将其视为 5 年捐赠（但在这 5 年期间，如果 Smith 夫妇还有额外的赠予将被征税）。如果捐助者在这 5 年内亡故，捐赠品的金额将按比例计算为捐赠者的应税遗产。

另外，Smith 夫妇应该考虑利用当前较低的长期资本利得税（15%）的优势。这个比率可能会根据税法修订定期更换。

总体而言，Smith 夫妇需要每月向 Vanguard Total Stock Market Index 组合（年平均回报率为 11.52%）中投入 $608，用于储备 Jackie 的教育基金。在前两年，以 Smith 夫妇目前的收入盈余计算，每月可投入 $443。Smith 夫妇的紧急备用金目标将会在两年内实现，Smith 夫妇的汽车贷款将在 15 个月内付清。因此，两年后，Smith 夫妇每月为 Jackie 的教育基金应增加至 $728。

退休准备

Don 的 403B 和 457 计划

Smith 夫妇的一个目标是增加税务优惠的储蓄。最大化 Don 的 403B 计划的投入将是一个很好的选择。Don 也有资格获得 457 计划，这是他可享受税收优惠的另一个退休计划，可以考虑好好利用。

Don 和 Rachel 的个人退休账户（IRA）

Smith 夫妇的一个目标是增加税务优惠的储蓄。最大限度地提高 Smith 夫妇的个人退休账户的投入将是另一个很好的选择。

可投入到退休账户中的额外资金

目前，Smith 夫妇没有额外的资金增加退休账户的投入以提高未来退休金。建议 Smith 夫妇卖出 4 只个股转投股票共同基金或 ETF。

遗产规划

医疗照护事前指示和律师权力

为 Don 和 Rachel 建立了医疗照护事前指示和律师权力。

Don 和 Rachel 的遗嘱

在遗嘱中增加关于生存条款的规定。

在遗嘱中为 Jackie 委任一个法定监护人和监管者（假设父母双方都亡故）。

Don 和 Rachel 的寿险保单

为 Don 的定期寿险设置一个不可撤销的人寿保险信托。

为 Rachel 的万能寿险设置一个不可撤销的人寿保险信托。

三年后，死亡赔付将不算作保险人的总遗产。

Smith 夫妇可以在 2015 年将 $28 000 转入该信托用于支付保险费，该资金的转移是免收赠予税的。

第五节　理财规划方案的实施

虽然制定和设计理财规划方案是未来理财目标实现的基础，但是从许多方面来说，在理财规划流程中最重要的步骤是理财规划方案的实施。如果客户没有实施理财方案，理财目标是难以达成的。另外，这还意味着理财规划师之前所有的努力都付诸东流。大家都不希望任何一种情况发生，因此，理财规划师应当督促客户采取行动完成理财计划。

一、贯穿理财规划方案实施始终的因素

无论何时实施某个理财方案，理财规划师都需要考虑该方案的实施对之前和之后理财方案的影响。举个简单的例子。假设一名客户非常厌恶借债。他/她不仅自己不愿意举债，而且从根本上反对借债这个理念。基于客户的这种情况，理财规划师可能会建议客户加快提前偿付长期债务，如房屋贷款或教育贷款。这个建议也许是合适的，但是会对客户产生一定的影响。

加速偿付债务会降低客户当前的自主现金流；提前偿付房屋贷款可能会带来税收的不利影响；影响客户的净资产水平并可能会需要重新审查当前的保单计划；延迟其他理财建议的实施。

图 3－4 展示了理财方案实施的整体性和循环性的特点。理财计划按照理财规划方案实施。实施一个或多个理财方案会导致客户当前和未来财务状况发生改变，随之影响未来的分析和理财建议。图 3－4 展示了理财规划方案实施的一个重要特点，即理财方案的实施需要监督。有些监督是短暂的，有些则需要持续很长的时间。

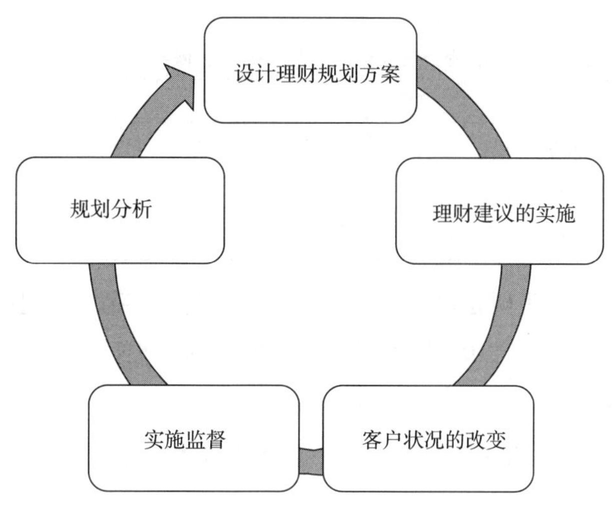

图 3－4 理财方案实施的整体性和循环性

二、沟通和执行

图3－4所展示的理财规划流程的循环性的特点揭示了理财规划对客户的重要意义。理财规划不仅是一个交易性的活动，还是一个综合性的服务。它不会随着产品或服务的售出而终结，理财规划师会继续监督客户对之前理财规划方案的实施情况。这种循环往复的理财规划流程会一直持续，直到客户解除与理财规划师的雇佣关系。

与客户充分沟通并详细解释理财规划方案中的细节是十分重要的。理财规划师需要口头表述并与客户讨论理财规划方案的内容。然而，将理财规划的实施方案书面化是更好地选择。理财规划师可以采取多种方式。最简单的方式是理财规划师向客户提供理财方案实施清单，将之前列举的七大问题（谁，什么，何时，何地，为什么，如何及多少钱）罗列其中。

表3－7　　　　实施方案清单

需要立即执行
利用银行账户中的现金偿还信用卡贷款余额
修订W－4税务表格，每月扣缴400美元
每期退休账户的缴款增加250美元
一年内执行
将退休计划由之前的雇主计划转为自有计划
用可变保单代替现在的现金价值寿险保单
更新遗嘱、生前遗嘱及律师权力
约见财产及意外伤害保险经纪，探讨当前保额覆盖范围及保额责任赔偿限额
未来18个月执行
利用出售邮票藏品的资金购买海滩小屋
出于保险保护的目的，完善家庭储备
考虑增加100万美元的责任保险

利用清单的方式列举理财建议的一个明显劣势是每个步骤的描述不是十分清楚。因此Lytton，Grable和Klock在2013年出版的《理财规划流程：制作理财规划》一书中建议理财规划师使用理财建议表格，如表3－8所示。虽然在表3－8中列举的理财建议与表3－7相同，但是却详细很多。另外，这个表格还向客户清楚展示了理财建议之间是如何影响现金流和净资产的。

表 3－8　　理财方案实施计划

理财建议（什么）	谁	何时	何地	为什么	如何	年现金流影响（多少钱）	年净资产影响（多少钱）
利用银行账户中的现金偿还信用卡贷款余额	客户	立即	网络在线	增加现金流	利用三星储蓄	＋$3 200	$0
修订 W－4 税务表格，每月扣缴 400 美元	客户	立即	工作地点的薪酬办公室	将代扣代缴金额与税收义务匹配	向薪酬办公室领取新的 W－4 税务表格，每月扣缴增加 400 美元	－$4 800	＋$4 800
每期退休账户的缴款增加 250 美元	客户	立即	工作地点的薪酬办公室	减少税务负担，增加退休收入	寻求薪酬办公室的帮助	－$2 250（税后）	＋$2 250
将退休计划由之前的雇主计划转为自有计划	理财规划师及客户	一年内	理财规划师办公室	整合所得	填写账户转移表格及新开户表格	$0	$0
用可变保单代替现在的现金价值寿险保单	理财规划师及客户	一年内	理财规划师办公室	减少保单成本增加投资灵活度	填写账户转移表格及新开户表格	$2 300	$0
更新遗嘱、生前遗嘱及律师权利	客户	一年内	律师办公室	遗产审核及维护	预约	$0	－$900
约见财产及意外伤害保险经纪，探讨当前保额覆盖范围及保额责任赔偿限额	客户	一年内	保险经纪办公室	年度保险审核	预约	$0	$0
利用出售邮票藏品的资金购买海滩小屋	理财规划师及客户	未来 18 个月	理财规划师办公室	资产多样化，为后代留有遗产	约见 Jim Brody of Empire 拍卖行	$0	＋$35 000
出于保险保护的目的，完善家庭储备	客户	未来 18 个月	家	年度更新所有资产资料记录	拍摄所有资产及编号，将记录存放在保险柜中	$0	$0
考虑增加 100 万美元的责任保险	理财规划师及客户	未来 18 个月	理财规划师办公室或保险经纪办公室	随着净资产增加，最小化可能的债务赔偿	约见保险经纪人，填写相关表格。可能需要增加其他责任险保额	－$350	$0

三、责任及义务

如表 3－8 所示，理财建议及理财方案的实施需要很多人的配合。通常情况下，根据理财规划师执业模式及客户需要，有 4 个人需要参与理财计划的实施。

客户；

理财规划师；

客户已雇佣的专业人士；

新的被推荐的专业人士。

有些理财规划师认为自己只充当分析师的角色。在这种情况下，客户需要承担理财计划执行的大部分责任。理财规划师一般不愿意向客户推荐执行理财计划所需要的专业人士。而有些理财规划师认为自己负有帮助客户执行理财计划并监督理财计划顺利执行的义务。这些理财规划师可能拥有提供不同保险经纪、保险及资金管理服务和产品的执照。理财建议执行的重担大部分压在了理财规划师身上。理财规划师可能会借助客户、其他理财规划师和相关专业人士的帮助完成理财建议的执行。客户有时会有自己的律师、会计师和银行业务员。在这种情况下，理财规划师可以考虑与这些专业人士共同合作。

极少数情况下，客户需要外界帮助执行理财计划。这就是为什么理财规划师需要组织专业团队帮助理财计划完成。这个专业团队的成员包括律师、会计师、税务专员、遗产遗赠专员、经纪人、代理人、财富管理经理、财务治疗师、社工、信托办公室、婚姻及家庭咨询师、保险经纪及代理人、房产经纪及房屋贷款经纪人。图 3－5 展示了理财规

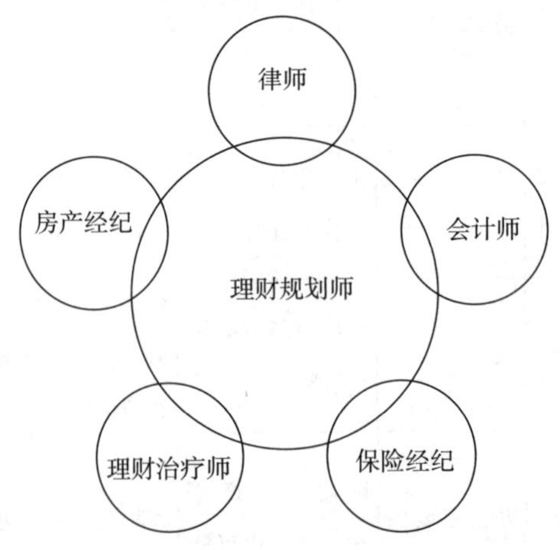

图 3－5　理财规划师是整个理财规划执行的协调者

划师是如何组织这些专业人士打造专业团队，并负责管理、协调及整理相关资料保证理财计划顺利实施的。另外，理财规划师还需要向客户推荐这些专业人士之前，披露有关的转介费用。

四、费用结构和计划

虽然每个国家的法律和风俗各不相同，但是以下是几种理财规划师在理财计划实施中常用的费用收取方法：

最简单但最不常用的方法是收取固定费用。理财规划师收取的费用主要是为了理财规划书的制作，但有时还会包含简单的理财规划方案的实施。这种情况下，理财规划师认为客户会实施理财计划并为其他理财建议的实施另外付费。

为富裕阶层客户服务的理财规划师越来越流行的费用支付方式是按小时收取理财规划分析及建议推荐费用。费用从 100 美元/小时至 300 美元/小时不等。

为富裕的个人和家庭服务的理财规划师通常会收取聘任费用。聘任费最少每年 5 000 美元。客户可以在一年内，随时找理财规划师咨询问题、分析问题及帮助实施个别的理财建议。

越来越多的理财规划建议实施收取资产管理费。费用按在管资产的 0.25% ~2% 不等。例如，如果一个拥有可投资资产 1 000 000 美元的客户需要每年支付 10 000 美元的理财规划费用。费用包含理财规划制作、所有的理财方案实施及随时的管理服务。

在美国及大部分东亚国家，佣金还是主要的费用收取方式。通常，理财规划是不收取费用的，因为理财规划师认为客户会和自己合作执行理财方案。

佣金收费的另一个变形形式是费用抵免。越来越多的理财规划师会收取理财规划费用。如果客户选择理财规划师帮助执行理财规划方案，这笔理财规划费用可以减少或者抵免。

在理财规划师中越来越流行的一种费用收取方式是不同费用收取方式的组合。最流行的一种是固定理财规划费用，结合资产管理费和少量的保险产品佣金。这种费用收取方式适用于能够提供多种产品服务的理财规划师。

虽然已经重复多次，但是还是应该强调的是，无论理财规划师采用何种费用收取方式，都需要充分披露他们是如何及何时为理财规划及实施收取费用的。表 3 -9 是一个简单的例子，说明在资产管理费模式下，理财规划师应如何披露报酬有关问题。

表3-9　　资产管理费用披露

XYZ公司

资产管理费用计划

根据XYZ公司管理资产金额，每季度商定理财规划及资产管理费用。该费用收取方式称为资产管理模式。费用在每年1月、3月、6月及9月计算并交纳。费用不可按比例分摊。

理财规划及资产管理费用安排如下：

$0至 $250 000	1.50%/年
$250 001至 $500 000	1.25% /年
$500 001至 $750 000	1.00%/年
$750 001至 $1 000 000	0.80% /年
$1 000 001至 $2 000 000	0.70% /年
$2 000 001以上	0.50%/年

例如，如果某客户在管资产为1 000 000美元，需要每年支付8 000美元（每季度支付2 000美元）的理财规划费用。费用将直接从客户的在管账户中划转。

客户：________________________日期：________________________

理财规划师：____________________日期：________________________

注：资产管理费用须在账单月月初缴纳。收取费用依据上一账单月月末最后一个工作日余额估算。

五、定期审核及修订

有时，理财规划师会疏忽理财规划流程的最后一步——监督客户的理财计划实施成果。理财规划师花费了大量的时间和精力分析客户的财务状况、制作理财规划方案并实施理财规划建议。理财规划师预想客户在理财规划方案实施后，其财务状况应该取得良好的改善。但现实不一定会与期望相符合。这就是为什么跟进监督理财规划方案的实施成果这一理财规划环节重要的原因。定期评估和长期监督能够帮助客户稳步实施理财计划并实现理财目标，同时，理财规划师还可以发现新的情况、问题和需求。

如果理财规划师与客户将保持一个长期的雇佣关系，那么理财规划师需要持续监督以下内容：之前的假设条件；之前进行理财规划时收集的信息；产品收益及经风险调整的收益表现；产品提供商排名；产品、服务及专业人士转介是否依然合适；客户风险容忍度；理财规划及产品费用。

客户发生的变化可能需要：调整资产配置；转换理财规划战略；重新分析当前财务

状况；理财目标实现进度。

经济状况及客户自身情况的改变可能需要理财规划师重新分析和调整规划方案。这就是为什么一些理财规划师会把理财规划方案称为“活着的文件”。这意味着之前的规划方案会基于客户当前的需要进行修订。

作为理财规划方案的最后一个环节，监督理财规划方案实施可以从三个方面加强理财规划师与客户的关系。首先，持续监督保证理财规划师与客户经常联系。经常沟通是理财规划内容中的一个价值增值内容。顺畅的沟通可以保证未来理财规划更加有效。其次，监督理财规划方案实施可以保证现有的产品和服务在成本和表现上对客户仍然适用。最后，理财规划方案监督是帮助理财规划师走在经济、法律、会计、税务及法规变化前面的工具。

如图 3 –6 所示，理财规划师在进行理财规划监督时要善于发现客户财务及生活状况的变化，并将其包含在理财规划协议中。换而言之，从历史的角度审视，理财规划过程永不停息。

图 3 –6　理财规划监督保证未来理财规划

六、或有规划

除个别情况外，大多数客户寻求理财规划师进行理财规划都是为了解决问题和困难，其中的含义是十分清晰的。表面上看，客户希望理财规划师给予明确、有的放矢及准确的建议。这些建议不仅针对客户本身，还应满足短期、中期及长期的利益。

最后一点是理财规划作为一个专业职业，是十分具有创造性和挑战性的。正如其他任何专业职业，理财规划方案没有唯一正确的答案。虽然错误的规划方案让人一眼就可以发现，但是对于客户的财务困境总是存在多种解决方式。例如，经过分析，理财规划师发现客户需要增加 400 000 美元的寿险保额。测算出这个需求差额的分析的过程十分烦琐和费时，但这只是理财规划建议的第一步。更重要的是，理财规划师必须做出明确的产品或服务的推荐建议。这取决于理财规划师的报酬方式、偏好、当前的环境、法律限制及客户的偏好。简而言之，针对这个客户的情况可能有多个效果相同的理财方案。理财规划师可能推荐 20 年期可续保定期保险。另一名理财规划师可能推荐某个保费水平的可变寿险产品。两个产品都是合适的。

与其陷入无意义的争论，理财规划师应该利用以下方法制作和呈现理财建议：选择符合客户需求的规划战略或方案；保证推荐是合适且公平的；披露有关规划方案的所有和任何限制条件；提供证据表明提供理财建议的理由；提供一个或多个其他解决方式。

从概念上讲，理财规划师认为第五步提供的依具体情况推荐的理财方案是次优的。如果存在一个或多个方案优于理财规划师提供的主要方案，那么理财规划师需要重新分析和评估理财计划。实际上，理财规划师提供或有计划是为了向客户展示这些方案经过评估，都不如之前的方案，因而是次优的。或有计划还可以防止今后若客户披露新的情况或者更正之前提供的信息时，现有的理财方案失效的情形。

七、理财规划的终结

越来越多的理财规划师定位自己为具有信托责任的客户咨询师。“工作联盟”表明了理财规划协议的长期性的特点。当然，有些理财规划师仍旧只是从事交易性的业务，但行业的整体趋势是理财规划师倾向与客户建立长达几年，甚至几十年的客户关系。

本章的内容表明，当所有的理财规划流程全部一一完成，理财规划才能达到最好的效果。理财规划监督流程保证理财规划师重新分析客户的新情况并延续理财规划关系。书面程序可以保证这种规划关系正式有序。客户需要在他们收到书面规划方案时签字确认。确认信也表明客户阅读了理财计划并给予充分时间向理财规划师询问有关报酬及产品或服务建议的问题。书面文件还应当详细记录“工作联盟”的相关假设和限制条件。例如，如果理财规划师希望成为所有理财方案实施的主要联系人，这点必须记录在案，并得到客户认可。

理财规划师—客户的关系总会终结。有时是因为客户搬离居住地，但也有可能是因为客户不满意理财规划师提供的服务而选择其他的理财规划师。不管是何种原因，理财规划师都需要谨慎地书面记录协议终止的事实，并规划客户要求的所有资料①。

有时，协议终止也许是理财规划师的意愿。新晋理财规划师往往对此不能想象，但是有经验的理财规划师会发现他们有时必须“解雇”某些客户。从理财规划师的角度讲，当维持协议的成本超过收益时，终止协议是必要的。80/20 法则可以帮助判断这一情形。通常，公司发现 80% 的利润来源于 20% 的客户。换而言之，20% 的客户占用了理

① 在美国，理财师要求保留现有及之前客户的文件和资料。之前客户资料的详细信息需要保留至少 5 年。

财规划师 80% 的时间和精力。只要 20% 的利润与 20% 的时间占用相匹配，维持现有的客户关系是没有问题的。但是，当利润贡献率低的客户开始占用理财规划师过多的时间和精力，问题就产生了。成功的理财规划师往往认为解除与这些“有问题”的客户的协议可以使自己有更多的时间和精力服务那些利润率高的客户。如果需要终止理财协议，理财规划师需要：（1）书面记录协议终止决定；（2）转介客户给其他合适的理财规划师；（3）继续以专业的精神保持与客户的合作。

第四章　打造成功的理财规划师职业生涯

在全世界建立、维护和推广 CFP 品牌的国际理财规划标准委员会认为，一个有竞争力的理财规划师应当能够有效运用自己的专业知识、技能和能力为客户提供理财规划服务。本章重点讨论一个理财规划专业人士不论其业务范围，如何能够成功打造自己的职业生涯。

第一节　理财规划师竞争力标准

保险经纪、银行职员、退休规划专员、股票经纪及其他提供理财规划服务的专业人士在市场上总是被人们误解他们的作用。消费者经常不能充分理解这些专业人士提供的金融服务的价值。其中一个原因是，与其他专业人士不同，金融服务行业的竞争是十分激烈的。市场上少有标准的产品和服务，这造成了消费者的困扰和疑惑。理财规划师就是在这样的市场环境中经营和打拼。但这也让消费者很难区分理财规划师与其他专业人士提供的服务。例如，消费者搞不清保险销售人员和股票经纪人的区别，更别说是理财规划师和其他金融服务人员的区别。正因为如此，消费者的态度往往就不那么积极。这种在规划服务当中的不决断是信任危机的一个直接结果。当消费者不清楚理财规划师提供的服务，不了解如何给理财规划师付费，那么他们就会要求理财规划师拿出证据证明他们的可信度。

以下这个案例是来自 2014 年美国理财规划师的一个真实的案例。2007—2008 年金融危机之后，很多的美国投资者都从股票投资转为固定收益投资。然而，这段时间的债券回报率很低（低于 1%）。从 2009 年开始，根据标普 500 指数、道琼斯指数及纳斯达克指数的数据，美国股票开始历史上新一轮大的牛市。许多股票的股价在 2009—2013 年之间翻了一番。许多转向固定收益投资的投资者大为懊恼自己失去了如此好的一个投资机会。有些理财规划师利用这个历史背景向那些不是很确定股票安全性，又愿意尝试的投资者售卖股票。电视、网络甚至收音机里都出现了这样的广告标语：

“你知道你可以不用承担任何风险就可以获得股票大涨的好处吗？许多年来，老道的投资者正是利用这些独特的产品在经济低迷的时候仍然能够增长和保护自己的财富。而今，你也了解拥有这些财富的秘密了。”

虽然这些广告语的设计并不是有意欺骗消费者，但这其中的信息十分具有误导性。消费者认为市场上出现了新的投资产品，或者新的投资产品至少更加适合不是那么富裕的投资者。但事实上，这个所谓的秘密产品就是一种形式的保险。投放这些广告的商家售卖的是可变指数型年金产品或是可变终身寿险产品。这些产品既不新颖也不独特。广告中没有披露的信息是与这些产品相关的大额的前端及维护佣金，也没有披露股票收益的上限和提前支取的罚金。虽然这些产品对有些客户来说是适合并合法的，但如果说这个产品适用于所有客户并能取得股票市场的最高收益却不承担一丁点风险，则是夸大其词。

这种激进的销售战略在一定程度上迷惑了消费者。这不是一个经营风险，有着多元化投资组合的理财规划产品，而是经过包装打上税收优惠创新标签，经过理财规划师之手售卖的传统保险产品。试问，一个正直经营，遵循理财规划流程，提供综合理财规划服务的理财规划师如何在这样一种市场上立足？获得竞争成功的一个途径就是以竞争力为标准提供与众不同的服务。

在美国，CFP 委员会为 CFP 资格认证创建了最基本的标准。CFP 委员会全力打造遵循理财流程的理财规划专业职业的市场地位。CFP 委员会的研究表明，遵循高标准的竞争力、道德及执业标准的理财规划师在市场受到消费者的高度认可。消费者愿意支付更多的费用雇佣拥有理财资格的理财规划师。从世界范围上看，有以下行为的人都不可以持有 CFP 资格：被逮捕或者犯有严重盗窃罪、贪污罪或者其他经济罪行；严重税务欺诈或其他有关税务的罪行；吊销金融职业执照，除非吊销只是行政性质的（如没有支付相关费用）；任何级别的谋杀或强奸的重罪；或 5 年内犯有其他形式的暴力罪行。

根据 CFP 委员会的规定，以下行为不予授予 CFP 资格：两次或以上的个人或公司破产行为；吊销或暂停非金融执业资格，除非吊销或暂停是行政性质的；5 年内有非暴力性质的重罪（包括伪证罪）；或 5 年前非谋杀或强奸性质的暴力性质犯罪。

其他因素可能也会限制理财规划师获得 CFP 资格，包括客户投诉，仲裁及其他民事行为，5 年前发生的非暴力形式的犯罪、违法行为、雇主调查及解雇。

国际标准

通过推行和监管 CFP 资格认证项目，国际理财规划标准委员会保证世界范围内执业标准的执行。在世界其他国家和地区推行的道德准则与在美国推行的道德准则大部分条款相同，在有些方面，国际准则更加简洁和具有条理。国际理财规划标准委员会定义理财规划是理财规划师通过设计理财战略帮助客户打理他们的财富，最终达成人生目标的过程①。作为理财流程的一部分，理财规划师需要审核客户财务状况的方方面面。这个标准定义清晰地区分了理财规划师与其他专业职业的区别。在国际理财规划标准委员会关于理财规划的概念中并没有要求理财规划师必须提供综合理财建议，或者书面综合理财规划方案。当然，理财规划师可以提供这些服务，但是不是强制性的。根据国际理财规划标准委员会的概念，理财规划师是具有一定知识、技能和能力审核客户的财务状况，帮助客户制定合理有效的理财战略的专业人士。

无论理财规划师的经营范围如何，他们必须具备以下能力：（1）向客户收集正确和合理的数据；（2）分析所收集数据的能力；（3）整合数据并分析，制作出以客户为中心的理财战略。理财规划师与证券经纪人或者理财咨询师主要的不同在于理财规划师在分析过程中整合定性及定量数据的能力，从而展示出对理财各个主要内容之间相互关系的掌握。对于一个税务专员来说，他们也需要收集、分析和整合客户的税务数据，但理财规划师的要求更高，他们需要将这些税务数据与客户整体的财务状况整合分析。换而言之，也许有些税务专员可以成为理财规划师，但不是所有的税务专员都具备这样的潜质。

第二节　道德准则和专业行为标准

在之前的章节，我们已经讨论了有关道德标准、准则和制度的问题。但是因为这个问题是相当重要的，所以我们在本章继续讨论。每个国家（地区）和每个专业职业都有自己的法律和准则。在有些国家，例如美国，特别针对理财规划执业的相关法规几乎没有。任何人都可以称自己的执业行为是理财规划服务。只有提供有偿投资服务、售卖产品或服务以获得佣金的行为才必须遵守相关规定和准则。提供有偿投资服务的理财规划

① Financial Planning Standards Board. 2011. *Financial planner competency profile*. Denver: FPSB.

师必须注册为投资顾问。管理资产在 1 亿美元以下的理财规划师需要在美国联邦证券及交易委员会注册。其他的理财规划师则需要在州级委员会注册。售卖证券的理财规划师还需要在金融管理当局注册并获得执照。售卖保险产品的理财规划师还必须获得保险相关执照。在世界有些地区，收取佣金的产品和服务是受限的。在这些国家，咨询师必须严格按照信托责任标准执业。而在其他国家和地区，咨询师则可以遵从适用性标准①。

理财规划师除了需要遵守联邦和州级的标准之外，通常都会隶属于某个专业组织或者认证团体，这些机构还要求理财规划师遵循相应的条款和规定。在美国，CFP 委员会颁布的道德准则被认为是最严格的。CFP 委员会希望自己的道德准则代表业内最高准则和规定。道德标准里的规定通常是协会希望 CFP 专业人士及会员能够在执业过程中达到的道德和专业行为的最高境界。道德准则是 CFP 委员会《行为准则》《执业标准》及《纪律规定》的基础。只有 CFP 专业人士才需要遵守 CFP 委员会颁布的这些准则和规定②。具体规定如下：

准则 1：正直诚信：本着正直诚信的宗旨为客户提供专业服务

正直诚信要求理财规划师在处理所有专业事务的时候都要做到诚实、坦诚并不因私欲而违反准则。客户诉诸理财规划师为其服务是基于他们对理财规划师的信任，而这种信任的最终来源是理财规划师个人正直诚信的品质。合理的意见分歧是允许存在的，但是正直诚信是不可能与欺骗或违背原则的行为共存的。

准则 2：客观公正：客观公正地为客户提供专业服务

客观公正准则对理财规划师提出了诚实、公正的要求。客观公正原则要求理财规划师在执业过程中对其提供的服务及所体现的理财规划能力做到正直诚信、客观公正，避免主观臆断。

准则 3：专业胜任：具备胜任专业服务所必备的各种能力、技能及知识

专业胜任准则要求理财规划师在提供专业服务时，在能力、技能和知识上达到并保持一定水平。专业胜任准则还要求理财规划师能够认识到自己的能力、技能和知识在某些领域的局限性，并能够在必要的时候主动咨询或向客户主动推荐其他更胜任的专业人士。专业胜任准则要求理财规划师承诺自己将不断进行专业提升。

准则 4：公平合理：理财规划师在所有专业执业关系中做到公平合理，披露利益

---

① 在美国，注册投资顾问必须遵从信托责任标准。只有注册证券经纪人和保险代理人才可以允许遵从适用性标准。

② 更多资料请参考：http：//www. cfp. net/for – cfp – professionals/professional – standards – enforcement/standards – of – professional – conduct/code – of – ethics – professional – responsibility#sthash. 7jf5QRlB. dpuf.

冲突

公平合理准则要求理财规划师保持公平合理、诚实守信并能披露重大利益冲突。这要求理财规划师能够控制自己的个人感受及偏见以达到利益平衡。只有公平对待他人才能得到他人的公平对待。

准则5：保守秘密：为客户所有信息保密

保密准则要求理财规划师为客户信息保密，仅允许授权人员了解客户信息。信任关系和客户的信心完全建立在理财规划师能够意识到不能违规泄露客户信息的基础上。

准则6：专业精神：行为上力求达到专业操作标准

专业精神准则要求理财规划师在业务活动中应保持尊严，谦恭、礼貌地对待客户、同行及其他业务相关人员。专业精神原则要求理财规划师与同行一起捍卫并提高本行业的公众形象，并不断提升为公众利益服务的能力。

准则7：恪尽职守：恪尽职守地提供专业服务

恪尽职守准则要求理财规划师能够及时、全面地履行专业服务的承诺，在理财规划、理财方案执行监督及提供专业服务时能够尽职尽责。

CFP 委员会还规定了理财规划师—客户关系的具体规定。除以上七点的规定外，CFP 持证人在向客户提供服务时还必须遵守以下规定。任何违反规定的行为都将受到 CFP 委员会的制裁。以下规定适用于当前及潜在客户：

如果 CFP 专业人士为客户提供的服务包括理财规划或理财规划流程中的某些重要环节，则 CFP 专业人士应在双方签订协议之前书面向客户提供以下信息并就以下问题与客户进行协商：

协议各方的义务和责任，包括客户的目标及需求；收集并提供相关数据；测算客户目前理财规划（不进行任何改变）可能导致的结果；明确表达理财规划的行动建议；执行理财规划建议；监控理财规划建议的执行。

协议中任何一方或任何一方的分支机构及会员机构根据协议规定应该或可能获得的报酬；决定成本及费用的因素或条件；CFP 专业人士如何利用理财规划决策获利或得到其他间接利益。

CFP 专业人士使用特许专卖产品的条款。

CFP 专业人士借助其他机构或专业人士来履行协议义务的条款。

终止服务关系的流程以及客户对 CFP 专业人士的服务提出投诉及索赔问题的解决办法。

如果 CFP 专业人士以书面形式提供以上信息，则 CFP 专业人士应当鼓励客户浏览信息，并随时回答客户的疑问。

如果 CFP 专业人士为客户提供的服务包括理财规划或理财规划流程中的某些重要环节，则 CFP 专业人士或其雇主应当与客户签订书面协议，内容应包括：协议各方的名称；协议的生效日及有效期；协议各方终止协议的条件和方式；及协议约定提供的服务内容。

协议可包含多个书面文件。书面文件应包括以上内容，供 CFP 专业人士或其雇主在联邦或州法律或任何使用的自律组织的条款和规定范围内使用。可能的文件有证券交易委员会的 ADV 表格或其他披露文件。

CFP 专业人士在任何情况下都应将客户的利益置于首位。当 CFP 专业人士为客户提供的服务包括理财规划或理财规划流程中的某些重要环节时，应当负有 CFP 委员会规定的信托责任。

其他与理财规划师如何与客户沟通交流的规定包括：

CFP 专业人士不得直接或间接向客户或其他相关人员提供与其专业资质或服务有直接或间接关联的错误或误导信息。

CFP 专业人士不得利用其专业服务可能带来的潜在收益误导客户或其他利益相关者。

CFP 专业人士在必要情况下应披露所有相关事实，以免误导客户或其他利益相关者。

CFP 专业人士不得进行不实、欺诈、欺骗或虚假陈述，不得故意向客户或其他利益相关者提供错误或误导性说明。

CFP 专业人士应向客户披露以下信息：

关于所收取报酬的明确及合理的说明。说明应当包括：有关客户成本、费用的信息，雇主基本收费项目及形式，雇主可以收取其他类型费用的条件及这些额外收费的内容和依据。

客户与 CFP 专业人士及其单位或其附属机构或任何第三方之间可能存在的利益冲突的扼要说明，包括但不限于可能会对客户造成重大不利影响的家庭成员关系、合约关系或代理关系。

任何可能会对客户是否聘用某位 CFP 专业人士产生实质影响的信息。

客户在了解服务合约的范围及性质时可能需要了解的其他相关信息，包括但不限于 CFP 专业人士的专业领域。

CFP 专业人士的联系方式，如果可能的话，提供其雇主的联系方式。

当 CFP 专业人士为客户提供的服务包括理财规划或理财规划流程中的某些重要环节时，这些披露内容必须以书面的形式提供。该书面披露可包含多个书面文件。书面文件应包括以上内容，供CFP专业人士或其雇主在联邦或州法律或任何使用的自律组织的条款和规定范围内使用。可能的文件有证券交易委员会的ADV表格或其他披露文件。

此外，CFP专业人士还应及时向客户通报有关上述信息的重大变更。

有关理财规划师如何处理客户信息及获得的资产的规定如下：

除以下情况外，CFP专业人士应对客户信息严格保密：依据正当的法律程序或法规要求必须披露的；向其雇主或合伙人履行义务时必须披露的；针对失职投诉，以申辩为目的必须披露的；与客户之间产生民事纠纷必须披露的；代表客户完成专业服务必须披露的。

理财规划师应妥善保护客户信息及财产，包括保护由其管理的客户实物资料和电子资料的安全。

为履行自己的专业职责，CFP专业人士应当获取必要的信息。否则，CFP专业人士须向客户披露任何及所有重大信息遗漏问题。

CFP专业人士应确认需要保管、投资或监管的客户资产。

CFP专业人士应当确认并保存客户受托管或CFP专业人士自己保管的任何资金或资产的全部资料。

除以下情况外，CFP专业人士不得向客户提供借款：客户是CFP专业人士的直系亲属；客户是开展信贷业务的机构，但借款与CFP专业人士提供的专业服务无关。

除以下情况外，CFP专业人士不得借款给客户：客户是CFP专业人士的直系亲属；CFP专业人士的雇主或其从业机构是开展信贷业务的机构，但提供贷款的一方不是其本人而是其雇主。

除法律允许且各方签订书面协议明确界定授权范围的情况外，CFP专业人士不得将客户财产与其个人财产、其雇主或其他客户的财产混同管理。客户只有在能够为每一位客户单独提供详细、准确的交易记录的前提下，才可以进行客户资产混同管理。

在客户提出要求后，CFP专业人士应尽快或在双方约定的期限内退还客户财产。

CFP专业人士还须遵守以下规定以保护客户免受伤害。具体规定如下：

CFP专业人士为客户制定的理财规划方案必须在自己专业胜任范围内。对于那些专业能力范围之外的领域，CFP专业人士应咨询或向客户推荐能够胜任的专业人士。

CFP专业人士在向客户提供专业服务时应守法遵规。

CFP专业人士在提供专业服务时应当遵循合理、谨慎的专业判断。

CFP专业人士应为客户制定和执行适合客户的理财规划方案。

对于接受理财规划师分配，向客户提供部分服务的下属或第三方，CFP 专业人士必须给予合理、谨慎的专业监督或指导。

如果 CFP 专业人士的 CFP 资质吊销或暂停，CFP 专业人士须告知其客户。

持有 CFP 商标的理财规划师还需要对他们的同事和雇主保持诚实守信的专业精神。相关规定如下：

CFP 专业人士在以雇员或代理人的身份提供专业服务时，应按照《CFP 专业人士道德准则和专业责任标准》的规定完成雇主/委托人下达的合法任务。

CFP 专业人士在以雇员或代理人的身份提供专业服务时，如其 CFP 资质吊销或暂停，CFP 专业人士须告知其雇主。

最后，CFP 专业人士负有在行业内维持和推广道德标准的义务。其中可以通过向 CFP 委员会履行以下职责完成义务：

CFP 专业人士应遵循 CFP 委员会制定的各种规则和章程，包括但不限于根据 CFP 委员会关于商标及专业审核的要求。

为拥有持续使用 CFP 商标的权力，CFP 专业人士必须达到 CFP 委员会制定的各种要求，包括进行继续教育的要求。

当电子邮件地址、电话号码及实际通信地址等联络信息发生变化后，CFP 专业人士应在 45 天内通知 CFP 委员会。

CFP 专业人士应书面通知 CFP 委员会除以下行为外的任何犯罪行为：交通违规除非涉及酒后或使用药物后违规行为，CFP 委员会接到 CFP 专业人士违法、违规或拘留通知 10 个自然日内的拘留行为。CFP 专业人士不得做出有损理财规划师正直、得体的专业形象，损害 FPSB 商标系列或理财规划行业专业性的行为。

这些规定仅适用于使用 CFP 商标的理财规划专业人士。在美国，大约有 25% 的理财规划师拥有 CFP 资格。然而，大多数的会员组织，例如理财规划师协会（Financial Planning Association）及个人理财规划师协会（National Association of Personal Financial Advisors）都有相似的道德准则的规定或约束，这些规定都比国家法律规定要严格。例如，以下是美国最大的独立理财规划师协会成员需要遵守的准则规定：

理财规划师需要尽全力按照客户的最大利益及诚信原则执业。

在签署业务协议之前及整个协议有效期内，理财规划师应向客户书面披露任何可能威胁到理财规划师独立性和公正性的利益冲突。

理财规划师及任何与理财规划师有财务往来的第三方，都不可以基于客户买卖理财产品而获得报酬或补偿。

理财规划师不可以因推荐客户或客户的某项业务而获得费用或报酬。

世界范围内，国际理财规划标准委员会（FPSB）规定了理财规划专业人士能够使用CFP商标的道德规定。FPSB的规定是基于客户希望信赖理财规划师的理念制作的。正因如此，FPSB坚信，只要理财规划师始终坚持客户利益至上，并维持和促进理财规划师职业的社会利益，那么理财规划职业便可以在市场上脱颖而出。

坚信并坚持高标准的道德标准是建立成功理财规划职业的关键。至少，它可以使每位理财规划师：与客户建立信任关系；当为客户提供服务和咨询时，以客户利益最大化为原则；展现有道德的判断；行为正直诚信；能够意识到个人能力的不足并积极寻求其他专业人士的建议和指导；声称理财规划师是负有公众信任的职业，因此总是以消费者利益为重；遵守所有的国家和地方法律法规；遵守相关执业准则和行为标准；维护经济、政治和法律环境意识；不断进行继续教育；在向客户提供产品和服务时，进行详细的尽职调查和研究；在与客户协议生效期间及以后，都保持良好的专业形象。

第三节　理财规划职业生涯

如前所述，一个有竞争力的理财规划师必须有能力收集信息、分析信息、整合信息并制作出以客户为中心的理财战略。这意味着要想成为一个理财规划师不仅要学习各种金融产品、理财技巧及一定的分析技巧，而且要想获得成功的专业和个人职业生涯，还需要遵从高标准的道德准则、获得足够的培训及自我监督进行持续不断的学习提升。

取得专业认证是理财规划师向客户传达自己力图成为一名有价值的理财规划师的信念。目前，有数十种有关理财规划的认证和执照。在美国，CFP资格被普遍认为是最受推崇也是最严格的项目。这是因为要想成为一名CFP持证人需要满足很多要求。例如，CFP持证人必须取得认可的美国大学或学院的本科学位，制作并提交一份书面的综合理财规划方案，另外还必须有三年以上相关工作经验。此外，CFP委员会要求CFP持证人坚持继续教育以保持自身的竞争力。CFP委员还会每两年对持证人进行一次道德及行为准则方面的审查。国际上，FPSB对CFP持证人也有同样的要求。除了CFP认证，其他认证也会帮助理财规划师迅速融入这个职业。例如，美国学院就有好几类专业认证。其中对于理财规划师来说，最重要的两个资格认证是认证寿险承销商（CLU ®）及注册金融顾问（ChFC®）。与 CFP 认证类似，这两个认证同样有继续教育的要求。对投资管理方面的专业培训有兴趣的理财规划师还可以考虑获取注册金融分析师（CFA®）。注册退休顾问资格（CRC®）适用于那些对提供退休规划服务感兴趣的理财规划师。世界范围内，理财规划师会选择适合当地市场和客户需求的认证和资格，但都需要得到消费者的认可和检验，特别是那些需要通过考试及不断继续教育才能持续使用的认证。

幸运的是，FPSB 及 CFP 委员会都会对执业人士进行经常的问卷调查来决定最低的竞争力水准。例如，CFP 委员会将考察理财规划师 78 个内容（如下所示）的掌握情况。他们认为无论是新晋理财规划师还是经验丰富的理财规划师都应具备针对以下内容收集、分析及制作理财战略的能力。

理财规划流程：

财务报表

现金流量表

融资战略

金融机构的功能、目的及监管

教育规划

特殊情况规划

经济学相关概念

货币时间价值

金融服务法规

经济法

消费者保护法

风险及保险原则

风险暴露分析及评价

健康保险及健康成本管理

个人残障收入保险

长期护理险

个人寿险

寿险的个人所得税

保险的商业用途

保险需求分析法

保单及公司选择

年金

投资工具的特征、用途及税收

投资风险的类型

投资的定量概念

投资回报的度量

债券型股票的概念

投资组合的构建及分析

投资战略

资产分配及资产多样化

个人所得税的基本原理

税收合规

个人所得税的基本原理及计算

商业机构的特征及税收

信托及遗产的所得税

税基

财产处置相关税收问题

其他最低税收

税收减免/管理技能

被动活动及风险准则

特殊情况的税收

慈善捐助及抵免

退休需求分析

社会保险

退休计划的类型

有资格的退休计划条款及选择

其他可获得税收优惠的退休计划

监管因素

影响企业选择退休计划的主要因素

有关退休计划的投资方面的问题

退休收入领取的选择及税收

财产产权的特征及结果

死后财产转移的方式

遗产规划文件

赠予策略

有关赠予的法律及税收计算

伤残规划

遗产税合规及税收计算

遗产流动性的来源

制定的效力

信托类型、特点及税收

许可的税收信托

慈善转移

寿险在遗产规划中的运用

婚姻减免

遗产税的递延及减少

家庭内部及其他商业转移技巧

GSTT

信托责任

继承者的收入

身后遗产规划

非常规家庭关系的遗产规划

客户及理财规划师态度、价值、偏见及行为特点对理财规划的影响

沟通及咨询的基本愿望

行为准则

纪律处罚规定

执业标准

国际视角

FPSB 通过进行问卷调查获得理财竞争力的基本标尺。在有些方面，FPSB 设计的竞

争力分类要优于 CFP 委员会制定的标准。尤其是在帮助新晋理财规划师理解他们需要在日常的理财规划活动中掌握的信息类型方面，FPSB 的设计更为合理。图 4 - 1 展示了理财规划师竞争力的主要构成。如图 4 - 1 所示，理财规划师需要掌握六大核心内容，并能在理财规划的数据收集、分析及整合过程中熟练运用。一个有能力的理财规划师必须具备在错综复杂、变幻莫测的经济、政治、社会及制度环境中设计制作有效理财规划的能力。这个要求使得理财规划师职业具备挑战性但也更有价值。虽然理财规划师的具体业务范围可能只涉及一个或两个内容，但是对理财规划师能力的评估却是全方位的。

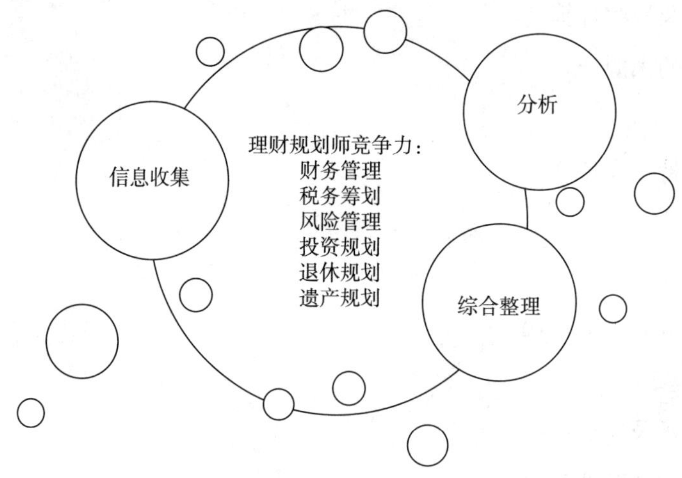

图 4 - 1　理财规划师竞争力的主要构成

FPSB 将理财规划知识体系归类为以下 11 个领域。每个知识领域都有关于核心竞争力的具体要求。这些要求是进入这个职业关于知识结构的最基本标准。虽然每个知识领域及核心竞争力要求的表述比较宽泛，但每个国家或地区的理财规划师可以根据自己的业务需要拓展每个知识领域的具体要求。

I. 税务

1. 评估规则
2. 个人税务
3. 公司税务
4. 财富转移
5. 国际税收问题

II. 保险

6. 商业保险

7. 人寿保险
8. 伤残保险/ 收入补偿保险
9. 健康保险
10. 重大疾病保险（包括重大疾病及外伤）
11. 财产保险
12. 意外保险

III. 投资

13. 投资种类
14. 投资结构
15. 投资风险的种类
16. 投资风险的测定
17. 投资组合管理技巧
18. 买卖交易技巧
19. 业绩评估
20. 现代投资组合理论

IV. 退休、储蓄和收入计划

21. 政府养老金
22. 政府储蓄计划
23. 雇主/雇员计划
24. 个人退休计划
25. 个人储蓄计划

V. 法律

26. 私法
27. 公司法

VI. 金融分析

28. 财务信息的分析
29. 个人财务比率
30. 现金管理和预算
31. 个人财务报表

VII. 债务

32. 消费者信用和信用管理

33. 按揭

34. 租赁

35. 无力偿债和破产

VIII. 经济和法规环境

36. 经济环境

37. 法规环境

IX. 政府福利计划

X. 行为金融学

XI. 道德和行为标准

38. 道德守则

39. 理财规划行为标准

以上要求虽然清晰列举了大多数理财规划师需要的知识结构，但是对基本的竞争力标准的表述却相对模糊。希望进入理财行业的人们可能需要一些具体的信息。FPSB 对此也做了具体的规定。表 4－1 列示了新晋理财规划师需要的一些基本能力。

表 4－1　　基本理财规划师执业能力

收集信息
确定客户的理财规划目标、理财规划需求和价值观
确定制定理财规划所需的信息
确定影响理财规划的相关法律问题
判定客户的理财规划态度和理财规划知识水平
鉴别客户个人和财务情况的重大变化
准备进行理财分析所需的信息
分析
分析客户的目标、需求、价值观和其他信息，从而把理财规划组成部分按优先顺序排列
考量各理财规划组成部分的相互关系
考量机会和限制条件及评估收集到的各理财规划组成部分的信息
考量经济、政治和政策法规的影响
衡量达成理财规划目标的进展情况
整理综合

在表 4－2 中，FPSB 将以上理财执业能力与具体的理财规划功能模块相结合，按照六大功能模块说明每个模块需要的收集、分析和整合的能力要求。一个有竞争力的理财规划师需

要在之前所述的11个核心知识框架下，达到这些能力要求，并能从某个方面改善客户的财务状况。能够达到这些能力要求的理财规划师只是满足了理财规划师竞争力的最低要求。将理财规划师职业视为一生职业生涯的理财规划师还需要在此基础上继续拓展这些能力。

表4－2　　　　按照理财规划功能模块整理的理财规划师执业能力矩阵

收集信息	
财务管理	收集客户资产和负债的信息 收集有关客户现金流、收入和/或债务的信息 收集预算所需的信息 准备客户净资产、现金流和预算的财务报表 确定客户的储蓄倾向 确定客户如何做出消费决定 确定客户对债务的态度
资产管理	收集投资组合明细报表信息 确定客户当前已有的资产配置 确定可以用于投资的现金流 确定客户的投资经验、态度和倾向 确定客户的投资目标 确定客户的投资风险承受能力 确定客户的假设和投资收益期 确定客户的投资期限
风险管理	收集客户当前的保险资料 发现潜在的负债 确定客户的风险管理目标 确定客户对风险的容忍度 确定相关的生活方式 确定健康问题 确定客户主动管理财务风险的愿望
税务筹划	收集制定税务情况报表所需信息 确定资产和负债的税务特征 确定当前的、递延的和未来的税负 确定与客户税收状况有关的其他信息 确定客户对税收的态度
退休规划	收集各种退休收入潜在来源的详细信息 收集预估退休费用的信息 确定客户的退休目标 确定客户对退休的态度 确定客户对退休规划假设的满意度

续表

收集信息	
遗产规划	收集影响遗产规划策略的各种法律合约和文件 确定客户遗产规划的目标 发现可能影响遗产规划策略的家庭动态和业务往来
分析	
财务管理	确定客户是否量入为出 确定客户资产和负债信息 确定客户的紧急情况备用金 考量潜在的现金管理策略 评估紧急情况备用金是否充足 评估收入和费用潜在变化的影响 发现相互冲突的现金流需求 评估融资替代方案
资产管理	计算实现客户目标所要求的投资收益 确定投资组合的特点 确定买入/卖出资产的依据 考量可能的各种投资策略 评估投资收益预期是否与风险承受能力相协调 评估资产组合是否与风险承受能力和要求的投资回报相一致
风险管理	确定目前保险额度和范围的特点 考量当前和可能的风险管理策略 评估承受的财务风险状况 评估针对当前的保险范围和风险管理策略客户所承受的风险状况 评估风险范围发生变化的影响 排列客户风险管理需求的优先次序
税务筹划	审查有关的税务文件 考量可能的税务策略和结构 评估现有的税务策略和结构的适宜性 评估税务筹划替代方案的财务影响
退休规划	根据现状制作财务预测 确定客户的退休目标是否现实 考量可能的各种退休规划策略 评估退休时财务方面的要求 评估财务预测假设发生变化时的影响 评估要达到退休目标所需的各种取舍

续表

分析	
遗产规划	预测去世时的资产净值 考量满足客户遗产规划目标时遇到的各种限制条件 考量可能的各种遗产规划策略 计算去世时潜在的费用和欠税 评估受益人的具体需求 评估去世后遗产的流动性
综合整理	
财务管理	制定各种财务管理策略 评估每种财务管理策略的优缺点 优化策略以提出财务管理建议 按优先次序排列帮助客户实施财务管理建议的行动步骤
资产管理	制定各种资产管理策略 评估每种资产管理策略的优缺点 优化策略以提出资产管理建议 按优先次序排列帮助客户实施资产管理建议的行动步骤
风险管理	制定各种风险管理策略 评估每种风险管理策略的优缺点 优化策略以提出风险管理建议 按优先次序排列帮助客户实施风险管理建议的行动步骤
税务筹划	制定各种税务筹划策略 评估每种税务筹划策略的优缺点 优化策略以提出税务筹划建议 按优先次序排列帮助客户实施税务筹划建议的行动步骤
退休规划	制定各种退休规划策略 评估每种退休规划策略的优缺点 优化策略以提出退休规划建议 按优先次序排列帮助客户实施退休规划建议的行动步骤
遗产规划	制定各种遗产规划策略 评估每种遗产规划策略的优缺点 优化策略以提出遗产规划建议 按优先次序排列帮助客户实施遗产规划建议的行动步骤

资料来源：FPSB，2011；国际理财规划标准委员会（中国），2012。

第四节　客户沟通的艺术和技巧

很显然，沟通技巧对于新晋理财规划师和资深理财规划师来说都是十分重要的技能。毕竟，客户有些时候需要面见理财规划师获得信息和指导，理财规划师也需要面见客户收集信息和提供理财建议。问题是，简单的会晤某人与最大化提升人际交往沟通能力是否等同？从根本上说，沟通是将信息从发送人传递到接收人的艺术。接收人可能只有1个人，也可能有百万人。虽然理财规划师肯定是会传递信息的，但是优秀的理财规划师会抓住沟通的机会与客户建立互动关系。达成信息创造和分享的效果以增进相互理解的交流是最有效的沟通方式。

要想成为沟通大师，就必须要知道沟通的过程是富有感性和知性的，同时具有一定的目的性。沟通是富有感性的，因为信息的发出人和接收人必须利用至少五种感官之一，比如听觉和视觉。这五大感官对信息的接收和传递都是很重要的。触觉、嗅觉及味觉也会帮助（或阻碍）信息的交流。例如在大多数西方文化中的握手礼仪。握手可以传递出温暖和友好的信息，同样会传递出焦虑的信息。此外，交流是一个学习的活动。要想成功交流并维持专业的合作关系就要懂得交流必需的技巧及正确解释沟通过程。这意味着沟通不仅包含文字和图片的使用，还需要了解对话的内容。比如，许多亚洲的专业人士在与客户、同事或者领导碰面的时候习惯鞠躬。这个沟通的方式就是需要学习的。对于生长在亚洲的理财规划师来说可能是很自然的，但是对于西方的理财规划师来说，这个鞠躬的见面礼就需要学习并且练习。

最后，沟通必须带有一定的目的性才是有效的。与客户、同事、员工或者其他人的交流应该带有一定的目的性，比如建立工作关系、获取信息、建立联系、说服他人、帮助他人做决定或者彰显权威，等等。无目的性的交流应当尽力避免，特别是在做理财规划的时候。无目的性的交流对构建强有力的客户—理财规划师关系有害无利，并可能造成客户抓不住理财规划师讲话的重点，产生误会。

一般说来，沟通可分为4种基本的类型：（1）个人内心的；（2）人与人之间的；（3）一小组人员内部的；（4）很多人（大众）的。个人内心的交流是指一个人自己在内心的独白。人与人之间的交流涉及两个或有时是在一小撮人，或家庭内部的交流。一小组人员的交流包括在一个小组内部人员及向另一个较多人构成的人群传递信息。大众传媒包括向较大的人群传递信息，通常是通过电子渠道。希望能够建立成功事业的理财规划师必须学会人际交流的技巧。

Robert Heath 及 Jennings Bryant① 这样定义人际交流：

人际交往是双重的。人们通过各种交流方式和渠道建立合作关系。人们希望通过这些交流方式和渠道减少他们自己、伙伴及人际关系的不确定性，沟通的有效性及提高自身的价值。

这个定义对理财规划师来讲有非常重要的含义。第一，人际交流建立在人际关系的基础上。第二，交流的意义超越了传递的信息的内容本身。人际交流不仅需要解释所听所见的内容，还需要解读所说内容的含义和影响。第三，只有当沟通的益处大于成本时，客户才愿意与理财规划师进行交流。相信理财规划师，并与他们通过沟通建立情感纽带的客户更愿意参与理财规划过程。当客户与理财规划师第一次见面时，唯一衡量交际关系成本的标准是理财规划师的言谈举止。也就是说，客户通过分析与理财规划师交流的内容，判断理财规划师的价值。这就解释了为什么那些收益回报标准设定得低，或者绩效表现次优的理财规划师往往很少失去客户。因为这些理财规划师知道许多客户通过衡量交际关系的收益和成本来决定是否继续进行接下来的理财规划。

交际关系的收益和成本

任何理财规划师—客户关系的优势取决于沟通的质量。如前所述，关系的价值是可以量化的。客户对和理财规划师关系的决定来源于成本收益的分析。Dalmas Taylor 及 Irwin Altma② 设计的公式可以清晰明了地说明这个问题：

关系的评估 = 关系的价值 - 关系的成本

评估结果有两种：

维持关系的决定 = 关系的价值 > 关系的成本，或

结束关系的决定 = 关系的价值 < 关系的成本

那么在理财规划师—客户关系中，到底什么是收益和成本呢？为了找到问题的答案，我们必须首先清除隐藏在这些公式中的一个重要的假设前提：一段关系的发展都不是一帆风顺的，都伴随着艰难和反复。正是理财规划师和客户如何评价关系产生的收益决定了一段危机将会如何改变他们的关系。对于客户来说，这段关系带来的明显收益包括增

---

① Heath, R. L., & Bryant, J. (1992). *Human communication theory and research: Concepts, contexts, and challenges.* Hillsdale, NJ: Lawrence Erlbaum Associates.

② Taylor, D. A., & Altman, I. (1987). Communication in interpersonal relationships: Social penetration processes. In M. E. Roloff & G. R. Miller (Eds.), *Interpersonal processes: New directions in communication research* (pp. 257 - 277). Newbury Park, CA: Sage.

长的财务知识、信息及财富。成本包括金钱、时间和精力。理财规划师也从这段关系中获益，包括增长的收入、满意度及声望。理财规划师的成本包括时间、精力及机会成本。

理财规划师—客户关系也可视为同时带来成本和收益。例如，一位理财规划师可能十分期待与某位客户见面即使这位客户的财务情况并不是十分吸引人。客户可能会觉得维持理财规划师—客户关系需要的成本太大。即使理财规划师看问题的角度不同，那也不能对自己带来什么好处。也许客户发现理财规划师的个性太过让人讨厌。如果从某种程度上，客户认为人际关系的维持成本大于理财规划师提供的建议的价值，那么他/她可能会选择结束这段关系。

客户对理财规划师同样会进行成本预测，他们会根据关系中当前的成本估算未来的成本，估算长期收益及成本。例如，理财规划师与一位客户会谈数次。在每次会议中，理财规划师都强调为退休进行股票投资。然后，每次会议之后，股票都是下跌的。那么客户就会推断理财规划师的建议是不正确且是高成本的。客户可能会根据可能发生的损失结束合作关系。当然，客户的这个预测也可能是不准确的。从长远角度看，在市场下跌的时候投资对于客户来说可能更有利，但是亏钱的精神成本可能会高于继续维持与理财规划师的合作关系带来的长期收益。

最后一点对理财规划师而言尤为重要。当信任关系是基于披露和自信时，建立这种关系的成本是很大的。当理财规划师与客户的会谈从浅显进入到深入的分析和评估时，理财规划师需要面对的是具有挑战性的、需要反应敏捷的并且是一对一的客户关系。因为这种关系会让客户感到压力很大，这从某种意义上来说也是一种成本。客户的反应反之也会让理财规划师备感压力。如果理财规划师认为客户会毫无反抗地接受这种关系，不对新的想法和观点提出质疑，那么就大错特错了。

理财规划师需要向客户询问有关收入、净资产、家庭生活、目标及人生梦想等话题。关键不是理财规划师是否应该讨论这些话题，而是什么时候及如何和客户探讨这些问题。最终，客户可能会基于与理财规划师沟通交流的过程评估决定是否继续与理财规划师合作。这个决定是相对主观的，并由理财规划师和客户共同决定。评估的重点是理财规划师与客户的交流如何，包括发出、接收、解释及再发出信息的整个过程。

为了能够顺利度过客户关系建立的整个过程并克服重重障碍，理财规划师必须从最开始的会晤掌握沟通过程的主导权。这不是意味着让理财规划师控制或掌控客户，而是确保每次沟通客户获得的收益多于成本。因为理财规划师的口头或者非口头的交流是客户评价与理财规划师关系收益与成本的主要方式。在理财规划师不断发展和更新的过程中，他们的人际交流技能是十分必要的。

第五节　客户关系管理：提升客户信任及忠诚度

提升人际交流技能有很多好处。首先，对于理财规划师而言，最重要的就是可以增加客户的信任和忠诚度。口头和非口头的交流对于塑造客户对理财规划师能力的印象是十分重要的。虽然技术熟练度、形象及声誉对建立客户的印象都是非常重要的，但是理财规划师沟通的能力能够有效地维持长期的客户关系。这有积极和消极两方面的影响。从积极方面看，理财规划师善于倾听，能够帮助客户设定目标和需求，解读客户表达的引申义，并积极对客户的表达做出支持或者引导性的反应，这样能够有更多的机会获得客户的信任。从消极方面看，一些理财规划师可能会利用自己的沟通技巧在某方面产生利益冲突。比如，如果理财规划师获取客户的信任，那么这个客户也更加容易被操纵。

本章绝不是关于如何操纵客户的，也不是讨论如何成为一个更好的销售人员。虽然具有良好沟通技巧的人往往是非常优秀的销售人员，但是理财规划师作为销售的角色是在提供杰出客户服务的功能之下的。对于每位理财规划师而言，最重要的问题是，通过理财规划想要向客户传达什么样的信息和服务。客户可分为两种，如图 4－2 所示的两个相反的箭头。左边的客户认为理财过程纯粹是一个交易性的商品。他们认为理财规划师与房产经纪、税务专员、水管工、电工及汽车修理工的服务性质是类似的。这一类型的客户愿意与任何可以为他们提供产品和服务的理财规划师合作。理财建议及长期客户关系对他们而言价值甚微。这当中的一些客户持有的观点可能不像我们描述的这样极端，但是他们仍然认为理财规划是一个产品递送机制而不是基于合作关系的财富最大化的过程。这类客户的理财规划师所使用的沟通技巧与希望追求合作关系的客户的理财规划师使用的沟通技巧是大为不同的。

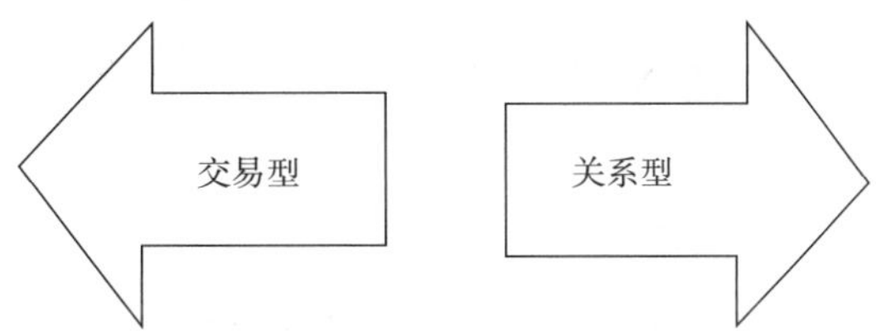

图 4－2　理财规划流程的连续统一

箭头的另外一端代表另外一种类型的客户。他们认为理财是一个人际沟通的过程，能够帮助自己实现理财目标。这些客户更加注重与自己信任的理财规划师合作，而对产品本身不是十分有兴趣。对于这种关系型客户，理财规划师—客户关系本身（而不是产品），服务或者理财规划师的表现决定了他们是否要与理财规划师合作。

关系型客户注重与理财规划师关系的持久性。他们视理财规划师为“治疗师”、“咨询师”、“教练”、“导师”或者“生活顾问”。这些客户愿意而且希望与理财规划师沟通交流并保持长期合作关系。他们可能会与理财规划师建立私人及职业关系。例如，这些客户在向理财规划师寻求意见之前都不会随意做出重大的生活上的决定。有些客户也不会这么极端。这些客户希望与他们信任的人分享自己财务上的秘密，但是他们也会把理财规划师的建议与其他信息来源做比较。

有时，由于文化或者雇佣合同的关系，有些理财规划师不得不使自己的业务专注在某一市场细分上。如果一个理财规划师大部分的客户都具有如下特点，那么他/她的客户就属于交易型客户：

寻求某一问题的帮助而不是进行综合理财规划；

喜欢简短的会议；

一年见一次面就足够；

喜欢一对一地探讨人生目标和梦想；

极少讨论遗产问题；

经常或者偶尔取消会议；

自己做调查研究然后询问信息来支持他们的发现和想法；

不愿意转介绍理财规划师给别人；

愿意购买产品但不愿进行综合理财规划。

对于理财规划师而言，箭头两端的客户都带来机遇。但是虽然这样讲，大部分成功的理财规划师都是注重与客户关系的发展。衡量理财规划师是否成功的标准通常有在管资产规模、执业规模、声誉及收入。对于所有的理财规划师而言，掌握沟通技巧是十分重要的，然而打造成功客户关系的唯一途径是掌握、联系并且提升沟通技巧。沟通技巧是基于客户关系而非产品交易的理财执业路径的基石。

沟通艺术早在客户步入理财规划师的办公室之前就开始发挥作用了。市场营销的方方面面，例如公司网络、宣传册、赞助及其他书面和广播媒介都为客户提供了参考。这些宣传资料以客观和主观的方式与客户沟通。例如，一家公司的宣传资料会传达公司深厚经验和良好声望的形象，也可能暗示公司较为随性的规划方式。

如果理财规划师希望将自己的职业发展建立在发展关系型客户的基础上，那么理财规划师就需要管理客户如何体会和解读整个规划过程。正如之前提及的，客户关系始于客户踏进办公室之前。如果客户感到轻松自在、舒心愉悦并且毫无压力，他们就会在会话中提供更加有价值的信息，更容易披露有关个人、家庭及财务方面的信息，更重要的是，能更好地执行理财建议。虽然理财规划师与客户的对话在低压的状态下持续进行，客户会逐渐将理财规划师当做可信任的咨询师。这种信任需要建立在共同的价值观、归属感及相互信任的基础上。

一、评估沟通方式

交流方式有口头和非口头的表达形式。词语的运用是口头交流的主要形式。如何将词语组织成句决定了交流过程的好坏。非口头交流也非常重要。非口头交流形式包括使用身体语言向他人表达有关口头表达内容方式的微弱（有时也不是微弱的）信息。例如面部表情、手势、身体方位及特殊方位。例如，一位顾客身体靠后坐在椅子上，双腿交叉，双手交叉于胸前。在这种情况下，客户表达的信息是她目前不打算接收任何现在及稍后所听到的信息。交叉的双腿和双手这样的非口头表达方式所传达的信息是听者“关闭”了自己的反应区，靠在椅子上也表达了听者不想参与对话。从另一方面讲，当某人讲话时，听者身体向前，微笑并且点头通常是积极的非语言表达形式。

但是，需要注意的是，非口头沟通方式有时会让人不解其意，社会和文化习惯总是会对有效的沟通方式产生影响。例如，交叉双腿在美国是一个很正常的举止。但是在有些文化中，如果鞋尖冲人，被视为非常粗鲁的行为。一个人觉得很自然的事情在他人看来可能很不可思议。正因为如此，理解并且适应一个社会的文化是十分重要的。

通常来说，沟通中产生的误解发生的原因是理财规划师和客户没有分享相同的“经验地图”。“经验地图”是指人们定义事实和解释行为的方式。这在学习和沟通方式的偏好上尤为显著。总体来说，人们倾向选择以下几种学习和沟通方式：（1）视觉；（2）听觉；（3）动觉触觉。但是，人们在谈话时并不是只用一种方式，而是每个人有偏好的交流模式。

以一个典型的视觉学习者为例。这类人比较容易通过眼睛观察数据、图标、影像及演讲学习。当理财规划师将理财规划报告交到这类客户手中，他们往往习惯迅速找寻适合视觉观察的分析表格和建议。之后，他们才会详细阅读整本报告。当和视觉学习者交谈时，他们往往会说："你说得很有道理，我可以看到你的意思"。

听觉学习者依赖他们所听到的，而非所看到的内容学习。这类人习惯参加讲座，而且比其他人更喜欢说话和参与讨论。如果有人说"我听到你说的了，我觉得很有道理"或者"你有没有听说去年房价下跌了3%？"我们可以据此判断出这个人可能是听觉学习者。

触觉动觉交流者则习惯通过参与活动学习。他们喜欢触摸，感知，记笔记。当理财规划师将理财报告递交到这类学习者手中，他们喜欢看推导出结果的公式，然后自己复算一遍。通常，触觉动觉学习者习惯画图，喜欢使用想象与人展开讨论。触觉动觉学习者可能会说"我实在不能想象退休后少于300万元存款，我该怎么办？"

作为理财规划师，首先要先判断自己的沟通类型，然后需要评估当前和潜在客户的沟通和学习类型。虽然看起来很简单，但是很多时候客户—理财规划师的关系之所以无法持续，就是因为理财规划师没有判断并使用客户偏好的学习方式展示理财规划。例如，一个听觉学习类型的理财规划师会觉得和一个视觉学习型的客户无法产生共鸣。对于客户而言，虽然理财规划师已经尽力表意清晰，他们还是会觉得理财规划师根本就没有听或者对自己的话毫无反应。

在美国，大部分的美国人是视觉型学习者，少部分是听觉型，最少的是动觉触觉型。因此，作为一条原则，理财规划师应该尽量适应客户的学习方式。表4-3为理财规划师判断客户是何种类型的学习者提供一些参考。

表4-3　　评估交流、学习类型的方式

个人特点	视觉型	听觉型	动觉触觉型
喜欢倾听			
听完报告后才会做出决定			
通过观察他人学习			
喜欢阅读			
喜欢做笔记			
在评估完所有的选择和完成所有的研究后才做决定			
通过动手学习			
通过评估过去的经验和结果做决定			

二、提问

理财规划师通过提问收集信息的方式与其他专业人士不同。以律师和医生为例。律师和医生很少将提问作为发现问题并快速诊断的依据。理财规划师一般不会太赶时间，因此会利用提问的机会增进与客户的了解。理财规划师通过从情感上建立信任的方式设计问题，进而加强与客户的关系，而不是仅把提问作为发掘信息的手段。

（一）开放式问题

问题可以分为开放式和封闭式。封闭式问题通常用简单的“是”或“不是”就可以回答。开放式问题往往以“什么时候”、“为什么”、“怎么”、“告诉我”、“在哪里”或者“什么”这样的词语开头。“为什么”开头的问题最好少用。客户会认为以“为什么”开头的问题有点像拷问的感觉，因此通常得到的回答会具有抵抗情绪。

（二）封闭式问题

封闭式问题通常仅有几个回答。封闭式问题通常这样开头：“你是……”，“你……”，“这个是”，“那个是”。律师非常不喜欢问这种封闭式的问题。理财规划师也应当尽量避免这种类型的问题，只在理财过程中需要收集特定问题时使用。

（三）介于开放性和封闭性之间的问题

当理财规划师需要促使客户行动时，封闭性问题会非常有效。例如以下场景：

理财规划师：“我们上个月进行了退休规划方面的计算。您还有什么问题吗？”

客户：“没有。”

理财规划师：“那么您准备好开始实施您的退休规划了吗？”

客户：“是的，我想我们可以进行下一步了。”

（四）模糊性问题

治疗师使用模糊性问题已经有几十年的历史了。模糊性问题是通过将开放性问题伪装成封闭性问题的方式来引导客户提供更多的信息。以“是否”、“请”、“请允许我……”等词语开始的问题让客户明确给予回答，但却提供客户可以增加信息完善他们答案的机会。例如以下几个问题：

“您能给我一个大概的概念，这个账户里有多少钱呢？”

“您能明天联系一下律师，询问一下关于披露条款还应当增加哪些信息吗？”

“您能再和我多谈一些关于雇主提供的寿险计划吗？”

“您是否愿意下周三与我们的内部会计师会面？”

（五）暗示及预测性问题

理财规划师经常使用暗示及预测性问题。暗示性问题通常以非直接的方式提问，类似前面提及的模糊性问题。暗示性问题只有当客户和理财规划师合作关系确立以后才可以使用。本质上来讲，暗示性问题通过类似“我想”或者“你必须”这样的词语来间接让客户回答问题。例如，理财规划师可能会问“我在想您对于退休后的生活有什么想法”。这实际是在暗示询问“当您退休时，您有什么计划”。

理疗师通常运用预测性问题挖掘更深层次的情绪反应、无意识的思想、价值及感觉。预测性问题通常这样开始“如果你”、“要是……会怎样”、或者“什么将……”例如，“如果你有三个愿望，您会如何许愿?”还比如，“如果您今天会留有一笔遗产，您希望为您的朋友、家人及同事留下怎样的印象?”这样的问题可以让客户憧憬，或者描绘他们的梦想。

（六）比例问题

比例问题可以有效帮助客户利用数字而非语言表达他们的想法、意见、希望、梦想及恐惧。比例问题也可以帮助理财规划师加强理财过程的积极因素。通常来说，当理财规划师希望客户表达一种印象、观察、预测或者相关比例问题，他们就会用比例问题提问。

理财规划师：“我们已经估计了您的退休资金需求。为了达到您的财务目标，您需要从现在开始多存储10%的工资。您觉得如何?”

客户：“我不是很清楚。”

理财规划师：“好。那我们换个角度来看这个问题。数字1至10，1代表完全没有自信，10代表非常自信，您对未来退休金的储蓄计划有多大的信心?”

客户：“这样说来，我觉得差不多7吧。”

（七）有关提问的规律总结

通常，新晋理财规划师提问时总是随心所欲。提问不是在某一时候随便提出的，而是需要提前进行详细计划和安排的。理财规划师通过提问，从客户那里获得答案和反应，推进理财规划过程。不管理财规划师使用哪种形式的问题，他们都应当遵循以下《心理咨询面谈技术》一书中有关治疗会谈的原则：

尽可能简洁地与客户分享信息并保持一致的与客户会谈的形式。

客户的每个回答都应当引导会话的继续进行。倾听及适时的反应是十分重要的。

问题应当与客户的每个需求和情况直接相关。

问题不仅应该引导客户提供信息还应当帮助客户专注理财规划过程的各个方面。

当涉及敏感问题时，理财规划师应当特别留意。因为在理财规划师看来不是十分敏感或重要的话题，也许可能伤害了客户。对于有关社会经济地位、性别偏好、个人及家庭困难或者其他类似话题，理财规划师要抱有谨慎和感同身受的态度和客户进行沟通。

第六节　持续提升理财规划师专业技能

本书，特别是本章节旨在帮助新晋理财规划师能够获得职业上的成功。作为帮助他人实现财务目标的过程及长期的职业发展路径，理财规划能够为那些充满智慧和激情的人士提供无限的可能。要想成为一个成功的理财规划师必须要学习、培养和完善多种技能。与其他专业领域不同，理财规划职业要求执业者在广泛的领域都具备一定的知识和技能。图 4－3 对打造成功理财规划职业生涯所需要的重要因素进行了展示说明。

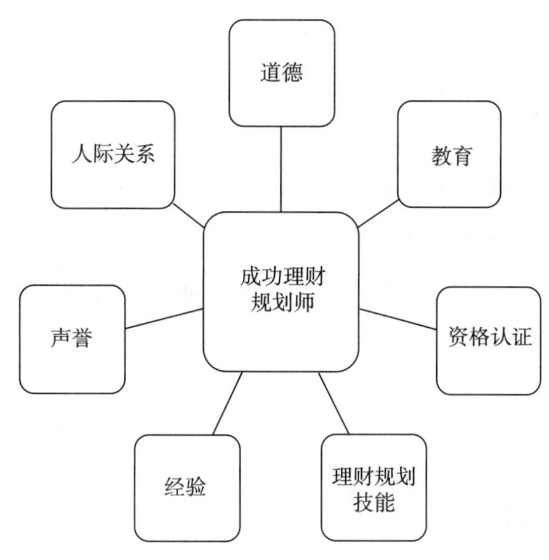

图 4－3　成功理财规划师应具备的素质

一、道德

成为一名成功理财规划师的首要条件是遵守道德。本章已经详细描述了作为一名理财规划师需要在执业中遵循清晰的道德准则。至少，理财规划师应该在为客户提供投资建议时，获得相关的当地、州及联邦颁发的专业许可。此外，理财规划师还应遵守书面的道德准则和执业标准。这些标准应包含如 FPSB 所倡导的"以客户利益为先并为社会公众利益维护和推广理财规划专业形象。"①

① Financial Planning Standards Board. 2011. *Financial planner competency profile*. Denver：FPSB.

二、教育

25 年前，理财规划专业学位还没有出现。大部分的理财规划执业者要么没有大学学位，要么持有其他学科的学位。20 世纪 80 年代初，大学开始提供理财规划专业的教学。如今，在美国，一些在全国最古老、规模最大及最有声望的教育机构开设了理财规划专业。消费者也越来越青睐拥有大学学位和理财规划专业的理财规划师。以往，理财规划师往往是通过专业培训或者资格认证项目满足客户的这个需求。通常情况下，认证项目会提供非学分制的培训，开设最多 6 ~ 7 门理财规划相关的课程。对于在保险、投资或者其他理财相关领域有丰富经验的理财规划师来说，这种资格认证培训是十分合适的。然而，对于刚起步踏入这个领域的理财规划师而言，获得一个理财规划专业的大学学位无疑是提升自己职业生涯水平的一个最好途径。

CFP 委员会的网站提供了全美提供认证项目及大学学位的机构名单：http：//www. cfp. net/become－a－cfp－professional/find－an－education－program。不在美国的人士可以通过在线学习或者参加当地与美国机构合作的大学或者学院完成理财规划的基本教育。当然，居住在美国以外的人士还需要通过当地的教育培训完成当地税务及遗产规划课题的学习。

三、资格认证

在金融机构里，财富管理专业人士是我们通常接触到的、直接跟客户打交道的群体。他们有各种各样的称呼，如客户经理、理财经理、理财顾问或是财富顾问等。具备大学学历，获得了一些监管门槛、在岗要求的资格证书，比如从业资格，专业执照，AFP、CFP、CFA、CPB 或是会计师等资格证书。但是单单拥有学历和专业证书是远远不够的，这些也仅仅只是一块敲门砖而已。全世界共有超过 150 000 名的 CFP 专业人士。这使得 CFP 资格成为世界最大的理财规划认证资格。消费者认为他们的理财规划师应当经过理财规划方面的专业训练，他们也希望自己的理财规划师能获得更高级的资格认证训练。认证资格是成功理财规划师有别于其他理财规划师的最好钥匙。富有并且有知识的客户往往希望他们的理财团队能够获得认证。正因如此，新晋理财规划师更应该投入时间、精力和资金获得一个或多个资格。除 CFP 资格外，理财规划师还应努力获得某个专业领域的资格，如投资管理、退休规划、税务规划及遗产规划。对于保险规划专业人士，有很多有名的资格认证项目可供选择。

四、理财规划技能

本章一直强调，理财规划不仅仅需要了解产品知识。一个有竞争力的理财规划师要想打造成功的职业生涯，必须具备成功收集、分析及整合数据并将其制作成理财规划的技能。这种能力不是什么人都可以拥有的。只有通过专业训练、自我学习、教育培训及认证进行刻苦的技能培训才可能获得这些技能。那么，如何鉴定一个财富管理人士是否“专业”呢？唯一标准就是看他服务过什么样的客户，解决了怎样的财务问题。这就要求财富管理专业人士也要具备甄别客户的能力。只有通过甄别客户才能帮助其选择具有针对性的产品、制定服务计划。但现阶段两大问题普遍存在：一是财务管理人员没能力鉴别客户的需求，需求都是客户自己讲出来的；二是即使能鉴别出客户的需求，却无法完成相应的后续服务。这其中存在一些客观原因，像制度平台的欠缺、相应产品和工具不足，也有业内人员的知识水平和服务能力不够等主观原因。

五、经验

新晋理财规划师经常会问为什么经验不是获得理财规划职业成功的首要因素。原因很简单，经验的作用总是被夸大，特别是在一个拥有悠久历史发展的职业。虽然，经验的激励对于磨炼规划熟练度是非常重要的，但是经验本身并不比培训、教育及继续教育重要。通常，新晋理财规划师会为这个职业带来新的知识和理财工具，这是年老的理财规划师所不具备的。当然，最终的理财事业的成功取决于培训、教育、认证资格、继续教育及经验。但是，如果简单认为一个人在理财行业从业时间长就可以保证他们提供的服务最能帮助客户实现理财目标，那么就错了。作为一名初级理财规划师，应该首先熟悉财富管理中的各个环节，比如家庭教育、风险规避和转移、退休后的生活方式、税负的有效管理及传承的计划和安排；家族企业与个人财务整合在一起的规划，涉及跨境问题的理财规划等。这些都是理财规划师可能会接触到的客户需求。如果一个理财规划师能够做到持之以恒为客户解决各种金融疑虑，他就会越来越专业。但现在国内理财规划师所存在的问题就是阅历有限又操之过急。在发达国家，财富管理专业人士不仅是全方面的，而且成为一名高端理财规划师是有多种途径的。

欧美许多优秀的财富顾问或是私人银行家都普遍在45岁以上，他们不仅积累了丰富的理财阅历，而且有着丰富的职业经历。有人当过警察、教师，有人曾经是一名医生或是会计师。他们最初从事理财也只是把它作为一个有发展前景的第二职业，后来随着业务量的增加才慢慢完成进一步的职业转型。

丰富的阅历既涵盖了丰富的经验，也可以铸就良好的信誉，它是一名财富管理专业人士可靠性的体现。客户在接触财富管理专业人士前都肯定想要知道这个财富管理专业人士帮助过多少人、打理过哪些财务问题、运作过多少资金量等等。就像国外招聘基金经理时，会重点关注他过去 14 年的投资理财经历。通常来讲 7 年为一个经济周期，要考察一个基金经理的投资水平至少要看他经历的两个经济周期的投资成果如何。市场好时挣到钱并不一定是他们的真实能力，但在市场低迷时，能够尽量减少客户的损失并实现资产的保值升值，才是财富管理专业人士应该做到的。

六、声誉

一个新晋理财规划师必须问自己两个重要的问题：

是否有人愿意接受自己的服务？

是否有人愿意转介其他客户给自己？

除非这两个问题的答案都是“是”，否则要想获得理财规划师事业的成功是非常困难的。这两个问题揭示了一个理财规划师在消费者心中的信任度。所以，新晋理财规划师该如何创造信任的氛围，从而让客户更愿意选择自己进行合作呢？

问题的答案总是让新晋理财规划师大吃一惊。大学和学院的课程告诉我们，理财规划，作为一个以流程为导向的执业，是非常讲究技术性、准确性，同时需要投入大量时间的战略过程。这个概念不十分准确。理财规划除了是一个技术职业外，还是一个非常人性，并以客户为中心的职业。许多年前，一个大型的理财规划公司认为一个伟大的理财规划师必须“拥有治疗师之心和资本家之脑”。简言之，这意味着一个成功的理财规划师必须与客户建立相互信任的关系，同时要利用自己的技能和能力制作可行的理财规划方案。

信任是建立在声誉的基础之上的。信赖自己理财规划师的客户会长期与自己的理财规划师合作并且会转介自己的朋友、同事和邻居。正因为如此，理财规划师，特别是新晋理财规划师，应尽快树立自己有能力有人性的职业声誉。通常，一个理财规划师总是在一定区域享有声誉，少有理财规划师在全国都很有声誉。建立良好声誉的方法通常包括：

志愿服务社区服务；在当地或者国家的专业委员会任职；出版文章或者书籍；为有名的杂志和书籍撰写专栏；发表网上市场评论；发表有关市场分析的博客；担当理财规

划学生的导师；志愿服务当地或者地区理财规划协会；加入全国理财规划组织；获得有声望的理财规划认证；与和自己不存在竞争关系的专业人士，如会计师、税务专员、律师及理疗师建立联系；为社会提供大家有兴趣的专业讲座。

以上列举的活动仅仅能够帮助理财规划师在消费者心中建立积极的职业形象。除了这些活动以外，成功的理财规划师往往能够将自己的个人和专业精力与执业相结合。例如一个生长在中国香港但是现居亚特兰大的理财规划师。与其花费大量的时间、精力和财力在亚特兰大地区拓展业务，不如利用自己的文化、语言及专业技能在美国华裔移民中建立声誉。这需要其学习有关签证、移民法、跨国税务及资产配置相关方面的技能。但这个回报是十分客观的。与其和当地的一般理财服务竞争，不如成为能够提供特殊服务的让人信赖的理财规划师。从这个角度来看，每位理财规划师都可以发展一项独特的技能，帮助最大化建立自己的声誉。

七、人际关系

回顾以上提及的为了建立声誉而需要做的活动清单。如果理财规划师每周都要做一至两项清单上的活动，那么会相当花费时间。如果要每周做三至四项活动，那么理财规划师大部分时间都被占用了。新晋理财规划师要有这个心理准备。通常，要想获得潜在客户 1 个小时的实际理财规划服务，一个新晋理财规划师需要花费 2 ~ 3 小时进行建立声誉的活动，市场营销服务及面谈客户。前三年的执业活动总是与建立关系网和客户关系有关。在这些年，人际交往的能力可以帮助理财规划师建立和铺平职业道路。具体的人际交往技巧包括：寻找新客户；接触相关专业人士，创造建立关系网的机会；志愿服务专业委员会；通过媒体广告进行宣传；乐于接受媒体采访并引用自己的言论。

人际交往能力取决于两个基本因素：第一，成功的理财规划师总是充满帮助他人的热情。当看到自己的建议被执行并对帮助客户实现生活目标产生积极的影响，这份热情也随之高涨。那些取得理财规划师事业辉煌的理财规划师往往视客户为家人。客户也会同样认为他们是最值得信赖的咨询顾问。正因为如此，对于理财规划师而言，真正的回报来自工作的满意度而不仅仅是金钱。第二，人际交往能力取决于沟通技巧。恰当的沟通是非常重要的。最成功的理财规划师并不一定是最聪明的那个，而是最能有效把握客户需求并收集、分析并整合获得的信息，有效减少客户财务恐惧的那个。这种才能是通过沟通技巧锻炼而得的。有人说，沟通能力决定着一个人的生活品质。理财规划师的成功与良好的沟通能力紧密相连。一个在客户面前表达不清、害羞甚至不敢面对客户的人，又该如何了解和帮助客户呢?

八、自我

除了上述几项因素，身为一名理财规划师最为关键的是要对自己有一个清醒的认识，这是从业者在从事一个职业1~3年内需要想明白的一个问题。只有对自己及自己所从事的职业有了更清楚的认知，才能制定一个更加清晰的职业规划，并为之不断努力。调查显示，国际理财规划标准委员会诞生至今，大约认证了10万名具备资格的理财从业人员，可其中只有占20%~30%的人群感觉自己非常适合这个行业，工作做得有声有色，如鱼得水，他们找到了恰当的角色定位；而也有相当一部分人在从事财富管理时会感到不适应，度日如年，工作压力很大，整天为完不成“指标”，找不到客户，做不出业绩等问题烦恼。不可否认，这其中有体制等客观原因存在的问题，但我们应该承认我们自身也有不可推卸的责任。所以，我们一定要对自身有一个更加清醒的认识。

综上所述，笔者认为当我们兼具了财富管理专业人士的资格、技能，寻找到了适合发展的职业通道，在完成了不断的自我认知后，才能更加清楚自身的角色定位。这样既是对自己、对客户负责，也是对这个尚待完善的金融事业负责。

当然，理财规划师也必须有足够的专业知识设计制作理财规划，但是如果没有人际交往能力，再好的规划也无法付诸实施。

打造理财规划职业并非易事。然而，没有几个职业像理财规划这样富有回报。最成功的理财规划师往往能成为客户最信任的同事和朋友。对于那些能够成功熬过前3~4年的理财规划师而言，今后的前途是不可限量的。正如本书一直谈论的，理财规划需求在全世界以不可思议的速度迅速增长，这对那些拥有教育、资格认证、理财规划技能、经验、声誉和人际交往能力的理财规划师而言，意味着更多的成功机遇。

附录　理财规划工具的使用

1. 金融计算器的使用

1.1　金融计算器的分类

金融计算器是针对银行、证券、保险、房地产、投资以及商业等相关行业的特点开发的专业计算器，它能轻松地将标准财务函数功能和高级函数功能融合在一起，使各种金融、财务计算变得更加便捷。以下以德州仪器 BA II PLUS 为例介绍金融计算器的使用。

1.2　计算器的基本设定

指示符	含义
2nd	使用下一按键的第二功能
COMPUTE	按下 CPT 键，计算器将计算显示变量的运算结果
ENTER	按下 ENTER 键，计算器以显示值给显示变量赋值
SET	按下 2ndSET 键，改变显示变量的设置
BGN	在货币的时间价值（TVM）计算中选择期初付款模式。如果没有显示 BGN，那么货币的时间价值计算将采用期末付款模式（END）

1.3　小数位数的设置

金融计算器默认显示两位小数。用户可根据自身需求更改计算器显示的小数位数。计算器最多可显示 8 位小数。

例如：将小数位数设置为 4。

按	显示
2nd [Format] 4 ENTER	DEC = 4.0000
2nd [QUIT]	0.0000

4 位小数设置将保持有效（即使将计算器关闭或者开启），直到用户再次对其进行更改。

1.4 功能键中数据的重新设置和清空

数字重新输入按 CE/C 键。一般计算重新设置，按 2ND CPT 键调用 QUIT，显示 0.0000，退出主界面。PV 、FV、N 、I/Y、PMT 这 5 个货币时间价值功能键中会存有上次运算的结果，通过 OFF 或 CE/C 键无法清除其中数据。正确的清空方法是按 2ND CPT 键调用 CLR TVM（注：为表述简单，凡直接书写第二功能键，即表示先按 2ND，然后按其所对应的主功能键）。

清除储存单元中保存的所有数据，可以进入 MEM 键，再按 CLR WORK 键。

如果需要清空所有数据，包括恢复所有计算器的设置，直接按 RESET 键即可，可以理解为计算器的“格式化”。

1.5 付款和复利计算设置

金融计算器可以假定付款发生在期初（BGN）或期末（END），默认设置为期末（END）。

将计算器设置为期初：

按	显示
2nd [BGN]	END
2nd [SET]	BGN
CE/C	0.0000

一个小的 BGN 字样出现在所显示的数字上方，表示当前为期初模式。

将计算器设置为期末：

按	显示
2nd [BGN]	BGN
2nd [SET]	END
CE/C	0.0000

一旦按了 2nd [BGN] 键，2nd [SET] 就变成 BGN 和 END 的切换键。

1.6　使用金融计算器的注意事项

PV 现值、FV 终值、PMT 年金、I/Y 利率、N 期数，是运用财务计算器计算货币时间价值的五大变量。只要输入任何 4 个变量，就可以求出剩下的一个变量。

输入时，数字在先，变量键或功能键（如 PV 键）在后。输出答案时先按计算的指令键（CPT），再按要求的变量键（如 FV），即可求出答案。

输入数字时，如投资、存款、生活费用支出、房贷本息支出都是现金流出，输入符号为负；收入、赎回投资、借入本金都是现金流入，输入符号为正。

1.7　货币时间价值（TVM）的计算

变量键	含义
N	计息周期
I/Y	年利率
PV	现值
PMT	年金
FV	终值

1.8　清除 TVM 工作表

按	显示
CE/C	0.0000
2nd ［CLR TVM］	0.0000

2. 用 Excel 计算货币时间价值

2.1　终值与现值的计算

终值是指现在的一笔资金按给定的利率计算所得到的未来某一时刻的价值，也称为未来值。现值是指未来的一笔资金按给定的利率计算所得到的现在时刻的价值。

2.1.1　单利终值与现值

单利是指仅对本金计算利息，以前各期产生的利息不再计算利息的利息计算方式。

2.1.1.1　单利终值

假设：P 为现在投入的一笔资金，i_s为单利年利率，n 为计息年数，F_s为 n 年末的单利终值。现在投入的一笔资金，n 年末的终值相当于 n 年末的本利之和，则：

$$F_s = P + P \times i_s \times n = P \times (1 + i_s \times n)$$

利用 Excel 计算单利终值非常简单，只需要在相应的单元格中输入上述计算公式即可。

例如，某人现在存入银行 1 000 元，单利年利率 5%，则 5 年后的本利和为 1 250 元，详见下图：

B4　=B1*(1+B2*B3)

	A	B	C	D	E
1	终值	1000			
2	利率	5.00%			
3	期间	5			
4	终值	¥1250			

2.1.1.2　单利现值

如果已知一笔现在的存款一定时期后按单利计息的终值，则可求出其等值的现值。由终值求现值又称贴现或折现，贴现时所使用的利率称为贴现率或折现率，其计算公式为：

$$P = F_s / (1 + i_s \times n)$$

利用 Excel 计算单利终值非常简单，只需要在相应的单元格中输入上述计算公式即可。

例如，某人打算在 5 年后从银行取出 1 000 元，单利年利率 5%，则现在需要存入银行的金额为 800 元，详见下图：

B4　=B1/(1+B2*B3)

	A	B	C	D	E
1	终值	1000			
2	利率	5.00%			
3	期间	5			
4	现值	¥800			

2.1.2　复利终值与现值

复利是指不仅对本金计算利息，而且对以前各期所产生的利息也计算利息的利息计算方式。

2.1.2.1　复利终值

复利终值是指一笔资金按一定的利率复利计息时，未来某一时刻的本利和。

假设：P 为现在投入的一笔资金，i 为复利年利率，n 为计息年数，F 为 n 年末的复利终值，则复利终值的计算公式为：

$$F = P(1+i)^n$$

利用 Excel 计算复利终值非常简单，只需要在相应的单元格中输入上述计算公式即可。

例如，某人现在存入银行 1 000 元，复利年利率 5%，则 5 年后的本利和为 1 276.28 元，详见下图：

B4　=B1*(1+B2)^B3

	A	B	C	D	E
1	现值	1000			
2	利率	5.00%			
3	期间	5			
4	终值	¥1276.28			

此外，复利终值还可以利用 FV 函数计算。

FV 函数：基于固定利率及等额分期付款方式，返回某项投资的未来值。

语法：FV（rate，nper，pmt，pv，type）

Rate：为各期利率。

Nper：为总投资期，即该项投资的付款期总数。

Pmt：为各期所应支付的金额，其数值在整个年金期间保持不变。通常 pmt 包括本金和利息，但不包括其他费用及税款。如果忽略 pmt，则必须包括 pv 参数。

Pv：为现值，即从该项投资开始计算时已经入账的款项，或一系列未来付款的当前值的累积和，也称为本金。如果省略 Pv，则假设其值为零，并且必须包括 pmt 参数。

Type：数字 0 或 1，用以指定各期的付款时间是在期初（1）还是期末（0）。如果省略 type，则假设其值为 0。

说明：

应确认所指定的 rate 和 nper 单位的一致性。例如，同样是四年期年利率为 12% 的贷款，如果按月支付，rate 应为 12%/12，nper 应为 4×12；如果按年支付，rate 应为 12%，nper 为 4。

在所有参数中，支出的款项，如银行存款，表示为负数；收入的款项，如股息收入，表示为正数。

上例中，用 FV 函数计算如下图所示：

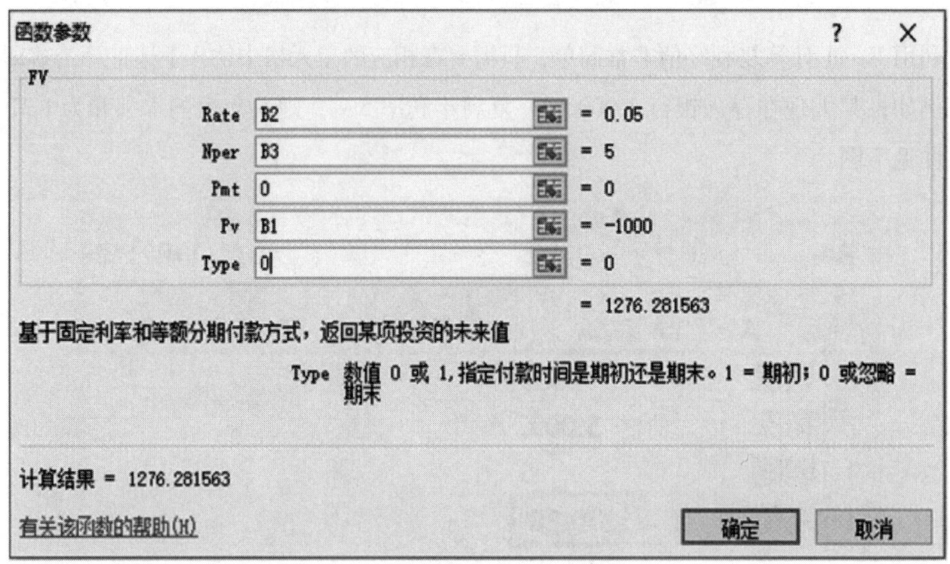

B4 =FV(B2,B3,0,B1,0)

	A	B	C	D	E
1	现值	-1000			
2	利率	5.00%			
3	期间	5			
4	终值	¥1276.28			

2.1.2.2　复利现值

复利现值是指未来时期的一笔资金按复利贴现的现在时刻的价值。贴现是复利的反过程。在已知复利终值、贴现率和贴现期数的条件下，可求得复利现值为：

$$P = F/(1+i)^n$$

利用 Excel 计算复利终值非常简单，只需要在相应的单元格中输入上述计算公式即可。

例如，某人打算在 5 年后从银行取出 1 000 元，复利年利率 5%，则现在需要存入银行的金额为 783.53 元，详见下图：

B4　　=B1/(1+B2)^B3

	A	B	C	D	E
1	终值	1000			
2	利率	5.00%			
3	期间	5			
4	现值	¥783.53			

复利现值利用 PV 函数计算。

PV 函数：返回投资的现值。现值为一系列未来付款的当前值的累积和。

语法：PV（rate，nper，pmt，fv，type）

Rate：为各期利率。

Nper：为总投资期，即该项投资的付款期总数。

Pmt：为各期所应支付的金额，其数值在整个年金期间保持不变。通常 pmt 包括本金和利息，但不包括其他费用及税款。如果忽略 pmt，则必须包括 Fv 参数。

Fv：为未来值，或在最后一次支付后希望得到的现金余额，如果省略 Fv，则假设其值为零（一笔贷款的未来值即为零）。并且必须包括 pmt 参数。

Type：数字 0 或 1，用以指定各期的付款时间是在期初（1）还是期末（0）。如果省略 type，则假设其值为 0。

说明：

应确认所指定的 rate 和 nper 单位的一致性。例如，同样是四年期年利率为 12% 的贷款，如果按月支付，rate 应为 12%/12，nper 应为 4 × 12；如果按年支付，rate 应为 12%，nper 为 4。

在所有参数中，支出的款项，如银行存款，表示为负数；收入的款项，如股息收入，表示为正数。

上例中，用 PV 函数计算如下图所示：

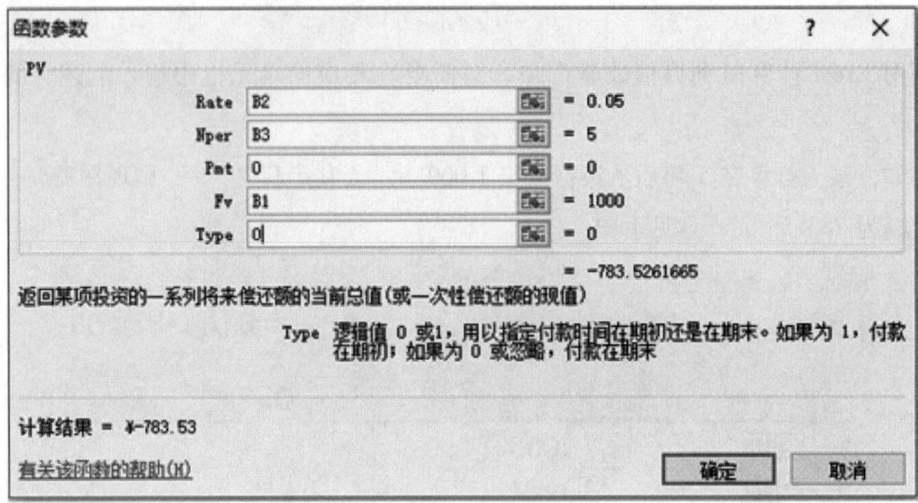

B4 =PV(B2,B3,0,B1,0)

	A	B	C	D	E
1	终值	1000			
2	利率	5.00%			
3	期间	5			
4	现值	¥-783.53			

2.2 年金的终值与现值

年金是指一定期限内每期都有的一系列等额的收付款项。年金可按发生的时间和期限不同划分为 4 种类型：

一是普通年金，又称后付年金，指一定期限内每期期末发生的等额款项。

二是先付年金，指一定期限内每期期初发生的等额款项。

三是永续年金，即无期限发生的普通年金。

四是延期年金，即一定时期以后才发生的普通年金。

2.2.1 普通年金的终值与现值

2.2.1.1 普通年金的终值

$$FV = PMT \times \left(\frac{(1 + r)^n - 1}{r}\right)$$

计算普通年金的终值，可以利用 Excel 中提供的 *FV* 函数。*FV* 函数的功能是利用固定利率及等额分期付款方式，计算年金的未来值。

例如，某人现在每年年末存入 2 000 元，在银行按 3% 的年利率复利计息的情况下，5 年后此人账户共有多少钱？

插入 FV 函数，参数如下图所示：

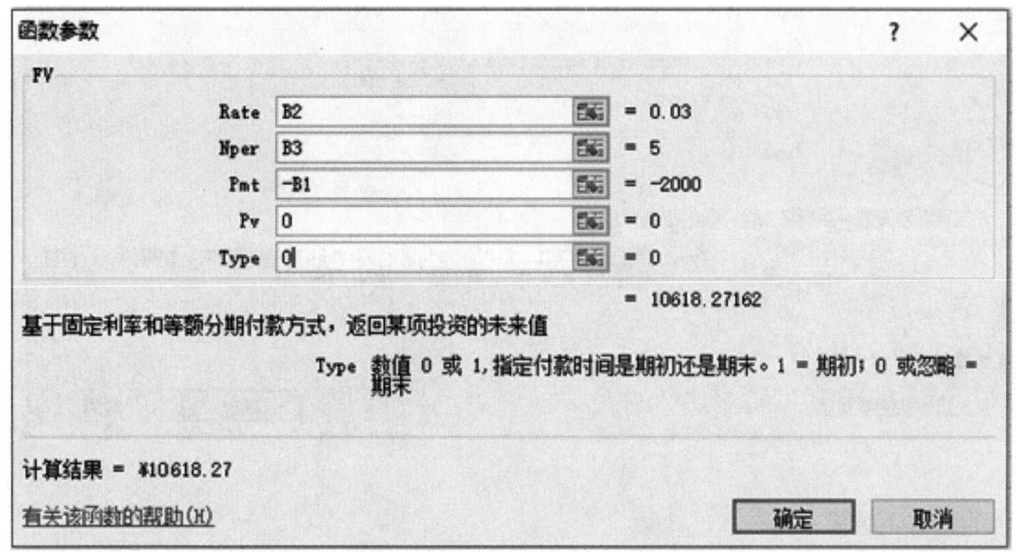

得到如下结果：

B4　=FV(B2,B3,-B1,0,0)

	A	B	C	D
1	年金	2000		
2	利率	3.00%		
3	期间	5		
4	普通年金终值	¥10618.27		

2.2.1.2　普通年金的现值

$$PV = PMT \times \left((1 - \frac{1}{(1 + r)^n}) / r \right)$$

计算普通年金现值，可以利用 Excel 中提供的 *PV* 函数。*PV* 函数的功能是返回未来若干期资金的现值。

例如，某人打算在今后的 4 年中每年等额从银行取出 2 000 元，在银行按 10% 的年利率复利计息的情况下，此人现在应一次性存入银行多少钱？

插入 PV 函数，参数如下图所示：

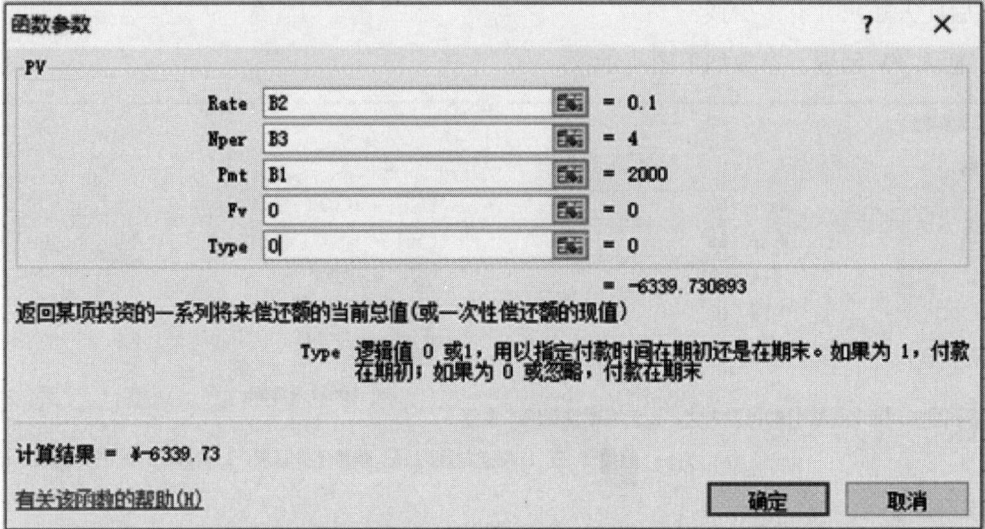

函数参数　? ×

PV

Rate　B2　= 0.1

Nper　B3　= 4

Pmt　B1　= 2000

Fv　0　= 0

Type　0　= 0

= -6339.730893

返回某项投资的一系列将来偿还额的当前总值(或一次性偿还额的现值)

Type　逻辑值 0 或1，用以指定付款时间在期初还是在期末。如果为 1，付款在期初；如果为 0 或忽略，付款在期末

计算结果 = ¥-6339.73

有关该函数的帮助(H)　确定　取消

得到如下结果：

B4　fx　=PV(B2,B3,B1,0)

	A	B	C	D	E
1	年金	2000			
2	利率	10.00%			
3	期间	4			
4	普通年金现值	¥-6339.73			

2.2.2　先付年金的终值与现值

2.2.2.1　先付年金的终值

先付年金发生在每期期初。

$$F = PMT(1+i) + PMT(1+i)^2 + \cdots + PMT(1+i)^{n-1} + PMT(1+i)^n$$

计算先付年金的终值利用终值函数 FV。

例如，某人准备在今后的 5 年中每年年初等额存入银行 8 000 元钱，如果银行按 4%

的年利率复利计息，那么第 5 年末此人可一次性从银行取出多少钱？

插入 FV 函数，参数设置如下：

函数参数 ? ×

FV

Rate B2 = 0.04

Nper B3 = 5

Pmt -B1 = -8000

Pv 0 = 0

Type 1 = 1

= 45063.8037

基于固定利率和等额分期付款方式，返回某项投资的未来值

Type 数值 0 或 1，指定付款时间是期初还是期末。1 = 期初；0 或忽略 = 期末

计算结果 = ¥45063.80

有关该函数的帮助(H)　确定　取消

此处，FV 函数的参数 PV 省略，Type 为 1，表示是先付年金。

得到如下结果：

B4　=FV(B2,B3,-B1,0,1)

	A	B	C	D	E
1	先付年金	8000			
2	利率	4.00%			
3	期间	5			
4	普通年金终值	¥45063.80			

2.2.2.2　先付年金的现值

先付年金发生在每期期末。

$$PV = PMT_1 + \frac{PMT_2}{(1+r)} + \frac{PMT_3}{(1+r)^2} + \cdots + \frac{PMT_n}{(1+r)^{n-1}}$$

计算先付年金的现值利用现值函数 PV。

例如，某企业准备在今后的 3 年期限内租用一台设备，按租赁合同的约定每年年初需要支付租金 6 000 元，若贴现率为 10%，那么全部租金的现值是多少？

插入 PV 函数，参数设置如下：

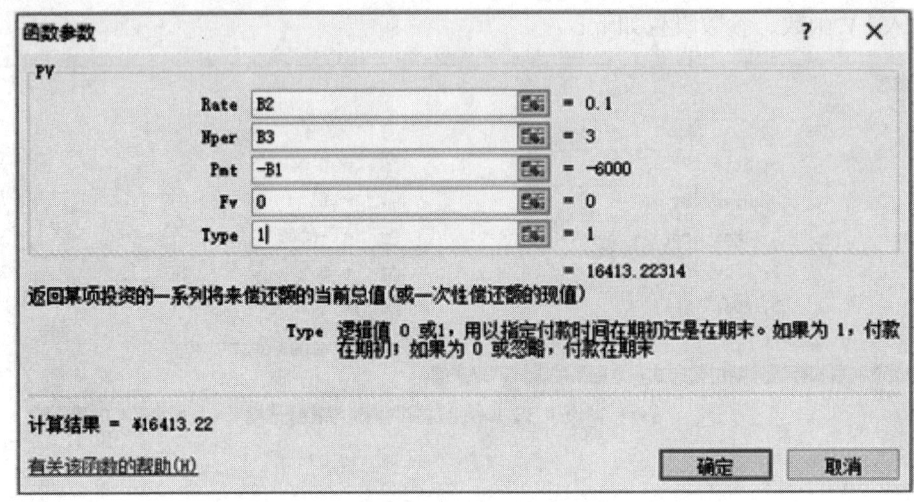

得到如下结果：

B4 =PV(B2,B3,-B1,0,1)

	A	B	C	D	E
1	先付年金	6000			
2	利率	10.00%			
3	期间	3			
4	普通年金现值	¥16413.22			

3. 实际应用举例

【例一】你的朋友在哥伦比亚新开了一个熟食店，邀请你对其进行投资。他承诺，现在借给他 20 000 元，他将在未来 5 年每月还款 400 元。假设你把同样数额的资金投放在银行，你的回报率为 6%。你会不会借钱给他？为什么？

通过资金的时间价值计算出投资熟食店的收益率，与银行的回报率 6% 进行比较。数值越大的方案越好。

ExcelL 算法：利用 RATE 函数。注意 $n = 5 \times 12 = 60$。

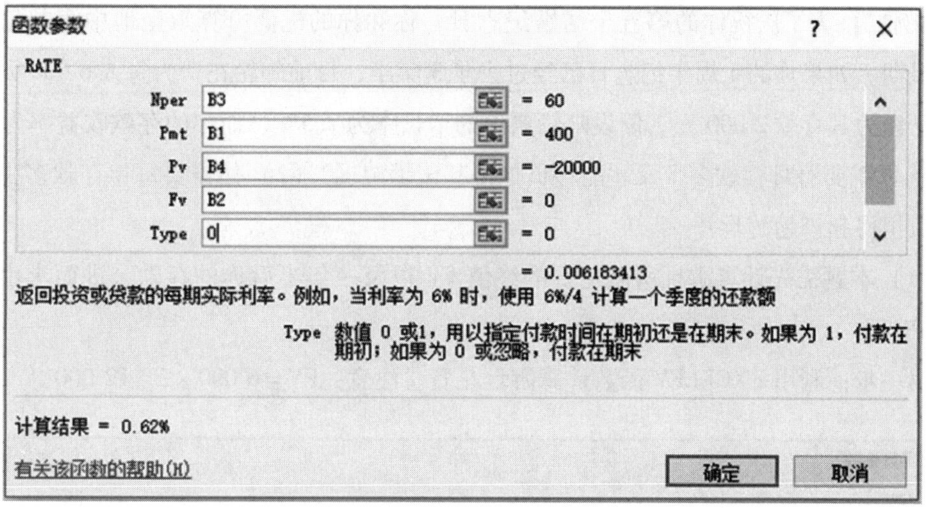

函数参数

RATE

Nper B3 = 60
Pmt B1 = 400
Pv B4 = -20000
Fv B2 = 0
Type 0 = 0

= 0.006183413

返回投资或贷款的每期实际利率。例如，当利率为 6% 时，使用 6%/4 计算一个季度的还款额

Type 数值 0 或1，用以指定付款时间在期初还是在期末。如果为 1，付款在期初；如果为 0 或忽略，付款在期末

计算结果 = 0.62%

有关该函数的帮助(H)　确定　取消

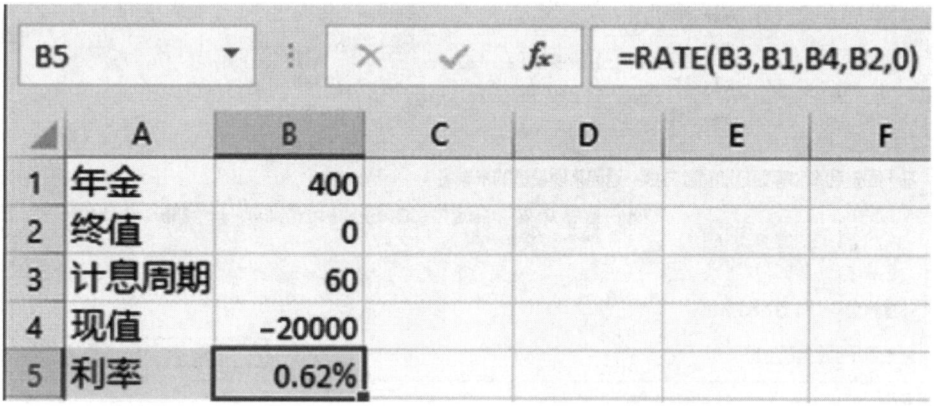

B5　=RATE(B3,B1,B4,B2,0)

	A	B	C	D	E	F
1	年金	400				
2	终值	0				
3	计息周期	60				
4	现值	-20000				
5	利率	0.62%				

金融计算器算法：

按	显示
2ndP/Y ↓ 1 ENTER	设置一年为一个计息周期
2nd ［QUIT］	0.0000
400 PMT	PMT＝400
0 FV	FV＝0
60 N	N＝60
20 000 +/－PV	PV＝－20 000
CPTI/Y	求出 i＝0.62%

因为投资熟食店的收益率为 0.62%×12＝7.42%，大于银行的回报率 6%，所以借

钱给朋友投资熟食店是更好地选择。

【例二】为了庆祝你的第五个结婚纪念日，你和你的配偶打算乘坐地中海邮轮游玩三个星期。如果你的5周年纪念日已经过去了3年半，目前邮轮花费为每人6 000元，并且你已经为其存款2 000元。假设邮轮票价的增长率为7.5%，而你的存款收益率为6%。（1）问你需要每月存款多少元才能够负担得起该趟游玩？（2）你需要每年存款多少元才能够负担得起该趟游玩？

（1）本题需先计算游玩所需花费的终值FV以及一年半后你的存款，进而求出每月存款PMT。

第一步：利用EXCELFV函数计算游玩花费。注意：PV = 6 000 × 2 = 12 000。

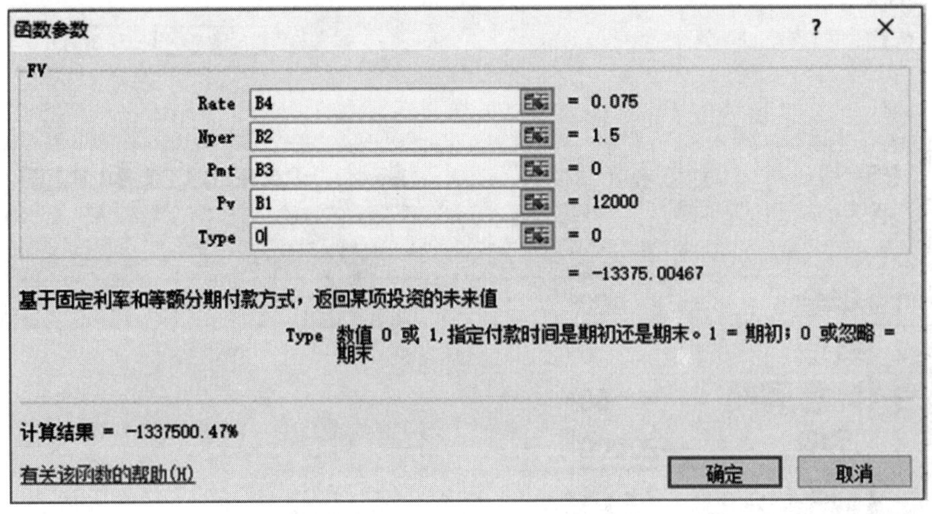

B5 =FV(B4,B2,B3,B1,0)

	A	B	C	D	E
1	现值	12000			
2	计息周期	1.5			
3	年金	0			
4	利率	7.50%			
5	终值	¥-13375.00			

金融计算器算法：

按	显示
[2ndP/Y ↓] 1 [ENTER]	设置一年为一个计息周期
[2nd] ［QUIT］	0.0000
0 [PMT]	PMT = 0
7.5 [I/Y]	i = 7.5%
1.5 [N]	N = 1.5
12 000 [PV]	PV = 12 000
[CPTFV]	求出 FV = 13 375

第二步，计算一年半后你的存款。

EXCEL 算法：利用 FV 函数。

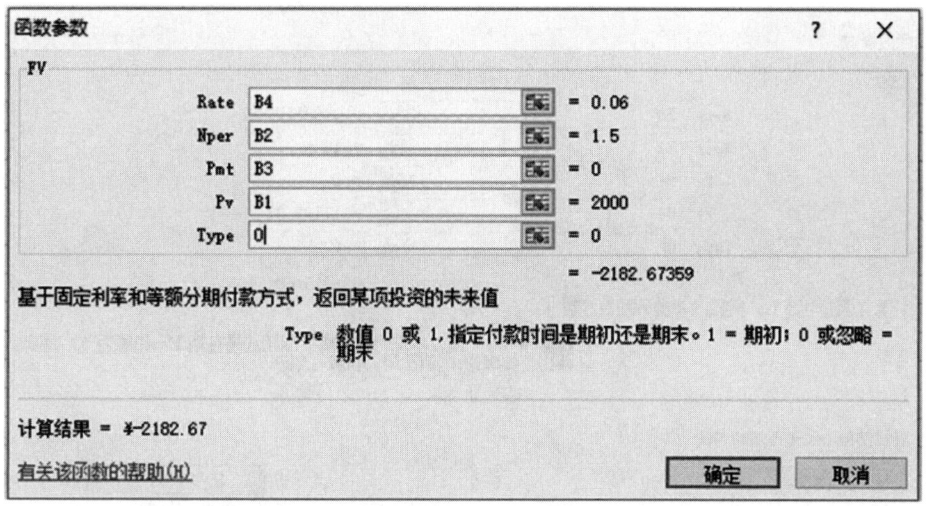

B5　=FV(B4,B2,B3,B1,0)

	A	B	C	D	E
1	现值	2000			
2	计息周期	1.5			
3	年金	0			
4	利率	6.00%			
5	终值	¥-2182.67			

金融计算器算法：

按	显示
2ndP/Y ↓ 1 ENTER	设置一年为一个计息周期
2nd ［QUIT］	0.0000
6 I/Y	i = 6%
0 PMT	PMT = 0
1.5 N	N = 1.5
2 000 PV	PV = 2 000
CPTFV	求出 FV = －2 182.67

求出游玩花费与存款之差：13 375 －2 182.67 = 11 192.33。这个差额是计算每月存款及每年存款时的 FV。注意：i = ［（1 + 0.075）/（1 + 0.06） －1］/12。

EXCEL 算法：利用 PMT 函数计算每年存款额。

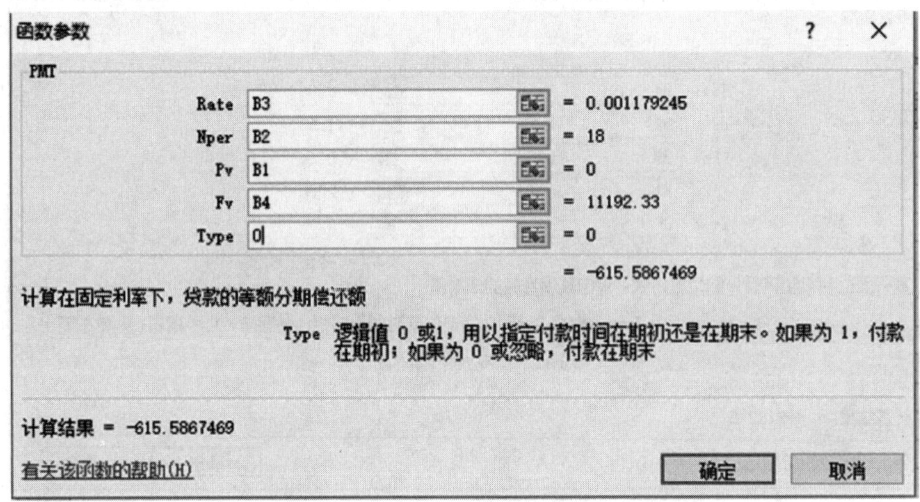

B5 =PMT(B3,B2,B1,B4,0)

	A	B	C	D	E
1	现值	0			
2	计息周期	18			
3	利率	0.12%			
4	终值	11192.33			
5	年金	¥-615.59			

金融计算器算法：

按	显示
2ndP/Y ↓ 1 ENTER	设置一年为一个计息周期
2nd ［QUIT］	0.0000
（（1+0.075）/（1+0.06）-1）/12 I/Y	i=0.12%
11 192.33 FV	FV=11 192.33
1.5×12 N	N=18
0 +/-PV	PV=0
CPTPMT	求出 PMT=-615.59

所以，需要每月存615.59元才能够负担得起该趟游玩。

（2）每年存款。注意：i=（1+0.075）/（1+0.06）-1。

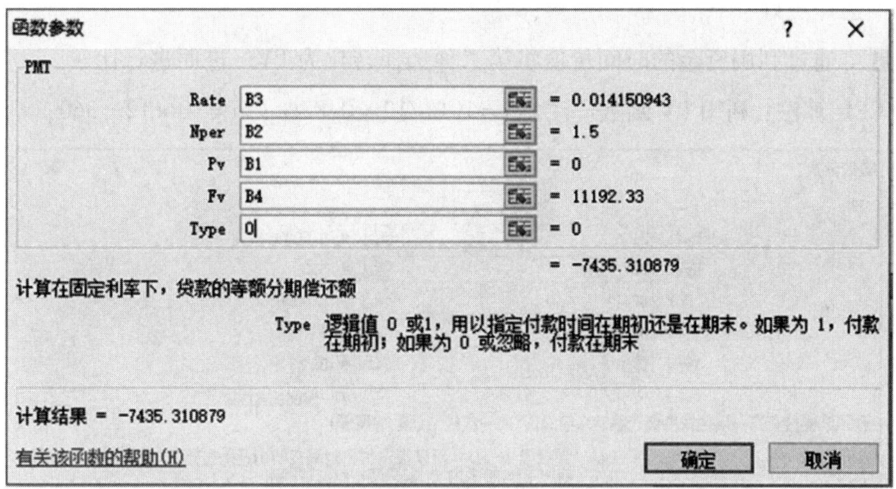

B5　=PMT(B3,B2,B1,B4,0)

	A	B	C	D	E
1	现值	0			
2	计息周期	1.5			
3	利率	1.42%			
4	终值	11192.33			
5	年金	¥-7435.31			

金融计算器算法：

按	显示
2ndP/Y ↓ 1 ENTER	设置一年为一个计息周期
2nd ［QUIT］	0. 0000
（（1 +0. 075）/（1 +0. 06）－1）I/Y	i = 1. 42%
11192. 33 FV	FV = 11 192. 33
1. 5 N	N = 1. 5
0 PV	PV = 0
CPTPMT	求出 PMT = －7 435. 31

【例三】你的叔叔刚刚赢得 3. 5 亿元的福利彩票头奖。现在他有两个选择，一是一次性获得 2. 57 亿元，二是每月获得 220 万元，持续 30 年。如果他能获得每年 10% 的回报率，哪个选择更好?

本题可通过利用资金的时间价值将第二种选择转化为 PV，进而进行比较。

EXCEL 算法：利用 PV 函数。注意 i = 10%/12 = 0. 83%；n = 30 × 12 = 360。

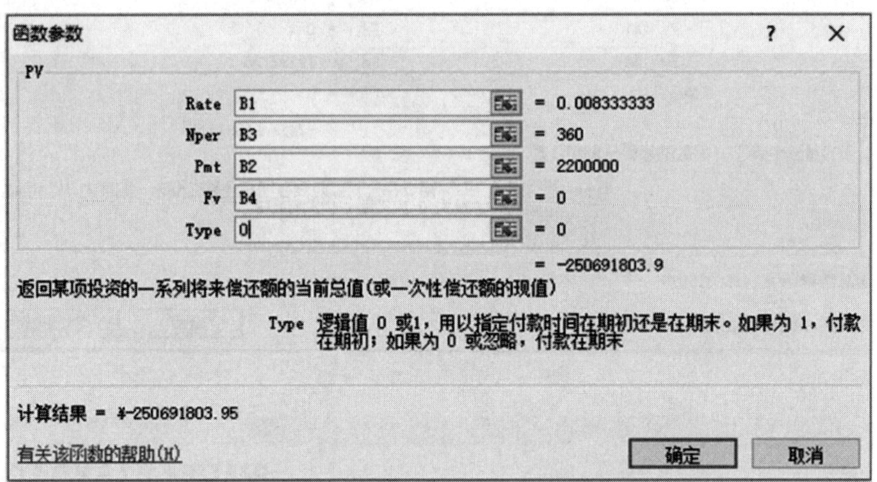

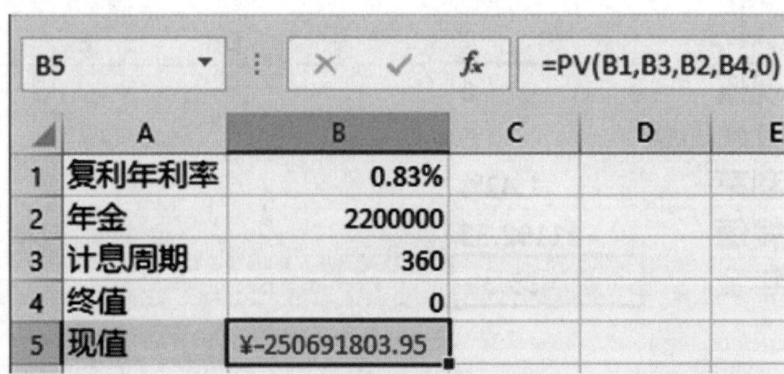
B5 =PV(B1,B3,B2,B4,0)

	A	B	C	D	E
1	复利年利率	0.83%			
2	年金	2200000			
3	计息周期	360			
4	终值	0			
5	现值	¥-250691803.95			

金融计算器算法：

按	显示
2ndP/Y ↓ 1 ENTER	设置一年为一个计息周期
2nd ［QUIT］	0.0000
10/12 =I/Y	i = 10%/12
0 FV	FV = 0
360 N	N = 360
2 200 000 PMT	PMT = 2 200 000
CPTPV	求出 PV = -250 691 803.9

所以，通过比较得出第一种选择，即一次性获得 2.57 亿元的选择更佳。

【例四】王刚借钱在成都郊区买了一套价值为 500 000 元的房子。他计划 5 年后搬走并且卖掉房子。假设他有一个 30 年的贷款，年利率为 7.25%。（1）当他出售房子的时候，还需还贷款多少元？（2）如果房子每年增值 10%，当他出售房子的时候，除了还清贷款，将获利多少元？

（1）当他出售房子的时候，还需还贷款多少元？

本题需先计算每月还款的数额 PMT，进而求出 FV。

第一步，计算年金。注意 i = 7.25%/12 = 0.6%；n = 30 × 12 = 360。

EXCEL 算法：利用 PMT 函数。

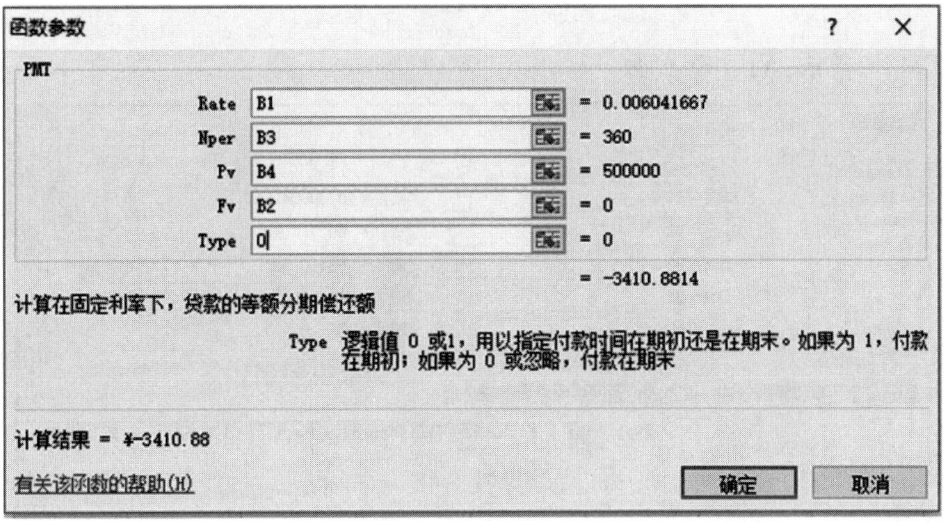

函数参数

PMT

Rate　B1　= 0.006041667

Nper　B3　= 360

Pv　B4　= 500000

Fv　B2　= 0

Type　0　= 0

= -3410.8814

计算在固定利率下，贷款的等额分期偿还额

Type　逻辑值 0 或1，用以指定付款时间在期初还是在期末。如果为 1，付款在期初；如果为 0 或忽略，付款在期末

计算结果 = ¥-3410.88

有关该函数的帮助(H)　　确定　　取消

B5 =PMT(B1,B3,B4,B2,0)

	A	B	C	D	E
1	复利年利率	0.60%			
2	终值	0			
3	计息周期	360			
4	现值	500000			
5	年金	¥-3410.88			

金融计算器算法：

按	显示
[2ndP/Y ↓] 1 [ENTER]	设置一年为一个计息周期
[2nd] [QUIT]	0.0000
7.25/12 [=I/Y]	i = 7.25%/12
0 [FV]	FV = 0
360 [N]	N = 360
500 000 [PV]	PV = 500 000
[CPTPMT]	求出 PMT = −3 410.88

第二步，计算终值，即出售房子后仍需还贷的金额。注意 i = 7.25%/12 = 0.6%；n = 5 × 12 = 60。

EXCEL 算法：利用 FV 函数。

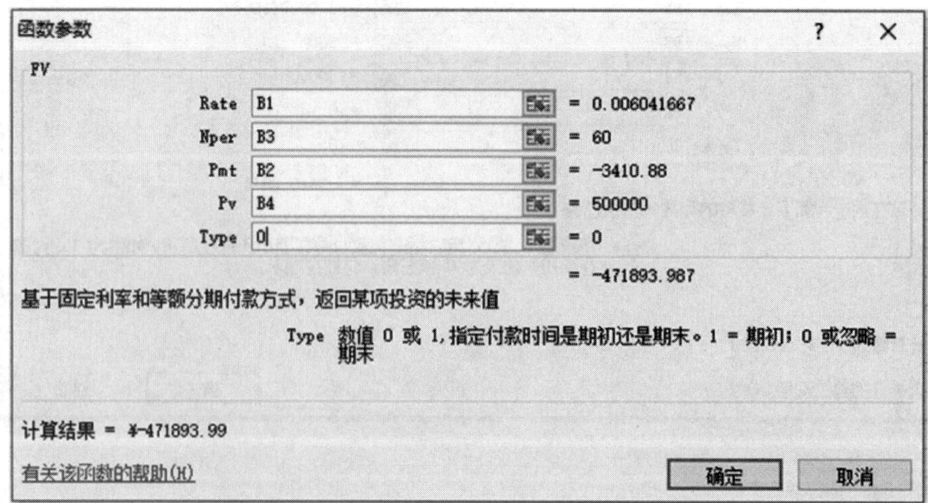

B5　=FV(B1,B3,B2,B4,0)

	A	B	C	D
1	复利年利率	0.60%		
2	年金	-3410.88		
3	计息周期	60		
4	现值	500000		
5	终值	¥-471893.99		

金融计算器算法：

按	显示
2ndP/Y ↓ 1 ENTER	设置一年为一个计息周期
2nd ［QUIT］	0. 0000
7. 25/12 =I/Y	i = 7. 25%/12
3410. 88 +/－ PMT	PMT = －3410. 88
60 N	N = 60
500 000 PV	PV = 500 000
CPTFV	求出 FV = 471 893. 99

所以，当王刚出售房子的时候，还需还贷款 471 893. 99 元。

（2）如果房子每年增值 10%，当他出售房子的时候，除了还清贷款，将获利多少元？EXCEL 算法：利用 FV 函数。

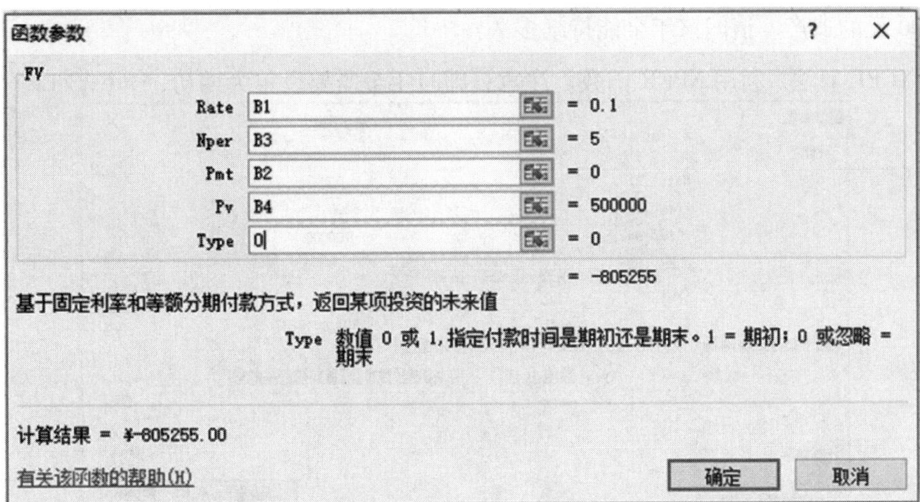

B5 =FV(B1,B3,B2,B4,0)

	A	B	C	D
1	复利年利率	10.00%		
2	年金	0		
3	计息周期	5		
4	现值	500000		
5	终值	¥-805255.00		

金融计算器算法：

按	显示
2ndP/Y ↓ 1 ENTER	设置一年为一个计息周期
2nd ［QUIT］	0.0000
10 I/Y	i = 10%
0 PMT	PMT = 0
5 N	N = 5
500 000 PV	PV = 500 000
CPTFV	求出 FV = －805 255

所以，如果房子每年增值10%，当他出售房子的时候，除了还清贷款，将获利805 255 – 3 410.88 × 5 × 12 – 471 893.99 = 128 708.2 元。

【例五】张琳向你咨询她的退休事宜。60岁的张琳想把700 000元积蓄存为即时年金。如果她的生活费（包括照顾残疾孩子的费用）为每年60 000元，并决定每月收到5 000元年金，请问年金能持续多久？（假设利率为6%）如果张琳想在死后为儿子留下200 000元的遗产，请问该年金能持续多久？

EXCEL算法：利用NPER函数。注意：即时年金需要设定为期初，i = 6%/12。

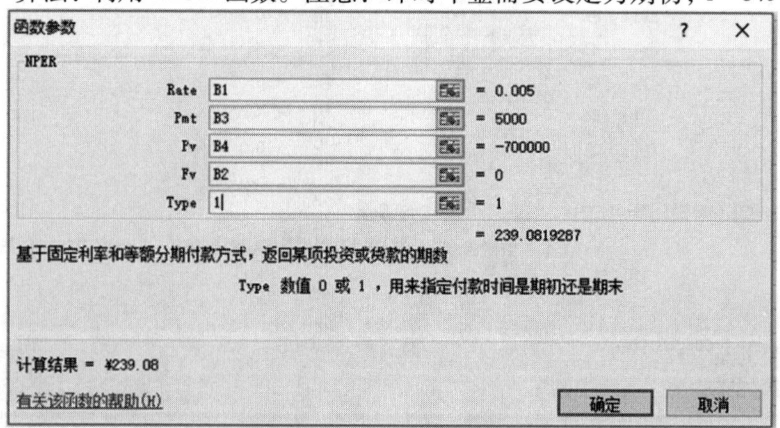

B5　=NPER(B1,B3,B4,B2,1)

	A	B	C	D	E
1	复利年利率	0.50%			
2	终值	0			
3	年金	5000			
4	现值	-700000			
5	计息周期	239.08			

金融计算器算法：

按	显示
2ndP/Y ↓ 1 ENTER	设置一年为一个计息周期
2nd [QUIT]	0.0000
2nd [BGN] 2nd [SET] CE/C	将计算器设置为期初
6/12 =I/Y	i=6%/12
5000 PMT	PMT=5 000
0 FV	FV=0
700 000 +/－PV	PV=－700 000
CPTN	求出 N=239.08

所以，年金持续时间为 239.08/12=20 年。

如果张琳想在死后为儿子留下 200 000 元的遗产：

EXCEL 算法：利用 NPER 函数。注意：即时年金需要设定为期初，i=6%/12。

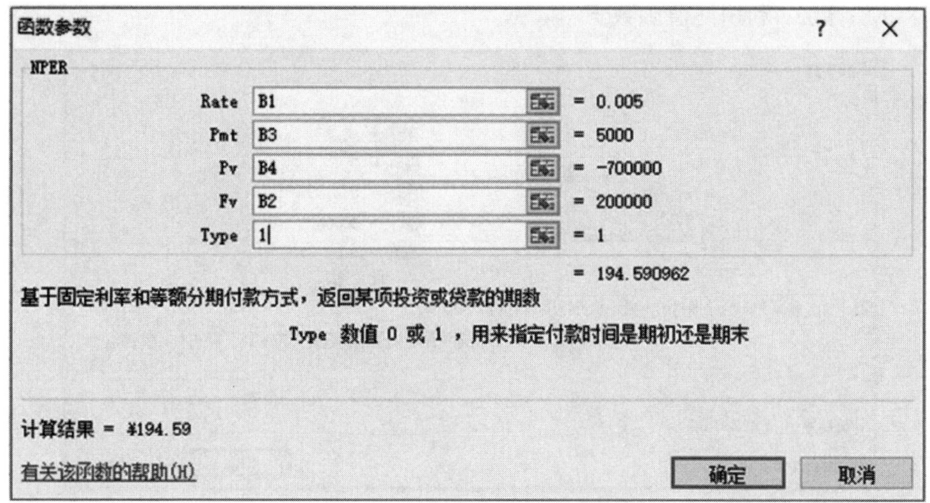

B5　=NPER(B1,B3,B4,B2,1)

	A	B	C	D	E
1	复利年利率	0.50%			
2	终值	200000			
3	年金	5000			
4	现值	-700000			
5	计息周期	194.59			

金融计算器算法：

按	显示
2ndP/Y ↓ 1 ENTER	设置一年为一个计息周期
2nd [QUIT]	0. 0000
2nd [BGN] 2nd [SET] CE/C	将计算器设置为期初
6/12 =I/Y	i=6%/12
5 000 PMT	PMT=5 000
200 000 FV	FV=200 000
700 000 +/-PV	PV= -700 000
CPTN	求出 N=194. 59

所以，如果张琳想在死后为儿子留下 200 000 元的遗产，则年金持续时间为 194. 59/12=16 年。

【例六】李强花费 30 000 元购买了一辆奇瑞 QQ。如果该车每年贬值 20%，请问三年后该车的价值为多少？5 年后该车的价值为多少？（提示：贬值意味着利率为负）

三年后：

EXCEL 算法：利用终值函数 FV。

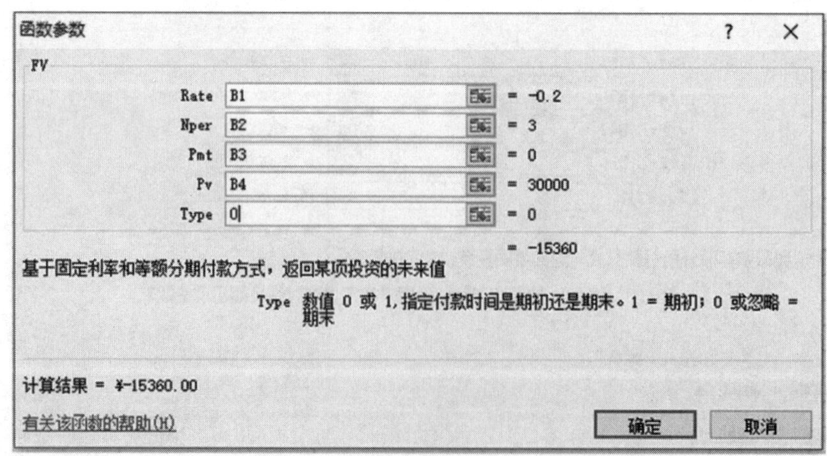

B5 =FV(B1,B2,B3,B4)

	A	B	C	D
1	复利年利率	-20.00%		
2	计息周期	3		
3	年金	0		
4	现值	30000		
5	终值	¥-15360.00		

金融计算器算法：

按	显示
2ndP/Y ↓ 1 ENTER	设置一年为一个计息周期
2nd ［QUIT］	0.0000
20 +/－I/Y	i = －20%
0 PMT	PMT = 0
3 N	N = 3
30 000 PV	PV = 30 000
CPTFV	求出 FV = －15 360

同样利用终值函数 FV 计算五年后汽车的价值，如下图所示：

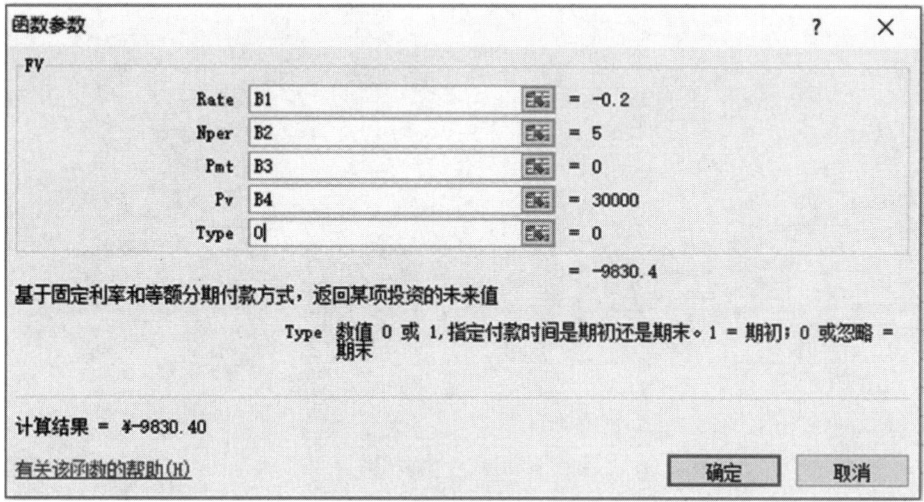

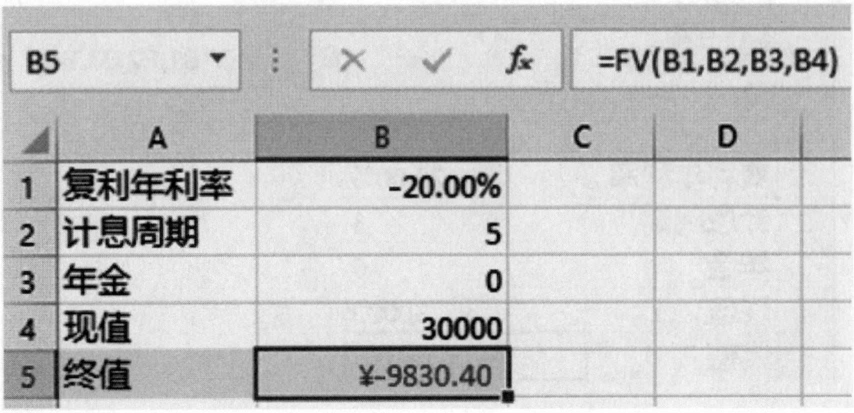

B5 =FV(B1,B2,B3,B4)

	A	B	C	D
1	复利年利率	-20.00%		
2	计息周期	5		
3	年金	0		
4	现值	30000		
5	终值	¥-9830.40		

金融计算器算法：

按	显示
[2ndP/Y ↓] 1 [ENTER]	设置一年为一个计息周期
[2nd] ［QUIT］	0.0000
20 [+/－I/Y]	i = －20%
0 [PMT]	PMT = 0
5 [N]	N = 5
30 000 [PV]	PV = 30 000
[CPTFV]	求出 FV = －9 830.4

Financial Planning：An International Perspective

Chapter 1 Financial Planning: A Definitional and Historical Review

The purpose of this book is to introduce the theory, process, and evolution of financial planning for those unfamiliar with this emerging profession. Given this objective, it is important to start with a useful definition of financial planning. At first glance, this may seem like a simple exercise. Upon further evaluation, however, it turns out that there are many different definitions floating around among practitioners, academicians, and media. Financial planning can mean different things to different people.

Although financial planning has been defined many ways over the past 40 years, today the phrase is generally meant to describe the "process of determining whether and how an individual can meet life goals through the proper management of financial resources." This framework for the profession was first proposed by the Certified Financial Planner Board of Standards, Inc. (CFP? Board) and has since become the core definition used by nearly all practicing financial planners working in the United States. What makes this definition unique is the focus on the application of a process when working with clients. CFP Board defines the process of financial planning as follows:

1. Establishing and defining a relationship with a client;
2. Gathering appropriate client data;
3. Analyzing and evaluating client data and measuring the client's financial status;
4. Developing and presenting recommendations and alternatives appropriate for the client's situation;
5. Implementing recommendations; and
6. Monitoring recommendations on an ongoing basis.

Technically, a written financial plan or document is the product or outcome associated with the financial planning process. Some financial planners write a comprehensive plan, while others write what have been called a targeted or modular financial plan. In order to appreciate the difference it is important to understand what core services financial planners provide when working with clients.

Types of Plans

The best and easiest way to understand what is meant by comprehensive financial planning is to identify the areas of expertise a planner brings to the table when working with a client. Generally, financial planners help clients address questions, concerns, problems, and opportunities associated with the following topic areas:

- Cash Flow and Net Worth Planning
- Tax Planning
- Insurance Planning, including Life, Disability, Property and Casualty, Long - Term Care, and Special Needs Insurance
- Retirement Planning
- Investment Planning
- Education Planning
- Special Situation Planning
- Estate Planning

By definition, a comprehensive financial plan should include a section or chapter devoted to each one of these topic areas.① A targeted or modular financial plan, on the other hand, would include only those topics of special interest to a client. For example, a client may only be interested in receiving help for a retirement question. The client may not have an interest or need, for instance, in an estate planning review (e. g., analysis of wills, trusts, and estate tax liabilities). If this were the case, a planner would deliver a targeted financial plan to the

① Lytton, Grable, and Klock (2013) defined comprehensive financial planning as: "The Process of helping clients achieve multiple financial goals and objectives through the application and integration of synergistic personal finance strategies" (p. 13).

client. However, in both the comprehensive and targeted/modular financial plan situations, the financial planner would be expected to follow the six-step planning process. Among financial planners working in the United States today, less than 50% write comprehensive financial plans, but among those who do deliver comprehensive financial plans demand for services is high.[①]

History of Financial Planning in North America, Europe, and Asia

Financial planning, as a term used to describe the use of a systematic process to assist clients reach financial goals and objectives, has become part of the modern business lexicon. What is most interesting to those who are just learning about financial planning theory and concepts is how new financial planning, as a professional activity, really is. Financial planning is among the youngest professions in the world today.[②]

While it is possible to now study financial planning at some of the leading academic institutions in the United States, this is a relatively new phenomenon. Consider that less than 10 universities worldwide offer a doctoral degree in financial planning. Over 100 undergraduate degree programs exist, but the opportunity for more programs to be created is immense. It is important to note that none of these academic degrees existed prior to 1980.[③] The demand for training in financial planning is something that gained momentum in the mid- to late-1980s when American consumers began to demand more complex, sophisticated, and proven products and services to meet their short-, intermediate-, and long-term financial goals. Prior to this time, the primary "financial planning" products sold in the United States were life insurance and annuities.

The life insurance industry played a very significant role in creating the modern financial

---

① College for Financial Planning, 2011.

② Profession is defined in this book as an activity that requires specialized training and where practitioners belong to a professional association, follow a universally recognized code of ethics, and undergo continuing education and training from distinguished institutions (see Magali, 1978).

③ Some Ph. D. programs were transformed from fields such as resource management and consumer economics.

planning profession. Until the 1960s, life insurance was the primary long – term savings vehicle used by most American families. Unlike today, very few individuals or families invested in stocks, bonds, or commodities. The reason for an insurance preference is relatively simple. In 1900, for example, the average life expectancy was 49 years of age.① The primary concern among households was less about saving for retirement and more about protecting income stability in the case of death. Life insurance was, and still is in many respects, the optimal product to help meet an income replacement need. Additionally, life insurance could be purchased with relatively little money, whereas investment products, such as stocks and bonds, often required a greater initial asset commitment.

One product stands out as the financial tool of choice by American families for most of the 20th century: whole life cash value insurance. Whole life insurance has traditionally been sold using two arguments. First, the product provided a tax – free lump sum benefit in the case of a breadwinner's untimely death. Second, insurance served as a retirement plan. To put the value of this second point in context, it is important to note that few Americans living in the period 1900 through 1940 were covered by any type of retirement plan. Social Security was not implemented until the 1930s, and even then, benefits were meager. Death benefits provided by life insurance products acted as a source of assets and income for many Americans.

The insurance industry was quite robust and growing quickly through much on the 20th century. Life insurance fit well with the American manufacturing and product distribution model of the time. The life insurance business model was based on mass marketing, streamlining underwriting decisions, and maximizing scales of economy. Whole life insurance was seen as a product that appealed to the mass market. The product was also reasonably priced, and the market valued the financial strength of insurance companies. Nearly all life insurance companies competed for business from an affordability and customer service vantage point. The motto of the pre – 1960s era was, 'If you offer whole life policies consumers will buy whole life policies.'

The marketplace for financial advice started to change in the early 1960s. By this point in history, the life insurance marketplace was nearly saturated, with shrinking opportunities for market share growth. This ushered in a change from a manufacturing and product distribution

---

① Society of Actuaries, 2005.

approach to one based on position marketing and company differentiation. While in earlier times one whole life insurance policy issued by a company might look similar to a policy issued by another firm, companies soon realized that consumers' attitudes, tastes, and expectations were changing. In effect, the marketplace was beginning to force some insurance firms, brokers, and agents to rethink their delivery of financial advice.

Whereas life insurance companies did relatively little to change their core products during the golden years of market growth, the landscape changed dramatically between 1960 and 1970. Firms attempted to counter flattening sales by increasing their hiring of insurance salespeople. Product delivery and sales approaches ranged from those based on seminars to door - to - door sales of insurance contracts. By 1970, nearly every town of any size had at least one life insurance office in operation. During this period, the insurance industry, in conjunction with regulators, standardized underwriting requirements, created more complex pricing structures based on improved mortality statistics, and agreed to uniformrisk classifications. All seemed to be going well. However, externally, the industry was being shaken by both cultural and economic changes.

Just as the life insurance industry was reaching a high level of whole life insurance market penetration two changes were occurring in American society that would forever alter the life insurance industry, and ultimately create what is known as financial planning as the profession. To begin with, the consumer movement was beginning to take shape. Consumer advocates, such as Ralph Nader, were leading consumer revolutions against high priced, low quality products and services. Issues related to product and commission disclosures became highly debated topics. Almost overnight, insurance companies were targeted as being engaged in deceiving consumers and profiting unduly from choice limitations. At the same time, the United States equities markets, both stock and real estate, were surging. Consumer income and wealth was increasing at historical rates.

The collision of consumer advocacy, increasing wealth, and market penetration left insurance companies scrambling to meet market challenges. It is with this background that a group of life insurance salespersons and a financial reporter met in Chicago. The year was 1969. Essentially, a small group of highly successful life insurance agents and company executives (13 people attended the meeting) met to talk about ways to provide a wider variety of services and products to consumers. This group was convinced that a one – size fits all products, such as whole life insurance and fixed annuities, was not the sole answer to meeting the needs of consumers. These industry leaders envisioned a point in time when a client would meet with an adviser to address a wide variety of financial issues that would then result in recommendations that included both products and advice. In other words, they hoped to see insurance salespeople transition into financial planners.

Life insurance companies did *not* immediately endorse the concept of financial planning. Some would argue that most life insurance firms today, who operate primarily in the North American market, still have not fully embraced financial planning. This did not deter those who met in Chicago. They went on, without great fanfare or corporate support, to create the International Association of Financial Planners (later changed to the International Association of Financial Planning (IAFP)) and the International College for Financial Counseling (later changed to the College for Financial Planning). Today the IAFP exists as the Financial Planning Association in the United States. The College for Financial Planning is also in existence and boasts the highest number of graduates who have completed Certified Financial Planner (CFP®) certification training.

In 1973, the College for Financial Planning graduated its first group of students who became the first 42 CFP certificants. Although the life insurance industry, in general, never claimed financial planning as its own, the growth of financial planning as an emerging profession was very quick and, in some ways, quite remarkable. In the early years, there were many skeptics of financial planning. Some viewed the IAFP, the College, and the CFP certification as mere gimmickry intended to hide the sale of insurance behind complex financial plans. The insurance industry was likewise reluctant to change their sales approach to include topics that were not typically "insurance" by nature. For example, insurance executives often would discourage a new planner from dealing with a client's tax or investment situation because they viewed this time better spent selling additional life insurance and annuity policies.

In many ways, those who adopted financial planning as their chosen profession were mavericks of their time. They faced consumer skepticism and industry backlash. Some new planners fell by the wayside, but others thrived. Consumers, it turned out, were hungry for advice and guidance that did not always involve the sale of an insurance product. The demand for financial advice that was based on proven strategic approaches was increasing. This demand was being driven by changing consumer preferences and a perception among consumers that planning for the future is not only prudent but necessary.

There was enough interest among practitioners and prospective financial planners in increasing ethical standards and implementing practice standards that by 1985 that the College for Financial Planning, which had previously taught courses and issued the CFP certification, was split into two entities. The College remained as a teaching organization and a new entity was created: the Certified Financial Planner Board of Standards, Inc. (CFP Board). The new CFP Board was formed to administer the CFP exam and to ensure that financial planners were competent, well trained, ethical, and working in the consumer interest. In 1987 the first college and university academic, for - credit, programs were introduced. In less than 50 years the number of Certified Financial Planners has grown from 42 to 76,724 as of March 2017 in the United States alone, with more than 150 academic - based programs throughout the United States.

Multiple Designations

It is important to note that in the United States, and worldwide, there are literally hundreds of certifications and designations that have been developed to help differentiate advisers in the marketplace. For example, the American College owns the Chartered Financial Consultant (ChFC ®) and Chartered Life Underwriter (CLU ®) marks. For many years, these certifications rivaled the CFP mark among financial advisers. There are also many specialized designations, such as the Accredited Asset Management Specialist, Certified Retirement Counselor, and Registered Financial Consultant that are valued by some practitioners and consumers. In addition, many associations have been created to support the efforts of financial planners. In the United States, the Financial Planning Association provides a professional home for many advisers. The Association of Professional Financial Advisers plays a similar role in the United Kingdom. Nearly every country in which financial planning has a presence has an association that promotes the work of financial planning.

International Trends

The growth of financial planning worldwide has mirrored that of the United States. The primary difference is that the concept of financial planning was introduced to international audiences a decade after the profession began to crystalize in the United States. An important milestone for the profession occurred in 2004 when the Financial Planning Standards Board Ltd. (FPSB) was established. The FPSB was created to manage, develop, and operate certification, education, and related academic efforts to promote financial planning outside of the United States. FPSB owns the CFP Marks outside the United States and establishes international competency, ethics, and professional practice standards for the financial planning profession. A primary function of FPSB involves administering the CFP certification program by entering into licensing and affiliation agreements with specific country members.

As of 2012, there were nearly 148,000 CFP practitioners working worldwide. While the majority of planners reside in the United States (67,000 + certificants), the highest growth rate for those practicing financial planning has occurred outside North America. Table 1 shows the total distribution of CFP professionals worldwide.

Table 1 Distribution of CFP Professionals (Listed By Size)

Country/Region	Number of Certified Professionals
Japan	18 548
Canada	17 368
China	13 850
Australia	5 437
Hong Kong	4 700
South Africa	4 335
South Korea	3 639
Malaysia	2 657
India	1 738
France	1 504
Germany	1 349
United Kingdom	965
Singapore	908
Brazil	907
Indonesia	831
Chinese Taipei	590
New Zealand	372
Austria	291
Switzerland	237
Ireland	148
The Netherlands	123
Thailand	84

Source: FPSB (http://www.fpsb.org/about/64.html).

Current State of the Financial Planning Profession

Financial planning, as currently conceptualized and practiced throughout the world, is comprised of a few very large firms and many small companies and individuals who provide financial advice, counsel, and management services to individuals, households, and other firms. ① Primary sources of income for financial planning firms include plan writing fees, money management fees, and product (e. g. , insurance and securities) commissions. It is important to note the following in relation to financial planning:

- While financial planners interact with portfolio managers—individuals and firms who actively manage assets in the form of mutual funds, variable annuities, hedge funds, exchange traded funds, and similar products—financial planners are not portfolio managers;
- Financial planners are not mutual funds, brokerages, hedge funds, or other entities that operate in the financial service marketplace; and
- The way in which financial planners are paid varies by firm and nation.

Although overly simplified, one way to differentiate a financial planner from, say, a portfolio manager is to think of the level of interaction each professional has with clients. Financial planners work directly with clients (e. g. , individuals and households) in clarifying financial goals, setting reasonable planning assumptions and time horizons, measuring risk tolerance and risk capacity, ② and developing plans that, when implemented, help improve the financial well - being of clients. Financial planners analyze, select, and recommend investment products, such as mutual funds, as implementation tools. In effect, financial planners play the role of selecting which portfolio manager to hire within a client's plan. Financial planning involves money management, whereas portfolio management entails the buying and selling of individual securities. ③

It is helpful to also note that some financial service professionals may be financial planners,

① Schmidt, 2012.

② Risk tolerance is defined as a person's willingness to take financial risk, whereas risk capacity refers to a client's ability to withstand financial losses.

③ It is possible for a financial planner to also act as a client's portfolio manager, but in practice, this is rarely done.

but not all financial services practitioners are financial planners. Consider the case of a life insurance salesperson. If the salesperson follows the financial planning process, as described above and specifically engages in comprehensive data gathering and analysis and provides a sufficient breadth and depth of recommendations and alternatives, he or she may rightfully say that they are "doing financial planning." If, on the other hand, the salesperson recommends an insurance product as the solution to nearly every possible financial situation the person is not acting as a financial planner. Similarly, stockbrokers are not generally considered to be financial planners. In the United States, brokers—those who buy and sell securities for clients—rarely provide advice and guidance using the six-step financial planning process. Additionally, brokers seldom deliver advice on topics and issues not directly related to investment planning.

Market Size

The current state of financial planning from a worldwide data perspective is difficult to assess. It is possible, however, to get a glimpse of the size and scope of the profession by evaluating the U. S. marketplace. In 2012-2013, American financial planners reported gross revenues of over $US50 billion. Profits during this period exceeded $US8 billion, for a gross profit margin in excess of 16%. Given the nature of the business, wages made up the largest expense incurred by planners ($US24 billion).①

Currently, there are approximately 136,000 financial planning firms operating in the United States. This figure is somewhat misleading however. Four firms control over 45% of the current market. The largest provider of financial advice and guidance is Morgan Stanley Smith Barney LLC. The three other largest firms include Wells Fargo & Company, Bank of America Corporation,② and Amerprise Financial Incorporated. Some find it confusing that these large firms are classified as financial planning enterprises rather than broker-dealers (i. e., brokerage firms). While it is true that financial advisers who work for these firms do transact buy

① All data reported in this section were gleaned from U. S. Department of Labor and IBISWorld. com publications (see Schmidt, 2012).

② Bank of America's role in the financial planning profession comes from its ownership of Merrill Lynch & Company, which employs nearly 17,000 financial advisers.

and sell orders for clients, they also follow the financial planning process and provide clients with a written financial plan (typically a targeted/modular plan). Firms such as Wells Fargo and Amerprise Financial actively encourage their advising staff to sit for the national CFP certification examination. Outside of the ultra large firms, financial planning is conducted in relatively small companies. The majority of firms operating in the United States employee five or fewer employees. A large percentage of firms are owned and operated by a single person.

Given the small number of planning firms and advisers relative to the population of the United States (i. e., approximately 2,200 people for each planning firm), firms face limited competition. In fact, according to one study, an untapped market for financial advice exists in the U. S. marketplace.① Limited competition in most markets means that firms can focus their marketing and sales efforts towards attracting high net worth (HNW) clientele. HNW clients are those who meet one of the following definitions:

- $ US750 000 in assets under management,
- $ US1 500 000 in net worth,② or
- $ US1 000 000 in investable financial assets.

Stated another way, few financial planning firms provide services to what could be called the middle market. Fewer than one quarter of households with incomes of $ US50,000 work with a financial planner. One reason this percentage figure is so low is because few firms are accessible to those with a modest incomes and/or limited investable assets. Typically, financial planning firms impose minimum qualifications on clients. For example, it is common for smaller firms to require a minimum of $ US500,000 or more in investable assets in order become a client. Another reason firms prefer to work with HNW clients is because the profit margins associated with activities is much higher. The amount of work necessary to help someone with $ 1,000,000 in assets is nearly the same as assisting someone with $ 100,000 in assets. Given the way financial planners are compensated in the United States, it almost always makes more sense to spend time with HNW clients.

---

① Schmidt, 2012.

② Net Worth = Total Assets less Total Liabilities.

Compensation Issues

The issue of compensation is quite contentious. Within the U. S. marketplace, financial planners tend to be compensated either via commission or by way of a set fee. ① The oldest and most widely used compensation form is a commission. Nearly all life insurance and investment products charge buyers (and sometimes sellers) a commission that is based on the sales price of the product. For example, some mutual funds sold by commission – based financial planners charge up to 8.25% of the initial purchase price as a commission (load). Some advisers also receive trailing commission, which are payments made to the adviser after the initial product sale. Trailing commission can last as long as the client owns the investment or insurance product.

Fees, as the name implies, are another way financial planners are paid. The most common fee arrangement is based on assets under management (AUM). Nearly all financial planners provide money management services, in addition to providing advice on non – investment related topics. When a fee is charged based on AUM, the client will incur a bill equal to between 0.50% and 2.50% of the assets being managed. Typically, the larger the assets under management, the lower than annual fee. Someone who has $ US1,000,000 under management would typically pay about 1.0% annually for planning and money management services ($ US10,000 per year).

Whereas 20 years ago commissions were the predominant form of compensation, today fees or some type of fee arrangement make up the bulk of payments to financial planners. Some financial planners, for example, use a fee – based system as a form of compensation. Under this arrangement, a flat fee is charged for the preparation of a financial plan and commissions are charged for products used to implement recommendations. A fee – offset system allows a client to either pay a relatively large planning fee or to waive the fee and use commissions from the sale of products to "offset" the initial planning fee. Fee – only financial planners, by law, may not take any form of commission. These planners, who are not in the majority, often charge for preparing and delivering a financial plan. Fee – only advisers sometimes also charge by the hour. In

---

① The situation is similar in Canada. By law, Canadian financial planners may be compensated as follows: (a) from front – end sales commissions (loads), (b) deferred sales charges (loads), (c) ongoing trailing commissions, (d) fees, (e) a percent of AUM, or (f) salary.

2012 – 2013, the typical rate was about $ US200 per hour. Among fee – only financial planners, however, AUM fees make up the primary source of ongoing annual income.①

The regulatory environment for financial planners, within the United States, is quite complicated. While this topic will be discussed in more detail in a later chapter, some regulatory familiarity is necessary to fully understand the state of financial planning today. In general, anyone who provides financial planning services and is paid any type of commission must be licensed to sell products. If the products being offered are securities (e. g., stocks, bonds, mutual funds), the adviser must hold a Series 7 and Series 63 license issued by the Financial Industry Regulatory Authority (FINRA), which is a self – regulatory body. Those who sell insurance and earn a commission must be licensed in the states in which they do business. Anyone who is paid a fee for services generally must be registered with the Securities and Exchange Commission or the State Securities Commissioner in the states in which they provide services. The SEC will require these advisers to hold a Series 65 or 66 Registered Investment Adviser Law license, which is overseen by FINRA. If this is not complicated enough, only those financial planners who manage more than $ US100 million for a fee are required to register as an Investment Adviser with the Securities and Exchange Commission. All others must register at the state level. It is possible, and actually likely, that many financial planners will be dually registered. That is, they hold a Series 7 license which allows them to sell securities and they are registered as an Investment Adviser, which allows them to charge a fee for services.

Although the United States may have originated the process and application of financial planning, other countries have moved well beyond the United States in terms of providing compensation clarity for consumers. Consider the case of Australia. According to the Australian Securities and Investments Commission, financial planners working in Australia may use one of three methods of compensation: (1) commissions on products sold to clients, (2) a percent of AUM, or (3) by the hour. Within the United Kingdom, compensation has been simplified to an even greater extent. Commissions earned on products sold are no longer allowed. Instead, financial advisers may either charge an hourly fee or a single sum that would cover the costs of all

① Advisers who work for firms such as Merrill Lynch & Company were once paid primarily via commission. Today, advisers at large national financial planning firms receive a high percent of their income in the form of fees from wrap accounts. A wrap account is similar to a fee – only AUM arrangement; however, a wrap account typically charges a slightly higher annual fee and may include other services and products beside money management advice.

planning and implementation.

Prospects for Financial Planning

It may not seem obvious, but the prospects for financial planning moving forward are tremendous. Across the world countries are faced with aging populations. This is particularly true in Europe, but also in many Asian countries as well. While this trend does not bode well for the financial capacity of some nations, aging populations create demand for financial planning professionals. Typically, older consumers control the greatest portion of a country's wealth. The downside associated with aging, however, is that aging is associated with increasing expenses associated with health care and living. How older consumers allocate their resources to conserve assets is one primary reason driving the growth of financial planning globally.

Growing worldwide prosperity is another factor that is having a positive influence on the growth of financial planning. The growth of HNW individuals and families across the globe means that the demand for financial planning services should increase dramatically in the future. Much of this demand will occur outside of Europe and the United States. Additionally, firms that cater to the needs of women will find a disproportionate opportunity for growth.

While the prospects facing financial planning, as a professional endeavor, are certainly positive, the profession faces distinct threats. As discussed above, it is likely that the way in which advisers are compensated will follow the British and Australian models. If this prediction holds true, profit margins for the largest firms may be squeezed initially. This is likely because consumers in most localities worldwide who purchase products do not pay a fee for service, nor do they understand the total cost of planning services. Most commissions are incorporated into the cost of products. Once the commission structure is removed, consumers will be forced to pay for services. Although the net cost may be similar, it will take time to socialize consumers so that they are willing to pay fees rather than commissions. Additionally, the financial planning profession can expect additional regulation in the future. *The Dodd – Frank Wall Street Reform and Consumer Protection Act of* 2010 was enacted in the United States to help protect consumers against fraudulent, misleading, and dishonest dealings in the financial marketplace. Although much of the regulatory reform has been, and will continue to be, directed at the largest firms in the financial services fields, increased regulatory burdens may hamper the growth prospects for small to medium sized financial planning firms.

What is Driving Consumer Interest?

Worldwide financial planning services① generate nearly \$ 1 trillion in gross revenues. ② IBISWorld has projected that annual growth of financial planning will increase by over 4 percent well into the next decade. There are six key demand factors that are driving the growth of financial planning throughout the world: (1) increasing discretionary income and wealth, (2) aging populations, (3) relatively high savings rates, (4) investor uncertainty, (5) corporate needs, and (6) gender demographics. Each of these factors is discussed in more detail below.

Increasing Discretionary Income and Wealth

Financial planning is a service that requires consumers to have enough discretionary cash

---

① As broadly defined in this book, financial planning refers to:

"The process of determining whether and how an individual can meet life goals through the proper management of financial resources. Financial planning integrates the financial planning process with the financial planning subject areas."

There are six steps to the financial planning process:

1. Establishing and defining the client – planner relationship
2. Gathering client data including goals
3. Analyzing and evaluating the client's current financial status
4. Developing and presenting recommendations and/or alternatives
5. Implementing the recommendations
6. Monitoring the recommendations

"Financial planning subject areas" denotes the basic subject fields covered in the financial planning process which typically include, but are not limited to:

- Financial statement preparation and analysis (including cash flow analysis/planning and budgeting)
- Insurance planning and risk management
- Employee benefits planning
- Investment planning
- Income tax planning
- Retirement planning
- Estate planning

See more at: http://www.cfp.net/for – cfp – professionals/professional – standards – enforcement/compliance – resources/frequently – asked – questions/financial – planning#sthash.5oPzc5Dj.dpuf

② Schmidt, D. (2012, March). *IBISWorld Industry Report* 52393: *Financial Planning and Advice in the US*. Los Angeles: IBISWorld.

flow① to both implement recommendations and to pay consulting fees. This is one reason the majority of financial planners, and the firms that employ them, tend to focus marketing and service efforts on high net worth (HNW) individuals and households. As shown in Figure 1, HNW households comprise approximately 10% of the general population. According to the U. S. Securities and Exchange Commission, someone is considered HNW is they have at least U. S. $ 750,000 in investable assets or at least U. S. $ 1.5 million in net worth. ② Some sources define HNW as anyone or household with at least U. S. $ 1 million in financial assets (excluding personal property and real estate). ③

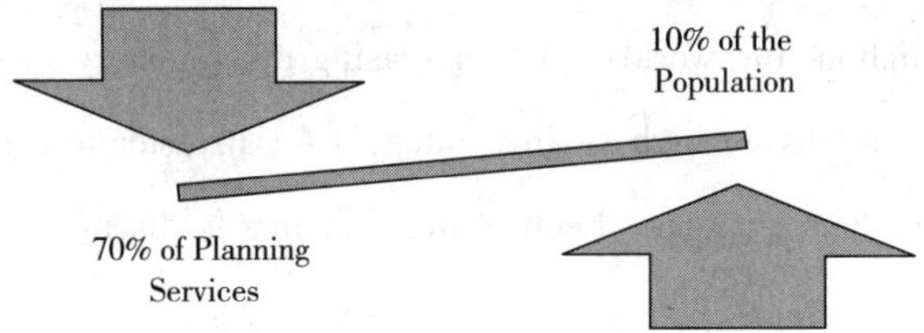

Globally, HNW households hold nearly U. S. $ 45 trillion in assets. A Capgemini and Merrill Lynch Global Wealth Management report noted that worldwide there are approximately 11 million HNW households. ④ North America has the highest number of HNW households. Asia is second with over 3 million falling into this category. HNW Europeans hold approximately U. S. $ 10 trillion in wealth. HNW individuals and families living in Latin America, China, and India are gaining in importance, although those living in the United States, Japan, and Germany comprise over 50% of all HNW households.

These statistics mask a growing phenomenon which will shape the demand for financial planning in the future. The number of HNW individuals is growing by approximately 10 percent annually throughout Asia. Outside of the Middle East, Asia – Pacific countries have seen the highest growth in net wealth. The following locations have seen the greatest growth in both the number of HNW individuals and the amount of investable assets held by these individuals: (1) Hong Kong, (2) Vietnam, (3) Sri Lanka, (4) Indonesia, (5) Singapore, and (6) India. Australia has quietly moved up in terms of the number of HNW households as well. This means,

---

① Discretionary cash flow is defined as gross household earnings less all fixed and variable expenses.

② Net worth = Assets – Liabilities.

③ See Schmidt, D. (2012).

④ Capgemini and Merrill Lynch Wealth Management (2011).

simply, that demand for planning services should continue to grow in step with the increase in wealth in this region.

Aging Populations

As the median age of national populations increases as a result of low birth rates, the number of older individuals, in comparison to working age adults, will continue to escalate. Two key concerns are common among those in old age. First is the issue of funding retirement. The second involves providing safeguards against health risks. Both of these factors are driving the demand for financial planning advice.

Another factor related to a general aging of populations worldwide involves the transformation of wealth accumulation goals to preservation and distribution objectives. For nearly a half century most households have focused on strategies to accumulate wealth for the future. For many individuals born in the 1950s and 1960s (i. e., baby boomers in the United States and Western Europe), the necessity for wealth management strategies is increasing demand for financial planning services. While competition for providing such services will come most directly from securities brokers and insurance companies, the size of the aging population ensures that demand for planning services will continue to keep ahead of potential supply.

Related to this issue is the asset mix held by older households. In North America, for example, households have a preference for equity investments. In most regions of Asia, which is also experiencing an age based demographic shift, real estate is the preferred asset.① Asset preferences by region can be a demand factor for financial planners. HNW households will continue to demand not only in - country diversification but also allocation strategies that maximize international opportunities. Institutions that provide comprehensive, internationally dynamic, planning opportunities that include access to commodity, currency, equity, fixed - income, and real estate alternatives stand to gain market share among HNW families.②

---

① According to Capgemini and Merrill Lynch Wealth Management (2011), Asians held 31% of their investment wealth in real estate, whereas American held over 40% of their wealth in equity securities. Japanese investors prefer fixed - income securities. The average Japanese HNW portfolio is comprised of nearly 50% bond holdings.

② HNW household demand for planning services also includes expertise related to sports investments, collectibles, gems, and jewelry.

Savings Rates

One positive worldwide outcome associated the Great Recession that began in 2007 – 2008 was an increased level of savings at the household level. Consumes either chose or were forced to reevaluate their sources of income and expenditures. Rather than rely on debt to finance future purchases, many households increased savings over this time period. At the same time, during the Great Recession, interest rates hit historical lows. This caused a conundrum for many consumers. On the one hand, they had more savings to invest. On the other hand, they had few alternatives in which to invest their money. As result, many consumers turned to financial planners for investment and asset allocation advice. While this demand trigger may slow in the future, the role of savings rates within a country can almost always be used to gauge the current and future demand for services.

Investor Uncertainty

During the period 2007 through 2009, the S&P 500, which is the key stock market index in the United States, fell by nearly 40 percent. At the same time, interest rates hit historical lows. Real estate values also declined substantially throughout thc United States. Concurrently, unemployment increased while household incomes decreased. This all resulted in reduced consumer and investor confidence. Similar experiences were shared by people living throughout the world. For example, the European debt crisis led to severe unemployment throughout much of southern Europe as well as reductions in governmental spending. Many investors found that what were once considered to be safe haven investments turned out to be quite risky. Consumer uncertainty related to investing and saving decisions has driven the demand for financial planning services to a dramatic extent. As long as financial matters continue to be complicated and uncertain, consumer demand, worldwide, for financial advice and counsel should continue tointensify.

In some respects, financial planning is an economic neutral activity. Some business domains move cyclically or counter – cyclically to the general economy or investment markets. Demand for financial planning services is benefited from both positive and negative changes in the markets. When economic activity improves, household income increases. As household wealth improves the demand for advice regarding the allocation of wealth also increases. On the other hand, economic and investment downturns often shine a light on less than optimal current planning strategies. As a market deteriorates consumer uncertainty and vulnerability increases. These factors combine to increase demand for financial planning advice and counsel.

Consider evidence from the Great Recession. Amidst this global financial meltdown, the financial planning marketplace experienced unprecedented growth. According to the U. S. Government Accountability Office (GAO),[①] the number of financial planners working in the United States doubled between 2000 and 2008. The GAO noted that rather than prompting a decline in the demand for financial planning services, the financial stress created by the Great Recession created even greater demand for financial planning help. The GAO has projected that by 2018 there will be more than 271,000 financial planners working the United States. What is interesting about this fact is the demand for planning services is expected to outstrip the supply. Currently, in the United States, which is considered a mature market, less than one quarter of Americans (22%) work with a financial planner. Institutional supply could increase four fold and still not meet the underlying demand for planning services.

Corporate Needs

Robust economic activity that results in corporate mergers, acquisitions, and multi-company integration can have a positive impact on the demand for financial planning services. Unlike demand for accounting, capital management, and underwriting services that disappear during period of economic malaise, cyclical changes can generate demand for personal finance advice among key executives and employees.

Gender Demographics

Traditionally, the worldwide demand for financial planning services has been driven primarily by the needs and desires of men. Men, for example, have been the primary breadwinners in households for centuries. This demographic fact is changing. The gender revolution is something that is happening quite quickly. Within the United States, for instance,

---

① GAO (2011).

women will control the majority of wealth held at the household level within 20 years. Today, the number of female financial advisers is both numerically and proportionately small. Women represent less than 10 percent of the adviser workforce. It is expected that women clientele will expect additional services and have a preference for working with planners who represent greater diversity. Firms that can create new products and services for women will find increasing demand over the next few decades.

As mentioned above, demand for financial planning services is growing globally due to the increasing number of HNW households. Today, nearly 75 percent of all HNW individuals are male. However, according to Capgemini and Merrill Lynch Wealth Management,① this concentration of wealth is likely to change dramatically and quickly over the next two decades. Financial planning firms should expect to see wealth shift to the hands of younger women in the future. In some respects, this shift is already taking place. In East Asia (excluding Japan), approximately 25 percent of HNW individuals are younger females. This is an important factor driving the demand for planning services because generational wealth transfers provide an opportunity for new firms to capture market share.

Case Illustration: Meet Your Clients

Throughout this book you will be asked to apply the financial planning process with a client family—the Fans. It is now time to meet your clients and work through the first two steps in the planning process: (1) establishing and defining a relationship with a client and (2) gathering appropriate client data.

Jing and XuanFan recently moved to a larger eastern city in China. They are both employed in well respected and secure positions. They noticed immediately after arriving in their new city that they need help managing their resources and saving for future goals. They each asked their work colleagues for the names of competent financial planners. After conducting research on the internet they decided to interview you. During your first meeting, which was free of charge, you noticed that Jing and Xuan asked good questions and listened attentively to your answers. After the initial one hour meeting they agreed to return to engage your service as their financial planner.

Jing and Xuan are now sitting in your office. While you learned a lot about Jing and Xuan

① Capgemini and Merrill Lynch Wealth Management(2011).

during your initial consultation, you know it is now time to start gathering appropriate data from your new clients. Prior to the meeting you sent them a client gathering intake form. Jing and Xuan did the best they could answering the questions, but like all clients, they sometimes did know the answers or were unsure of what was being asked. Here is what you learned from analyzing the in – take form:

Personal Profile

JingFan

Age:47 years

Employment: Associate Professor in the Marketing Department at China State University. This is Jing's second academic position. Previously, he was employed at China Rural University for four (4) years. Jing currently contributes to a retirement plan through work, but his university does not contribute to the plan.

Health status: Jing appears to be in good health. He expects to live to age 90.

Expectation to receive inheritance: Jing's parents have indicated that he and his sister will be the sole beneficiaries of their estate. His expected share of the inheritance is $ 300,000. His parents are currently in good health. Jing does not expect an inheritance sooner than 10 years from today.

XuanFan

Age: 37 years

Employment: Xuan is employed as an accountant. She has held several financial management positions. In order to support Jing, she gave up her job in rural China to relocate with him to the city. Luckily, she found a job soon after the relocation. Xuan currently contributes to a retirement plan. Her employer matches 100% for her contribution up to 3% of her salary and then matches 50% for her contribution until her total contribution reaches 5% of her salary.

Health status: Xuan appears to be in good health, although she suffers from a neck pain and goes to anacupuncturist every other week. She expects to live to age 85.

Expectation to receive inheritance: Xuan expects to receive $ 100,000 from her mother, who is currently in good health. Like Jing, the earliest she expects to receive this money is in 10 years.

LuFan

Jing and Xuan have one daughter who is currently in primary school.

Age: 9 years

Health status: In good health.

The Fan's Goals and Financial Situation

Jing and Xuanhave come to you primarily to think about ways to fund their retirement. They just assumed that you would recommend a single product or service; however, after learning that you provide comprehensive financial planning services they have decided to work with you on a comprehensive basis.

The couple has similar risk tolerance levels. Jing is the one who executes all investment decisions. He also manages their separate and combined wealth. Xuan pays all bills, and she prepares personal financial statements and tax returns for the family.

When the couple moved to the city, they purchased an apartment for \$ 300 000. They financed it with a 4.0% 30 – year fix – rate mortgage loan.

Financial Goals (amounts in today's dollars)

Jing's goals (importance)

1. Spend \$ 12 000 per year to travel with Xuan and Lu (10) and \$ 3 000 per year on sky – diving until he retires (6);

2. Build up enough savings to live comfortably in retirement (9).

Xuan's goals (importance)

1. Increase tax – advantaged savings (10);

2. Save enough to build an emergency fund within the next two years (7).

The Fans (importance)

1. Save enough to build aneducation fund to send Lu to college. They plan to support her with \$ 15,000 tuition and fees per year for four years (10);

2. Become debt – free in 15 years (7);

3. Remodel one of their guest bedrooms into a home office next year; they expect the cost to be \$ 18,000 (8);

4. Remodel their kitchen in the next two years; they expect it to cost \$ 15,000 (7);

5. Retire together in 2035 with \$ 120,000 to spend per year; after Jing's death, Xuan can

live on \$ 75,000 per year; if Xuan were to die before Jing, he can live on \$ 80,000 per year (9).

Economic Information/Assumptions

1. Inflation rate: 4.35% per year;

2. Educational inflation: 8.0% per year;

3. Apartment value increases in value by3.5% per year;

4. Current 30 – year mortgage rates: 3.125%. 15 – year mortgage: 2.500%.

Insurance Information

Auto	100/300/300 renewed every six months on 08/15
Life	\$ 240 000 term policy on Jing with Xuan listed as the beneficiary; Jing is the policy owner. \$ 50 000 universal life policy on Xuan; annual growth rate: 4.8% ; Lu is the beneficiary; the benefit is not to be used to fund any goals; Xuan is the policy owner.
Health	Deductible: \$ 2 000; Co – insurance: 90/10; Stop loss: \$ 5 000; Lifetime cap: \$ 3 million
Disability	Jing pays 100% of the premium on a long – term any occupation disability policy offered through MU (premium paid is after – tax dollars; benefits received are tax – free). It includes 60% benefit coverage for both sickness and accidents, with a 180 – day elimination period and defined disability. Benefits will be paid until end of disability or age 65, whichever occurs earlier.
Homeowners	A typical homeowner's policy with no separate endorsements; the policy is renewed annually on February 20th of each year
Inland Marine	Covers their collections ; renew annually on 02/20
Umbrella	\$ 1 million coverage; renew annually on 02/20

Investment Information

1. Jing and Xuan agree that their investments are not doing as well as they have expected (no particular plan).

2. When Xuan left her job, she rolled over the entire balance of her pension to an IRA.

3. All financial assets (except where specified) are used to fund all goals.

4. They do not intend to sell their use assets to fund any goals.

Taxes Information

They would like to minimize their income tax burden.

Retirement Information

1. Jing and Xuan are both fully insured for Social Security retirement benefits. They plan to use Social Security payments to fund retirement only.

2. Jing has a defined benefit plan at his university, which has a five – year cliff vesting schedule. It is jointly funded by the university and Jing with an annual contribution of 2.2% of his salary. The annual rate of return during accumulation has been around 5.7%. At age 70, he would be entitled an annual benefit of $ 203,845 in future dollars for the remainder of his life. This amount will be adjusted for inflation once payments start.

3. They plan to contribute the maximum amount to Jing's individual retirement plan every year.

4. They plan to contribute the maximum amount to Xuan's individual retirement accounts every year.

Estate Information

They executed wills eight years ago; however, that was done in a different province. Their wills leave everything to each other. Beneficiaries (Jing for Xuan; Xuan for Jing) have been listed on all retirement accounts. Most nonretirement assets are titled under both Jing and Xuan. Personal items are separately titled.

You asked that Jing and Xuan complete the investment attitude's form shown below:

Investment Attitude Risk Questionnaire – Jing & Xuan Fan

Check the box next to the number in answer to each of the six risk tolerance questions below. These answers will help select your Asset Allocation Target Portfolio.

1. How important is capital preservation?

Not at all Moderately important Very important

■1 ■2 ■3 ■4 ■5 ■6 ■7 ■8 X9

2. How important is growth?

Not at all Moderately important Very important

■1 ■2 ■3 ■4 ■5 ■6 ■7 ■8 X9

3. How important is low volatility?

Not at all Moderately important Very important

■1 ■2 X3 ■4 ■5 ■6 ■7 ■8 ■9

4. How important is inflation protection?

Not at all Moderately important Very important

■1 ■2 ■3 ■4 X5 ■6 ■7 ■8 ■9

5. How important is current cash flow?

Not at all Moderately important Very important

■1 X2 ■3 ■4 ■5 ■6 ■7 ■8 ■9

6. How much risk are you willing to take to achieve a higher return?

Not at all A Moderate amount A lot

■1 ■2 ■3 ■4 ■5 ■6 X7 ■8 ■9

What Average Annual Rate of Return * do you want to earn on your portfolio to reach your financial goals?

(Enter a number between 5% and 14%.)

Average Annual Rate of Return * You Want: ____ 10 ____ %

* This rate of return is hypothetical and used for comparison purposes only. It is not related to any specific investment and there is no guarantee you will actually receive this rate.

Based on this information you are now ready to start working through the additional steps of the financial planning process. You should expect to ask for and receive information from the Fans throughout the financial planning process.

References

Capgemini and Merrill Lynch Wealth Management. (2011). *World wealth report*. New York: Author.

College for Financial Planning. (2011). *Survey of Trends*. Denver, CO: College for Financial Planning.

GAO. 2011. "Report to Congressional Addressees: Consumer Finance." www.gao.gov/new.items/d11235.pdf.

Lytton, R. H., Grable, J. E., &Klock, D. D. (2013). *The process of financial planning: Developing a financial plan* (2nd ed.). Erlanger, KY: National Underwriter.

Magali, S. L. (1978). *The rise of professionalism: a sociological analysis*. Berkeley, CA: University of California Press.

Schmidt, D. (2012, March). IBISWorld industry report 52393: *Financial planning & advice in the US*. Santa Monica, CA: IBISWorld.

Society of Actuaries. (2005). A strategic analysis of the U.S. life insurance industry Part I: Customers. The Actuary. http://www.soa.org/library/newsletters/the-actuary-magazine/2005/april/str2005april.aspx.

Chapter 2 The Global Experience in Financial Planning

As discussed in the previous chapter, the demand for financial planning services has seen a dramatic increase globally over the past two decades. Much of this demand stems from changing demographics and expectations among consumers. Financial institutions have responded to this increased demand by exploring ways to incorporate financial planning services into their core practice areas. The purpose of this chapter is to provide greater context for the adoption of financial planning within larger financial institutions.

The evolution of financial planning in the United States provides a useful case study for those interested in understanding institutional support for financial planning. Recall that financial planning, as originally conceptualized and practiced in the United States, was based on a life insurance and annuity sales platform. The origination of financial planning, as a distinct field of study and practice, began in the late 1960s and early 1970s. This time frame was not coincidental. As illustrated in Figure 1, the life insurance industry specifically, and the financial service profession more generally, has moved through seven primary phases of development. Financial planning emerged only during the middle maturation of this developmental cycle

The developmental phases of the financial service field are shared by nearly all industrialized countries. It is important to note, however, that the speed at which a country moves from one phase to the next is not precise. Some countries, especially those in East Asia, may move quite quickly from emerging status to maturity. Today, the United States can be classified as a very mature market. Many East Asian countries, such as China, can be classified as emerging, whereas some nations, like South Korea, are at a point in between. The following discussion

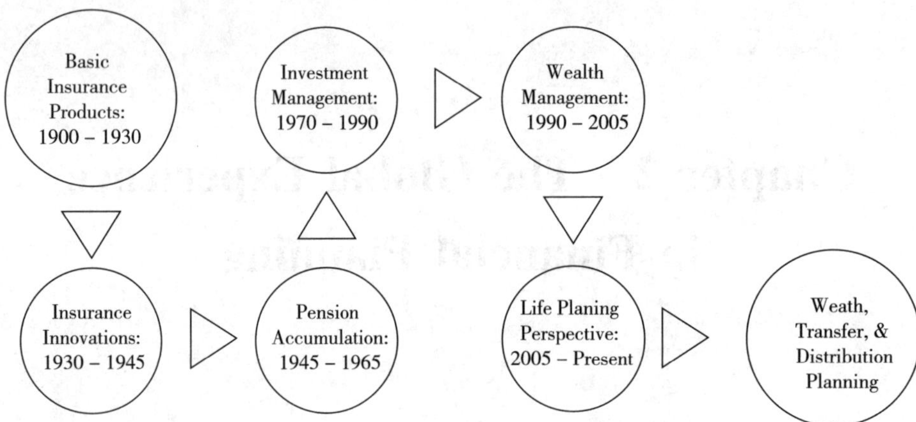

Figure 1 Primary phases of professional development

highlights each phase of development.

Phase One

An emerging market is one characterized by a number of firms whose primary business involves selling term① and cash value life insurance② through a large network of salespeople. In almost all emerging marketplaces, the distribution of insurance products is conducted by commissioned salespeople. Generally, the sales staff has little training in household or personal finance topics. An emphasis tends to be on sales generating tools and techniques. Additionally, those who are hired to distribute insurance products tend to be hired based on their sales skills rather than through academic training.

① Term life insurance is "pure" coverage provided by a firm for a set period of time. For example, a person may purchase a 10 – year term policy with a face value of \$ 100,000. If the insured dies within the 10 year time horizon, the policy beneficiary will receive the full face value of the policy. If the insured dies after the policy lapses (i. e. , 10 years and 1 day or more) then the beneficiary receives nothing.

② Cash value life insurance combines pure insurance with a forced level of savings. A portion of each premium paid is allocated to fund the underlying term insurance costs. The remainder of the premium is split among insurance company underwriting expenses, policy expenses, and a cash value account that is credited interest. The policy owner may use the cash value of and earnings on the account to help offset future premiums or as a source of borrowing. A traditional whole life insurance policy provides for both a fixed premium and rate of return for the life of the policy. Cash value policies tend to cost 10 to 20 times the premium of a term policy.

Phase Two

As a nation industrializes, the need to meet new consumer demands causes financial service companies to create innovative products. In the United States, industrialization led to greater urbanization of the population. The same phenomenon is apparent in China today. A byproduct of urbanization is the movement away from family support to one based on the earnings and savings of a single breadwinner. As such, products are needed to meet lost income needs in the case of death or disability. Products such as accidental death and dismemberment, disability, and group life insurance plans mark this phase of development.

Phase Three

The combination of industrialization and urbanization generally results in national prosperity and greater financial stability at the household level. Consumers, at this phase of development, begin to focus less on present financial demands and more on providing for their financial future. Additionally, corporate competition for well trained and productive employees causes firms to compete based, in part, on employer - provided benefits. A key benefit tends to be providing employees with some type of guaranteed pension plan. At this phase of the financial service field development, life insurance and annuities are used almost exclusively to fund pension plans. It is during this third phase of development that insurance companies and affiliated firms experience great growth and stability. The combination of consumer and corporate demand for insurance based products leads to enormous profitability within among firms in the field.

While financial service firms would be content to level off at phase three of the developmental process, there are usually environmental events that are beyond firm control that occur to shape the next phase of development. It is important to note that up until this point the marketplace for financial service products has been limited and somewhat generic. Whole life cash value life insurance tends to be the primary product being sold at this time. While quite profitable for insurance companies, many firms fail to capitalize of trends that will impact consumer demand in the future. During the fourth phase of development consumer preference undergoes a dramatic shift. Rather than being satisfied with bank - like rates of return, households begin to dabble with riskier forms of investment, including direct stock, mutual fund, and real estate ownership. This period of development sees greater market regulation and lower barriers to entry from firms competing for consumer savings expenditures.

Phase Four

It is precisely during this period (i. e. , phase four) of development that financial planning begins to be seen as a technique to add greater value to the consumer – adviser relationship. As consumer appetite for risk and returns increases, the demand for investment management services also increases. Institutions begin to ask more from their sales staffs than simply delivering fixed rate insurance and annuity products. In fact, sales teams begin to demand that their firms innovate once again as a way to compete against investment advisory firms, brokerages, and others who offer comprehensive investment management services. Within the insurance field firms begin to introduce variable return products, such as variable life insurance and annuities.

Another important trend typically occurs during phase four. The way in which financial advisers begins to shift away from purely commissions to include fees for services. This is an important step in the developmental process because for the first time consumers begin to pay for services directly, rather than through commissions affiliated with products.

Phase Five

The transformation from the fourth to fifth state of development occurs when traditional cash value life insurance no longer makes up the bulk of products and services provided to either consumers or corporations. In the United States, this transition occurred in the 1990s when variable annuity premiums exceed premiums earned on life insurance products. This period can be identified by the types of market activities employed by those in the financial service field. An emphasis on wealth management, rather than simply on investment supervision, takes center phase. Consumers tend to be more interested in overall household wealth performance than on one single aspect of their wealth. Firms that can offer a more comprehensive perspective on the accumulation and management of wealth tend to have a competitive advantage in the marketplace. Stated another way, firms that adopted a financial planning perspective early on emerge as leaders in the fifth state of development.

Phase Six

The sixth phase of development is marked by both a maturing economy and population. While each nation and region will be faced with unique economic activity, interest rates, and population longevity, this sixth phase of development finds consumers increasingly fixated on issues of legacy. Legacy refers to how someone hopes to be remembered after death. For many people, the thought of leaving a legacy beyond a simply monetary bequest to another person or charity becomes a driving passion. The concepts of financial planning and life planning become intertwined at this phase of development. Financial planners move from mere managers of client wealth to stewards of client hopes, dreams, and aspirations. Rather than focus on the sales of a product, financial service professionals tend to engage their clients both on financial and emotional matters.

A distinct change in the way financial advisers are viewed takes place during this phase of development. A consumer perception of financial service providers moves from viewing their adviser as a salesperson to that of a trusted counselor. Consumers begin to expect their financial adviser to provide unbiased and comprehensive advice that will improve the well - being of the client and their immediate family. In many respects, this point of development is the pinnacle of achievement. This marks the first point in the development process when financial advisers are regarded similarly to accountants and attorneys. By this phase of development, only a small percentage of advisers still earn their living 100 percent by way of commission. A larger percent of adviser charge fees for services or they charge some combination of fees and commissions. It is also worth noting that the qualifications for entry into the field have, by now, increased dramatically. A college education is almost certainly a requirement. Consumer demand for appropriate certifications and education is also an important development at this phase of development.

Phase Seven

The sixth and seventh phases of development are, in some respects, interwoven. Financial planning has emerged in the United States, during this late phase of maturity, as a means to help clients accumulate, manage, and distribute wealth. Financial planning is not only by definition, but in practice as well, comprehensive. Consumers have now come to expect disclosure information regarding fees, expenses, and conflicts of interest. While there are certainly firms still operating as product sales organizations, the shift in the marketplace now favors those organizations that focus on helping clients achieve life dreams.[①] In general, consumers expect to pay for advice rather than purchasing a product.

Market Segmentation

Institutions operating in the United States compete in a mature marketplace. Consumer demand has slowly shifted from accepting product recommendations to meet specific needs to a preference for broad financial service delivery. Financial planning, as a comprehensive process driven service model, fits well within this type of environment. It is important to note, however, that the phase of development within the financial marketplace differs across the world. Some firms operate in economies in which basic insurance products dominate. Others compete in environments where investment management is the preferred consumer choice. As such, the level of adoption of financial planning within financial institutions tends to be driven by local markets.

Figure 2 illustrates the developmental phases within the financial services field. As shown, a sales model dominates the first three phases of industry development. During these phases, firms tend to be focused primarily on developing networks of sales teams to distribute products to consumers. Although a few companies may enter the market by providing comprehensive financial planning services, these firms play only a small role in the industry. Phase four marks a turning point for many institutions. As consumer demand shifts from product to service, some firms will move with and help shape the marketplace. Others will opt out and attempt to maintain market share through more aggressive sales approaches.

Phase four is a pivotal point in the adoption of financial planning methods within individual firms. A few leading companies will adopt models of financial planning; however, some will explicitly reject the notion that their sales force is anything more than an intermediary between the consumer and the firm. For example, few property and casualty insurers operating in the United States have ever adopted a financial planning approach when working with consumers. Large

---

① More information on the industry state of development can be found in *CIPR Study WPS* 2013: *State of the Life Insurance Industry issued* by the National Association of Insurance Commissioners and the Center for Insurance Policy and Research.

property and personal automobile policy insurers have consistently maintained the perspective that they are selling a generic product. Further, these firms have often argued against more comprehensive evaluations of client situations on the grounds that consumers, in this particular market, are interested solely in transacting business rather the developing client - planner relationships built on quality of advice. As such, offering other planning services might create a liability for the firm and its sales force.

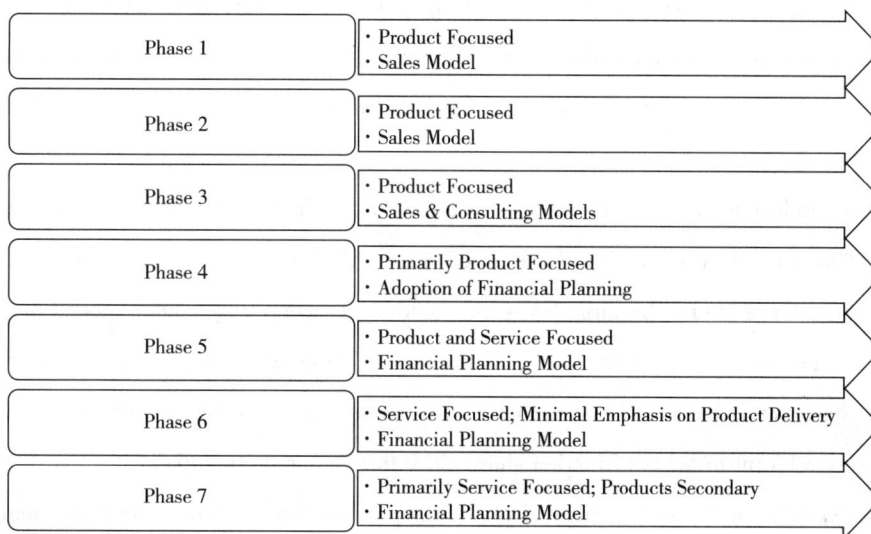

Phase 1	· Product Focused · Sales Model
Phase 2	· Product Focused · Sales Model
Phase 3	· Product Focused · Sales & Consulting Models
Phase 4	· Primarily Product Focused · Adoption of Financial Planning
Phase 5	· Product and Service Focused · Financial Planning Model
Phase 6	· Service Focused; Minimal Emphasis on Product Delivery · Financial Planning Model
Phase 7	· Primarily Service Focused; Products Secondary · Financial Planning Model

Figure 2 Product and service delivery associated with phases of development

Regardless if a firm adopts a financial planning approach or not, consumer demand, within the context of industry development, continues to evolve. During periods where wealth management is of primary importance a clear shift away from products to service occurs. Institutions that failed to transition towards a consultative model (i. e., a financial planning approach) often find that their market share deteriorates during this phase of market development. On the other hand, firms that spent resources earlier in training their sales force to move from a purely product driven model of client interaction to one based on counseling often experience phenomenal growth. As the market matures, a clear differentiation among firms emerges. The leading firms, by phase six, have all adopted, in one form or another, aspects of financial planning as the key service and product delivery mechanism.

Figure 3 illustrates the five primary types of institutions that remain in a competitive position when a country's financial service field enters maturity. At this phase of development, consumer demand has clearly shifted towards a preference for advice and counsel on the accumulation, management, and distribution of wealth. It is important to note that wealth is defined very broadly to include both financial and qualitative factors, such as issues related to human capital and legacy planning.

As shown in Figure 3, even though consumer demand has clearly shifted towards client – centered financial advice at the point of market maturity, there will be at least three types of firms that have yet to fully adopt a financial planning perspective. The first are firms focused on meeting the needs of independent consumers. In any market there will be consumer who can be classified as "do – it – yourself" investors. These consumers simply need a company to take custodianship of their assets so that the consumer can make their own financial decisions. Stated another way, independent consumers neither want nor need financial advice or financial planning services. The second type of firm focuses on transacting services directly with consumers. Although rare, these tend to be large firms that continue to use a fully commissioned based sales force. It is interesting to note that these "transactional" firms were the dominant players during the early phases of industry development. At this phase of development, transaction oriented firms are less relevant in terms of market share. The third example includes firms that have yet to decide whether they will adopt a financial planning approach, or to what extent they should adopt financial planning. These institutions can be classified as "uncommitted." Oftentimes, these firms are forced into moving from a strictly transactional orientation to one based on planning services by the actions of their competitors.

The fourth type of firm is one that has fully adopted financial planning as its primary client interaction tool. These institutions can be labeled as "relational client centered firms." Although these firms may still sell products to consumers, the bulk of earnings are derived directly from fees charged for service. The large bubble indicates the myriad of typical small firms operating at this phase of market maturity. In the United States, these companies—the fifth type of company—may be classified as investment advisory firms, asset management institutions, or simply financial planning organizations. Also shown in Figure 3 are smaller bubbles circling the large sphere. As in any marketplace, there will be firms that provide some type of financial service to consumers, but are not defined traditionally. ①

① Examples include pawn shops, cash advance and title loan operations, and other consumer lending services.

Hidden within this visual representation lies the underlying reason financial institutions have, and ought to continue to, embrace financial planning over other product or service models. The final phase of market development tends to be driven by consumer expectations and preferences. Firms that can meet the needs of consumers tend to be more profitable over the long run.

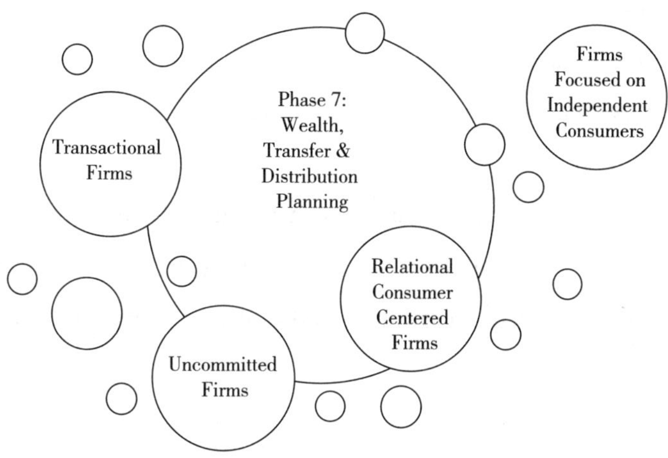

Figure 3 Adoption of financial planning during market maturity

The Dominance of Financial Planning in a Mature Market

As stated at the outset of this chapter, the United States provides a useful case study for firms operating in other countries that might be interested in adopting a financial planning model. The United States market for financial planning services generates approximately $ 47 billion in annual revenue. ① Over 135,000 firms operate in this space, but among these firms, four control over 45 percent of the total market. ② The key drivers of demand are related to increasing levels of discretionary income among an older population, a relatively high savings rate, and investor uncertainty regarding the direction of interest rates and security prices.

---

① Data for this discussion were obtained from: Schmidt, D. (2012, March). *IBISWorld Industry Report* 52393: *Financial Planning and Advice in the US*. Los Angeles: IBISWorld.

② Morgan Stanley Smith Barney LLC, Wells Fargo and Company, Bank of America Corporation, and Ameriprise Financial Inc.

It is worthwhile to note that among the leading firms that have adopted the financial planning model in the United States, all are recent adopters. Bank of America is the third largest provider of financial planning services. This transformation from a traditional commercial bank to becoming a leading planning institution occurred very quickly. In 2008, Bank of America purchased Merrill Lynch & Company. Merrill Lynch has traditionally operated in the securities/brokerage marketplace. Although Merrill Lynch was one of the first firms to introduce a fee structure within the brokerage industry, it is only recently that the firm's compensation structure has shifted towards fees for advice rather than commissions for products. This shift in approach, which was brought about by emphasizing financial planning processes, has helped the firm capture a significant portion of market share.

Other firms have taken notice. Institutions that traditionally hired transaction salespersons now encourage their staff to obtain credentialing in financial planning. Firms such as LPL Financial and Raymond James have grown their market share to nearly 4 percent and 3 percent, respectively.

The Delivery of Financial Planning Services: Planning Models and Approaches

Insurance Platforms

The original practice of financial planning is tied very closely to the life insurance industry. In fact, as discussed in Chapter 1, the origination of financial planning as a service model was first conceptualized by those working in the insurance field. Given its role in shaping the modern practice of financial planning, it is important to understand how the life insurance industry has changed over time.

Life insurance has a long and colorful history in the United States. The first life insurance contracts were sold by the Presbyterian Minister's Fund in 1759. From these humble beginnings, the life insurance industry has grown to a mammoth size. In 2012, for example, life insurance companies held U. S. $ 5. 5 trillion in financial assets. [①] This growth has occurred using a two model distribution system. It is important to understand these two models as a way to understand life insurance trends in the United States.

Life insurance companies originally operated as stock firms. That is, companies were formed and stock was sold to the general public. These assets were then invested in securities to provide a pool of resources to pay claims. As more policies were sold, premiums were used to increase the pool of securities held, and during profitable years shareholders received a dividend, as well as the possibility of an increasing stock price. The early – to mid – 1880s witnessed significant economic fluctuations. The result was that just prior to and during the U. S. Civil War it became very difficult for life insurance companies to raise capital by selling stock. As a result, an entirely different type of insurance company came into existence.

Mutual companies were built on the premise that policy owners should own the insurance company. Because no stock was issued to the general public, it became essential that life insurance firms market their products to the fullest extent. The only way an insurer could increase market share, and thus it capital base, was to issue more policies. This required hiring and training large sales forces to penetrate cities and towns across the country. If a mutual insurance company did well financially, [②] the policy holders would receive a dividend that could be spent or used to offset future premiums. [③]

Given the potential for fraud and mismanagement, it was not long before individual states took action to regulate the sale of life insurance products. In 1849, New York was the first state to require stock companies to maintain minimum deposits to support issued policies. New Hampshire created a new regulatory position called an insurance commissioner shortly thereafter. By the 1870s, nearly every state had implemented some form of life insurance regulation. In 1871 insurance regulators joined forces to provide uniform guidance on insurance issues by forming the National Association of Insurance Commissioners.

---

① National Association of Insurance Commissioners and the Center for Insurance Policy and Research. (2013). *State of the life insurance industry: Implications of industry trends.* http://www. naic. org/documents/cipr_home_130823_implications_industry_trends_final. pdf

② Defined as earnings on assets held, plus premiums earned, being greater than policy payouts and ongoing expenses.

③ In an interesting twist, the majority of mutual insurance companies have since reverted back to being publically held stock corporations. In 2013, for example, the top 10 publically traded firms controlled 40 percent of the life insurance premiums. Mutual companies play a relatively small role in the marketplace today.

The life insurance industry continued to grow and prosper throughout the late 19th and early - to mid - 20th century. Term life insurance and basic whole life (cash value) insurance were the predominant products sold in the United States during this time, although other products were slowly introduced into the marketplace. ① Dramatic shifts in consumer preferences began to emerge after World War Two. This period ushered in the baby boom generation. With the large influx of children being born, an increased demand for life insurance was put into place. At the same time, consumer sophistication was intensifying. While basic life insurance demand remained high, consumers began to search for alternative products that provide both protection of current earnings and future growth potential. In 1952, the Teachers Insurance and Annuities Association - College Retirement Equity Fund (TIAA - CREF) issued the first variable annuity product. Essentially, this annuity allowed premiums to be invested in equity investments through mutual funds. Previous to this point, all annuity holders were credited with a fixed rate that was based on the after - fee performance of the insurance company's investment performance. ②

It is now possible to look back at this dynamic point in history to see the beginnings of financial planning taking shape. By the early 1960s the life insurance industry had come together to develop the field's first designation. One of the first broad based financial service designations was created at this time. The American College of Life Underwriters created, marketed, and regulated the Chartered Life Underwriter (CLU ®) designation. This abbreviated time line leads directly to 1969 and the birth of financial planning.

The consumer movement flourished during the 1960s and 1970s. The insurance industry came under increased scrutiny. Sales tactics, which included door - to - door sales, hidden commission structures, and selling replacement policies that were either overpriced or unwarranted make media headlines. The result was a shift in consumer demand towards services related to investment and wealth management and away from product delivery. Increased consumer awareness and shifting demand preferences led many within the insurance industry to create the first models of financial planning. These entrepreneurial individuals were driven by two primary goals. First, they wanted to expand the market for insurance products and services.

---

① Examples of products introduced in the 1920s and 1930s include key personnel insurance, group life and health insurance, disability coverage, and double indemnity clauses within cash value policies.

② These products still exist and are known as fixed annuities.

Second, they had a strong desire to help consumers not only accumulate wealth but also to manage the wealth in the form of legacy planning. Prior to this time, insurance products (both life insurance and annuities) were considered to be estate planning and wealth transfer tools. Suddenly, the life insurance and other insurance products, under the guise of financial planning, began to be seen as a way for households to achieve a myriad of concurrent financial goals through tax - efficient investing.

The flurry of activity within the life insurance industry that occurred with the development of financial planning as a field of practice and study was relatively short lived. Throughout the 1980s, the industry continued to be innovative in relation to the forms of life insurance and annuities being sold, but the field failed to capitalize on consumer demand for comprehensive investment and wealth management services. In many respects, the life insurance model was hampered by the fact that life insurance and annuities were, and continue to be, the only products that a salesperson could use to help clients reach financial goals.

Consider, for example, how the competitive nature of the marketplace shifted throughout the 1980s and 1990s. The insurance industry, while attempting to meet consumer demand, developed several pioneering life products, including variable, universal, and variable/universal life insurance. On the accumulation and distribution side of the equation, firms modified and continued to sell fixed and variable annuities. The primary sales feature associated with these products, as mentioned above, was the opportunity for policyholders to accumulate wealth in a tax - deferred account. The history of variable - universal life (VUL) insurance encapsulates the industry's attempt to compete with other types of financial service providers.

VUL policies were developed in response to consumer demand for exposure to the equity markets using tax - deferred vehicles. A VUL, in the most simple of terms, allows a policyholder to fund an equity linked account within a traditional cash value life insurance policy. Unlike a variable life policy, premiums can fluctuate. For better or worse, cash values can also fluctuate. During the 1990s, when the worldwide equity markets were generating excess rates of return, those who held a VUL experienced phenomenal tax - deferred growth. A common retirement strategy at the time involved over funding a VUL and investing the cash value of the account very aggressively. Assuming that the cash account were to grow large enough, a policyholder could then take policy loans out against the cash value. As long at the equity markets continued to move ahead, both premiums and policy loan payments could be made from account earnings. In effect, it was theoretically possible to save money on a tax – deferred basis, pull money from the account in retirement on a tax free basis,① and at death the full face value of the policy, and any remaining cash value, would transfer tax free to a beneficiary. Conceptually, the VUL seemed like the perfect product among all competing products and services in the financial marketplace.

It turns out that the VUL phenomenon lasted only a few years. First, the insurance industry priced VUL products at the high end of the market. Ongoing fees were very high. Policyholders did not mind paying these fees when the equity markets were increasing dramatically, but when the equity markets turned negative, and cash values plummeted, policyholders found themselves forced to add extra premium to declining policies. Second, as noted above, the VUL retirement planning strategy only works in markets where equity returns move steadily higher. Beginning in the late 1990s, and extending throughout the first decade of the 21st century, equity prices moved downward. The majority of existing VUL policies lapsed, leaving policyholders with losses that were not insured or subject to a tax benefit.

Today, life insurance is primarily a secondary source of revenue to the insurance industry. By the mid – 1990s, annuity sales surpassed life product premiums.② Annuities, while a particularly useful tool for those who want to save money for retirement outside of a traditional qualified retirement plan or individual retirement account, have become a niche product. It is important to note that the insurance industry is still a major player in the broad financial marketplace, but the industry that created financial planning is no longer the leader in shaping how financial planning is perceived by consumers today. In many respects, financial planning has moved well beyond what it was originally designed to do; namely, add value to the consumer – agent relationship.

Figure 4 illustrates the primary financial planning target markets and distribution channels used by insurance firms today. As illustrated, the majority of firms operating in this space tend to be large regional or national insurance companies. Almost all of these industry players employ a captive sales force that sells primarily the firm's products and services. This is particularly true at the mass, middle, and affluent market levels, although nearly all firms have also developed

---

① Policy loans are not considered income for tax purposes.

② National Association of Insurance Commissioners and the Center for Insurance Policy and Research (2013).

specialized services and products designed to meet the needs of affluent and high net worth clients. These products and services can generally be sold by independent advisers and non – captive insurance agents. Nearly all insurance companies have either hired in – house financial planning specialists or created affiliated wealth management firms to meet the needs of high net worth clients. Clients of these affiliated organizations can gain access to traditional insurance products and services, as well as obtain direct wealth management services typically provided to institutional clients.

Figure 4 Insurance platform target markets and distribution channels

Banking Platforms

Prior to the early 1980s, banks maintained a complete and separate wall between their deposit and loan functions and what might be called financial planning services. Traditionally, banks have always offered high net worth clientele individual tax, estate, and investment services through their private banking structures and through trust departments. Although available, these services were almost always reserved for a bank's top tier customers. This changed in 1984. The Bank of Boston allowed any customer to ask a branch manager about financial planning services beyond deposit accounts and loan alternatives. The reality was that the Bank of Boston had outsourced planning services to another firm. This marked, however, a turning point in the bank industry. Rather than limiting access to planning services to those bank customers who qualified for trust services, the Bank of Boston endorsed the concept that financial planning might be beneficial to a wide segment of clientele.

Other banks soon began offering planning services by outsourcing planning and investment advice to a third party firms. Some large banks countered this by lowering minimum account requirements so that private banking and trust services could be expanded. This was the status quo until 1999. In November 1999 the U. S. Congress repealed sections of the 1933 *Glass – Steagall Act* that had prohibited banks from directly owing other banks, investment banks, or providing a more diverse mix of investment products.

What emerged were bank holding companies. Wells Fargo & Company provides an example of how many banks today have incorporated financial planning into their customer product mix. The bank holding company is comprised of four distinct business segments. The first is called community banking. This is what most people think of in terms of a bank. The community bank segment operates local branches and provides consumer deposit, credit card, business banking, and other personal and commercial lending services. Mortgage lending falls under the community banking umbrella. Wholesale banking comprises the second segment. This bank – within – a – bank provides mutual fund, asset – based lending, real estate, trust, and commercial loan services primarily to other commercial operations. The third segment is called Wells Fargo Securities. This is essentially the bank's investment banking division.

Financial planning services fall under the fourth segment of operations, which is called Wells Fargo Advisors. This business segment provides wealth management, brokerage, and retirement planning services to the general population. The firm's private bank and high net worth family division are also housed in this market unit. Wells Fargo, like many other large bank holding companies, entered the financial planning marketplace through acquisitions of other firms. In the case of Wells Fargo, the firm purchased Wachovia Corporation. ①

The target markets and distribution channels for large banks that operate in the financial planning field resembles the insurance industry. Figure 5 illustrates these markets and the primary ways banks meet demand for services. It is also important to note that many local and regional banks also continue to promote financial planning services. Typically, these activities are outsourced to other firms, and in some situations, these banks own a brokerage firm that can

---

① Bank of America purchased Merrill Lynch, which gave the bank a significant presence in the planning marketplace.

both act as an account custodian and clear trades for clients. In either the bank holding company situation or the small/regional firm case, it is common for investment management and financial planning advisers to be housed in the same building as the bank.

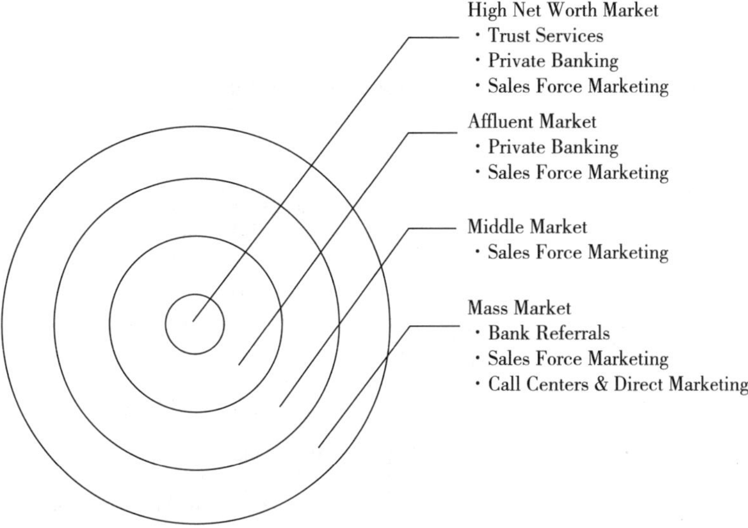

Figure 5 Banking platform target markets and distribution channels

Investment Platforms

The delivery of financial planning through investment platforms occurs almost exclusively through broker – dealer firms and networks. Among the general public, the concept of financial planning is often confused with brokerage services. This is strictly not true; however, the perception does exist. Broker – dealer advisers tend to provide transaction – based services by recommending equities, bonds, annuities, mutual funds, some types of insurance, and asset management (wrap) accounts. The typical compensation structure tends to be fee – based. This means that advisers working within broker – dealer firms earn a commission on the sale of products. They may also earn a fee for providing planning services or by bundling investable assets into a management account.

Prior to the Great Recession, which began in the late 2000s in the United States, the majority of advisers working in the United States were employed by a broker – dealer firm. After the Great Recession, many of these firms merged with or were purchased by bank holding companies. Today, this model of financial planning delivery is represented by smaller regional firms, such as LPL Financial and Raymond James. Similar to insurance and bank holding companies, firms operating in this sector tend to focus their marketing efforts on the mass and middle markets, the affluent, and high net worth sectors. Similar to insurance platforms, nearly all services and products are sold by captive representatives (see Figure 6). Members of a firm's sales force are known as brokers, financial service representatives, registered representatives, or financial advisers.

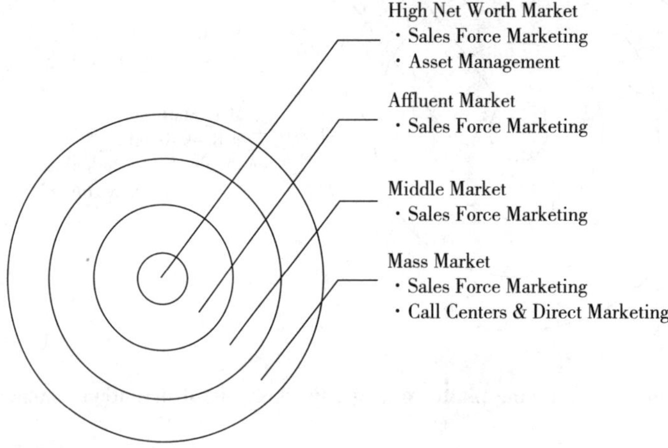

Figure 6 Investment platform target markets and distribution channels

Comprehensive Product Platforms

The number of truly comprehensive financial planning firms operating in the United States is rather limited. As will be discussed below, the majority of such firms fall under an independent service platform. However, there are several large national firms that do provide comprehensive financial planning services to the mass and middle markets, the affluent, and the high net worth sectors.

Two of the largest financial planning firms are Ameriprise Financial and Waddell & Reed. By far, Ameriprise is the largest company that utilizes the financial planning process when working with clients. In 2012, Ameriprise employed more than 12,000 planners and had a customer base of nearly 12 million. In total numbers, Ameriprise employs the largest number of CFP® certificants in the United States. Waddell & Reed is a smaller national firm that focused on investment management and insurance delivery within a financial planning environment.

The Ameriprise model provides an insight into this market delivery platform. The firm utilizes two approaches to meet the needs of consumers. Some financial planners are employed directly by the firm and provide services through branch offices located throughout the United States. In some respects, this approach to product and service delivery is similar to traditional sales force models. Financial planning employees receive less in commissions on products sold, but their expenses for operations tend to be lower as well. The larger delivery platform consists of franchise owners who use the Ameriprise name, systems, and marketing power to attract, work with, and retain clients. Currently, about 60 percent of all financial planners in the Ameriprise system work as independent contractors.

Firms operating in this space are the most likely to meet the needs of the mass and middle markets, although franchise owners tend to provide services to more affluent clients. Figure 7 illustrates the distribution channels most often used by comprehensive financial planning firms.

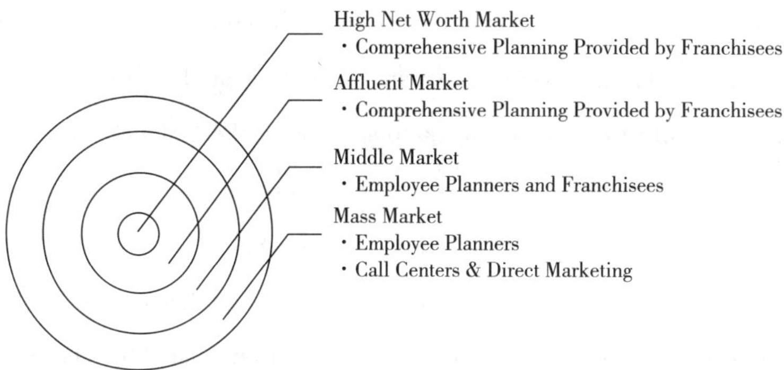

Figure 7 Comprehensive product platform target markets and distribution channels

Independent Service Platforms

Although a handful of firms dominate the financial planning marketplace in the United States, at least in terms of advisory staff and gross revenues, nearly all financial planning firms operate within an independent service platform or structure. For example, there are over 12,000 financial advisers who are registered with the national Securities and Exchange Commission. Even more operate at the state level. While not all of these firms provide comprehensive financial planning advice, nearly all deliver some aspect of planning services to clients (primarily investment advice). Together, these firms manage nearly U. S. $ 45 trillion in assets, with the vast majority of firms overseeing less than U. S. $ 100 million in client investable assets.

A unique feature of this financial planning segment of the market is the size of the typical firm. It is not unusual, for example, for firms to have fewer than five employees. Many financial planning companies are operated by one or two principal owners who have no staff members. According to Securitas and Exchange records, two – thirds of advisers employ 10 or fewer staff members. As these data suggest, the delivery of financial planning products and services tends to be fragmented and diverse.

In general, the majority of firms operating in the United States today do so using a third – party custodian. This means that client assets are held by a larger broker – dealer, such as Charles Schwab, Fidelity, or TDAmeritrade. Financial planners typically hold discretion over client assets. This allows the adviser to trade securities and make portfolio changes at any time; however, adviser do not have direct access to client assets. The delivery of other products and services is almost always handled by a third party firm. In other words, few financial planners working in this segment of the market are captive to one product provider. Instead, these financial planners are able to shop the marketplace and make product recommendations from among competing firms.

Independent financial planners typically work with a smaller number of clients compared to advisers who are employed by insurance, investment, or comprehensive competitors. In 2012, for example, the average independent financial adviser had few than 150 total clients. As such, these advisers tend to seek out and work with affluent and high net worth clientele. A primary reason for this market segment preference is the way in which these financial planners are paid. A fee and commission structure of compensation is very typical, with a one percent of assets under management fee very common. That is, independent financial planners generate revenue equal to approximately one percent of the assets they manage. Given that the time needed to assist a client with U. S $ 100,000 in assets is roughly the same as helping someone with U. S. $ 1 million in investable assets, most independent financial planners prefer to work at the upper end of the marketplace. This is shown in Figure 8. As noted, independent financial planners are the most likely, among all those who deliver planning services, to focus on the high net worth market. They are also very active in the affluent market. If any mass or middle market services are provided, these activities are almost always delivered by staff.

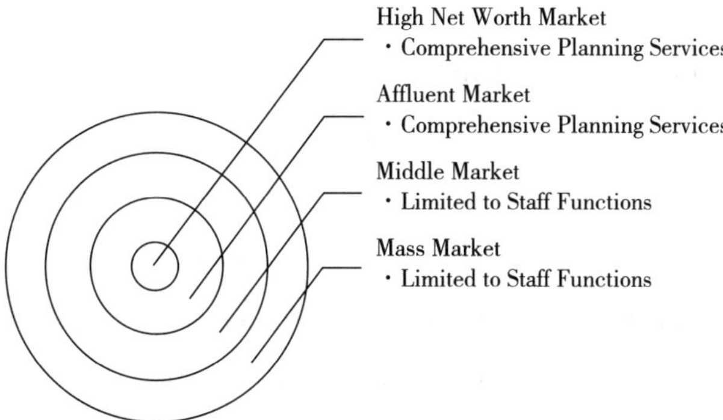

Figure 8 Independent service platform target markets and distribution channels

Fee and Compensation Structures

A review of fee and compensation models used by financial planners operating in the United States shows that there are at least eight ways advisers get paid. ① While no financial planner is rewarded using each method, it is possible for a single practitioner to receive compensation from several sources. The following discussion introduces the concept of fiduciary and suitability standards as a way to frame the discussion regarding the primary fee and compensation methods in force in the United State today. This is followed by a review of the primary compensation structures within the profession.

Case Illustration: The Fan Family

The Fan family (Jing, Xuan, and Lu), who you met in Chapter 1, chose you as their financial planner because they like the fact that you provide comprehensive financial planning services. Prior to engaging your services, they met with several advisers who were primarily interested in selling securities or insurance. The Fan family is much more comfortable working with you under a comprehensive product platform.

---

① Lytton, R. H., Grable, J. E., &Klock, D. D. (2013). The Process of Financial Planning: Developing a Financial Plan (2nd ed.). Erlanger, KY: National Underwriter.

The Fiduciary and Suitability Standards Debate

The debate focused on what role a financial planner should play when working with clients has become heated, and in some situations, hostile. Within the United States, there are two distinct models of practice. On the one hand are the planners who view their relationship with a client in a fiduciary manner. This means that they always offer recommendations that they believe are in the absolute best interest of their clients. On the other hand are advisers who see their primary role when working with clients as a product and service provider in which recommendations are made based on matching clients with suitable products and services. Often, the financial planner has little choice regarding which side of the argument they are on. This happens because either the firm they work for or consumer financial laws will dictate whether the planner works under a fiduciary or suitability standard. In order to better understand the difference between the two standards it is best to work from a common definitional framework.

Here is how fiduciary is defined by the Legal Information Institute at the Cornell University Law School:[①] A fiduciary has a "legal duty to act solely in another party's interests. Parties owing this duty are called fiduciaries. The individuals to whom they owe a duty are called principals. Fiduciaries may not profit from their relationship with their principals unless they have the principals' express informed consent. They also have a duty to avoid any conflicts of interest between themselves and their principals or between their principals and the fiduciaries' other clients. A fiduciary duty is the strictest duty of care recognized by the US legal system." Here is another definition. The U. S. Department of Labor[②] defines a fiduciary under the Employee Retirement Income Security Act (ERISA) as someone who acts prudently and solely in the interest of the client. This definition prohibits self-dealing and provides judicial remedies when violations of these standards cause harm to clients.

A key distinction in the debate is that fiduciaries, under the broadest of definitions, include anyone who gives investment advice for a fee and has the authority and responsibility to act in the best interest of another person. In 1975, the Department of Labor issued a five-part regulatory test for investment advice that gave a very narrow meaning to this term. Under the regulation,

---

① See http://www.law.cornell.edu/wex/fiduciary_duty.

② See http://www.dol.gov/ebsa/newsroom/fsfiduciary.html.

before a person can be held to the Department of Labor's fiduciary standards with respect to their advice, they must (a) make recommendations on investing in, purchasing or selling securities or other property, or give advice as to their value (b) on a regular basis (c) pursuant to a mutual understanding that the advice (d) will serve as a primary basis for investment decisions, and (e) will be individualized to the particular needs of the plan. Under federal law, an investment adviser, and by default a financial planner, is not treated as a fiduciary unless each of the five elements of this test is satisfied for each instance of advice. More recently, the Department of Labor has recommended key changes to the definition. The Department has proposed that a fiduciary is someone who provides the following type of advice for a fee:

- Appraisals or fairness opinions about the value of securities or other property;
- Recommendations on investing in, purchasing, holding, or selling securities; or
- Recommendations as to the management of securities or other property;

And meets one of the following conditions:

- Represents to a plan, participant or beneficiary that the individual is acting as an ERISA fiduciary;
- Is already an ERISA fiduciary to the plan by virtue of having any control over the management or disposition of plan assets, or by having discretionary authority over the administration of the plan;
- Is an investment adviser under the Investment Advisers Act of 1940; or
- Provides the advice pursuant to an agreement or understanding that the advice may be considered in connection with investment or management decisions with respect to plan assets and will be individualized to the needs of the plan.

The Certified Financial Planner Board of Standards, Inc. (CFP® Board) has also weighed in with a definition of fiduciary. This organization's definition is broader. According to CFP Board, "The Standards require that all CFP® professionals who provide financial planning services will be held to the duty of care of a fiduciary, as defined by CFP Board—A CFP® professional shall at all times place the interest of the client ahead of his or her own." It is important to note that all CFP professionals, regardless of the manner in which they are paid, must follow this basic guideline.[①]

The largest Fee - Only association of financial planners—the National Association of Personal Financial Advisors (NAPFA)—also follow a fiduciary definition. NAPFA defines a fiduciary as follows: "A financial advisor held to a Fiduciary Standard occupies a position of special trust and confidence when working with a client. As a Fiduciary, the financial advisor is required to act with undivided loyalty to the client. This includes disclosure of how the financial advisor is to be compensated and any corresponding conflicts of interest." Few firms operating from the insurance, banking, or investment perspective require their advisory staff to follow this, or any, fiduciary standard.

Instead, financial planners who earn some or all of their income from commissions, rather than fees, generally adhere to the suitability standard. A helpful rule to remember is this: if an adviser has either an insurance or securities license to sell products, he/she most likely falls under the suitability standard. The Financial Industry Regulatory Authority (FINRA)[②] defines the suitability standard as follows:

- A member or an associated person must have a reasonable basis to believe that a recommended transaction or investment strategy involving a security or securities is suitable for the customer, based on the information obtained through the reasonable diligence of the member or associated person to ascertain the customer's investment profile. A customer's investment profile includes, but is not limited to, the customer's age, other investments, financial situation and needs, tax status, investment objectives, investment experience, investment time horizon, liquidity needs, risk tolerance, and any other information the customer may disclose to the member or associated person in connection with such recommendation.

- A member or associated person fulfills the customer - specific suitability obligation for an institutional account, as defined in Rule 2111, if (1) the member or associated person has a reasonable basis to believe that the institutional customer is capable of evaluating investment risks independently, both in general and with regard to particular transactions and investment strategies involving a security or securities and (2) the institutional customer affirmatively indicates that it

① See Rule 1.4: http://www.cfp.net/for-cfp-professionals/professional-standards-enforcement/compliance-resources/frequently-asked-questions/fiduciary-duty#sthash.D2egdxxY.dpuf.

② See http://finra.complinet.com/en/display/display_main.html? rbid=2403&element_id=9859.

is exercising independent judgment in evaluating the member's or associated person's recommendations. Where an institutional customer has delegated decision making authority to an agent, such as an investment adviser or a bank trust department, these factors shall be applied to the agent.

To summarize, those who believe strongly in holding to a fiduciary standard believe that all recommendations and products delivered to a client must minimize conflicts of interest, be made with reasonable, fully disclosed compensation, and always be made with the client's best interest in mind. The suitability standard requires advisers to always make a reasonable recommendation given client, market, and employer constraints. Here is an example that will clarify the debate.

Suppose a financial planner who lived in Kansas was working with a client. The client has a long – term time horizon to fund retirement needs, a moderate risk tolerance, and the financial ability to withstand some market volatility. The financial planner searches the marketplace and identifies two mutual funds that would work to meet the client's investment objectives. The first fund is a no – load (no upfront commission) fund with an expense ratio of 0. 50 percent. The second fund is a load fund sold with no upfront commission but with a trailing 4. 5 percent commission. The expense ratio is higher than the no load fund. In this case, the expense ratio is 0. 60 percent. The load fund currently also has an incentive attached to it. Although not disclosed to the public, the fund family has offered to provide any adviser who sells $ 100,000 of the fund with a one week trip for two to Hawaii. If both the no – load and load fund have approximately the same 3 – , 5 – , and 10 – year annualized returns, which fund should be recommended?

The answer is quite simple for someone who follows the fiduciary standard. The no – load fund with the lower annual expense ratio is the best product for the client. An adviser who obeys the suitability standard can rightfully choose either mutual fund. Why? Because both funds are suitable in meeting the client's needs. In all likelihood however, the adviser will probably recommend that load fund. While the expense ratio is high, the adviser would likely note that the difference is marginal. Besides, the load fund does provide something the load fund cannot; namely, a vacation to Hawaii. It is also important to note that some advisers may not be allowed, under securities laws, to ever sell the no – load mutual fund. Broker – dealers must maintain pre – approved lists of investments that are screened for use with clients. If a no – load fund is not on the list—even though it is a superior product—it would be impermissible for the product to be recommended. This is one reason those who adhere to the fiduciary standard claim that other advisers sometime mislead or deceive clients. ①

In actuality, the manner in which a financial planner is paid is only a reason for concern in cases of payment non – disclosure. All advisers must be paid. The way in which compensation is generated should not be an issue unless conflicts of interest and fee structures are hidden from clients. In situations where a planner openly shares how he/she is paid then it is up to each client to determine if the payment method is reasonable and appropriate. The following discussion reviews five common compensation structures used within the United States.

Fee – Only

Fee – only planners generally receive 100 percent of their compensation② in the form of fees for assets under management (AUM), fees for plan development, or fees for advice. Fee – only excludes the receipt of current or trailing commissions. While this definition seems straightforward and reasonable, the term fee – only has been misinterpreted for many years. Some advisers have claimed to offer fee – only advice when they concurrently have been receiving commissions. This is technically incorrect and inappropriate; however, this dual relationship sometimes occurs because some advisers believe that if they have the ability to provide advice for a fee that they are also a fee – only adviser. Again, the clearest definition of fee – only advice is the one that specifically excludes anyone who receives a commission or payment from a secondary source other than the client. There are four primary fee – only models: (a) AUM fee, (b) plan fee, (c) retainer fee, and (d) hourly fee.

The vast majority of financial planners working in the fee – only arena charge an AUM fee. The typical fee ranges from 0.50 percent to 2.50 percent of assets under management, with the

---

① There is a counter to this argument. Fee – only fiduciary planners also face conflicts of interest that are not always fully disclosed. Consider a client who asks his/her adviser if he should pay off his current mortgage with assets that are being managed by the planner. If the planner says, "no" how can the client be sure that the recommendation was made in good faith. It is possible, but not likely, that the planner said "no" because his/her income would drop based on the reduction in assets under management. They key issue then is for all financial advisers and planners to fully disclose conflicts of interest and compensation arrangements.

② The largest "fee – only" association in the United States allows its members to receive up to 2 percent of annual income in the form of commissions and other forms of remuneration.

fee falling as the assets managed increases. About 50 percent of financial planners charge a flat fee for writing and delivering a financial plan. Fees range from U. S. $ 250 to well over U. S. $ 5,000 for this service. Some planners charge what is called an annual retainer fee. This is a flat fee that allows the client to access planning services and advice throughout the year. This model of compensation is similar to retainer fees charged by attorneys. Increasingly, fee – only planners have added an hourly fee schedule that allows clients to obtain very specific advice and counsel on an hourly basis. Hourly fees run from U. S. $ 100 to U. S. $ 500 per hour. Most often, more advanced planners charge a higher annual fee. It is possible for a single planner or planning firm to offer services that utilize more than one of these fee structures.

Fee – Based

Planners who use a fee – based model charge both a fee and commission. This approach is sometimes called a "fees plus commission" approach. For example, a financial planner might charge a modest planning fee (e. g. , U. S. $ 250) for the development of a financial plan. The planner would then charge a standard commission of products sold to implement plan recommendations. This often occurs whenever an insurance product is recommended. ① Closely related to this form of compensation is something called fee – offset. Planners who used this model charge a fee for planning services. However, they allow their clients to "offset" the fee through commissions earned on products sold within the planning process.

Commissions

The use of commissions has been discussed in earlier sections of this chapter. A commission is compensation generated from the sale of product. Generally, a commission is based on a set percentage of the dollar amount sold. If, for example, the commission rate is 5 percent of the gross sale, and a planner were to sell U. S. $ 100,000 in product, the commission would be U. S. $ 5,000. Most often, the financial planner shares the commission with his firm. The split can range from 30 percent/70 percent to 80 percent/20 percent for the adviser and firm,

① Currently in the United States it is difficult to place insurance with clients on a non – commission basis. Fee – only advisers are generally forced to provide referrals for insurance product implementation. Fee – based planners, on the other hand, can implement recommendations using commission products.

respectively. The vast majority of financial planners operating today earn at least some of their base compensation through the sale of products. ①

Assets under Management

Assets under management (AUM) has already been described as a fee – only method of compensation. Some large investment and banking firms offer a similar service referred to a wrap account. Wrap accounts provide clients who might otherwise pay a commission on products purchased the opportunity to obtain portfolio management services based on the value of the assets managed. The AUM model and wrap account approach are, in today's marketplace, the predominant way in which advisers who work with affluent and high net worth clients charge for services. Often, for instance, planning firms provide basic financial planning services for free as long at the AUM are sufficient to cover ongoing expenses.

Hybrid Approach

Many firms have introduced hybrid compensation models. It is increasingly common for financial planners to charge fees based not only on AUM but also on a combination of total client assets or income. As already mentioned, the combination of fees and commissions is another form of hybrid compensation. The primary reason financial planners and firms like the hybrid approach is that it diversifies the way in which clients are paid. The AUM model, for example, can cause planners to experience decreases in income when the market environment is negative. Likewise, commission planners can experience significant swings in income based on their ability to sell products (no client buys a U. S. $ 1 million life insurance policy every year). Using a hybrid model reduces these income swings.

---

① It is important to note that often commission based products provide what are called trailing commissions. As long as the client continues to own a product, the salesperson will receive between 0.25 percent and 1.00 percent in commissions into the future. The purpose of trailing commissions is to incentivize planners to provide continuing service to clients.

Compliance and Regulation

The issue of compliance and regulation of financial planners and planning firms is quite complex. The discussion that follows is intended to provide a broad overview of the topic as a way to frame regulatory issues in China and other Asian countries.

The Principle Compliance and Regulatory Frameworks

The manner in which financial planners work with clients should be guided by ethical standards. These ethical standards are arrived at through consensus among practitioners, regulators, and consumers. Within the financial planning, investments, and financial consulting fields ethical considerations are normative in nature. This means that rules, laws, and practice standards are based on what an adviser should do when working with a client. Stated another way, an ethical standard serves as a benchmark for performance and behavior.

Although this definition of ethics seems somewhat obvious, in practice the application of ethical standards is much harder to apply. Consider the fiduciary example from earlier in this chapter. In the example, a Kansas financial planner was faced with a product recommendation. She identified two mutual funds that would work well within a client's investment account. Both funds had a similar after – tax return. The first alternative was a no – load fund with an expense ratio of 0.50 percent. The second fund had a deferred load of 4.5 percent. This fund had an expense ratio is 0.60 percent. What made the example interesting is that the second fund offered to provide any adviser who sold $ 100,000 of the fund a one week trip for two to Hawaii.

Advisers working as a fiduciary would always choose the no – load fund for their client. This choice is shaped in part by the value orientation of the planner and by the normative standards of practice that fiduciaries must follow. When an adviser is faced with a clear choice situation this is called a deontological perspective. Fiduciaries must always choose the best product and service for their clients, regardless of the outcomes for the planner.

A financial adviser who does not adhere to a fiduciary standard would likely use a teleological perspective when making the fund decision. Teleological ethics is based on relativism and consequences. Those who would justify the higher expense ratio as reasonable as a way to obtain a free trip would be engaging in situation ethical decision making. This is, by far, the way in which most people make daily decisions. Individuals frequently speed while driving, snack on fruit at the grocery store, and tell inconsequential lies so as not to hurt someone's feelings. In other words, people break laws and social norms nearly every day, but they do so because the consequences of these actions are considered minor.

Although some financial planners may use a teleological ethical lens when formulating financial plans and interacting with clients, policy makers, regulators, and credentialing organizations almost always apply a deontological rule making perspective. Rarely does the argument that no one was hurt relieve a financial planner of liability or penalties. All rules, regulations, and practice standards are based on normative applications. This means that regulators write and interpret rules in a black and white manner; that is, a financial planner is considered to either fall under the rules or outside the rules. Penalties will be assessed to those outside the boundaries of the rules.

Government Regulatory Bodies

The regulatory landscape was quite barren in the United States, Europe, and Australia up until 1933. Prior to this time, nearly anyone could legally be involved in promoting investment securities and providing financial advice. ① This was a period of financial caveat emptor, which means that consumers during that time had to beware of the advice and counsel received because there would be limited recourse for misleading, fraudulent, or deceptive financial practices.

The Great Depression that began in 1929 significantly altered the way in which financial advisers and planners were regulated at the governmental level. Three important pieces of legislation were passed that forever altered the manner in which financial planning services are delivered to consumers. In 1938 the Maloney Act was passed by the U. S. Congress. This Act

① Even today it is possible in the United States to provide pure financial planning and counseling services without being licensed or certified. A loophole exists in the current regulatory structure that only requires those advisers who provide investment advice and counsel for a fee to be registered with the Securities and Exchange Commission or their state securities regulator. (All advisers who charge a commission on products sold must be licensed to do so.) While it is practically impossible to deliver financial planning advice without also providing investment advice, there are advisers operating in the United States who are, nonetheless, totally unregulated because they claim not to discuss or recommend investment solutions.

helped to create the National Association of Securities Dealers, which was the first self – regulatory organization within the brokerage industry. In 1940, the U. S. Congress passed the Investment Advisers Act. This Act has had the most profound impact on the financial planning profession.

The Investment Advisers Act of 1940 mandated that any financial adviser who charged consumers directly for investment advice or services must register with the Securities and Exchange Commission (SEC). ① Following the Great Recession that began in the United States in 2007, the Dodd – Frank Act was passed by the U. S. Congress. This Act passed through the most sweeping changes to securities and investment adviser regulations since the 1930s. A key change that occurred with Act's passage was the separation of financial advisory firms into two categories: those that manage U. S. $ 100 million or more and those that mange less. In effect, any firm that today manages at least U. S. $ 100 million in combined client assets must maintain registration with the federal SEC. Financial planning and investment advisory firms that manage fewer assets are required to register with the state securities regulators in the states in which they operate.

Under both federal and state requirements then, nearly everyone who provides investment advice to the public must be registered. Registration information is publically available through Form ADV, the Uniform Application for Investment Advisers Registration. ② This two – part document requires advisers to provide information about their business, employees, and regulatory history. More detailed information about an adviser's education, business background, certifications, fees charged, types of clients served, methodological approaches, types of investments recommended, conflicts of interest, ethical and privacy standards, and general advisory service procedures is also required. This detailed information must, by law, be provided to each client. Some firms give their clients Form ADV, while others rework the information into

① The 1940 Act did provide four exclusions for those who occasionally give investment advice. Exclusion for registration is available to: (1) banks and bank holding companies; (2) lawyers, accounts, engineers, and teachers whose investment advice is incidental to their core business; (3) publishers of newspapers, magazines, financial publications, and new sources of general circulation; and (4) advisers who deal only with U. S. government securities.

② Consumer access to this documentation is available through the Securities and Exchange Commission.

a detailed disclosure brochure. ① In addition to registering with the appropriate regulatory body, nearly every individual state requires investment advisers to sit for and pass the Series 65 examination. ② In 48 out of the 50 states anyone who holds the CFP ® certification or a ChFC ®, PFS ®, or CFA ® is exempt from the examination process.

It is possible that a financial planner may also fall under regulatory oversight of the National Association of Insurance Commissioners (NAIC). This national, but not federal, organization is comprised of representatives from each state's insurance regulatory office. ③ The NAIC was formed in 1871 to provide oversight of the sale of insurance products. Anyone who sells insurance must be licensed in the state in which they do business. Thus, it is conceivable for a financial planner to maintain both an insurance licenses and registration as an investment adviser.

Self – Regulatory System

The Maloney Act of 1938 created a new regulatory definition. Self – regulatory organizations (SRO) were allowed to be formed so that broker – dealers and other financial service firms could engage in self – monitoring and discipline. As previously mentioned, the NASD was formed to act as the SRO for brokerage firms and their employees. The name for the NASD was later changed to the Financial Industry Regulatory Authority (FINRA). FINRA oversees the activities of nearly 4,500 firms and close to 630,000 of these firm's employees. FINRA's primary role is to license and regulate firms within the brokerage industry. Of special importance is the licensing of registered representatives. A registered representative is a commission – based adviser who works for an investment bank or securities firm.

All registered representatives must hold an appropriate securities license. While there are numerous licenses, the most common is the General Securities Representative License, which is also known as a Series 7 license. This FINRA issued license is comprised of 250 questions that cover a wide spectrum of investment specific items. The test is six hours in length and considered

① It is important to note that generally the firm registers as the investment adviser. In the United States, most firms are organized as a corporation or limited liability company. Once the firm has been registered, each employee of the firm must then register as an Investment Adviser Representative. It is possible, however, for a sole proprietor to be both the "firm" and "adviser".

② States will allow an adviser to substitute completion of the Series 7 and Series 66 exams.

③ Insurance is regulated at the state, rather than federal level, in the United States.

quite difficult. Anyone who recommends investment securities to consumers must hold the Series 7. Another popular license is the Investment Company Products/Variable Contracts Limited Representative license (Series 6). Although less popular than in times past, this license allows someone to recommend mutual funds and annuity products. ①

Market and Consumer Based Disclosures

Under federal and state investment adviser rules, financial planners are required to provide prospective and current clients with relatively detailed disclosure information. As currently written, these rules mandate minimum levels of disclosure, which include the following:

- Past disciplinary events
- Previous bankruptcy filings
- Forms of compensation (but not the amount of income earned)
- Outside business interests
- All disciplinary information
- Background data
- Past experience
- Relevant financial information
- Information about discretion over client assets
- Custody disclosure and procedures
- Account review procedures
- Market analysis procedures
- Conflicts of interest
- Privacy rules
- Risk and diversification strategies
- Profile of other clients (but not names of clients)
- Comprehensive list of services offered
- Certification and designation information
- Personnel information

---

① The test is 2 hours long and consists of 100 questions.

Disclosure rules for investment advisers are different than rules for registered representatives. Stated another way, financial planners who charge clients directly (fees) must generally disclose more information that advisers who charge clients a commission (those who are regulated by FINRA). Policymakers advocate this unbalanced disclosure system based on the concept of the client – planner relationship. It is thought that financial planners who charge a fee have a fiduciary duty to provide the best services and product recommendations to their clients. This, by default, requires a higher level of disclosure. Commission – based planners, on the other hand, are generally considered to be transaction oriented. The difference is that a registered representative (broker) need only recommend a product or service that is reasonable for a client's situation. Under this policy, the level of consumer disclosure is much more limited. The same general rule applies to insurance salespeople.

All of the regulatory and disclosure discussion, up until this point, has dealt with federal, state, and SRO compliance issues. It is important to acknowledge that it is possible for one financial planner to fall under SEC, FINRA, and state insurance commissioner mandates at the same time. Although this is not common, when it does happen, the adviser is required to spend a great deal of time, effort, and resources on compliance issues.

As if this was not enough, an entirely different level of disclosure rules applies to financial planners who hold a professional certification. The most popular and well recognized financial planning certification in the United States is the Certified Financial Planner (CFP ®) mark. Financial planners who complete CFP training and pass the rigorous certification examination must follow ethical rules and practice standards as outlined by CFP Board.① Currently, close to 70,000 individuals hold the mark and provide services to clients. These advisers, regardless of their national, state, or SRO regulatory status, are required to provide extensive disclosure to their clients.②

All CFP ® professionals, for example, must follow a code of ethics and professional responsibility that include the following six principles:

1. Principle of Integrity

---

① CFP Board of Standards, Inc. owns the CFP ® mark.

② Unlike federal and state regulators, CFP Board only has the power to limit the use of the CFP mark. Federal, state, and SRO organizations have the ultimate power to revoke an adviser's legal ability to provide services to clients.

2. Principle of Objectivity

3. Principle of Competence

4. Principle of Fairness

5. Principle of Confidentiality

6. Principle of Professionalism

7. Principle of Diligence

Specific rules apply to each of these principles. In general, those who hold the CFP ® mark must disclose information to prospective and current clients that is comprehensive, easy to read, and indicative of conflicts of interest. Of particular disclosure importance is the role of compensation. Unlike FINRA standards, anyone holding the CFP ® mark must indicate how they are paid and from whom they receive compensation.

Figure 9 illustrates the different levels of disclosure within the financial planning field at this time. At the bottom of the pyramid are rules dictated by SROs and state insurance commissioner's guidelines. The level of disclosure tends to be limited. Advisers who are subject to SEC or state investment commissioner standards must adhere to a much higher level of disclosure. In general, investment advisers who charge a fee for service are held to a fiduciary standard when working with clients. As such, the level of disclosure is much higher. At the top of the pyramid are those financial planners who are certified by organizations such as the Certified Financial Planner Board of Standards, Inc. These planners must follow licensing rules, and sometimes SEC requirements, in addition to disclosure and practice standards as dictated by the Board.

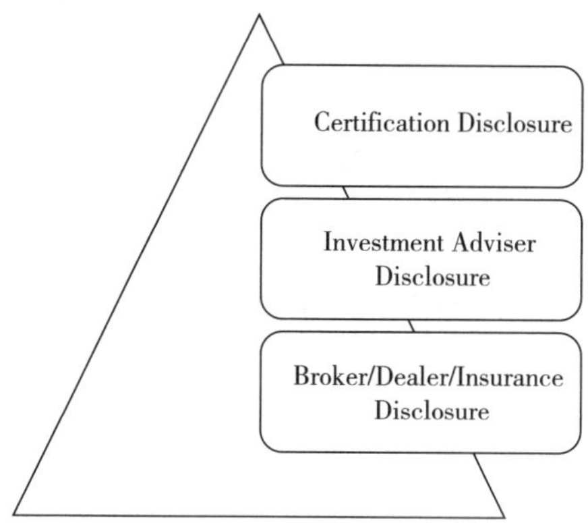

Figure 9 Hierarchy of disclosure

Case Illustration: The Fan Family

Working within a comprehensive financial planning platform you know that you must follow the rules and guidelines prescribed by your firm, as well as all governmental regulations. Working with your firm, you know that it is in your best interest—as a way to develop a strong client - planner alliance—to provide full disclosure of anything that might be considered a conflict of interest when working with the Fan family. For example, you should let them know if, for example, your spouse has a commercial interest in a home supply store. You know that the Jing and Xuan would like to make improvements to their apartment. Without fully disclosing the fact that one of your family members is in the business of providing home repair services, the Fans may not know for certainty whether your advice, in relation to spending money on home repairs, is unbiased. During the beginning phases of the financial planning process you should also disclose restrictions on products or services that you can provide, guidelines on compensation, and information about your expertise.

Chapter 3 Financial Planning Practice

The Financial Planning Process

By its very definition, financial planning is process oriented. The development of financial planning coincided with the advancement of strategic management, which is also process oriented. Within the context of financial planning, the process begins with the establishment of the planner – client relationship. This step involves defining relationship boundaries, disclosing fee and compensation methods, and clarifying working assumptions. Once the relationship has been established and defined, the next phase of the process involves gathering appropriate client data. This step of planning requires the adviser to determine the client's personal and household goals, financial needs, and financial situation. In addition to purely quantitative data, financial planners are expected to gather qualitative analytical inputs, such as measures of risk tolerance, goal expectations, and other information that could impact the way in which data is used in an analysis.

An important third step in the planning process involves an analysis and evaluation of the client's current financial situation. While such an analysis can be comprehensive in nature, it is also possible for financial planners to focus their evaluation on specific client derived goals and objectives. Typically, however, this third step in the planning process entails a review of a client's financial situation in relation to the following topics:

✓ Cash Flow and Net Worth Situation

✓ Income Tax Situation

✓ Risk Management Coverage, including:

- ○ life
- ○ disability
- ○ health
- ○ long – term care
- ○ property, casualty, and liability

✓ Investment Situation

✓ Retirement Situation

✓ Estate Planning Situation

✓ Special Needs Situation(s), including

- ○ education funding
- ○ elder care funding
- ○ charitable and legacy funding
- ○ child – specific funding

Once a client's financial situation has been evaluated, the process revolves to developing and presenting financial planning recommendations. This step in the financial planning process brings together a financial planner's creativity and technical competencies. A crucial next step in the process entails prompting a client to take action through recommendation and plan implementation. For many financial advisers this is the point of compensation, especially for those who are paid on a commission basis. It is during the implementation phase of the planning process that advisers select products and services that they believe best meet the needs of their clients. Rather than ending with implementation, the planning process requires financial advisers to continue to monitor the status of the client's situation in relation to recommendations made and implemented plans.

The six – step financial planning process is illustrated in Figure 1. As shown, the process is circular rather than linear. In effect, the planning process only ends when the planner – client relationship is dissolved. The continuing nature of the planning process can be seen in the association between monitoring and the establishment and defining of the planner – client relationship. Sometimes planning services will be strictly transactional. In these situations, once a product or service is delivered, the relationship comes to an end. Most times, however, the monitoring process, which can entail ongoing portfolio reviews, annual goals reviews, and other forms of supervision, leads into more in - depth planner - client relationships, new scopes of engagement, and additional service opportunities. When this happens, the financial planning process continues in the same step - by - step manner.

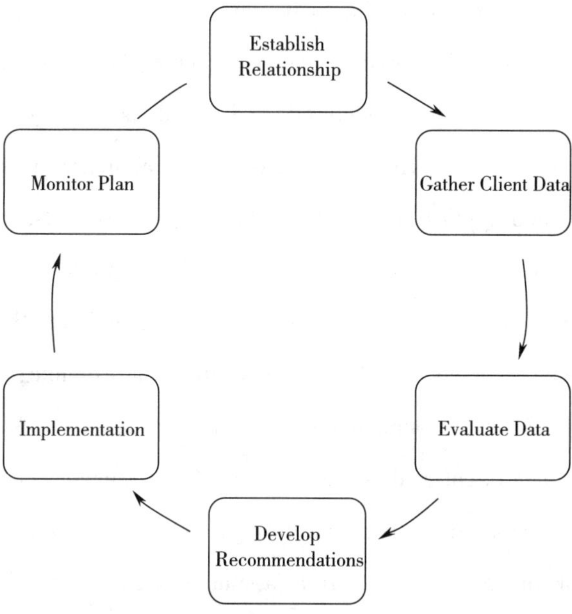

Figure 1 The Financial Planning Process

Elements of the Financial Planning Process

The complexity of the financial planning process is based, in a large part, on the practice management decisions made by individual financial planners. The following discussion highlights the role cash flow plays in shaping financial plans for most households. A brief review of how financial goals and objectives are formulated and analyzed is also presented. This is followed by a discussion of the key financial planning statements used at the outset of the planning process: the cash flow statement and the balance sheet. This is followed by an overview of the many ways macroeconomic factors shape assumptions made within a financial plan.

The Principle of Financial Planning: Cash Flow Planning

Financial planners generally fall into one of two schools of thought regarding the way in which the process of financial planning should be carried out. The first viewpoint is called goal based asset planning. The second approach is client centered, based on cash flow planning. The primary difference between a client centered and agoal based assetapproach is the way recommendations are formulated. The goal based asset approach uses institutional money management techniques and applies these to individuals and households. Institutional managers, particularly those in the non - profit sector, tend to build portfolios that are designed to fund current and future liability needs. When applied at the household level, this means that a client's goals are first determined as a specific funding liability. For example, a client may indicate wanting to retire at age 67 with an annual retirement income equal to $ 90,000, adjusted for inflation for 25 years. Each client goal is then ranked. Once ranked, goals are evaluated in the context of a client's balance sheet, rather than through a cash flow analysis. If it turns out that a goal is not attainable or unrealistic using current assumptions, then the planning process focuses on estimating the exact inputs needed to accomplish one or multiple goals. For example, a goal based asset financial planner might indicate to a client that she needs to take significantly more portfolio risk with her assets in order to reach a goal.

It is this last point that makes goal based asset financial planning unique. Goal based asset planning can be quite beneficial as a way to determine the likelihood of planning success by matching current assets to specific goals. Within this approach, it is possible to estimate funding liabilities as the difference between the future value of assets and expected goal costs. The method also provides for flexibility in portfolio development. Rather than having one portfolio, each goal can have a unique portfolio allocation. This is the point of divergence between a goal based asset methodology and a client centered approach. Those who advocate goal based asset financial planning are not as concerned with a client's risk profile, investing attitudes, past experience, or other qualitative planning inputs. What really matters, for a goal based asset financial adviser, is a client's risk capacity, not the client's willingness to engage in financial behavior in which potentially negative outcomes exist. Risk capacity refers to a client's ability to withstand a financial loss. Capacity is most directly tied to a person's net worth situation. Nearly all financial capacity factors are found on a client's balance sheet and in their tax and risk management profile. Goal based asset financial planning has a unique appeal. The approach attempts to remove as many non – quantifiable factors from the planning and portfolio development process as possible.

From a financial planner perspective, goal based asset planning seems both intuitive and very practical. Each client goal has a price. The key aspect associated with goal based asset planning is estimating that price. Given that few client goals are ever quickly fully funded, a portfolio can be developed, using a combination of stochastic and tax – adjusted strategies, which will eliminate funding liabilities over time.

The simplicity of goal based asset planning is also its shortfall. It is precisely the fixation on the quantitative nature of financial planning that causes many goal based asset financial plans to fail. It is helpful to think of goal based asset planning this way: the fact that recommendations are made with minimal regard to a client's attitudinal, emotional, or psychological preferences often leads to plan failure at some point in the future. It is important to remember that clients tend to be risk – averse. This means that when faced with prolonged and unexpected asset losses, clients will tend to step back and reevaluate their risk taking choices. The very nature of goal based asset planning involves forcing clients to sometimes take more risk than they may otherwise be comfortable taking. This is not a problem when portfolio assets increase; however, when portfolio assets decrease the stage is set for plan failure. In simple terms, goal based asset financial planning is ideally suited for clients who have excess risk capacity. Clients who must make sometimes painful asset and purchase choices with limited cash flow may find the goal based assetfinancial planning approach more problematic.

The client centered cash flow approach to financial planning provides an alternative for those financial planners who are most interested in helping their clients develop meaningful goals that have the highest probability of being funded over time. A client centered cash flow perspective forces clients to realistically define their financial objectives. Financial planning recommendations are then shaped by a thorough analysis of the client's goals, lifetime and legacy aspirations, time horizon, risk attitude, and other factors, with an emphasis on how goals can be funded over time through a combination of asset commitments and cash flow allocations. While the use and allocation of current assets is, of course, a key element in any financial plan, those who follow a cash flow approach tend to first look for ways to maximize discretionary cash flow, which is defined as:

- Discretionary Cash Flow = Gross Income - Fixed Expenses - Variable Expenses - Regular Savings

Financial planners who utilize a client centered cash flow approach acknowledge that the use of attitudinal factors, such as risk tolerance and emotions, play a key role in shaping future client behavior. Recall again the retirement example from above. A client centered financial adviser would predict, quite reasonably, that agoal based asset retirement plan may fail in the future. What evidence exists to predict failure? The answer to this question comes from the link between risk tolerance and future behavior. The evidence is clear that risk tolerance and wealth are positively associated①, and over time, clients strive to reach equilibrium between their willingness to take risk and the actual level of risk in their portfolio. Few individuals can withstand the pressure of taking ongoing risks beyond their comfort level. ②

From a purely practical point of view, conducting a cash flow analysis, which will be discussed later in this chapter, for each current and prospective client is useful for two reasons. The first is to determine whether or not someone has the wherewithal to fund their financial goals currently and in the future. While it is true that there are households that can allocate current assets to fully fund their goals, the reality is that these households are not at all common. Nearly all clients must rely, to some extent, on current cash flow to fund their goals. Second, it is important to understand a client's cash flow situation as a basis for compensation. In other words, clients must have sufficient discretionary cash flow to both fund goal achievement and to pay for ongoing financial planning services.

Financial Objectives and Demand Analysis

Regardless of which approach a particular financial planner uses in practice on a daily basis, a requisite step in the planning process involves establishing financial goals and

---

① Finke, Michael S., and Sandra J. Huston. 2003. "The Brighter Side of Financial Risk: Financial Risk Tolerance and Wealth." *Journal of Family and Economic Issues* 24 (3): 233 - 256.

② Grable, John E. 2013. "Gender, Wealth, and Risk: Why are Baby Boomer Women Less Risk Tolerant than Baby Boomer Men?" *Journal of Financial Service Professionals* 67 (3): 7 - 8.

objectives. Think of a goal as the outcome of the financial plan. A financial objective can be thought of as a step towards goal achievement. For example, a client may have a goal to fund a child's college education when the child turns age 18. The goal may include having enough money on hand to fully fund four years of education, including room and board and books. In order to reach the goal, it will be necessary to have implementable financial objectives clearly defined. In this case, one goal may include saving a specific dollar amount on a monthly basis into a tax – advantaged college saving plan. As this example illustrates, goals and objectives are tightly linked; it generally is not possible to achieve a financial goal unless a client is simultaneously working to meet financial objectives along the way.

Financial goals and objectives need to be clearly defined at the outset of the financial planning process. If the process is conceptualized as a journey, with the financial plan as a map, it becomes very apparent that goals and objectives are needed to determine both progress during the journey and also as a measure of financial planning success.

Many financial planning practitioners and decision – making academicians use what is called the "SMART" method to help clients identify and define their financial goals. SMART, as shown in Figure 2, is an acronym that means, (1) specific, (2) measurable, (3) attainable, (4) realistic, and (5) trackable.

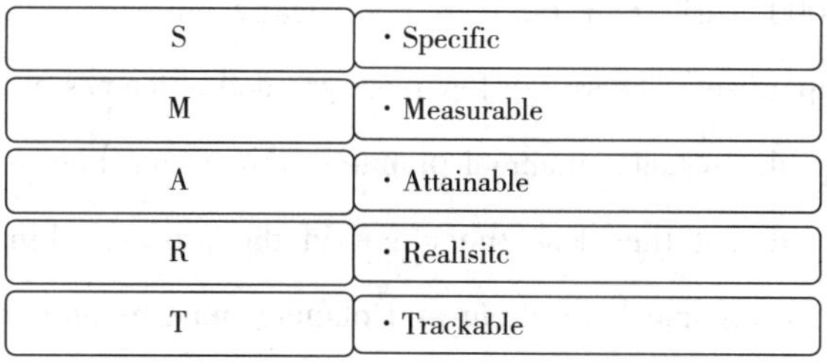

S	· Specific
M	· Measurable
A	· Attainable
R	· Realisitc
T	· Trackable

Figure 2 Components of a SMART Financial Goal

Applying the SMART approach to goal and objective formation is essential in helping clients fully understand where they are starting financially. The approach is also useful in helping clients stay on track towards goal achievement. For example, assume one client, age 58, states that she would like to take an once – in – a – lifetime world vacation. She further states that she would like to take the vacation within two years of her retirement and that she is hopeful her financial planner can develop a plan to make her dream come true. It should be obvious that the way in which the client has stated her goal does not provide the financial planner with enough information. Without more clarity on the goal it is likely that the client will find the planner's efforts to be lacking.

Rather than accept what the client has laid out, a financial planner could have helped define the goal using the SMART approach. The specific element of the goal was partially answered. She would like to take a dream vacation within two years of retirement. The question is then when does she plan to retire? Is it 5, 10, 15, or 20 years in the future? As stated, her goal is not measurable. The planner really needs to know, in today's dollars, what the dream vacation would cost. Answering this question may require an in – depth review of travel plans to determine the level of comfort the client expects. Achieving a \$ 10, 000 goal may entail different recommendations than paying for a \$ 100,000 goal. This leads to the issue of attainability. Every client has dreams and wants. Few people would turn down an all – expenses paid luxury tour of the world. The real issue is whether someone who wants such a tour can actually afford to pay for it. Stated another way, it is crucially important for financial planners to ascertain whether a client has the financial capacity to achieve the goal they have set. Financial capacity is a function of current assets, available cash flow, and expected future wealth. Related to this issue is the concept of having each goal be as realistic as possible. If, for example, the client has opted for the \$ 100,000 world tour but can realistically only afford a \$ 25,000 tour goal achievement will be jeopardized. There are few positive good outcomes associated with attempting to meet an unrealistic goal. In fact, financial planners who set out knowing that a client's goal is unrealistic most often find that they lose the client in the process. Finally, goals need to be trackable. This simply means that both client and planner must be able to determine, from time to time, if the client is on track to reaching the goal. In this case, trackability could include measuring the annualized return on investments dedicated to the world tour goal and measuring directly the level of savings dedicated towards goal achievement.

In reality, financial planners rarely deal with one goal in isolation. Given the integrative nature of financial planning, which is based on the notion of viewing a client's financial situation comprehensively, goals tend to be intertwined. Often, accomplishing one goal has an impact on achieving other goals and objectives. A key element when helping clients establish goals involves placing clear timelines for goal achievement. As shown below, time horizons can be defined as short, long, or somewhere inbetween. ① It goes almost without saying, but if a client's goal has an ultra – short or short time horizon, then the types of recommendations made need to be more conservative.

Table 1 **Goal Time Horizons Defined**

Time Horizon	Length of Time
Ultra – Short Term	9 months or less
Short – Term	More than 9 months to 2.5 years
Short – Intermediate Term	More than 2.5 years to 5.0 years
Long – Intermediate Term	More than 5.0 years to 10.0 years
Long Term	More than 10.0 years

It is relatively easy, using the SMART system, to establish goals. Clients may find goal setting exercises to be, quite simply, enjoyable. This can often lead to an over – abundance of client established goals and objectives. While having clients actively engaged in goal setting is an important input into the planning process, this can also cause financial planning difficulties. Unless a client holds limitless wealth, financial goals and objectives must be ranked within a financial plan. This is easier said than done. Think back to the example from above. While the client's goal is to fund a world tour, it might be concluded that this should not, or cannot, be her primary financial goal. Other issues, such as funding retirement, paying bills, or some other factor may rise to the top of the list of goals to be achieved. The following questions can be used to help rank goals. ②

➢ How important is the goal to the client?

➢ How important is it within the comprehensive plan that the goal be achieved?

➢ Is the goal a need or something the client wants?

➢ Does an alternative exist?

➢ Is the goal a one – time funding event?

➢ What is the likelihood that the goal will be achieved?

---

① Grable, John E., Kristy Archuleta, and David A Evans. 2009. "Hey Buddy, Do You Have the Correct Time (Horizon)?" *Journal of Financial Service Professionals* 63(4): 49 – 56.

② This list was adapted from: Slade, Stephen. 1994. "Goal – Based Decision Making: An Interpersonal Model." Hillsdale, NJ: Lawrence Erlbaum Associates.

- When is funding needed?
- Can the goal time implementation be delayed?
- How long will it take to fully fund the goal?
- How serious is the outcome if the goal is not achieved?

There are no set answers to these questions. For example, answering how serious it would be if the world tour goal was not achieved can only be determined by the client. If her answer is, "It would be nice but I can live with it one way or the other" this would indicate a lower ranking than if the client answered, "I would find my life to be incomplete and I would regret it the rest of my life." In general, however, high priority goals and objectives should be those marked by importance and seriousness if not accomplished. Balancing both short - and long - term goals is important as a way to show clients that they are progressing in their financial journey.

Financial Diagnosis and Financial Statements

The establishment of client goals and objectives tends to be the foundation of all financial planning processes. Once goals and objectives have been identified, clarified, and ranked it is important to begin evaluating a client's financial capacity to begin working towards goal achievement. Two documents form the basis of all financial planning work: a cash flow statement① and a balance sheet.

Before moving forward, it is important to clarify a few key terms. The cash flow statement, which is described in some detail in this chapter, is simply a report of what a client earned and spent over a given time period. This differs from a budget. A budget is a financial counseling and planning tool designed to help a client decide where they will spend their income in the future. Sometimes a budget is called a spending plan. While all financial planners utilize cash flow statements—as a retrospective tool showing a client's past actions—the use of budgets is less universal.② There are, however, financial planners who incorporate

---

① Occasionally a cash flow statement is called an income and expense statement.

② Financial counselors are more likely to use budgets when working with clients. A financial counselor, as defined in practice, is someone who helps a client deal with problematic spending, borrowing, and saving behavior. Often, those who seek the help of a financial counselor are facing bankruptcy or reductions in their credit score. For simplicity, financial counseling can be thought of as a process designed to stabilize a client's financial situation. Financial planning, on the other hand, is almost always intended to help move a client forward towards goal achievement.

both into the planning process. That is, these planners insist that their clients create and maintain a spending plan. The determination of how well the client stayed on track with spending can then be evaluated using a cash flow statement. The use of budgeting techniques is generally used whenever a client has trouble saving money or in situations when income fluctuates from period to period.

The Cash Flow Statement

As described earlier in the chapter, the role of discretionary cash flow within the financial planning process cannot be over - emphasized. The primary factor in determining whether a client will reach some or all of their financial goals is their ability to fund, from cash flow (and assets), saving objectives. Table 2 illustrates a typical cash flow statement. ① This template can also be used as the foundation of a budget.

As shown, income is listed at the top of the statement. It is useful to split income into three categories: earned, unearned, and non - taxable. The primary reason for separating income into categories is the distinction will facilitate tax planning later in the planning process. For example, earned income may be taxed at a different rate than unearned income.

Expenses are generally split between those that are fixed (non - discretionary) and variable (discretionary). Fixed expenses include those that have a high degree of regularity. For instance, housing payments, either in the form of a mortgage or rent, must be paid on a regular basis, and as such, this expense is considered to be fixed. It is important to note that savings can be classified as a fixed expense if the savings occurs at a regular interval. Retirement savings that is tied to a client's salary is an example of fixed savings expense. Reinvested dividends, interest, and capital gains would also be included as fixed expenses. In fact, failing to "expense" these sources of income will lead to an inflated, and inaccurate, level of discretionary cash flow. Variable expenses are those in which the client has more freedom to adjust expenditures. Expenses for food, for example, provide a good example. Nearly any client can vary their expenses on food. This may not be something the client would prefer to do, but it is an option as a way to increase cash flow.

---

① For simplicity purposes, the cash flow analysis is assumed to be conducted on an annual basis.

The determination of a client's level of discretionary cash flow is relatively straight forward. Once income has been established, both fixed and variable expenses should be subtracted from this dollar figure. The resulting number indicates if the client has excess cash flow to devote to financial planning goals and objectives. Table 2 illustrates a typical cash flow statement.

Table 2 **Cash Flow Statement**

Income	Client	Co – Client	Total
Earned Income			
Wages & Salaries			
Bonuses			
Other			
Unearned Income			
Interest			
Dividends			
Business Income			
Pensions			
Rent			
Royalties			
Other			
Non – Taxable Income			
Gifts			
Loans			
Scholarships			
Other			
Total Income			
Fixed Expenses	Client	Co – Client	Total
Taxes			
Federal			
State			
Total			

Concluded

Income	Client	Co – Client	Total
Local			
Personal			
Other			
Salary Reductions			
Health Care			
Retirement			
Other			
Debt Payments			
Housing (Principal & Interest) or Rent			
Home Equity Loan			
Auto Loan			
Student Loan			
Secured Loan			
Unsecured Loan			
Credit Cards			
Other			
Insurance			
Auto			
Home or Renter's			
Life (not salary reduction)			
Disability (not salary reduction)			
Health (not salary reduction)			
Long – Term Care			
Other			
Dedicated Savings and Investments			
General Savings			
Retirement			
Education			
Special Needs			
Specific Goals			
Reinvested Interest, Dividends, & Capital Gains			

Concluded

Total Fixed Expenses			
Variable Expenses	Client	Co – Client	Total
Housing and Utilities			
House Maintenance and Repairs			
Lawn/Yard Maintenance			
Utilities			
Other			
Household Expenses			
Clothing and Accessories			
Laundry and Dry – cleaning			
Personal Care			
Furnishings			
Hired Help			
Allowances			
Child Care			
Other			
Food			
Groceries			
Eating Out			
Entertainment			
Internet, TV, & Cable			
Hobbies			
Recreation			
Travel			
Club Dues			
Other			
Medical			
Deductibles			
Prescriptions			
General Health Care			
Unreimbursed Heath Expenses			
Other			
Transportation			
Gas and Maintenance			
Licenses and Registration			

Concluded

Variable Expenses	Client	Co – Client	Total
Parking and Tolls			
Public Transportation			
Other			
Miscellaneous			
Subscriptions			
Phones			
Gifts			
Charitable Giving			
Business			
Tobacco, Gambling, and Alcohol			
Child Support			
Alimony			
Pet Care			
Mail			
Bank Fees			
Investment Feeds			
Legal Fees			
Other			
Total Variable Expenses	Client	Co – Client	Total
TOTAL INCOME			
– TOTAL FIXED EXPENSES			
– TOTAL VARIALBE EXPENSES			
= DISCRETIONARY CASH FLOW			

Case Illustration: The Fan Family

When you first met the Fan family in Chapter 1 you spent a lot of time gathering data about the family's lifestyle, goals, insurance, and general financial situation. At this point in the financial planning process—gathering appropriate client data—it is essential that you uncover all of their sources of income and expenditures. The following cash flow statement summarizes their yearly (and monthly) cash flow position. It is worth noting that this statement of cash flows contains different headings than the example shown in Table 2. The reason the two statements differ is because cash flow and balance sheets are meant to be adaptable and flexible.

Estimating a client's cash flow position marks a key transition point in the financial planning process. Once you have a definite cash flow figure in hand it is time to begin analyzing and evaluating the data to measure the client's financial status. As shown below, the Fan family is doing an excellent job managing their household financial situation. They are currently able to generate monthly and annual savings. Having a positive cash flow offers greater opportunities for you to make recommendations that can be funded.

CASH FLOW STATEMENT

January 1, 20 × × to December 31, 20 × ×

INFLOWS	ANNUAL	MONTHLY
Salary (H)	$ 150 000	$ 12 500
Salary (W)	65 000	5 417
Interest and Dividends	1 326	111
Capital Gains	5 787	482
Total	$ 222 113	$ 18 509
OUTFLOWS		
403b Contribution (H)	$ 17 000	$ 1 417
401k Contribution (W)	$ 17 000	$ 1 417
Individual Investment Account Contribution (H)	5 000	417
Individual Investment Account Contribution (W)	5 000	417
Flex Spending Contribution (H)	3 000	250
Flex Spending Contribution (W)	1 000	83
Savings Account Contribution (JT)	1 000	83
Federal Income Tax Withholding	33 617	2 801
State Income Tax Withholding	9 511	793
Social Security	10 472	873
Mortgage Payment	12 780	1 194
Property Tax	6 319	527
Vehicle Loan Payments	8 625	719
Utilities Electricity	1 350	113
Gas	1 560	130
Water	660	55
Phones	1 440	120
Cable TV	480	40

Concluded

INFLOWS	ANNUAL	MONTHLY
Internet	720	60
Insurance: Auto	1 250	104
Health	4 200	350
Disability	220	18
Umbrella	260	22
Inland Marine	60	5
Term Life	90	8
Universal Life	250	21
Homeowners	620	52
Medical/dental/vision care	3 000	250
Child care	5 760	480
Hardware/Software	5 200	433
Cleaning Service	960	80
Lawn Service	1 580	132
Gas/oil/maintenance	2 600	217
Food	10 800	900
Clothing/personal care	7 260	605
Professional Memberships	1 050	88
Sky Diving	3 000	250
Vacation	12 000	1 000
Donations	18 000	1 500
Total	$ 205 314	$ 17 238
SURPLUS = DISCRETIONARY CASH FLOW		
Available for goals & savings	$ 16 799	$ 1 271

The Balance Sheet

The second important planning statement is the balance sheet. The purpose of a balance sheet is to provide a summary of what a client owns (assets) and owes (liabilities). Table 3 illustrates elements found in a typical balance sheet. It is important to note that the specific assets and liabilities listed can and should be changed to match each client's specific situation. What is less likely to be changed is the order in which assets and liabilities are listed. Generally, assets are categorized according to their liquidity; that is, those assets that can be converted to cash quickly in an active market are listed at the beginning of the asset listing. For example, checking and savings account assets typically are the first items shown on a balance sheet. Assets with low liquidity, such as collectibles, household furnishings, and boats are listed towards the bottom.

Similarly, liabilities are listed according to their payoff time horizon. Short – term debts, including credit cards, are typically shown first in the liability section. A short – term liability is any bill, loan, or expense that is currently outstanding but payable within the next year. For simplicity, utility bills and other recurring short – term payments are generally only listed if a client is past due in terms of making a payment.

Clients should be reminded, whenever they are involved in helping establish asset estimates and liability values, of the following two rules. First, assets should always be valued at fair market value. Fair market value is equivalent to the cash value of the asset in the open market. Sometimes clients use the cost of an item when originally purchased. This can be problematic because the point of a balance sheet is to provide the client and planner with a realistic estimate of asset values as a measure of liquidity. Valuing monetary and investment assets is generally easier than estimating the worth of personal and use assets. In the United States and Canada, it is possible to obtain valuations for cars through the use of online services, such as Edmunds. com and KBB. com. For other assets, such as boats and furnishings, thrift store values can sometimes be used to arrive at a conservative valuation. Second, the dollar amount of liabilities should equal the amount needed to fully payoff the debt. For example, if a client owns a car with three years remaining on the loan, the amount shown on the balance sheet should be the liability listed on the monthly statement.

The ultimate outcome associated with a balance sheet is an estimate of a client's net worth, which is defined as follows:

Net Worth = Assets - Liabilities

There are no hard and fast rules associated with what constitutes an appropriate level of net worth for a client at any given time. In general, net worth should increase over a client's lifecycle, but the absolute level of net worth will be different for each client based on factors such as age, attitudes (e. g., level of debt aversion), level of discretionary cash flow, and past financial windfalls.

Sometimes clients easily confuse the purpose of a cash flow statement versus a balance sheet. These two financial statements serve as the foundation of all financial plans, and as such, financial planners sometimes assume that clients recognize the distinct purpose of each document. This assumption can lead to confusion between a client and his or her financial planner. It is important for financial planners to remind their clients—especially those clients who are new to the planning process—that the cash flow statement is used to record earnings, savings, and spending. A balance sheet is used exclusively to record assets and liabilities. Confusion often arises in relation to the role of savings in the two statements. Cash flow items, such as saving for retirement in a tax - deferred plan, will increase a client's assets on the balance sheet. Likewise, paying off debt with assets will increase a client's cash flow but leave their net worth unchanged. For maximum clarity, it can be useful for financial planners to describe these processes in a stepwise manner; that is, rather than assume that a client can differentiate between a cash flow item (e. g. , saving monthly for retirement) and an asset or liability, financial planners should consider drawing figures (both actual and figurative) that show the link between the two statements. An example is shown in Figure 3.

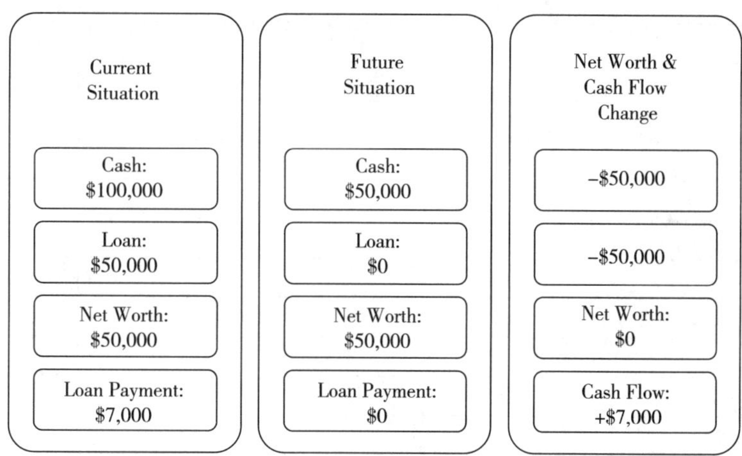

Figure 3 Net Worth and Cash Flow Example

A simple example, as shown in Figure 3, can be an effective tool to help client distinguish between the purpose of a cash flow and balance sheet statement. Figure 3 illustrates how using assets to reduce liabilities has no impact on a client's net worth position, but also how paying down debt can increase discretionary cash flow. This very simple concept is, in many ways, the foundation of financial counseling and planning practice. A key step in the planning process involves identifying ways to increase useable cash flow that can be allocated towards financial goals. Paying down debt with assets is a fundamental strategy associated with accomplishing this activity. Other common planning actions designed to increase cash flow include refinancing existing debts, trimming current discretionary expenses, increasing yields and returns on assets, and balancing the use of debt in ways that increase a client's financial flexibility.

Table 3 **Balance Sheet**

Assets	Client	Co – Client	Value
Monetary Assets Checking			
Saving			
Money Market			
Certificate of Deposit			
Other			
Investment Assets			
Stocks			
Bonds			
Mutual Funds			
Commodities			
Other			
Real Assets			
Primary Residence			
Second Home			
Vacation Home			
Other			
Retirement Assets			
Tax – Deferred Retirement Plan			
Tax – Free Assets			
Other			
Insurance Assets			
Employer Provided Life Policy			
Cash Value Policy			
Other			
Education Assets			
Tax – Advantaged Plan			
Savings Bonds			
Other			
Personal Assets			

Concluded

Assets	Client	Co – Client	Value
Automobile			
Automobile			
Watercraft			
Collectibles			
Other			
Use Assets			
Household Furnishings			
Electronics			
Other			
Liabilities	Client	Co – Client	Amount
Current Liabilities			
Credit Cards			
Short Term Installment Loans			
Other			
Long – Term Liabilities			
Mortgage			
2nd Mortgage			
Auto Loan			
Auto Loan			
Consumer Loans			
Other			
TOTAL ASSETS			
TOTAL LIABILITIES			
NET WORTH			

Case Illustration: The Fan Family

A balance sheet showing the asset and liability position for the Fan family is shown below. Similarly to the cash flow statement, this example looks different than Table 3. In this example, assets are listed on the left side of the sheet, whereas liabilities are identified on the right side. The following terms are used as shortcut identifiers:

JT = Joint Ownership

H = Owned by Husband (Jing)

W = Owned by Wife (Xuan)

As illustrated, the Fan family is doing a good job managing their assets and liabilities. Their current net worth position is high relative to their age. The use of financial ratios will be introduced later in the chapter to help evaluate their overall financial status.

STATEMENT OF FINANCIAL POSITION: BALANCE SHEET

As of January 1, 20 × ×

ASSETS	TITLE	BALANCE	BASIS	LIABILITIES	TITLE	BALANCE
Cash and Cash Equivalents				Auto Loan *	JT	$ 10 513
Checking and Savings	JT (Entirety)	$ 5 200		Mortgage **	JT	231 284
Money Market Mutual Fund	JT (Entirety)	16 800				
Brokerage Account	W	5 032				
Cash Value of Life Insurance	W	3 647		* 3 year, 3.00% annual rate		
		Total	$ 30 679	**4.00% annual rate; original balance:	$ 250 000	
Investments						
Stocks – Investment Technology Group	H	$ 10 518	$ 6 000	TOTAL LIABILITIES	$ 241 797	
Stocks – Dick's Sporting Goods Inc.	H	33 839	18 000			
Stocks – Wells Fargo & Company	W	30 849	15 000			
Stocks – Walgreen Company	W	27 678	20 000			
Vanguard Energy (Mutual Fund)	JT (Entirety)	84 782	65 000			
		Total	$ 187 666			
Retirement Assets						
Non-vested Defined Benefit *	H	$ 38 463				
403b – Vanguard Target Retirement 2035 Fund	H	70 263		NET WORTH	$ 862 577	
401 (k) – Vanguard Target Retirement 2035 Fund	W	73 776				
401 (k) – previous employment (see details)	H	135 837				
IRA – Domestic Mutual Funds (see details)	H	53 814				
IRA – International Mutual Funds (see details)	H	9 460				
IRA – Domestic Mutual Funds (see details)	W	82 435				
IRA – International Mutual Funds (see details)	W	5 524				
		Total	$ 431 109			
Use Assets						
Home	JT (Entirety)	$ 315 920				
Vehicles	JT (Entirety)	61 000				
Furniture	JT (Entirety)	30 000				
Computer (hardware software network)	H	5 000				
Jewelry	W	20 000				
Collections	W	23 000				
		Total	$ 454 920			
TOTAL ASSETS			$ 1 104 374	TOTAL LIABILITIES & NET WORTH	$ 1 104 374	

note: H = husband's separate property; W = wife's separate property; JT = jointly held property

* Jing would like to count his DB plan as retirement income

Evaluating the Current Situation using Financial Ratios

Financial planners, as well as their clients, need to know whether a client is on or off target in terms of asset accumulation, debt structure, and cash flow management. Whereas 30 or 40 years ago it was generally assumed that those with more assets and high income were in a better position to implement financial planning recommendations, it is now known that it is the relative value of assets to liabilities and total discretionary cash flow that really matters. Often, individuals and families who appear to possess the greatest wealth are, upon objective analysis, the most leveraged and illiquid.

Today, financial planners use a number of financial ratios to gauge their clientele's financial capacity to implement recommendations. Financial ratios are also used to measure progress towards goal achievement. Table 4 shows the most widely used financial ratios in the profession. (Not shown are the front - and back - end ratios that measure mortgage viability; these ratios will be discussed in greater detail later in the book.) For those familiar with security analysis, these ratios may look similar to analytic tools used by financial managers. In fact, financial planners adopted the use of corporate measures and applied these ratios to the household unit. Notice in Table 4 that a benchmark is provided for each ratio. It is important to note that these benchmarks are based on consensus opinion within the financial planning literature. For example, some financial planners insist that their clients need only two month's worth of emergency savings. Other financial planners are uncomfortable if their clients have less than nine months of expenses saved or accessible through life insurance cash value. In general, however, these benchmarks provide guidance on what is considered acceptable in the profession.

Table 4 **Financial Planning Ratios**

Ratio	Formula	Benchmark
Current Ratio	Monetary Assets / Current Liabilities	Greater Than 1.0
Emergency Fund Ratio	Monetary Assets / Monthly Living Expenses	3 to 6 Months
Savings Ratio	Total Savings / Gross Income	Greater than 10%
Debt Ratio	Total Liabilities / Total Assets	Less Than 40%
Long - Term Debt Coverage Ratio	Annual Gross Income / Total L - T Debt Payments	Greater Than 2.5
Debt to Income Ratio	Consumer Credit Payments / After - Tax Income	Less Than 15%

It is worth remembering that financial ratios are meant only as objective measures of financial health. As such, the absolute value of a ratio will depend on each client's stage of the life cycle. For example, someone just entering the workforce after graduating from college may not meet, or be close to meeting, the current or debt ratio benchmarks. Their level of student loan and consumer debt may exceed all accumulated assets. This is perfectly acceptable, assuming the debt was used to purchase human capital—an investment in the income generating capability of the client. Over time the client should expect to pay down debt as assets increase. As such, the financial ratio benchmark becomes more of a financial objective. On the other hand, a client who is already entering the glide path towards retirement should easily exceed most of the benchmarks shown in Table 4. A serious underachievement in any of the listed financial ratios would indicate the need for immediate remedial action for that particular client.

Case Illustration: The Fan Family

Analyzing and evaluating client data and measuring a client's financial status typically begins, within a comprehensive financial planning framework, by estimating financial ratios. Information provided by the Fan family was used to calculate the financial ratios described above. As shown below, the Fan family is doing very well in respect to the management of their resources. Their current and debt - to - income ratios cannot be computed because they have no short - term consumer debt. This means that they have more cash flow to allocate towards savings and other goals. Their emergency fund ratio falls between one month and nearly three and a half months. The reason for this wide variation is related to the inputs used. If the Fans' total monthly expenses are incorporated into the formula then then the ratio is below the benchmark threshold; however, if retirement plan savings and taxes are removed, then their emergency fund is sufficiently large. The Fan family's savings ratio is an indication that Jing and Xuan are doing a fantastic job of living within their means. The ratio was determined by adding their end - of - year discretionary cash flow with other forms of savings, including retirement plan contributions. Finally, their liability ratios show that they are in an excellent position, and if needed, they should be able to access credit easily.

Fan Family Financial Ratios

Ratio	Benchmark	Actual
Current Ratio	Greater Than 1.0	n. a.
Emergency Fund Ratio	3 to 6 Months	1.78 to 3.53

Concluded

Ratio	Benchmark	Actual
Savings Ratio	Greater than 10%	28%
Debt Ratio	Less Than 40%	22%
L - T Debt Coverage Ratio	Greater Than 2.5	10.38
Debt to Income Ratio	Less Than 15%	n. a.

It is at this stage of the financial planning process the general strengths and weaknesses of the client's situation should be summarized. The following is a list of strengths and weaknesses—areas for improvement—related to the Fans' overall financial situation:

Strengths

- The Fans' have excellent net worth.
- They have excellent annual income and cash flow position.
- Jing contributes to his retirement plan account.
- Xuan contributes to her retirement plan account.
- Jing has disability insurance coverage.
- They have a high level of liability coverage.
- All household members have adequate health insurance coverage.
- The Fans' have appropriate insurance coverage for their collections.

Weakness

- The Fans' need to take additional estate planning action; they do not appear to have living wills or medical directives; the Fans' may need to update their will as it was last done 8 years ago.
- The Fans' are not adequately covered for the loss of their jewelry.
- They do not have adequate life insurance coverage.
- The policy ownership of Jing and Xuan's life insurance policies should be reviewed; current ownership status may increase estate tax liability upon either of their deaths.
- Their current mortgage interest rate is higher than market rates.
- The Fans' emergency fund is likely underfunded.
- The Fans' do not have sufficient college funds set aside for Lu.
- Xuan does not have adequate disability insurance coverage.
- Neither have long - term care insurance coverage.

The Macroeconomic Environment and Fundamental Assumptions in Financial Planning

Financial planning, unlike many other professional endeavors, relies heavily on the use of carefully chosen and applied assumptions. Lytton, Grable, and Klock (2013)① defined a financial planning assumption as an inference based on "premises, reasoned conclusions, facts, or circumstantial evidence that affects a client's planning need and the quantification of that need" (p. 265). Rate of return, interest rate, longevity, health, wellness, and economic assumptions, just to name a few, form the backdrop for all financial planning calculations and recommendations. Of critical importance is the use of economic indicators as a tool to help financial planners derive appropriate planning assumptions. These assumptions are used from the initial stages of client engagement through the monitoring processes associated with financial plan implementation. The following discussion highlights some of the key macroeconomic indicators that nearly all financial planners monitor on an ongoing basis.

Understanding and predicting future inflation in the economy is of particular importance. Actual and perceived inflation levels are a key determinant of asset prices. In general, rising consumer prices are reflected in decreased financial asset prices, particularly the prices of fixed - income securities. Financial advisers who believe that inflation will increase in the future will incorporate this assumption into nearly every financial calculation made in a client's financial plan. For example, increasing inflation will result in an increased retirement asset need, an increased educational savings need, and a portfolio allocation that is protected from potential falling security prices. On the other hand, an assumption of decreasing inflation will result in a much more aggressive asset allocation strategy than would otherwise seem appropriate. Financial planners watch, and try to anticipate, the following indexes as a way to derive inflation rate assumptions. In general, rising consumer, producer, salary, employment, housing, import, and GDP prices are considered to be harbingers of future inflation.

- Consumer Price Index: A seasonally adjusted index of prices paid for common household items for urban consumers.

---

① Lytton, R. H., Grable, J. E., &Klock, D. D. (2013). *The process of financial planning: Developing a financial plan* (2nd ed.). Erlanger, KY: National Underwriter.

- Producer Price Index: A seasonally adjusted index of the price of finished goods within the economy.
- Employment Cost Index: A salary, wage, and benefit index for civilian workers.
- Employment Situation Index: A measure of civilian unemployment.
- Housing Price Index: An index of quarterly price changes in real estate markets.
- Import and Export Price Indexes: Measures of prices of imported and exported goods and services.
- Gross Domestic Product Price Index: An indicator of period - over - period changes in gross domestic product.

In addition to forecasting inflation, financial planners tend to be particularly concerned with tracking changes in major investment and asset markets. Activity in these markets serves as the basis of all rate of return assumptions used within a financial plan. It is important to note that nearly all professional software programs incorporate rate of return, price correlation, and standard deviation (price volatility) assumptions; however, such assumptions should only be used as a starting point in estimation of planner specific assumptions (software assumptions are either made by an individual, a group of experts, or estimated using trend analysis methodologies). Regardless of the assumption development method, the following market indexes typically serve as the historical foundation for rate of return assumptions, with those in bold dominating the development of global rate of return assumptions:

Stock Markets

- All Ordinaries Australian Index
- AMEX Composite Index
- Bovespa Brazilian Index
- CAC 40 France Index
- DAX Germany Index
- Dow Jones Euro Stoxx 50 Index
- Dow Jones Industrial Average Index
- Dow Jones Wilshire 5000
- FTSE 100 English Index

- FTSE Burse Malaysia Index
- FTSE Emerging Market Index
- FTSEurofirst 300 Index
- Hang Seng Index
- IBEX 35 Spanish Index
- Indice de Precios y Cotizaciones Mexican Index
- ISEQ 20 Ireland Index
- JSX Indonesia Index
- KOSPI Korean Index
- MSCI EAFE Index
- NASDAQ Index
- Nikkei 225 Index
- NZX 50 New Zealand Index
- RTS Russian Index
- Russell 3000 Index
- S&P 500 Index
- S&P Asia 50
- S&P CNX Nifty India Index
- S&P Europe 350
- S&P MIB Italian Index
- SSE Composite China Index
- ST Singapore Index
- Swiss Market Index
- TA – 25 Israel Index
- TSEC Taiwan Index

Currencies

- Canadian Dollar
- European Euro
- Japanese Yen

- U. K. Pound
- U. S. Dollar

Commodities

- Gold
- Light Crude Oil
- Natural Gas
- Corn

Bonds

- 3 – Month U. S. Treasury Bill
- 10 – Year U. S. Treasury Bond
- 30 – Year U. S. Treasury Bond
- 3 – Month LIBOR

In general, financial planning assumptions can be classified as either client specific or global. Examples of client specific assumptions include estimates of a client's lifespan, which, in turn, are based on client data related to health, family history, and expectations; future income tax rates;, and risk – adjusted rates of return. Most often, client specific assumptions are arrived at through dialog and negotiation with a client. For example, whether or not a client will increase savings over the duration of a goal funding time horizon is an assumption that needs to be determined jointly with a client. Global assumptions are those that are used to form the overall planning strategies used in multiple client plans. Examples of global assumptions, some of which flow from an analysis of the indexes and markets listed above, include:

- Average inflation
- Average nursing home costs
- Average fixed – income returns
- Average real estate returns
- Average stock market returns
- Benchmark safe withdrawal rates
- College tuition inflation

- Current and future estate and gift tax rates
- Current and future ordinary income tax rates

Life Cycle and Simulation of Cash Flows

The term "lifecycle" refers to the process of transformation that occurs to changes in economic, attitudinal, and physiological factors over the course of a person's life. Earlier in the chapter, a basic cash flow statement was presented and described. It was stressed that the cash flow statement serves as the foundation of nearly all financial planning work. In effect, a single year statement of cash flows shows all sources of income and all expenses incurred by a client.

Simulation of cash flows, over the course of a life cycle, is a method that can add a great deal of value to the process of financial planning. Financial planners, and their clients, face the ongoing challenge of "proving" that one or a set of recommendations, if implemented, will result in positive long – lasting financial outcomes. The use of a simple cash flow statement (or balance sheet for that matter) cannot possibly provide the necessary proof. Cash flow simulation provides a means to illustrate how the implementation of a comprehensive financial plan will change a client's financial situation over the life cycle. It is important to note that lifecycle, when linked with cash flow simulation, is loosely defined. The duration of a lifecycle analysis will vary based on each client's unique situation. The length of analysis can be quite short, or it can extend literally from the point of analysis through the death a client.

Table 4 provides a simple example of a cash flow simulation. The analysis illustrates how funding four years of college will impact a client's cash flow situation. Essentially, this analysis was conducted to help a client determine if they could afford to send their child to a relatively expensive college and if the family should insist that the child and family incur debt or chose another institution of higher education. The analysis helped the client see that over the four years of college the family's cash flow situation would be reduced. In fact, the client would need to borrow money in order to balance income and expenses. However, the amount of borrowing to pay for college, as shown, is not substantial in relation to the client's annual income. By using a cash flow simulation, the financial planner was able to show the client that after paying for four years of college the cash flow situation would improve dramatically, which would allow for any loans to be repaid quickly.

Typically, lifecycle analyses tend to be more complex than what is shown in Table 5. Within a comprehensive financial plan the impact of all recommendations should be illustrated. These types of historical reviews are very useful from a client's perspective. Nearly all clients are concerned about the current year's cash flow situation. Being able to balance income and expenses is critically important; however, financial planners need to constantly remind their clients to stay focused on longer – term goal achievement. Cash flow simulations are an excellent tool for this purpose.

Simulations can also be used as a plan monitoring system for a financial planner. For example, if the cumulative effect of financial planning recommendations leads to consistent negative cash flows in the future, a financial planner can reasonably assume that the plan will likely fail. Given this almost inevitable conclusion, the cash flow simulation can then be used to help refine recommendations and generate new ways to balance income and expenses.

Table 5 **Cash Flow Simulation Example**

	Year1	Year2	Year3	Year4	Year5	Year6	Year7	Year8	Year9	Year10
Yearly Income										
Salary Client One	$ 152 000	$ 158 080	$ 164 403	$ 170 979	$ 177 819	$ 184 931	$ 192 328	$ 200 022	$ 208 022	$ 216 343
Salary Client Two	$ 65 000	$ 67 275	$ 69 630	$ 72 067	$ 74 589	$ 77 200	$ 79 902	$ 82 698	$ 85 593	$ 88 588
Interest Received	$ 3 600	$ 3 744	$ 3 894	$ 4 050	$ 4 211	$ 4 380	$ 4 555	$ 4 737	$ 4 927	$ 5 124
Group Benefit Income	$ 475	$ 494	$ 514	$ 535	$ 556	$ 578	$ 601	$ 625	$ 650	$ 676
Total Income	$ 221 075	$ 229 593	$ 238 441	$ 247 630	$ 257 175	$ 267 089	$ 277 387	$ 288 082	$ 299 192	$ 310 732
Fixed Yearly Expenses										
Principal&Intereston Home	$ 18 037	$ 18 037	$ 18 037	$ 18 037	$ 18 037	$ 18 037	$ 18 037	$ 18 037	$ 18 037	$ 18 037
Education Funding	$ 13 000	$ 13 000	$ 13 000	$ 13 000	$ 2 400	$ 2 400	$ 2 400	$ 2 400	$ 2 400	$ 2 400
Child's School Tuition	$ 9 600	$ 10 080	$ 10 584	$ 11 113	$ 11 669	$ 12 252	$ 12 865	$ 13 508	$ 14 184	$ 14 893
Credit Cards	$ 3 800	$ 3 914	$ 4 031	$ 4 152	$ 4 277	$ 4 405	$ 4 537	$ 4 674	$ 4 814	$ 4 958
LoanPaymentTotal	$ 44 437	$ 45 031	$ 45 653	$ 46 303	$ 36 383	$ 37 095	$ 37 840	$ 38 619	$ 39 435	$ 40 288
Life Insurance	$ 7 344	$ 7 564	$ 7 791	$ 8 025	$ 8 266	$ 8 514	$ 8 769	$ 9 032	$ 9 303	$ 9 582
Disability Insurance *	$ 748	$ 770	$ 794	$ 817	$ 842	$ 867	$ 893	$ 920	$ 948	$ 976
Medical Insurance *	$ 9 600	$ 9 888	$ 10 185	$ 10 490	$ 10 805	$ 11 129	$ 11 463	$ 11 807	$ 12 161	$ 12 526
Homeowner's Insurance	$ 2 265	$ 2 333	$ 2 403	$ 2 475	$ 2 549	$ 2 625	$ 2 704	$ 2 785	$ 2 869	$ 2 955
Automobile Insurance	$ 3 600	$ 3 708	$ 3 819	$ 3 934	$ 4 052	$ 4 173	$ 4 299	$ 4 428	$ 4 560	$ 4 697

Concluded

	Year1	Year2	Year3	Year4	Year5	Year6	Year7	Year8	Year9	Year10
GroupBenefitInsurance	$ 475	$ 489	$ 504	$ 519	$ 535	$ 551	$ 567	$ 584	$ 602	$ 620
OtherMisc. Ins. Premiums	$ 588	$ 606	$ 624	$ 643	$ 662	$ 682	$ 702	$ 723	$ 745	$ 767
Insurance Total	$ 24 620	$ 25 359	$ 26 119	$ 26 903	$ 27 710	$ 28 541	$ 29 398	$ 30 279	$ 31 188	$ 32 123
FederalIncomeTaxes	$ 30 573	$ 31 643	$ 32 750	$ 33 896	$ 35 083	$ 36 311	$ 37 582	$ 38 897	$ 40 258	$ 41 667
State&LocalIncomeTaxes	$ 8 632	$ 8 934	$ 9 247	$ 9 570	$ 9 905	$ 10 252	$ 10 611	$ 10 982	$ 11 367	$ 11 764
FICA	$ 14 226	$ 14 724	$ 15 239	$ 15 773	$ 16 325	$ 16 896	$ 17 487	$ 18 099	$ 18 733	$ 19 388
RealEstateTaxes	$ 4 800	$ 4 968	$ 5 142	$ 5 322	$ 5 508	$ 5 701	$ 5 900	$ 6 107	$ 6 321	$ 6 542
PersonalPropertyTaxes	$ 3 200	$ 3 312	$ 3 428	$ 3 548	$ 3 672	$ 3 801	$ 3 934	$ 4 071	$ 4 214	$ 4 361
Other Taxes	$ 1 900	$ 1 967	$ 2 035	$ 2 107	$ 2 180	$ 2 257	$ 2 336	$ 2 417	$ 2 502	$ 2 590
Tax Total	$ 63 331	$ 65 547	$ 67 841	$ 70 216	$ 72 673	$ 75 217	$ 77 849	$ 80 574	$ 83 394	$ 86 313
Regular/AllocatedSavings	$ 4 200	$ 4 368	$ 4 543	$ 4 724	$ 4 913	$ 5 110	$ 5 314	$ 5 527	$ 5 748	$ 5 978
Unallocated Savings	$ 3 750	$ 3 900	$ 4 056	$ 4 218	$ 4 387	$ 4 562	$ 4 745	$ 4 935	$ 5 132	$ 5 337
ReinvestedDiv/CG/Interest	$ 3 600	$ 3 744	$ 3 894	$ 4 050	$ 4 211	$ 4 380	$ 4 555	$ 4 737	$ 4 927	$ 5 124
RetirementPlanContributions *	$ 17 350	$ 18 044	$ 18 766	$ 19 516	$ 20 297	$ 21 109	$ 21 953	$ 22 831	$ 23 745	$ 24 694
After - TaxRetirementSavings	$ 10 000	$ 10 400	$ 10 816	$ 11 249	$ 11 699	$ 12 167	$ 12 653	$ 13 159	$ 13 686	$ 14 233
Savings Total	$ 38 900	$ 40 456	$ 42 074	$ 43 757	$ 45 507	$ 47 328	$ 49 221	$ 51 190	$ 53 237	$ 55 367
VariableYearlyExpenses										
Utilities	$ 6 900	$ 7 142	$ 7 391	$ 7 650	$ 7 918	$ 8 195	$ 8 482	$ 8 779	$ 9 086	$ 9 404
Telephone	$ 1 500	$ 1 553	$ 1 607	$ 1 663	$ 1 721	$ 1 782	$ 1 844	$ 1 908	$ 1 975	$ 2 044
Utility Total	$ 8 400	$ 8 694	$ 8 998	$ 9 313	$ 9 639	$ 9 977	$ 10 326	$ 10 687	$ 11 061	$ 11 448
HomeMaintenance&Repair	$ 3 000	$ 3 105	$ 3 214	$ 3 326	$ 3 443	$ 3 563	$ 3 688	$ 3 817	$ 3 950	$ 4 089
HomeExpenseTotal	$ 3 000	$ 3 105	$ 3 214	$ 3 326	$ 3 443	$ 3 563	$ 3 688	$ 3 817	$ 3 950	$ 4 089
FoodatHome&EatingOut	$ 9 000	$ 9 315	$ 9 641	$ 9 978	$ 10 328	$ 10 689	$ 11 063	$ 11 451	$ 11 851	$ 12 266
Clothing	$ 3 600	$ 3 726	$ 3 856	$ 3 991	$ 4 131	$ 4 276	$ 4 425	$ 4 580	$ 4 741	$ 4 906
Automobile Repairs	$ 5 200	$ 5 382	$ 5 570	$ 5 765	$ 5 967	$ 6 176	$ 6 392	$ 6 616	$ 6 847	$ 7 087
DailyLivingExpenseTotal	$ 17 800	$ 18 423	$ 19 068	$ 19 735	$ 20 426	$ 21 141	$ 21 881	$ 22 647	$ 23 439	$ 24 260
Entertainment&Vacation	$ 6 000	$ 6 210	$ 6 427	$ 6 652	$ 6 885	$ 7 126	$ 7 376	$ 7 634	$ 7 901	$ 8 177
Gifts&Donations	$ 12 000	$ 12 420	$ 12 855	$ 13 305	$ 13 770	$ 14 252	$ 14 751	$ 15 267	$ 15 802	$ 16 355
OtherExpenseTotal	$ 18 000	$ 18 630	$ 19 282	$ 19 957	$ 20 655	$ 21 378	$ 22 127	$ 22 901	$ 23 703	$ 24 532
UnreimbursedMedicalExpenses	$ 3 000	$ 3 105	$ 3 214	$ 3 326	$ 3 443	$ 3 563	$ 3 688	$ 3 817	$ 3 950	$ 4 089
Miscellaneous Expenses	$ 5 400	$ 5 589	$ 5 785	$ 5 987	$ 6 197	$ 6 414	$ 6 638	$ 6 870	$ 7 111	$ 7 360
MiscellaneousExpenseTotal	$ 8 400	$ 8 694	$ 8 998	$ 9 313	$ 9 639	$ 9 977	$ 10 326	$ 10 687	$ 11 061	$ 11 448
DiscretionaryCashFlow										
Total Income	$ 221 075	$ 229 593	$ 238 441	$ 247 630	$ 257 175	$ 267 089	$ 277 387	$ 288 082	$ 299 192	$ 310 732
TotalFixedExpenses	$ 171 288	$ 176 393	$ 181 687	$ 187 179	$ 182 274	$ 188 181	$ 194 307	$ 200 662	$ 207 254	$ 214 091
TotalVariableExpenses	$ 55 600	$ 57 546	$ 59 560	$ 61 645	$ 63 802	$ 66 035	$ 68 347	$ 70 739	$ 73 215	$ 75 777
Discretionary Cash Flow	$ (5 813)	$ (4 346)	$ (2 807)	$ (1 193)	$ 11 099	$ 12 873	$ 14 733	$ 16 681	$ 18 724	$ 20 863
* pre - taxitems										

Financial Planning Components

Financial planners are engaged, on a daily basis, helping shape an individual's or family's financial objectives andmeeting these objectives with the development and implementation of strategies to achieve them. Bernheim summarized the ongoing day - to - challenge faced by financial planners as follows:

The problem of developing an appropriate personal financial plan is extraordinarily complex. Ideally, a plan should account for earnings, growth, assets, current and future rate of return, pension benefits, social security benefits, special needs (e. g. , college tuition, weddings, down payments on houses), household composition, current and future tax law, mortality probabilities, disability probabilities, insurance rates, risk - return trade - offs, and a host of other factors …"①

Considered within context of the financial planning process is the analysis of client data and the development of recommendations that can be implemented to help each client reach their unique financial and life goals. A financial planner's job does not end with strategy development or implementation. The periodic reviewing of a client's overall financial plan on a regular basis is an important financial planning task. Topics under consideration when working as a comprehensive financial planner include analyzing a household's investment and portfolio situation, savings plans and alternatives, insurance needs and opportunities, retirement plans, income tax situation, and estate planning opportunities.

When viewed within the context of the process of financial planning, the plan document—which is often written—should be comprehensive in that each of the planning elements is considered holistically and in relation to the other elements. Financial planning gets easier with experience, but for those who are new to the profession, a common question is, "Where should I begin?" Although it is a cliché, the answer is really to "Begin at the beginning," as the King said, very gravely, in Lewis Carroll's *Alice in Wonderland* and go on till you come to the end:

① Bernheim, B. D. (1994). Personal saving, information, and economic literacy: New directions for public policy. In *Tax Policy for Economic Growth in the* 1990*s*. Washington, DC: American Council for Capital Formation, pp. 53 - 78.

then stop." As illustrated earlier in the chapter, the financial planning process tends to be circular in nature. This means that as long as the client – planner relationship exists, the step's in the planning process will be repeated. The continual practice of the planning process gets easier with time, as does the ability to think creatively and holistically.

As noted above, the components of personal financial planning—or what financial planners do on a daily basis—include gathering data related to, analyzing, developing strategies associated with, implementing, and monitoring aspect of: (1) Risk Management; (2) Asset Management; (3) Retirement Planning; (4) Tax Planning; and (5) Estate Planning. The following discussion briefly reviews these topics with an emphasis on how financial planners manage their work in these domains. Readers who are interested in the analytical details associated with each topic should consult manuals and books written specifically for each topic.

Risk Management

Risk management is a broad term often used to describe a client's insurance needs. Insurance provides clients and their families with a level protection against financial losses occurring because of (1) premature death, (2) disability, (3) medical care expenses, (4) property and liability losses, and (5) unemployment. Each is described below.

Premature Death. The stark reality is that people die. Unfortunately, few people know when or how they will pass. This level of uncertainty causes significant financial planning complications because few clients like to think about their own death or the impact death can have on survivors. Premature death refers to a condition where death happens before life and financial objectives and goals have been met. The premature death of a family income earner removes this person's future earning power from the household. The premature death of a stay at home child caregiving spouse may necessitate hiring childcare, thereby increasing expenses that had not been in the budget before. Obligations of all sorts, financial, emotional, and familial, progress toward completion through time. When the time line changes, so must the plan. For example, house loans and other debts are amortized over time, children are raised and educated, and retirement savings accumulate; premature death before these goals are completed can cause significant financial disruption within a household. Death at any time, premature or otherwise, brings with it expenses, such as burial costs, possible estate taxation, and family transition expenses.

An important financial planning solution designed to reduce the financial impact of premature death is to transfer the risk to an insurance company by buying life insurance. Clients desiring to be covered by life insurance need to provide the life insurance company some proof of insurability (reasonable health) and pay a periodic payment or premium for the coverage. Obviously, life insurance does not replace the lost life, but the proceeds from a policy can replace financial resources lost by a death, premature or otherwise. The role of a financial planner is to estimate the amount of life insurance needed to pay off outstanding debts, fund future household goals, and continue income for survivors. Another role played by financial planners is determining whether life insurance should be purchased by the client directly from an insurance company or through an employer provided plan at work. If purchased in the private market, a financial planner needs to decide whether a cash value plan—one that provides protection and a savings component—or term life insurance should be purchased. Clients who use an employer plan will nearly always be offered an annually renewable term life insurance policy with an annually increasing premium.

Disability. Disability is a condition where a client's ability to perform daily activities is or will become impaired or limited. Impaired or limited abilities impact the quality of life and often the ability to produce income through normal activities, including employment. The odds of becoming disabled are higher than death until a client reaches age 60. As such, disability insurance planning is something every financial planner needs to do with each client. The process of assessing a client's disability need entails reviewing the client's risk factors, which can include their current type of employment and health factors (smoking, drinking, and engaging in risky lifestyle activities). The risk of becoming disabled can be transferred to an insurance company through the purchase of disability insurance.

It is well known that the probability of suffering a period of disability severe enough to disrupt employment during a person's working years is considerably greater than the risk of death. That said, disability insurance is often overlooked. In the United States there are more people covered by life insurance than disability insurance. The analysis of a client's disability insurance need provides an opportunity to add value to the client - planner relationship. Disability insurance can provide income to replace lost earnings and to provide an opportunity for additional care that may be required by a disabled person. Disability coverage is an important element associated with increasing a client's risk capacity, which is related to a client's ability to withstand a financial shock.

Disability insurance usually requires the payment of a periodical payment or premium for which the insurance company will typically provide a monthly income to the disabled person for some predetermined period of time. Disability insurance can be purchased directly from an insurance company by the individual or through the person's employer as a group benefit. There are potential tax differences on the benefits depending on how the premium is paid that should be considered. Basically, if a client pays the premium with after tax money the benefit will not be taxable; however, if the cost is pretax the benefit will be taxable when received. Sick pay provided by employers can also help to offset some disability expenses, but this should generally not be considered a replacement for disability insurance.

Before making a disability insurance recommendation, financial planners need to be aware of the different types of policies available—own occupation versus any occupation. Clients should be steered towards the purchase of an own or modified own occupation policy. These policies provide a benefit if the client cannot reasonably work in their field or a closely related field. An any occupation policy will be less expensive; however, the chances of receiving compensation are lower because the insurance company may require the client to work in a position that is not suited for the client. While some clients purchase disability coverage in the private marketplace, most buy coverage through their employer. This can be problematic, however, if the client loses or changes jobs. As a practical matter, financial planes need to understand how Social Security benefits influence disability insurance recommendations. Social Security does provide disability coverage, but only under the strictest definitions of disability—that is, it is very difficult to obtain a benefit. Financial planners can add value to the client - planner relationship by steering clients away from relying solely on Social Security disability benefits.

Medical care. Sickness or injury and related medical care expenses can be very disruptive to the personal and financial lives of clients. One of the most prevalent causes of personal bankruptcy is from incurring medical expenses. In the United States, clients can buy insurance in the marketplace, through their employer, or through federally mandated exchange programs. Unlike other countries, clients must pay premiums for their health insurance coverage. This is a very complex arrangement and promises only to become more complicated.

Of all the risk management areas, medical care insurance is the one where financial planners have the least direct influence on client choices. Nearly all clients purchase employer - provided coverage. This is due to the fact that employer - provided coverage tends to be less expensive and more comprehensive. The role of the financial planner is to understand the different options provided by a client's employer and suggest the most appropriate choice from the plans provided.

Another important role for a financial planner is making sure a client's emergency savings fund is sufficient to cover potential deductibles and copayments associated with a health insurance plan. Details about the specific cost and coverage should be understood in sufficient detail. Typically, the client pays the health insurance company a periodically payment or premium for which the insurance company will cover or pay for health costs within some predetermined parameters. Even though covered by insurance there are likely to be uncovered expenses and some out of pocket expenses that can add up. Financial planners can add value to the client - planner relationship by focusing on and communication plan details to clients. Financial planes should also monitor plan costs over time. As clients age, issues related to Medicare and Medicaid become more important. At age 65, clients become eligible for Medicare—federally provided basic life insurance. The role of a financial planner in helping client's transition from employer - provided benefits to Medicaid is very important.

Property and liability coverage. Losses can occur if a client owns property or is exposed to other liability risk. In fact, liability—damage caused by a client to another person or entity—should be a primary financial planning concern. Ensuring that a client has sufficient liability coverage is of paramount importance. Owning a house, other real estate property and buildings, cars or other types of property exposes people to potential financial losses and liabilities. For example, if a client's commercial investment property burns down, the client will suffer a financial loss of value and income. If someone is hurt in the fire the client may be held personally responsible for all medical expenses and loss of income for the injured party. Transferring this loss exposure risk to an insurance company is an economic equation that all clients must consider. It is each financial planner's responsibility to analyze a client's risk exposures and determine how much of the risk can be retained (i. e., self - insured). Liabilities that are both probable and potentially large should be transferred to an insurance company.

Case Illustration: The Fan Family

Insurance Analysis: Homeowner Insurance

One weakness associated with the Fans' personal property coverage is the lack of separate endorsements for the loss of some items, such as jewelry.

Liability exposure and potential loss comes from legal exposure from others. Liability coverage might protect from loss incurred by someone getting injured on the insured property. If a visitor to a client's property falls, becomes injured, and is owed a financial sum because of this injury the insurance company will pay expenses and/or defend the client in court. Property and liability insurance usually requires the payment of a periodical payments or premiums for which the insurance company will typically provide coverage to offset losses to or of property, sometimes lost income from the property, and exposures to financial liability. The analysis of client's property and liability needs can get complicated quickly. It is important to consider the specified insurance policy contract and its limitations and coverages. In general, clients should also purchase what is none as excess liability insurance or umbrella insurance coverage. As the name implies, this policy provides an extra layer of liability protection for clients. Coverage includes strict liability protection, as well as protection against other types of lawsuits. It is prudent practice for financial planners to remember that most every activity may cause some liability exposure—owning property, a house or car, for example, or a business or rental property all expose the owner to liability claims by others. Having appropriate liability coverage in place is important as a factor that increases a client's risk capacity.

Unemployment. Unemployment exposes people to income loss. In many, if not most, cases clients derive a significant amount of their financial wealth from employment income and wages. During those years when a client's major source of economic stability comes from employment, becoming suddenly or involuntarily unemployed can cause significant household financial disruption. Clients can insure against becoming unemployed in several ways. The first and most obvious strategy is to self-insure; that is to create an adequate reserve (emergency) fund to cover expenses that might be incurred during times of unemployment. Having an adequate reserve fund to cover living expenses during times of unemployment requires personal financial resources to be allocated or earmarked for this purpose.

Often unemployment insurance is provided by local or state governments. During times of employment employers pay into a government pool that pays a benefit to people who become unemployed in the future. The amount paid into the pool varies by the applicable rate and the specific experience of the employer. If an employer consistently has a significant number of people collecting unemployment compensation, the employer will pay a higher rate than an employer who has few employees collecting benefits. People collecting government unemployment payments usually get a specified amount for a specified period of time. The government often subsidizes the resource pool if it runs low and will also extend the time someone may collect benefits if they find it desirable. Rarely do clients have individual unemployment insurance, although it is possible to purchase policies that will pay specific bills, home mortgage payments for example. Sometimes financial planners recommend that clientspurchase supplemental income coverage either through their employer or through specialized insurance companies but this is relatively rare. Financial planners most often attempt to manage unemployment possibilities through emergency funds and asset management strategies.

Asset Management

Individuals and households accumulate capital for various purposes, including: (1) providing a financial cushion in case of emergencies, (2) funding general household expenses, (3) developing a general investment portfolio, and (4) managing investments and properties. Financial planners tend to spend the majority of their day - to - day activities thinking about and managing client assets. This occurs because the strategic use of client investment assets tends to be the primary way in which financial objectives and goals are met over time. Additionally, the management of client assets is the principal way financial planners are compensated. Fee - only financial planners most often charge an assets under management (AUM) fee of approximately 1% of assets managed (the fee moves inversely with the level of assets managed by a financial planner). The analysis and strategic work in other areas of a client's financial situation are usually incorporated into this fee. Financial planners who are commission based also earn a significant proportion of their income from asset management fees. For instance, a financial planner may recommend and sell an insurance policy, but the likelihood of selling a similar product to the same client in the future is quite low. As such, commissioned based financial planners often develop an expertise in investment management, where opportunities exist to implement stock, bond, exchange traded fund, mutual fund, and alternative investment recommendations on an ongoing basis. Financial planners who deal primarily with life insurance and annuity products also focus heavily on asset management issues. Opportunities to make investment recommendations within variable life and annuity products are almost never ending.

Regardless of a financial planner's compensation structure, an important asset management task involves establishing and managing a client's emergency savings fund. Life has a tendency to present financial situations that cannot be predicted with any degree of accuracy; yet these events do occur. Emergency funds can be used to cover bills during periods of unemployment, to pay for outsized expenses from unexpected events, such as health bills not covered by insurance, home and auto expenses, and special needs. Householdpurposes generally motivate clients to accumulate money, but the gentle prodding of a financial planner can enhance a client's saving habit. Families often wish to possess desirable housing and cars, pay monthly expenses in a timely manner, take a vacation, and have money for entertainment allowances. Many families also wish to provide for the education of their children and provide for retirement resources. General investment portfolio assets can be managed to help clients meet each of these needs. An important role of a financial planner is to monitor asset values and incorporate the management of assets into a client's estate plan to ensure that assets ultimately pass to the client's heirs in an efficient and cost effective manner.

Case Illustration: The Fan Family

Educational Analysis

Jing and Xuan should set aside \$ 37,600 today for Lu's education. Jing and Xuan will still be working while Lu is in school. They expect the tuition to be \$ 15,000 annually (today's cost), increasing by 8% annually. They expect Lu, beginning at age 18, will attend four years of college. Thus, it is important to estimate the amount needed to fully fund Lu's educational need in order to develop a reasonable portfolio to the meet the need.

Retirement Planning

While all households can benefit from proactive financial planning, few households engage the services of a financial planner until questions regarding retirement readiness come to mind. This usually happens when the head of a household is 40 years of age or older. The role of a financial planner in helping clients conceptualize retirement is significant. The process typically begins by helping clients visualize what they would like to do and where they intend to live in retirement. Questions associated with when retirement will occur, how much income will be needed at that time, the types of activities the client hopes to engage in, and what level of health care may be needed help shape retirement planning calculations.

Sometimes financial planners need to report bad news to their clients. For example, some clients have retirement goals that are simply not fundable given current levels of assets and savings and/or investment returns. Even so, financial planners can add value to the client - planner relationship by helping clients realistically estimate future retirement income and expenses. An important financial planning task involves managing a client's retirement assets using appropriate asset allocation and portfolio management strategies. Once a client retires, the process of retirement planning changes from resource accumulation to one of asset decumulation. Familiarity with distribution rules—for example the 4% income distribution standard—is an essential competency for financial planners.

Retirement income is necessary if clients are to accumulate the necessary resources to retire. Retirement and not having to work to provide income is often a client's most important goal. Like most financial objectives, achieving a retirement goal is problematic without proper planning. Reaching a retirement goal has more moving parts than nearly any other financial planning topic area. Issues related to taxable versus tax - free accounts, pre - tax versus post - tax savings, and accessible versus tax - deferred options all intertwine to create complications in planning. Furthermore, retirement planning tends to be influenced directly by short - term changes in the markets, interest rates, and client expectations. Retirement planning is also influenced by longer - term fluctuations in a client's preferences and motivations. From a day - to - day practice point of view, financial planners spend a great deal of their analytic work ensuring that clients are on track to meet their retirement objectives. This analytic work entails corresponding retirement monitoring with changes in the tax code, variations in the macro economy, and fluctuations in the investment markets.

Case Illustration: The Fan Family

Retirement Analysis

Retirement Account Distributions

If the Fans' need additional cash, the net proceeds from the sale of their domestic mutual fund retirement account, listed on his personal Statement of Financial Position, including any taxes and penalties and assuming no basis will be $ 19,200. Proceeds from the account will be considered as ordinary income. Taxes will be calculated at ordinary rates. A 10% distribution penalty will apply because neither Jing nor Xuan is older than 59 1/2 years of age.

Jing and Xuan Retirement Need Analysis

Both Jing and Xuan expect to retire in approximately 20 years. Jing expects to live until age 90 and Xuan expects to live until age 85. They have estimated that they need $ 120,000 per year in today's dollars for retirement. This amount will drop if only one were to survive. The following analysis assumes a pre – tax portfolio. They will pay income taxes out of their gross retirement income. Xuan can live on $ 75,000 per year if Jing were to pass away first. Jing can live on $ 80,000 per year if Xuan were to pass away first. Thus, the Fans' need $ 2,765,462 today to fund their retirement. This amount does include spending $ 12,000 per year for Jing to travel with Xuan and Lu. Lowering this amount would also lower the amount needed to have available for the start of retirement.

Tax Planning

Tax planning involves developing and implementing strategies to reduce, shift, or postpone a client's tax burden, thereby enhancing alternative uses for resources. The level of involvement an individual financial planner has in the tax planning process varies based on each financial planner's business model. Some financial planners, for instance, provide tax preparation services. For these advisers, tax planning is an important and central component of their practice. For other financial planners, tax planning involves simply evaluating the overall tax structure of a client's situation. For example, financial planners who are engaged in asset management services need to know the marginal tax bracket of their client in order to determine the optimal mix of stocks, bonds, and other assets in a portfolio. Tax planning also plays an important role in retirement, education, and estate planning. IN some ways, tax planning is the one topic that is infused in every other aspect of a client's financial situation. Taxes are paid during a client's life, even upon the transfer of a client's assets to subsequent owners. Financial planners do need to be aware of the tax code, Internal Revenue Service rules and regulations, and tax filing procedures; however, many financial planners refer actual tax preparation to other professionals, including Certified Public Accountants and Enrolled Agents.

Estate Planning

Estate planning entails the accumulation, management, and distribution of a client's assets over the lifecycle, with a special emphasis on the distribution and transfer of assets accumulated during a person's lifetime. It is important to take note that unless a financial planner is also a licensed attorney, he or she may not draft legal documents for clients. It is, however, legal and appropriate for a financial planner to evaluate a client's current estate planning situation and recommend essential changes to a client's situation.

Clients fail to plan for many reasons. Without an estate plan, the odds of assets getting to the desired location—heir or charity—after the death of the owner becomes marginalized. It has been said that "not having a plan is a plan to fail." In relation to estate planning this is certainly the case. If a client does not spell out plans in some detail, prior to death or disability, the state where they live will dictate the terms of asset distribution. This is known as the probate process. Probate is a public legal process that ultimately dictates the distribution of assets. Estate planning techniques can be used to help clients avoid probate, if they do want to maintain privacy. Tools and techniques include the use of living trusts, irrevocable trusts, irrevocable life insurance trusts, and property titling can and should be recommended, when appropriate, by a financial planner. Additionally, a baseline standard of practice requires financial planners to consider the role of wills, living trusts, powers - of - attorney, and other legal documents as tools to help clients manage their present and future financial situation. Clients rarely enjoy thinking or talking about their own demise; however, it is important for financial planners to remind clients of the troubles that await for those who fail to plan for the efficient management and eventual distribution of assets. The cost associated with not planning may not be obvious but the costs can be very high. Without the intervention of a financial planner, clients can be left with inadequate resources to accomplish goals or pay excess taxes prior to and after death.

Case Illustration: The Fan Family

Estate Analysis

Jing's Probate Estate, Gross Estate, and Estate Tax Liability

If Jing were to die today, his probate estate will be \$ 1,567,098. His gross estate will be \$ 1,870,990, and his estate tax liability will be \$ 0.

Xuan's Probate Estate, Gross Estate and Estate Tax Liability

The estimates shown below are based on the current Statement of Financial Position valuations, assuming a funeral and administrative cost of \$ 100,000. If Xuan were to die today, her probate estate will be \$ 0. Her gross estate will be \$ 967,467, and her estate tax liability will be \$ 0.

Second - To - Die Estate Tax

The estimates shown below assume funeral and administrative costs will be \$ 100,000 each. It was also assumed that Xuanretains her term insurance through her employer. Based on future projections, if Jing were to die in 10 years, followed by Xuan's death in an additional 10 years, the total tax liability of both will be \$ 1,365,640 at that time.

Important Steps in the Personal Financial Planning Process

Data Gathering

The personal financial planning process involves the translation of client objectives into specific outcomes and then moving these outcomes into financial strategies that can be implemented to reach intended outcomes. In addition to the lockstep financial planning process, there are some general logical steps that can be followed to help a client move from outcome conceptualization to goal achievement. Gathering information about where the process is starting and where it is going is a logical first step. As described earlier in the chapter, this involves the development of personal financial statements. These statements include a balance sheet, income statement, and some cash flow schedules. Information needed to complete these forms can be obtained during the data gathering phase of the planning process. Asking clients to bring copies of their tax returns, pay stubs, bank statements, brokerage statements, and receipts to a data gathering meeting is common. Financial planners are increasing using online client income and expense monitoring platforms to help complete these types of documents. Retirement plan statements can provide significant information about the saving and spending behavior of clients, so it is reasonable to request that a client bring recent statements to meetings. Other useful information includes loan documents and statements, home loan information, and auto loan and credit card statements. Bank and credit card statements can also be useful sources of information to help facilitate the development of cash flow and income statements.

Case Illustration: The Fan Family

Cash Flow Analysis

A weakness in the Fans' current plan is their low level of emergency fund savings. A safe amount to have is approximately 3 to 6 months of living expenses saved in a liquid account. Currently, they are on the low end of the range, depending on the level of expenses used in the calculation. They need to accumulate approximately $ 25,000 in a safe liquid account to reach their goal.

Balance sheet items can also provide a valuable starting point when evaluating a client's estate planning situation. It is also important to have all client insurance policy information, in particular life insurance data, such as death benefits and cash values. Wills and trust documents, if they exist, provide some insight into past planning activities. Places to look for this information and data include banks, mutual funds, company employer benefit statements, insurance companies, lawyers, and accountants. In most cases, the client will need to reach out to other institutions and professionals or provide his or her financial planner with a limited power of attorney allowing the financial planner access to these sources of information. Many times banks or investment companies have sample financial information gathering inventory forms that can be helpful in this process and will provide them at no cost. Once this information has been gathered, more information will likely become necessary as the process moves from data gathering to the analysis stage. The development of a periodic checklist is useful. A checklist can not only ensure the completion of tasks but also provide a mechanism for documenting the receipt of data and forms.

Client Objectives and Goals

Once relevant data has been collected, a financial planner's attention will almost always turn to discovering a client's life and financial objectives and goals. As it has been said, "If you don't care where you are going, any path will get you there." This statement has a ring of truth to it.

The process of personal financial planning is, if nothing else, the charting of a course to help a client move from a starting point to some desired point in the future. If a client does not care where they are going financially or where they want to end post retirement, then there is little reason to expend effort in the personal financial planning process.

Fortunately, nearly every person who reaches out for financial planning help does have some notion of where they are currently at financially and where they want to be in the future. They may not know the exact numbers or the timeline, but with the correct prompting from a financial planner their dreams and aspirations can be identified. Personal financial planning objectives should be stated as explicitly as possible. Forcing clients to think creatively and define goals explicitly helps clients think through exactly where they are current and where they want to be financially in the future. Defining goals explicitly helps ensure that clients do not overlook important outcomes or concentrate too heavily on one expected outcome at the determinant of other outcomes.

It is important to note that things will inevitably change and so will a client's objectives and goals. It is important for financial planners keep previously obtained documents current, review as necessary, and update them when required. The only thing that is certain in financial planning is that client financial objectives will change—children are born, marriages, divorces, deaths, disabilities, sickness, inheritances, market and investment volatility, and career changes happen. Financial planner flexibility and understanding help clients manage these changes.

Analysis and Strategy Development

Once a financial inventory has been made, other statements have been constructed, and goals and objectives have been formalized, strategies to accomplish these objectives need to be developed. Strategy development emerges from a thorough analysis of a client's quantitative and qualitative data. Reasonable people and advisers can and will differ on ways to proceed in meeting a client's goals. This is natural and informative. The correct solution or course of action can vary, but whatever path is chosen, it should make sense financially and emotionally. It is always the responsibility of a client's financial planner to document, at a minimum, how each recommended strategy is appropriate and suitable. While the starting point in the planning process may be well documented, it is important to remember—as stated above—that a client's goals will almost necessarily be more fluid. Objectives and goals will change over time. It is expected that every financial planner will develop a periodic review process designed to facilitate plan revision. As each client's circumstances change so should the client's financial plan.

Implementation and Monitoring

As a financial planner and his or her client move through the financial planning process. It is worth keeping in mind that financial planning is, in the end, a person – centered professional activity. It is sometimes easy to get too focused on products, services, and strategic development. What really matters, in the end, is client satisfaction and well – being. While maximum accumulation of wealth may be a lofty goal, helping a client live a life filled with opportunity through the prudent management of household resources is also an important element of financial planning. Each client's goals and objectives must be taken in context with what the client hopes to accomplish over their life. Consider againthis insight from Lewis Carroll's Alice in Wonderland: "Alice came to a fork in the road. 'Which road do I take?' she asked. 'Where do you want to go?' responded the Cheshire Cat. 'I don't know,' Alice answered. 'Then,' said the Cat, 'it doesn't matter.'" Within the financial planning process, both financial planner and client should know where the client is going so that the financial planning process can be used to it highest purpose.

Developing Recommendations

Developing and presenting recommendations is a key outcome associated with the financial planning process. In some respects, this is the moment of truth for a client. That is, the type and quality of recommendations presented by a financial planner indicate the planner's skills and abilities as they relate to data gathering, synthesis of data, and integration of planning components. Well drafted recommendations can easily be implemented. Appropriate recommendations also lead a client towards goal achievement. Weak recommendations tend to be more difficult to implement, harder to understand, and unproven in terms of goal outcomes.

Recommendations can be classified into one of two primary categories. The first are *procedural or service recommendations. Lytton and her associates* (2013)[①] described a procedural recommendation as one that emphasizes a particular process or service situation within a client's financial plan. Common procedural strategies involve altering a plan assumption, retitling the ownership of an asset, and reminding or encouraging a client to take a particular action. The second classification of recommendations is what can be described as product oriented. A product strategy, as the name implies, focuses on the use of specific product or product attributes to help a client achieve their goal. It is worth noting that many novice financial planners assume that financial planning is a technique to help sell more products. While it is true that a combination of procedural and product recommendations make up the strategic planning aspect of the planning process, the fact is that the majority of recommendations within a plan tend to be procedural in nature. Table 6 provides examples of both procedural and product recommendations.

Table 6　　　　Procedural and Product Recommendation Examples

Plan Content Area	Procedural Strategy	Product Strategy
Life Insurance Planning	Add a contingent beneficiary to an existing life insurance policy.	Transfer a cash value life insurance policy to an irrevocable life insurance trust.
Education Planning	For federal financial aid purposes, postpone year - end bonus into next calendar year.	Transfer $ 34,000 from savings into a UTMA custodial account.
Investment Planning	Reallocate portfolio in such a way that the weighted average annualized rate of return increases by 200 basis points.	Purchase 100 shares of Stock XYZ, 500 shares of Fund ABC, and 600 shares of ETF MNO.
General Insurance Planning	Consider increasing policy deductibles as a way to decrease policy premiums.	Increase policy liability limits from $ 25,000 to $ 100,000, at a minimum.

In some respects, developing financial planning recommendations is the most rewarding part of the financial planning process. This is the step within the process that allows a financial planner to be creative and insightful. Novice planners sometimes are quick to rush to recommendation development and suggestions. This temptation should be avoided. Consider the following recommendation: "You need to reallocate your portfolio in order to obtain higher returns in the future." While this statement may, in fact, be true, from a client perspective this form of

① Lytton, R. H., Grable, J. E., &Klock, D. D. (2013). *The process of financial planning: Developing a financial plan* (2nd ed.). Erlanger, KY: National Underwriter.

recommendation is nearly useless. The reason for the ineffectiveness of this type of statement is that the recommendation is too vague to be implemented. Often financial planners worry that if they are too specific when making a recommendation the client may move towards implementation without the financial planner. This fear is overstated. Client confidence tends to be highly associated with recommendation and plan implementation. Vagueness on the part of the financial planner does not lead to confidence. If the end goal of the planning process involves providing a client to take action—implement recommendations—then it is of crucial importance for recommendations to be framed consistently and precisely.

Lytton, Grable, and Klock (2013) developed a recommendation checklist that can be adapted by any practicing financial planner. Their checklist was created to help both financial planners and their clients understand the exact steps to be taken, and the costs involved, in the implementation of a recommendation. The inputs into a recommendation include answering the following seven questions:

1. Who should implement the recommendation? Is it the client, the planner, a third - party, or the client and planner working together? For instance, reallocating a client's portfolio may be a financial planner implemented recommendation in the planner manages the client's assets. The same recommendation may be something a client implements if the assets are held in a qualified retirement plan.

2. What should be done? The answer to this question should be as specific as possible. Rather than say something vague like, "reallocate your portfolio," it is almost always better to state specifically how the portfolio should be reallocated. Creating action lists can be one way to illustrate what should be done.

3. When should the recommendation be implemented? Although this seems like something every financial planner would answer anyway, it is worth repeating that clients should be given precise timeframes for recommendation implementation. For example, should a particular recommendation be implemented within the week, month, year, or at some other point in the future? It is worth remembering that the more specific the recommendation, the more likely the suggestion will be implemented.

4. Where should the recommendation be implemented? It is likely that within any client's plan the points of implementation will vary to a large extent. Some recommendations can be

implemented with a planner. Other recommendations can only be implemented through an employer or a second party, such as an insurance agent or a governmental agency.

5. Why should the recommendation be implemented? Showing a client why it is important to implement a recommendation is just as an important as indicating how the suggestion should be implemented.

6. How should implementation take place? While it is certainly true that many financial planning recommendations can be implemented with the help of a financial planner, there are many other suggestions, particularly those that are procedural in nature, that will require the client to take action alone. As such, it is imperative that the client be provided an "implementation road map" that can be put into effecteasily and efficiently. Say, for example, that a recommendation involves having a client increase their withheld savings into a qualified retirement plan. Answering the how question could include instructing the client to:

a. "Meet with your benefits administrator at corporate headquarters and ask for Form T;

b. Fill out Form T with your benefits administrator by indicating an increase in paycheck withholding from 4% to 7%; and

c. Turn in Form T with your firm's payroll department."

7. How much will it cost? Sometimes financial planners are reluctant to indicate the cost of plan implementation. Rather than shy away from this issue, financial planners should use this step in the recommendation development process to fully disclose the costs and benefits associated with a suggestion. Some recommendations have a direct cost associated with implementation. For example, increasing insurance liability coverage can be shown to produce an increase in policy premiums. Other recommendations have less transparent costs associated with implementation. In general, however, nearly every product recommendation will either impact a client's cash flow or net worth position. Sometimes the effect is positive. At other times, the impact is negative. Consider a typical cash flow and net worth recommendation. Refinancing a mortgage is a commonly recommended strategy. Most often this recommendation is made to increase monthly cash flow; however, implementation may also decrease net worth by depleting cash assets to pay for closing costs. Implementation of a refinancing strategy can also provide a tax benefit, which, in turn, further increases cash flow on an annual basis. Planners who fully disclose all aspects of recommendation costs can build client confidence. Additionally, tracking all plan costs and

benefits makes the task of cash flow tracking, as described later in this chapter, much easier.

As discussed above, the development of a recommendation within a financial plan is more complex than simply suggesting a client take action. It is worth noting, at this point, that there is active debate within the planning profession regarding the role of a financial planner when it comes time to make recommendations. The discussion from above assumes that a financial planner's primary role is to gather and analyze client data in an effort to develop and present one or more recommendations that will help a client achieve their financial goal(s). This implies that the presented recommendation is, in the planner's professional opinion, the best solution for the problem at that time, given the client's current situation. There are some financial planners who argue, however, that it is not the planner's responsibility or duty to "force" a recommendation on a client. Instead, these advisers argue that clients should be presented a menu of acceptable alternatives that can be chosen by the client to meet a question or objective.

The difference in these two planning approaches cannot be over - emphasized. The traditional approach places a financial planner in the role of trusted adviser, similar to that of an accountant, attorney, or physician. Planners who hold this perspective argue that it would be disconcerting, at a minimum, to visit a doctor only to have the physician provide three or four possible remedies, and then to have the client chose the remedy that feels right. The counter argument is that the client, or patient, is always in the best position to understand their own needs, desires, and wishes. Using this framework, it is the adviser's job to provide alternatives that are appropriate for the client's situation. Every financial planner, at some point in their professional development, must deal with the approach they will take when working with clients. The vast majority of currently practicing financial planners do follow the expert model. That is, they provide what they consider to be the best and highest outcome recommendation to their client. They then follow this optimal strategy with acceptable alternatives. The difference between the recommendation and alternatives is that the recommendation provides superior outcomes. For example, a financial planner may recommend that a client refinance their mortgage. If the recommendation is made as a way to increase cash flow, then a 30 - year refinance suggestion may be made, with 15 - and 20 - year refinancing alternatives also presented. Within the recommendation it would be clear why the 30 - year strategy is best for the client; namely, the recommendation maximizes the client's level of discretionary cash flow. If the client were debt averse—something that would emerge from further planner – client discussion—then one of the alternatives could then be accepted.

Case Illustration: The Fan Family

As has been illustrated throughout this chapter, the Fan family's financial situation provides ample opportunity to develop a comprehensive financial plan. The following examples represent just a few of the possible recommendations that could be made to help the Jing and Xuan meet their short – , intermediate – , and long – term financial goals.

Prior to making one or more financial planning recommendations it is important to review, once again, the client's goals and the assumptions used during the analysis process. This secondary review may provide additional insights into opportunities for further analysis and recommendation development. The following list describes the additional information that would be useful to have before making a recommendation:

Additional Information Needed

- Does the disability coverage cover both sickness and accidents? What is the term of benefits?
- Who is the beneficiary of the pour – over trust? What has changed since the wills were originally drafted?
- How stable has family income been over the past five years?
- Do Jing and Xuan have durable powers of attorney for health care and financial emergencies?
- What was the original purchase date and basis of all currently held investments?

Assuming answers to these questions can be obtained from the clients, the next step in the planning process involves drafting and presenting financial planning recommendations. The following recommendations represent a sample of client – centered recommendations that could be included in a comprehensive financial plan:

Insurance Recommendations

Personal "Umbrella" Liability Coverage

While the Fan family currently has a $ 1 million personal excess liability policy in place, they should consider purchasing more coverage. Given the size of their net worth and gross estate, coverage of at least $ 2 million is recommended. Additional insurance can be purchased efficiently from their current property and casualty insurance company for approximately $ 150 in additional premium per year. This recommendation should be implemented within the next 30 days.

Long – Term Care Coverage and Medicare

Jing and Xuan are too young currently to need long – term care insurance; however, they are entering the point, based on age, where long – term care insurance is most affordable. An alternative is to rely on government provided long – term care coverage; however, governmental programs generally limit benefits to skilled nursing care rehabilitative services for only 100 days. They should revisit this planning need yearly.

Homeowners Insurance

The Fans' property is currently valued at $ 315,920. Their homeis estimated to have a replacement cost of $ 425,000. It is essential that the Jing and Xuan maintain coverage equal to 80% of the replacement value of the home ($ 340,000). In order to do this, they should confirm that their current policy is based on full replacement value with an automatic inflation adjustment. In order to address the fact that their personal property is covered on an actual cash value (AVC) basis, the Fans'should purchase an endorsement to cover the property on a replacement cost basis. Jing and Xuan should also purchase additional endorsements to cover potential losses to their jewelry in the amount of $ 20, 000. The total cost for such an endorsement will be approximately $ 250 per year. These insurance recommendations should be implemented in the next 30 days.

Xuan's Disability Insurance Coverage

It is recommended that Xuan purchase a disability insurance policy to protect her income in the event of injury or illness. She can begin the insurance search process with her current life insurance agent or by obtaining a referral. At a minimum, she needs an "own occupation" policy that pays at least 60% of her income. As an alternative, a modified own occupation policy can be substituted. An annual premium of $ 1,500 is typical for her age, occupation, and income. The purchase decision should occur within the next 60 days.

Investment Recommendations

Because of the Fans' relatively long planning time horizon and their greater than average willingness to take on risk (measured as 7 on a 10 – point scale), they can afford an asset mix that is more aggressive than average. Rather than focusing on fixed – income securities and other low yield investments, they should seek out—with the guidance of their financial planner—a mix of equities, real estate, and other investments that provide prospects for above – average capital gains. Currently, the Fans' portfolio could be classified as conservative; this is not in line with their individual risk tolerance levels and goals. The reallocation process should begin immediately.

Tax Recommendations

Given their high income and the limited availability of tax deductions and credits, the Fan family should reallocate regular savings to tax – advantaged savings and investments. For example, they should hold dividend paying stocks, bonds, and other interest bearing securities in tax – deferred retirement plans. They should also utilize other forms of tax deferral to minimize current taxation. At the current time, they are not liable for estate or gift taxes. Tax planning should begin immediately.

Retirement Recommendations

Retirement Plan Account

Currently Jing is contributing the maximum possible to his employer sponsored retirement account. He needs to continue this behavior until retirement. At age 50, Jing should take advantage of any additional opportunities to make "catch – up" contributions. Xuan is not currently maximizing all retirement plan accounts. Within the next 90 days she should increase her contribution rate to her retirement account. Additionally, she should allocate contributions to investments that provide above – average potential returns.

Estate Recommendations

Jing and Xuan's Life Insurance Policies

Jing and Xuan need to immediately change the ownership provisions in their life insurance policies. The current policy ownership status causes the inclusion of the proceeds from a policy to be included in the deceased gross estate. While the current estate planning implication is minimal, this status defeats the privacy goal of the Fan family (assets included in probate are public information). The use of an irrevocable life insurance trust is highly recommended. An attorney can establish such a trust for less than $ 1,000. The trust will retain ownership of any insurance held in the trust. Further, the trust will become the beneficiary of the ultimate payout. Implementation of this recommendation needs to occur within the next 30 days. Under IRC Section 2035, if the decedent transfers (by trust or otherwise) an interest in property, or relinquished a pore with respect to property, during the three – year period ending on the date of his death, the full amount of the transfer will be added back to the decedent's gross estate. This is known as the "three – year rule."

Living Wills and Durable Powers of Attorney

Within the next 30 days both Xuan and Jing need to draft living wills (or health care directives), along with creating durable powers of attorney in the even to injury or illness. Only an attorney (or the clients themselves) can draft these documents. Combined, the total cost for drafting and executing these documents should be less than $ 1,000.

Exploring Client Implementation of Financial Plans

While developing and presenting recommendations serves as the foundation of future goal achievement, plan implementation is, in many respects, the most important step in the planning process. Without client implementation of recommendations goal achievement becomes problematic. Additionally, lack of plan implementation means that a financial planner's analytical efforts will have been wasted. Neither outcome is desired. As such, it is imperative that financial planners position their clients to take action by implementing recommendations.

Factors That Integrate Across the Elements of Financial Planning That Ensure Proper Financial Plan Implementation

A key element to consider whenever implementing a financial recommendation is the impact implementation of one recommendation will have on previous and future recommendations. A simple example illustrates this point. Assume a client is extremely debt averse. That is, the client not only dislikes going into debt, the client actually finds the notion of debt to be disagreeable. Based on the client's disposition, a financial planner might recommend that the client accelerate repayment of long – term debts, such as prepaying loans used for the acquisition of a home or education. While this course of action may be appropriate, implementation of the strategy will certainly have repercussions throughout the client's financial plan. For example, the client can expect the following outcomes, at a minimum, to arise from loan prepayment implementation:

- Acceleration of debt payments will decrease current discretionary cash flow;
- Prepaying the mortgage may cause negative tax implications;
- Recommendation implementation will impact the client's net worth statement and require a review of current insurance policies; and
- Implementation may force the client to postpone implementation of other recommendations.

The integrative and recursive nature of plan implementation is illustrated in Figure 4. As shown, implementation follows the development and presentation of a recommendation. By definition, implementation of one or more recommendations means that the client's current and future financial situation will change. This change in situation then has an impact of future analyses and recommendations. A key element in Figure 4 is the concept that all implementations need to be monitored. Some monitoring occurs on a short – term basis, whereas other forms of monitoring occur over longer periods of time.

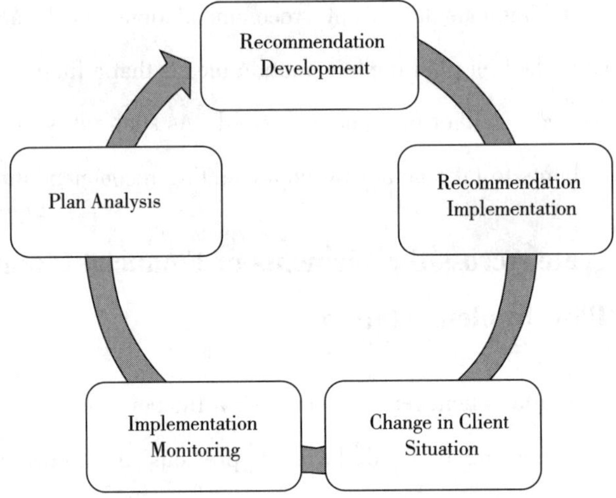

Figure 4 The Integrative and Recursive Nature of Recommendation Implementation

Communication and Execution

The circular nature of the financial planning process, as illustrated in Figure 4, highlights the important role financial planning can play in the lives of clients. Rather than viewing the practice of financial planning as purely transactional and ending when a product or service has been purchased by a client, the comprehensive financial planner continues to work with clients through constant monitoring of previously implemented strategies. This ongoing, circular or recursive, process continues until the planner - client relationship has been dissolved or as defined in the engagement agreement.

Communicating the details of recommendation implementation to clients is of critical importance. Of course, plan recommendations and implementation strategies should be verbally discussed with clients. However, it is always a good idea to formalize implementation procedures in written form. There are multiple ways this can be accomplished. One simple method involves providing clients with a list of activities that need to be implemented by addressing the seven implementation questions (i. e., who, what, when, where, why, how, and how much) described earlier in the chapter. Table 7 illustrates an implementation checklist.

Table 7 Implementation Checklist

Implement Immediately
o Pay off credit card debts using cash from bank account. o Amend W - 4 tax form to withhold an additional $ 400 from each paycheck. o Increase retirement plan contributions at work by $ 250 each pay period.
Implement Within the Year
o Rollover retirement plan from previous employer into a self - directed IRA. o Exchange current cash value life insurance policy into a variable policy. o Update your will, living will, and power of attorney. o Consult with your property and casualty insurance agent about current coverage and liability limits.
Implement in the Next 18 Months
o Sell stamp collection and invest proceeds in beach front condominium. o Complete a household inventory for insurance purposes. o Consider purchasing an additional $ 1 million excess liability insurance policy.

The one disadvantage associated with a checklist approach to implementation communication is that often the steps necessary to complete action are too vague. This is the reason Lytton, Grable, and Klock① advocated the use of an implementation table, such as the one shown in Table 8. Notice how the same recommendations from Table 6 are shown but also how much more detail is provided to help the client implement strategies. Additionally, the table can be used to show clients how implementation of any recommendation will impact both cash flow and net worth.

① Lytton, R. H., Grable, J. E., &Klock, D. D. (2013). *The process of financial planning: Developing a financial plan* (2nd ed.). Erlanger, KY: National Underwriter.

Table 8 **Recommendation Implementation Table**

Recommendation (What)	Who	When	Where	Why	How	Annual Impact of Cash Flow (How Much)	Impact on Net Worth (How Much)
Pay off credit card debts using cash from bank account.	Client	Immediately	Online	Increase Cash Flow	Use Samsung Savings	+ $3 200	$0
Amend W – 4 tax form to withhold an additional $400 from each paycheck.	Client	Immediately	With Payroll Office at Work	Match Tax Liability with Withholdings	Ask Payroll Office for New W4 and to Increase Withholdings by $400	– $4 800	+ $4 800
Increase retirement plan contributions at work by $250 each pay period.	Client	Immediately	With Payroll Office at Work	Decrease Tax Liability and Increase Retirement Savings	Ask Payroll Office for Assistance	– $2 250 (after taxes)	+ $2 250 + Employer Matching & Account Appreciation
Rollover retirement plan from previous employer into a self – directed IRA.	Planner & Client	Within the Year	Planner's Office	Consolidate Holdings	Complete Account Transfer Form and New Account Form	$0	$0
Exchange current cash value life insurance policy into a variable policy.	Planner & Client	Within the Year	Planner's Office	Reduce Policy Costs and Increase Investment Flexibility	Complete Account Transfer Form and New Account Form	$2 300	$0
Update your will, living will, and power of attorney.	Client	Within the Year	Attorney's Office	Estate Review and Maintenance	Make Appointment	$0	– $900
Consult with your property and casualty insurance agent about current coverage andliability limits.	Client	Within the Year	Insurance Agent's Office	Annual Insurance Review	Make Appointment	$0	$0
Sell stamp collection and invest proceeds in beach front condominium.	Planner & Client	Within the Year	Planner's Office	Diversify Assets and Prepare Assets for Heirs	Meet With Jim Brody of Empire Auctions	$0	+ $35 000
Complete a household inventory for insurance purposes.	Client	Within the Year	Home	Annual Update of Assets Owned	Video Record all Owned Items and Serial Numbers; Place Record in Safe Deposit Box	$0	$0
Consider purchasing an additional $1 million excess liability insurance policy.	Planner & Client	Within the Year	Planner's Office or Insurance Agent's Office	To Minimize Possibility Liability Claims in the Future as Net Worth Increases	Meet with Insurance Agent to Complete Necessary Forms; May Require Increasing Other Liability Coverages	– $350	$0

Definition of Responsibilities

As illustrated in Table 7, recommendation and plan implementation typically involves a number of individuals. Four individuals are typically involved with implementation procedures, depending on each financial planner's model of practice and a client's preferences:

1) The Client

2) The Planner

3) Existing Network Professionals

4) New Referred Professionals

Some financial planners define their role primarily as an analyst. Using this approach, clients are given the most responsibility within a plan to implement recommendations. Planners who see themselves as analysts typically stay at arm's length in terms of recommending the use of one or more professionals to implement recommendations. On the other end of the spectrum are those advisers who see their primary role as helping their client's implement and monitor nearly all financial planning recommendations. Sometimes these financial planners are licensed to provide different brokerage, insurance, and money management services and products. The burden of plan implementation falls squarely on the planner for these advisers. It is most common, however, for a planner to use a combination of client, planner, and outside professionals to implement recommendations. Clients sometimes have their own attorney, accountant, and banker. In these situations, it is a good idea to include these professionals in the planning process.

Occasionally, however, a client will need outside help to implement a plan recommendation. This is the reason it is important for financial planners to develop strategic alliances with affiliated professionals. These referral networks can include attorneys, public accountants, tax professionals, charitable giving specialists, brokers, dealers, wealth managers, financial therapists, social workers, trust officers, marriage and family therapists, insurance brokers and agents, real estate agents, and mortgage brokers. Figure 5 shows how a financial planner, using a referral network of strategic alliances, takes center stage in managing, coordinating, and documenting the work of each of the professionals used in plan implementation. Of course, it is important to disclose any referral fee arrangements to clients before recommending someone within a referral network.

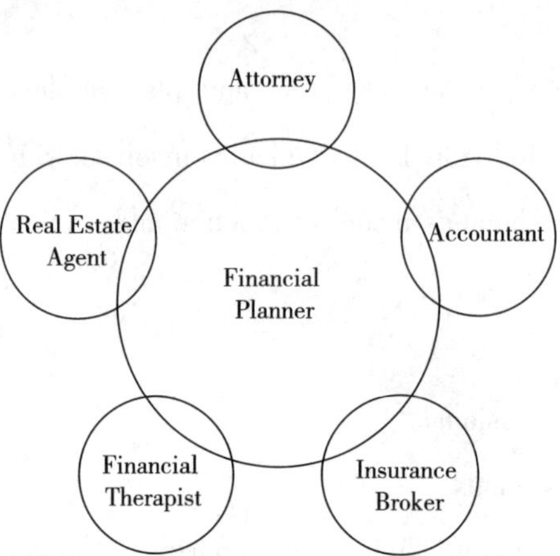

Figure 5 Financial Planner as Coordinator of Plan Implementation

Case Illustration: The Fan Family

The previous Fan family illustration provided examples of recommendations that would be appropriate within a comprehensive financial plan. The following example shows how one of these recommendations can be summarized into a Recommendation Implementation Table.

Recommendation (What)	Who	When	Where	Why	How	Annual Impact of Cash Flow (How Much)	Impact on Net Worth (How Much)
Purchase an "Own Occupation" Disability [or Modified Own Occupation] Policy	Xuan	Within the next 60 days	Locally with XYZ insurance company [the same firm that services the family's life insurance policies]	Protect family income and cash flow in the case of Xuan's disability	Meet with Haidong Tun within the next 60 days at this office on 36 Victoria Street	- $ 1,500	$ 0

Fee Structure and Schedule

Although laws and customs are different in each country, there are seven general ways in which financial planners are paid to implement recommendations. Each method is briefly described below:

1) The simplest, but least common, form of compensation is a flat fee arrangement. Financial planners who use this method basically charge for the development of a financial plan. The fee sometimes also includes basic implementation of plan components, but it is expected that the client will take steps to implement, and pay for, most other recommendations within the plan.

2) A growing trend, especially among financial planners serving the mass affluent market (clients with investable assets of less than U. S. $ 500,000, involves charging hourly fees for plan analysis and recommendation implementation. Fees typically range from $ 100 to $ 300 per hour.

3) Financial planners whose client's consist of affluent individuals and households often charge a retainer for planning activities. Retainer fees often start at U. S. $ 5,000 per year. The retainer guarantees access to the planner and planning staff on a year round basis for problem analysis, consultation, and limited recommendation implementation.

4) Increasingly, plan and recommendation implementation is included in an annual assets – under – management (AUM) fee. Planners who use this approach charge a fee ranging from 0.25% to over 2.00% of the dollar value of assets being managed. A client, for example, with U. S. $ 1,000,000 in investable assets would pay approximately $ 10,000 a year for planning services. This fee would include plan preparation, nearly all implementation procedures, and ongoing management services.

5) In the United States, and throughout most East Asian countries, commission based compensation continues to be the primary way in which planners are paid to implement recommendations. Often, planning services are provided at no cost, with the assumption that clients will implement recommendations with the adviser who prepared the plan.

6) A variation of commission compensation is called fee – offset. Increasingly, planners are beginning to charge a flat fee for plan preparation. This planning fee is then reduced or eliminated (offset) if the client implements with the financial planner.

7) Lastly, a growing trend among those in the profession involves combining aspects of different compensation methods. A popular approach is to combine a set plan preparation fee, coupled with an AUM fee and limited commissions based on the use of insurance products. This

multi – source compensation method is most widely used by financial planners who have the ability to implement a wide variety of recommendations made within a financial plan.

It should go without saying, but is worth repeating nonetheless, that financial planners, regardless of compensation method, need to fully disclose how and when they are paid for plan preparation services and implementation of recommendations. Table 9 provides a minimal example of how a financial planner working under an AUM model might disclose compensation issues.

Table 9 AUM Compensation Disclosure Form

XYZ Firm

Asset Management Fee Schedule

Financial planning and asset management fees are determined on a quarterly basis by the total amount of assets managed by XYZ Firm. This method of compensation is referred to as Assets Under Management. Fees are calculated and due in January, March, June, and September of each year. Note that fees are not prorated.

The ongoing plan development and portfolio management fees are as follows:

- $ 0 to $ 250 000 — 1.50% annually
- $ 250 001 to $ 500 000 — 1.25% annually
- $ 500 001 to $ 750 000 — 1.00% annually
- $ 750 001 to $ 1 000 000 — 0.80% annually
- $ 1 000 001 to $ 2 000 000 — 0.70% annually
- $ 2 000 001 + — 0.50% annually

For example, someone with $ 1,000,000 in assets under management will pay $ 8,000 per year in planning fees ($ 2,000 per quarter), which will be deducted directly from the managed accounts or directly by the client.

Client: ______________________ Date: ______________________

Planner: ______________________ Date ______________________

Note: Asset management fees must be paid in advance at the beginning of each billing month. Fees are assessed on the total value of all accounts on the last business day of the previous billing period.

Periodical Review and Modification

Sometimes it is easy for financial planners to forget the sixth step in the planning process—monitoring client outcomes. Financial planners spend much of their time analyzing a client's financial situation, developing recommendations, and implementing strategies. A reasonable assumption is that clients should experience positive and meaningful improvement in their financial situation when recommendations are implemented. The reality is that this assumption may or may not be true in practice. This is the reason ongoing monitoring of implemented recommendations is so important. That is, periodic evaluations and ongoing monitoring help ensure that a client is on track meeting goals and that new issues, situations, and demands are evaluated in the context of previously implemented strategies.

Assuming that the planner – client relationship involves an ongoing relationships, financial planners should constantly monitor the following factors:

- Previously made assumptions
- Previously determined financial plan inputs
- Portfolio returns and risk – adjusted performance
- Ratings of companies and product providers
- Suitability of referrals
- Client risk tolerance
- Plan and product fees
- Changes in the client's situation that would warrant
  - Adjustments to portfolio allocations
  - Alterations to strategies
  - Reanalysis of the current financial situation
- Progress towards goal achievement

It is reasonable to anticipate that changes in the economy and a client's personal situation will entail a need for renewed analyses and adjustments to plan recommendations. This is the reason some financial planners refer to a written financial plan as a "living document." This means that an original plan is always subject to change and revision based on the current needs of the client.

As the final step in the financial planning process, monitoring a client's progress towards goal achievement provides three opportunities to strengthen the planner – client relationship. First, ongoing monitoring ensures that a planner will maintain contact with each client. Constant contact is one way to add value within a planning context. Communicating with clients promotes a more proactive approach to future financial planning. Second, monitoring a client's situation helps make sure that the products and services being used by a client are still appropriate, both in terms of costs and performance. Finally, plan monitoring is a tool that allows a financial planner to stay abreast of economic, legal, accounting, tax, and regulatory changes.

As illustrated in Figure 6, plan monitoring takes cues for changes in a client's financial and life situation. These changes, as identified in the monitoring process, are then folded into the ongoing financial planning engagement. In other words, when viewed holistically, the process of planning never truly ends.

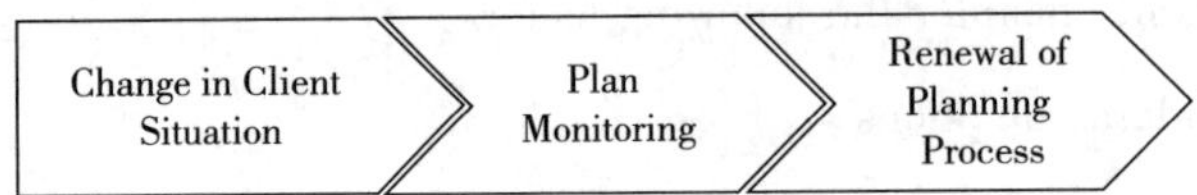

Figure 6 Plan Monitoring Promotes Future Planning

Contingent Plan

Although there are exceptions, most clients engage the services of a financial planner to obtain specific financial recommendations to solve a problem or to answer a question. The implication of this insight is clear; namely, clients expect financial planners to make specific, targeted, and precise client – specific recommendations. These recommendations, by definition, should not only be suitable for a client but also offer the greatest short – , intermediate – , and long – term benefits.

It is the last point that makes financial planning, as a professional endeavor, a creative challenge. Like nearly every other profession, there are no single correct solutions or approaches when it comes to financial planning recommendations. While there may be obviously wrong strategies, there is usually more than one way to solve a client's financial dilemma. Consider, for example, an analysis indicating a client needing an additional $ 400,000 in life insurance coverage. Determining the need, while time consuming as an analytical exercise, is only the first step in the recommendation and implementation process. More importantly, the financial planner must make a recommendation regarding the precise type of insurance to purchase. This decision should be based on the financial planner's compensation structure, preferences, the current environment, legal restrictions, and client preferences. In short, there may be several equally useful recommendations for this situation. One financial planner may recommend a 20 – year guaranteed renewable term policy. Another financial planner may recommend a level premium variable life insurance product. Both may be appropriate and suitable.

Rather than get caught up in a debate about which product or service may be better or best, financial planners should instead consider utilizing the following approach when developing and presenting recommendations for implementation:

(1) Choose a strategy that meets the need of a client;

(2) Ensure that the recommendation is appropriate and fair;

(3) Disclose any and all limitations associated with the strategy;

(4) Provide evidence showing why the recommendation is optimal for the client; and

(5) Provide one or more alternatives (contingent recommendations).

By definition, the contingent recommendations at step five should, in the financial planner's opinion, be sub - optimal to the recommendation made to the client. If it turns out that one or more of the alternative suggestions are equal to or better than the recommendation, in any way, a reanalysis and evaluation of choices should be made. In effect, the contingent recommendations should be made to provide evidence to the client that other alternatives were evaluated but dismissed as being less than optimal. Alternatives should also be shown in case a client discloses new information or factual details later that would make the current recommendation problematic.

The Termination of a Financial Plan

Increasingly, financial planners are positioning themselves to become trusted client advisers. The term *working alliance* describes the long - term nature of most financial planning engagements. While there certainly are advisers who are engaged in transactional business, the trend is increasingly moving towards building planner - client relationships that last several years, and in some case, decades.

As alluded to throughout this chapter, the financial planning process works best when all of the steps in the process are followed, with plan monitoring leading to renewed analyses and stronger planner - client engagements. One way to make sure this occurs is to formalize the planning relationship in writing. Clients should sign a letter indicating that they received a written planning document. The acceptance letter should also indicate that the client has reviewed the plan and had an opportunity to ask questions about planner compensation issues and product/service recommendations. Documentation should also be used to clearly and explicitly describe the working alliance assumptions and limitations. For example, if a financial planner intends to be the primary contact for all implementation procedures, this assumption should be discussed and agreed upon.

There are times when planner – client engagements terminate. Sometimes terminations result when a client moves. There may be times when a client decides to end a relationship because they are dissatisfied or have chosen to take a different life journey. In either case, it is always prudent to conclude the relationship in writing and return any documents that are requested by the client. ①

There are also times when a financial planner may wish to terminate the planner – client relationship. Novice planners often cannot imagine this scenario; however, more experienced planners find that they must, on occasion, "fire" clients. Terminating the planner – client relationship, from a financial planner's point of view, makes sense whenever the costs associated with maintaining the relationship exceeds the revenue gained. The 80/20 rule is a useful measure in this respect. Typically, firms find that 80 percent of revenue is generated by 20 percent of clientele. Alternatively, 20 percent of clients utilize 80 percent of a financial planner's time and resources. As long as the 20 percent of revenue matches the 20 percent of time use, there should be no problem; however, whenever low revenue clients start to consume more time and effort, problems arise. Successful financial planners often conclude that terminating relationships with "problem" clients creates additional time and resources to cultivate relationships with more profitable clients. ② When it comes time to ending a planner – client relationship, financial planners should (1) document the decision in writing, (2) refer the client to another financial planner when appropriate, and (3) continue to be professional in any future dealings with the individual.

Summary

The profession of financial planning is unlike many other professional activities. A financial planner can make a very good living, but more importantly, a financial planner is in a unique

---

① Note that in the United States, financial planners are required to maintain files and documentation for every current and former client. Former client details should be maintained for at least five years.

② Profitability, in this context, is measure broadly as both financial and emotional gains.

position to make a significant positive impact in the lives of clients. Something as simple as helping a client formalize a life dream into a fundable goal can be a life altering turning point for a client. Celebrating with a client as they reach a goal, such as purchasing a beach house, fully funding a child's education, or taking a dream vacation, can be a rewarding milestone for both client and financial planner. Moments shared with a client are a unique and important outcome associated with the practice of financial planning.

Sometimes people assume that a financial planner's job involves sitting in an office contemplating the markets, making trades in a client's account, occasionally monitoring a chart, and analyzing the economy. While these are all important aspects of financial planning, it is worth noting that the life of a financial planner is much more dynamic. The day - to - day practice of financial planning is fast paced, always changing, and eventful. Consider the typical day of a financial planner:

7:00 am	Start morning by reviewing previous day and overnight market trends
9:00 am	Morning meeting with staff
10:00 am	Communicating with clients
Noon	Lunch with client
2:00 pm	Developing strategies for one or more clients
3:00 pm	Meetings with clients
5:00 pm	Meet with staff to review notes and update future plans
6:00 pm	Dinner with client or home with family

What surprises many novice financial planners and nearly all clients is the amount of time spent communicating and meeting with clients. While it is certainly true that financial planners engage in analytic activity almost every day, the most effective and successful financial planners allocate the majority of their day listening to and discussing events with clients. This is an effective method that can be used to help clients formulate goals, establish funding objectives, and maintain progress towards goal achievement. In the end, the most successful financial planners—those who love what they do and are loved by their clients—are those who have a passion for helping others achieve life success while simultaneously enjoying working in the world of personal finance. It takes this combination—heart and mind—to maximize the outcomes associated with the financial planning process.

As this chapter concludes it is worth reviewing some of the most important elements from the chapter content. To begin with, financial planning is a process, one that can continue and evolve over time as a client's dreams, aspirations, perceptions, preferences, and resources change. The most successful financial planners tend to be those who are empathetic to the needs of their clients, creative, strategic, and adaptive. Life changes. Things happen. People's goals evolve. A financial planner's role is to help each client manage these and other life events.

A key emphasis in this chapter has been on the systematic implementation of tools and techniques as a means to help clients reach their goals. The use of repeatable processes, from the development of objectives and goals to the conceptualization of strategies, is an important aspect of financial planning. This approach helps ensure that every client is treated fairly and that the most suitable product and service is being offered to clients. Financial planners who following the financial planning process, as described in this chapter, will find that as their experience deepens, their client - planner relationships will evolve into partnerships based on trust and commitment. It is likely that the financial planner will emerge as the client's most trusted adviser.

Chapter 4 Building a Successful Financial Planning Practice

According to Financial Planning Standards Board (FPSB), the organization that establishes, upholds, and promotes the worldwide use of the Certified Financial Planner (CFP®) mark, a competent financial planner is someone who can deliver financial planning to consumers using specialized skills, knowledge, and abilities effectively. The purpose of this chapter is to describe how a financial service professional—regardless of their scope of service—can build a successful financial planning practice.

Financial Planner Competitive Standards

Insurance agents, bank employees, retirement plan specialists, stock brokers, and others who provide financial advice to consumers provide services that are often misunderstood in the marketplace. Often, consumers do not fully appreciate the value provided by a financial service provider. One reason is that unlike other professions, the level of competition among financial service providers is quite intense. There are few standard products and services, which tends to cause confusion among consumers. Financial planners operate in this very competitive marketplace. This makes it difficult for consumers to differentiate services provided by a financial planner from offers made by others. Consumers, for example, cannot easily distinguish between an insurance salesperson and a stockbroker, let alone describe how a financial planner is different from or the same as either of these financial service providers. This creates confusion that often leads to inaction on the part of consumers. This indecisiveness in planning behavior is a direct result of trust erosion. That is, consumers who are unsure of the services offered by an adviser, and how the adviser is compensated, develop defensive mechanisms that require advisers to prove their trustworthiness.

Consider this example originating from certain advisers working in the United States in 2014. Following the Great Recession that started in 2007 – 2008, a large proportion of the U. S. population moved out of equities into fixed – income securities. Unfortunately, during this time, the yield on fixed – income debt was very low (i. e. , less than 1 percent). Beginning in 2009, the U. S. equity markets, as represented by the S&P 500, the Dow Jones Industrial Average, and the NASDAQ began one of history's greatest bull market runs. Many stocks nearly doubled in value between 2009 and 2013. Investors who were sitting in fixed – income securities felt a strong tinge of regret for missing out on the specular gains realized in stocks.

Some advisers used this historical backdrop as a way to sell products to those wanting to invest in stocks but who were unsure about the safety of equities. Advertisements began to appear on television and online, as well as on the radio, that went something like this:

"Did you know that you can obtain stock market returns without taking any stock market risk? For years, savvy investors have used these unique products to grow and protect their wealth in good and bad times. Now you too can obtain the secret to wealth."

While these advertisements were not designed specifically to deceive consumers, the ads were misleading. Consumers were led to believe that some sort of new investment had been created, or at least made available to non – wealthy consumers. In reality, the secret product was a form of insurance. The advisers running the advertisements were either selling variable indexed annuities and/or variable universal life insurance. The products advertised were neither new nor unique. What was not advertised were the huge upfront and ongoing commissions associated with the sale of these products, or disclosures regarding caps on equity gains or distribution penalties for early withdrawals. While the products were legitimate and appropriate for certain clients, the generalized sales pitch that any consumer could capture the upside of the equity markets with no downside risk was clearly overstated.

These types of aggressive sales tactics tend to cause confusion among consumers. Rather than being a financial planning product designed to manage the risk associated with a diversified portfolio, the products being sold by these advisers were traditional insurance contracts marketed as innovative tax havens. How, then, can someone who is honestly attempting to follow the financial planning process by providing comprehensive financial advice and counsel to clients compete in such a marketplace? One clear path to competitive success involves differentiation based on character and fitness standards.

In the United States, the CFP Board of Standards, Inc. has established baseline standards for CFP ® certification. CFP Board has a vested interest in establishing a financial planning marketplace that reflects well upon those following the planning process. CFP Board research demonstrates that those who follow high character, ethical, and professional standards are more highly valued by consumers. Consumers are willing to pay more for services provided by those who hold a planning certification. Worldwide, the following conduct is considered unacceptable for someone holding the CFP mark:

- Being arrested and found guilty of felony theft, embezzlement, or another financially - based crimes;
- Felony conviction for tax fraud or other tax - related crimes;
- Revocation of a financial professional license, unless the revocation is administrative in nature (i. e. , not paying the required fees);
- Felony conviction for any degree of murder or rape; or
- Felony conviction for any other violent crime within the last five years.

Under CFP Board rules, the following conduct can bar someone from becoming a CFPP:

- Having two or more personal or business bankruptcies;
- Revocation or suspension of a non - financial professional, unless the revocation is administrative in nature;
- Suspension of a financial professional license, unless the suspension is administrative in nature;
- Felony conviction for non - violent crimes (including perjury) within the last five years; or
- Felony conviction for violent crimes other than murder or rape that occurred more than five years ago.

Other factors that may limit someone's ability to obtain the CFP mark include customer complaints, arbitrations and other civil proceedings, felony convictions for non - violent crimes that occurred more than five years ago, misdemeanor convictions, and employer investigations and terminations.

International Standards

Internationally, FPSB ensures practice standards by promoting and regulating the use of the CFP ® certification. Ethical standards worldwide follow those of the United States in most regards; however, in some ways, FPSB standards are more streamlined and concise. FPSB defines financial planning as the process of developing strategies to assist clients in managing their financial affairs to meet life goals. ① As part of this process, financial planners are expected to review all relevant aspects of a client's financial situation. This definitional framework clearly helps financial planners differentiate their work in the marketplace. The FPSB definition of financial planning does not require that a financial planner provide a comprehensive advice or write a comprehensive financial plan. Of course, a financial planner may provide these services but it is not required. Instead, a financial planner, using FPSB guidelines, is someone who has the skills, knowledge, and ability to review a client's complete financial situation and develop a strategy that is appropriate and effective.

A financial planner, regardless of their scope of practice, must exhibit the following three performance abilities: (1) ability to collect correct and appropriate data from a client; (2) ability to analyze data collected; and (3) ability to synthesize data and analyses into client – centered strategies. A key factor that distinguishes a financial planner from, say, a stockbroker or financial counselor, is the planner's competency related to integrating both quantitative and qualitative financial information during the analysis phase of the process, and, just as importantly, demonstrating mastery of the interrelationships between and among planning components. Whereas a tax preparer, for example, may collect, analyze, and synthesize client tax data this is not the same competency level of a financial planner who must be able to integrate tax information throughout a client's financial situation. Stated another way, it is possible for a tax preparer to be a financial planner, but not all tax preparers are, or can be, financial planners.

---

① Financial Planning Standards Board. 2011. *Financial planner competency profile*. Denver: FPSB.

Ethical Standards and Professional Conduct

Ethical guidelines, rules, and regulations were discussed in earlier chapters; however, the topic is so important that it is worthy of additional discussion. As a reminder, every country and every professional activity has its own rules and laws that must be followed. In some countries, such as the United States, specific rules regarding the practice of financial planning are almost non - existent. Anyone can call their activity financial planning. Only those who provide investment advice for a fee or those who sell a product or service for a commission, must follow any type of prescribed rules or regulations. Specifically, planners who provide services for a fee must register as an investment advisor. Those who manage or advise less than U. S. $ 100 million register with the U. S. Securities and Exchange Commission. All others register at the state level. Advisors who sell securities must hold a license issued by the Financial Industry Regulatory Authority (FINRA). Advisors who sell insurance products must also obtain insurance specific licenses. In other parts of the world, commission - based sales of products and services have been limited. In these countries, advisors must follow a fiduciary standard of conduct. In other regions, a suitability standard exists. ①

In additional to local and federal standards, financial planners generally belong to professional organizations or certification bodies that add a layer of additional rules and requirements. In the United States, CFP Board adopted a code of ethics that is generally considered to be the most robust. CFP Board established their code of ethics with the goal of representing the highest principles and standards. Within the code, Principles are general statements expressing the ethical and professional ideals CFP professionals and registrants are expected to display in their professional activities. Principles are aspirational. The Principles form the basis of CFP Board's *Rules of Conduct*, *Practice Standards and Disciplinary Rules*. It is very important to remember, however, that only CFP professionals must abide by these

---

① In the United States, anyone who is registered as an investment advisor must follow a fiduciary standard. Only licensed stock brokers and insurance agents are allowed to follow a suitability standard of care.

Principles, rules, and standards.[①] CFP Board's specific Principles are as follows:[②]

Principle 1 – Integrity: Provide professional services with integrity.

Integrity demands honesty and candor which must not be subordinated to personal gain and advantage. CFP professionals are placed in positions of trust by clients, and the ultimate source of that trust is the CFP professional's personal integrity. Allowance can be made for innocent error and legitimate differences of opinion, but integrity cannot co – exist with deceit or subordination of one's principles.

Principle 2 – Objectivity: Provide professional services objectively.

Objectivity requires intellectual honesty and impartiality. Regardless of the particular service rendered or the capacity in which a CFP professional functions, CFP professionals should protect the integrity of their work, maintain objectivity and avoid subordination of their judgment.

Principle 3 – Competence: Maintain the knowledge and skill necessary to provide professional services competently.

Competence means attaining and maintaining an adequate level of knowledge and skill, and application of that knowledge and skill in providing services to clients. Competence also includes the wisdom to recognize the limitations of that knowledge and when consultation with other professionals is appropriate or referral to other professionals necessary. CFP professionals make a continuing commitment to learning and professional improvement.

Principle 4 – Fairness: Be fair and reasonable in all professional relationships. Disclose conflicts of interest.

Fairness requires impartiality, intellectual honesty and disclosure of material conflicts of interest. It involves a subordination of one's own feelings, prejudices and desires so as to achieve a proper balance of conflicting interests. Fairness is treating others in the same fashion that you would want to be treated.

Principle 5 – Confidentiality: Protect the confidentiality of all client information.

Confidentiality means ensuring that information is accessible only to those authorized to have access. A relationship of trust and confidence with the client can only be built upon the

---

① CFP Board has spent millions of dollars on consumer awareness advertisements to help consumers understand the value of working with someone who is certified.

② More information can be found at: http://www.cfp.net/for-cfp-professionals/professional-standards-enforcement/standards-of-professional-conduct/code-of-ethics-professional-responsibility#sthash.7jf5QRlB.dpuf.

understanding that the client's information will remain confidential.

Principle 6 – Professionalism: Act in a manner that demonstrates exemplary professional conduct.

Professionalism requires behaving with dignity and courtesy to clients, fellow professionals, and others in business – related activities. CFP professionals cooperate with fellow CFP professionals to enhance and maintain the profession's public image and improve the quality of services.

Principle 7 – Diligence: Provide professional services diligently.

Diligence is the provision of services in a reasonably prompt and thorough manner, including the proper planning for, and supervision of, the rendering of professional services.

CFP Board also outlines specific aspects of the client – planner relationship. In addition to the seven Principles from above, anyone holding the CFP certification must follow prescribed rules when working with clients. Violation of any one rule may subject the planner to sanctions imposed by CFP Board. The following rules define a financial planner's relationship with a prospective or current client:

- The CFP professional (CFPP) and the prospective client or client shall mutually agree upon the services to be provided by the CFPP.
- If the CFPP's services include financial planning or material elements of financial planning, prior to entering into an agreement, the CFPP shall provide written information or discuss with the prospective client or client the following:
- The obligations and responsibilities of each party under the agreement with respect to:
  - ○ Defining goals, needs and objectives,
  - ○ Gathering and providing appropriate data,
  - ○ Examining the result of the current course of action without changes,
  - ○ The formulation of any recommended actions,
  - ○ Implementation responsibilities, and
  - ○ Monitoring responsibilities.
- Compensation that any party to the agreement or any legal affiliate to a party to the agreement will or could receive under the terms of the agreement; and factors or terms that determine costs, how decisions benefit the CFPP and the relative benefit to the CFPP.

- Terms under which the agreement permits the CFPP to offer proprietary products.
- Terms under which the CFPP will use other entities to meet any of the agreement's obligations.

If the CFPP provides the above information in writing, the CFPP shall encourage the prospective client or client to review the information and offer to answer any questions that the prospective client or client may have.

- If the services include financial planning or material elements of financial planning, the CFPP or the CFPP's employer shall enter into a written agreement governing the financial planning services ("Agreement"). The Agreement shall specify:
  - The parties to the Agreement,
  - The date of the Agreement and its duration,
  - How and on what terms each party can terminate the Agreement, and
  - The services to be provided as part of the Agreement.

The Agreement may consist of multiple written documents. Written documentation that includes the items above and is used by a CFPP or CFPP's employer in compliance with state or federal law, or the rules or regulations of any applicable self - regulatory organization, such as the Securities and Exchange Commission's Form ADV or other disclosure documents, shall satisfy the requirements of this Rule.

- A CFPP shall at all times place the interest of the client ahead of his or her own. When the CFPP provides financial planning or material elements of financial planning, the CFPP owes to the client the duty of care of a fiduciary as defined by CFP Board.

Additional rules apply to the manner in which a financial planner deals with clients. Specific communication rules include the following:

- A CFPP shall not communicate, directly or indirectly, to clients or prospective clients any false or misleading information directly or indirectly related to the CFPP's professional qualifications or services. A CFPP shall not mislead any parties about the potential benefits of the CFPP's service. A CFPP shall not fail to disclose or otherwise omit facts where that disclosure is necessary to avoid misleading clients.
- A CFPP shall disclose to a prospective client or client the following information:
  - An accurate and understandable description of the compensation arrangements being

offered. This description must include:

○ Information related to costs and compensation to the CFPP and/or the CFPP's employer, and

○ Terms under which the CFPP and/or the CFPP's employer may receive any other sources of compensation, and if so, what the sources of these payments are and on what they are based.

○ A general summary of likely conflicts of interest between the client and the CFPP, the CFPP's employer or any affiliates or third parties, including, but not limited to, information about any familial, contractual or agency relationship of the CFPP or the CFPP's employer that has a potential to materially affect the relationship.

○ Any information about the CFPP or the CFPP's employer that could reasonably be expected to materially affect the client's decision to engage the CFPP that the client might reasonably want to know in establishing the scope and nature of the relationship, including but not limited to information about the CFPP's areas of expertise.

○ Contact information for the CFPP and, if applicable, the CFPP's employer.

○ If the services include financial planning or material elements of financial planning, these disclosures must be in writing. The written disclosures may consist of multiple written documents. Written disclosures used by a CFPP or CFPP's employer that includes the items listed above, and are used in compliance with state or federal laws, or the rules or requirements of any applicable self - regulatory organization, such as the Securities and Exchange Commission's Form ADV or other disclosure documents, shall satisfy the requirements of this Rule.

○ The CFPP shall timely disclose to the client any material changes to the above information.

Rules related to how a financial planner handles information and property obtained from a prospective or current client include:

- A CFPP shall treat information as confidential except as required in response to proper legal process; as necessitated by obligations to a CFPP's employer or partners; as required to defend against charges of wrongdoing; in connection with a civil dispute; or as needed to perform the services.

- A CFPP shall take prudent steps to protect the security of information and property, including the security of stored information, whether physically or electronically, that is within the CFPP's control.

- A CFPP shall obtain the information necessary to fulfill his or her obligations. If a CFPP cannot obtain the necessary information, the CFPP shall inform the prospective client or client of any and all material deficiencies.
- A CFPP shall clearly identify the assets, if any, over which the CFPP will take custody, exercise investment discretion, or exercise supervision.
- A CFPP shall identify and keep complete records of all funds or other property of a client in the custody, or under the discretionary authority, of the CFPP.
- A CFPP shall not borrow money from a client. Exceptions to this Rule include:
  - The client is a member of the CFPP's immediate family, or
  - The client is an institution in the business of lending money and the borrowing is unrelated to the professional services performed by the CFPP.
- A CFPP shall not lend money to a client. Exceptions to this Rule include:
  - The client is a member of the CFPP's immediate family, or
  - The CFPP is an employee of an institution in the business of lending money and the money lent is that of the institution, not the CFPP.
- A CFPP shall not commingle a client's property with the property of the CFPP or the CFPP's employer, unless the commingling is permitted by law or is explicitly authorized and defined in a written agreement between the parties.
- A CFPP shall not commingle a client's property with other clients' property unless the commingling is permitted by law or the CFPP has both explicit written authorization to do so from each client involved and sufficient record – keeping to track each client's assets accurately.
- A CFPP shall return a client's property to the client upon request as soon as practicable or consistent with a time frame specified in an agreement with the client.

CFPPs must also follow rules designed to protect clients from harm. Specific obligations include:

- A CFPP shall treat prospective clients and clients fairly and provide professional services with integrity and objectivity.
- A CFPP shall offer advice only in those areas in which he or she is competent to do so

and shall maintain competence in all areas in which he or she is engaged to provide professional services.

- A CFPP shall be in compliance with applicable regulatory requirements governing professional services provided to the client.

- A CFPP shall exercise reasonable and prudent professional judgment in providing professional services to clients.

- In addition to the requirements of Rule 1.4, a CFPP shall make and/or implement only recommendations that are suitable for the client.

- A CFPP shall provide reasonable and prudent professional supervision or direction to any subordinate or third party to whom the CFPP assigns responsibility for any client services.

- A CFPP shall advise his or her current clients of any certification suspension or revocation he or she receives from CFP Board.

In addition to clients, financial planners who hold the CFP mark must also be truthful and professional to colleagues and their employer. Rules related to employer obligations include:

- A CFPP who is an employee/agent shall perform professional services with dedication to the lawful objectives of the employer/principal and in accordance with CFP Board's *Code of Ethics*.

- A CFPP who is an employee/agent shall advise his or her current employer/principal of any certification suspension or revocation he or she receives from CFP Board.

Finally, CFPPs have an obligation to uphold and promote high ethical standards within the profession. One way to do this is by adhering to the following obligations to CFP Board:

- A CFPP shall abide by the terms of all agreements with CFP Board, including, but not limited to, using the CFP® marks properly and cooperating fully with CFP Board's trademark and professional review operations and requirements.

- A CFPP shall meet all CFP Board requirements, including continuing education requirements, to retain the right to use the CFP® marks.

- A CFPP shall notify CFP Board of changes to contact information, including, but not limited to, e-mail address, telephone number(s) and physical address, within forty five (45) days.

- A CFPP shall notify CFP Board in writing of any conviction of a crime, except misdemeanor traffic offenses or traffic ordinance violations unless such offense involves the use of alcohol or drugs, or of any professional suspension or bar within ten (10) calendar days after the date on which the CFPP is notified of the conviction, suspension or bar.

- A CFPP shall not engage in conduct which reflects adversely on his or her integrity or fitness as a CFPP, upon the CFP® marks, or upon the profession.

It is important to note that these rules only apply to financial planning practitioners who hold the CFP mark. In the United States, only about 25 percent of planners are currently obliged to follow these rules. However, most membership organizations, such as the Financial Planning Association and the National Association of Personal Financial Advisors require their members to adhere to similar ethical guidelines and constraints. These ethical rules are above and beyond basic legal principles statutory rules all advisers must follow. For example, the following code is one in which members of the largest Fee – Only financial planning association agree to follow:

✓ The advisor shall exercise his/her best efforts to act in good faith and in the best interests of the client.

✓ The advisor shall provide written disclosure to the client prior to the engagement of the advisor, and thereafter throughout the term of the engagement, of any conflicts of interest, which will or reasonably may compromise the impartiality or independence of the advisor.

✓ The advisor, or any party in which the advisor has a financial interest, does not receive any compensation or other remuneration that is contingent on any client's purchase or sale of a financial product.

✓ The advisor does not receive a fee or other compensation from another party based on the referral of a client or the client's business.

Internationally, FPSB has identified the ethical skill set a financial planning professional must follow in order to hold the CFP mark. FPSB rules are based on the notion that clients expect the financial adviser to be trustworthy. As such, FPSB insists that financial planners differentiate them work in the marketplace by always working in the interest of clients while upholding the promoting the interests of the profession as a force for social benefit.

It should be clear that believing in and practicing high ethical principles and standards is the keystone to establishing a successful financial planning practice. At a minimum, it is up to each financial planner to:

➢ Establish trust with clients;

➢ Act in the best interest of each client when providing advice and counsel;①

➢ Demonstrate ethical judgment;

➢ Exhibit intellectual honesty;

➢ Demonstrate impartiality;

➢ Recognize personal limits on competency and seek professional advice and guidance from other professionals when appropriate;

➢ Acknowledge that financial planners hold a position of public trust, and as such, always act in the consumer interest.

➢ Comply with all local and federal laws and regulations;

➢ Adhere to relevant professional codes and standards of practice;

➢ Maintain awareness of economic, political, and regulatory environments;

➢ Engage in ongoing professional continuing education;

➢ Perform due diligence and research on all products and services offered to clients; and

➢ Act professionally by acting responsibly during and after a client engagement.

Jumpstarting a Career in Financial Planning

As noted earlier, a competent financial planner must be able to collect data from a client, analyze the data, and synthesize information to develop appropriate client - centered strategies. This implies that jumpstarting a career in financial planning means much more than learning about product lines, sales techniques, or a limited number of analytical techniques. Those who are just beginning their career as a financial planner will find that if they adopt and follow high standards of ethical conduct, achieve adequate training, and continually push for professional continuing education will be in the best position to achieve professional and personal success.

Pursuing a professional certification is the primary way a financial planner signals to consumers that he/she is serious about being valued as a financial planning professional.

---

① FPSB specifically avoids referring to suitability and fiduciary standards. Whether or not someone follows a suitability or fiduciary standard is less important than always acting in the best interest of a client.

Currently, there are dozens, if not hundreds, of financial planning certifications and designations. In the United States, the Certified Financial Planner (CFP®) certification is generally considered to be the most prestigious and rigorous program of study. This perception is based on the requirements necessary to become a CFP professional. For example, new CFPs must hold a bachelorette degree from an accredited university or college, write and present a written comprehensive financial plan, and obtain three years of professional experience prior to using the CFP marks. In addition, CFP Board requires all CFP certificants to maintain their competency through ongoing continuing education that includes bi-annual reviews of CFP Board standards of conduct and ethics. Internationally, the FPSB maintains standards for CFP professionals. There are, however, other certifications that help to jumpstart a new planner's career. The American College offers several proprietary certifications. The two most important, from the perspective of financial planners, are the Chartered Life Underwriter (CLU®) and Chartered Financial Consultant (ChFC®) certifications. Similar to the CFP, holders of these marks must maintain competence through continuing education. Those who are interested in specialized training often pursue the Chartered Financial Analyst (CFA®) certification if they are interested in investment management issues. The Certified Retirement Counselor (CRC®) designation is favored by those whose interests include providing retirement planning services. Financial counselors and debt advisers often pursue the Accredited Financial Counselor (AFC®) certification. Worldwide, financial planners will likely be attracted to certifications and designations that match their particular market and customer based. In general, any mark of achievement is valued by consumers, especially credentials that require an examination and ongoing continuing education.

Fortunately, FPSB and CFP Board conduct regular surveys of practitioners to determine minimum levels of competency. CFP Board, for example, tests all new CFP professionals on 78 topics.[①] It is expected, for example, that novice, as well as veteran, financial planners will be proficient in collecting data on these topics, analyzing the data, and creating strategies that integrate aspects from one or more of the following topic areas:

1. Financial Planning Process
2. Financial Statements

① The topic list was accurate as of 2014.

3. Cash Flow Management
4. Financing Strategies
5. Function, Purpose, and Regulation of Financial Institutions
6. Education Planning
7. Financial Planning for Special Circumstances
8. Economic Concepts
9. TVM
10. Financial Services Regulation and Requirements
11. Business Law
12. Consumer Protection Laws
13. Principles of Risk and Insurance
14. Analysis and Evaluation of Risk Exposures
15. Health Insurance and Health Care Cost Management (individual)
16. Disability Income Insurance (individual)
17. Long Term Care Insurance
18. Life Insurance (individual)
19. Income Taxation of Life Insurance
20. Business Uses of Insurance
21. Insurance Needs Analysis
22. Insurance Policy and Company Selection
23. Annuities
24. Characteristics, Uses and Taxation of Investment Vehicles
25. Types of Investment Risk
26. Quantitative Investment Concepts
27. Measures of Investment Returns
28. Bond – Stock Valuation Concepts
29. Portfolio Development and Analysis
30. Investment Strategies
31. Asset Allocation and Portfolio Diversification
32. Income Tax Law Fundamentals

33. Tax Compliance
34. Income Tax Fundamentals and Calculations
35. Characteristics and Income Taxation of Business Entities
36. Income Taxation of Trusts and Estates
37. Basis
38. Tax Consequences of the Disposition of Property
39. Alternative Minimum Tax (AMT)
40. Tax Reduction/Management Techniques
41. Passive Activity and At – Risk Rules
42. Tax implications of Special Circumstances
43. Charitable Contributions and Deductions
44. Retirement Needs Analysis
45. Social Security (OASDI)
46. Types of Retirement Plans
47. Qualified Plan Rules and Options
48. Other Tax – Advantaged Retirement Plans
49. Regulatory Considerations
50. Key Factors Affecting Plan Selection for Businesses
51. Investment Considerations for Retirement Plans
52. Distribution Rules Alternatives and Taxation
53. Characteristics and Consequences of Property Titling
54. Methods of Property Transfer at Death
55. Estate Planning Documents
56. Gifting Strategies
57. Gift Tax Compliance and Tax Calculation
58. Incapacity Planning
59. Estate Tax Compliance and Tax Calculation
60. Sources for Estate Liquidity
61. Powers of Appointment
62. Types, Features and Taxation of Trusts

63. Qualified Interest trusts

64. Charitable Transfers

65. Use of Life Insurance in Estate Planning

66. Marital Deduction

67. Deferral and Minimization of Estate Tax

68. Intra – Family and Other Business Transfer Techniques

69. GSTT

70. Fiduciaries

71. Income in Respect of a Decedent (IRD)

72. Postmortem Estate Planning Techniques

73. Estate Planning for Non – Traditional Relationships

74. Client and Planner Attitudes, Values, Biases and Behavioral Characteristics and the Impact on Financial Planning

75. Principles of Communication and Counseling

76. Standards of Professional Conduct

77. Disciplinary Rules and Procedures

78. Financial Planning Practice Standards

The International Perspective

FPSB also conducts surveys to obtain benchmark indicators of planning competency. In some ways, FPSB's competency categorization efforts are superior to those used by CFP Board, especially in helping novice financial planners understand the type of information that they need to be familiar with day – to – day when in practice. Figure 1 illustrates the core areas of planner competency. As shown, a financial planner must have a strong familiarity with the six core topic areas. This familiarity needs to extend to data collection and analysis, as well as synthesis of data into recommendations. As with all complex systems, a competent financial planner must be able to create effective and efficient financial plans within ever changing environments—economic, social, political, and regulatory. This is precisely what makes financial planning such a rewarding and challenging career; namely, the ability to view a client's financial situation holistically, even if the planner's scope of practice is limited to one or two competency areas.

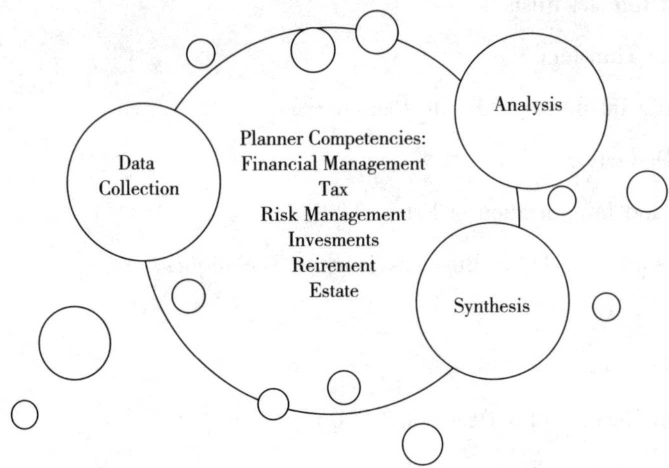

Figure 1　Aspects of Planner Competency

FPSB categorizes the financial planning body of knowledge into 11 topic categories. Within each category a number of core competencies are identified. These competencies comprise the minimum expectations of knowledge some entering the profession should possess. The categories and specific competencies are purposely broad. This approach allows each adviser to build nation specific frameworks of practice within the categories. These categories include:

1. Taxation

a. Assessment Rules

b. Personal Taxation

c. Corporate Taxation

d. Wealth Transfer

e. International Tax Issues

2. Insurance

a. Business Insurance

b. Life Insurance

c. Disability Insurance/Income Replacement

d. Health Insurance

e. Critical Illness Insurance, including Dread Disease and Trauma

f. Property Insurance

g. Casualty Insurance

3. Investments

a. Investment Types

b. Investment Structures

c. Types of Investment Risk

d. Measurement of Investment Risk

e. Portfolio Management Techniques

f. Selling and Buying Techniques

g. Performance Measurement

h. Modern Portfolio Theory

4. Retirement, Savings, and Income Programs

a. Government Pension

b. Government Savings

c. Employer/Employee Programs

d. Personal Retirement

e. Personal Savings

5. Law

a. Private Law

b. Corporate Law

6. Financial Analysis

a. Analysis of Financial Information

b. Personal Financial Ratios

c. Cash Management and Budgeting

d. Personal Financial Statements

7. Debt

a. Consumer Credit and Credit Management

b. Mortgages

c. Leases

d. Insolvency and Bankruptcy

8. Economic and Regulatory Environment

a. Economic Environment

b. Regulatory Environment

9. Government Benefit Plans

10. Behavioral Finance

11. Ethics and Standards

a. Code of Ethics

b. Financial Planning Practice Standards

While the listing of competencies from above is useful in describing the broad topics of practice encountered by most financial planners, the list does little to describe minimum competency standards. Someone who is hoping to jumpstart their financial planning career needs additional specific information. Fortunately, FPSB provides this information. As shown in Table 1, there are a number of minimum expectations in place for those just starting their career as a financial planner. The listing can best be viewed as necessary skills to be a competent financial planner.

Table 1 Minimum Financial Planning Functions

Data Collection
1. Identify a client's objectives, needs, and values that have financial implications
2. Identify information required for the financial plan
3. Identify client's legal issues that affect the financial plan
4. Determine client's attitudes and level of financial sophistication
5. Identify material changes in client's personal and financial situation
6. Prepare information to enable financial analysis
Analysis
7. Analyze client's objectives, needs, value, and information to prioritize financial planning components
8. Consider inter – relationships among financial planning components
9. Consider opportunities and constraints and assess collected information across financial planning components
10. Consider impact of economic, political, and regulatory environments
11. Measure progress toward achievement of objectives of the financial plan
Synthesis
12. Prioritize recommendations to optimize client's situation
13. Consolidate recommendations and action steps into a financial plan
14. Determine appropriate cycle of review for the financial plan

The listing shown below in Table 2 illustrates how FPSB links particular competency tasks with data collection, data analysis, and data synthesis activities. The list is grouped by planner competency topic—financial management, tax, risk management, investments, retirement, and estate. Essentially, a competent financial should be able to complete the following tasks, within the framework of the 11 core topic categories, in a way that improves the financial situation of clients. A financial planner who can conduct these tasks is considered to be minimally competent. Those wishing to jumpstart their career as a financial planner should focus on developing these necessary skills.

Table 2 Financial Planning Competency Tasks Grouped by Competency Topic

Data Collection	
Financial Management	Information regarding client assets and liabilities Information client cash flow income, and/or obligations Information necessary to prepare a budget Prepare statements of client's net worth, cash flow, and budget Determine client's propensity to save Determine how client makes spending decisions Determine client's attitudes toward their debt
Asset Management	Information necessary to prepare detailed statement of holdings Determine client's current asset allocation Identify cash flows available for investment Determine client's investment experience, attitudes, and biases Determine client's investment objectives Determine client's tolerance for investment risk Identify client's rate of return assumptions and expectations Identify client's investment time horizon
Risk Management	Information about client's existing insurance coverage Identify potential financial obligations Determine client's risk management objectives Determine client's tolerance for risk exposure Determine relevant lifestyle issues Determine client health issues Determine client's willingness to manage financial risk

Concluded

Data Collection	
Tax Planning	Information necessary to establish client's tax situation Identify taxable nature of assets and liabilities Identify current, deferred, and future tax liabilities Identify parties relevant to the client's tax situation Determine client's attitude toward taxation
Retirement Planning	Details of potential sources of retirement income Details of estimated retirement expenses Determines client's retirement objectives Determine client's attitudes toward retirement Determines client's comfort with retirement planning assumptions
Estate Planning	Identifies legal agreements and documents that impact estate planning Identifies client's estate planning objectives Identifies family dynamics and business relationships
Analysis	
Financial Management	Determine whether client is living within their financial means Determine the issues relevant to the client's assets and liabilities Determine client's emergency fund provision Consider potential cash management strategies Assess whether emergency fund is adequate Assess the impact of potential changes in income and expenses Identify conflicting demands on cash flow Assess financial alternatives
Asset Management	Calculate required rate of return to reach client objectives Determine characteristics of investment holdings Determine implications of acquiring/disposing of assets Consider potential investment strategies Assess whether investment return expectations match risk tolerance Assess whether asset holdings match risk tolerance Assess whether asset holding match return requirements

Concluded

Data Collection	
Risk Management	Determine characteristics of existing insurance coverage Consider current and potential risk management strategies Assess exposure to financial risk Assess client's risk exposure and risk management strategies Assess implications of change to insurance coverage Prioritize client's risk management needs
Tax Planning	Review relevant tax documents Consider potential tax strategies and structures Evaluate existing tax strategies and structures for suitability Assess financial impact of tax planning alternatives
Retirement Planning	Develop financial projections based on current position Determine if client's retirement objectives are realistic Consider potential retirement planning strategies Assess financial requirements at retirement date Assess impact of changes in assumptions of financial projections Assess trade – offs necessary to meet retirement objectives
Estate Planning	Project net worth at death Consider constraints to meeting client's estate planning objectives Consider potential estate planning strategies Calculate potential expenses and taxes owed at death Assess specific needs of beneficiaries Assess liquidity of the estate at death
Synthesis	
Financial Management	Develop financial management strategies Evaluate advantages and disadvantages of each strategy Optimize strategies to make financial management recommendations Prioritize actions steps to assist client implement recommendations
Asset Management	Develop asset management strategies Evaluate advantages and disadvantages of each strategy Optimize strategies to make asset management recommendations Prioritize actions steps to assist client implement recommendations

Concluded

Data Collection	
Risk Management	Develop risk management strategies Evaluate advantages and disadvantages of each strategy Optimize strategies to make risk management recommendations Prioritize actions steps to assist client implement recommendations
Tax Planning	Develop tax planning strategies Evaluate advantages and disadvantages of each strategy Optimize strategies to make tax planning recommendations Prioritize actions steps to assist client implement recommendations
Retirement Planning	Develop retirement planning strategies Evaluate advantages and disadvantages of each strategy Optimize strategies to make retirement planning recommendations Prioritize actions steps to assist client implement recommendations
Estate Planning	Develop estate planning strategies Evaluate advantages and disadvantages of each strategy Optimize strategies to make estate planning recommendations Prioritize actions steps to assist client implement recommendations

Source: Financial Planning Standards Board Ltd., 2011.

The Art and Science of Client Communication

It may seem obvious that communication skills are an essential attribute for those beginning or furthering their career as a financial planner. After all, clients must meet, at some point, with their financial planner to obtain information and guidance, whereas planners have got to meet with clients to gather data and make recommendations. ① The question is whether simply meeting with someone is the same as maximizing interpersonal communication strategies. At its base

① Client – planner communication can certain occur virtually; however, for the purposes of this chapter, the tools and techniques discussed involve face – to – face meetings and interactions.

level, communication is the act of transmitting information from a sender to a receiver.① The receiver can be one person or millions of people. While financial planners certainly do transmit information, the best planners use communication opportunities as a way to enhance interactions with their clients. The most effective forms of communication are process oriented with the intended outcome being the creation and sharing of information to enhance mutual understanding.

In order to be a masterful communicator it is important to acknowledge that the process of communication is sensual, learned, and intentional. Communication is sensual because both sender and receiver must use at least one of the five senses, such as sight and hearing, which are essential to both the transmittal and receipt of communicated messages. Touching, smelling, and tasting can also aid (or hinder) communication. Consider the traditional handshake used in most western cultures. A handshake can send a message of warmth and friendliness or a message of anxiety. Second, communication is a learned activity. Obtaining the skills necessary to communicate and to interpret communication properly is required to successfully establish and maintain professional relationships. This means that communication is as much about the context of dialog as it is about the word or pictures used. Consider how many Asian business professionals automatically bow appropriately when meeting a client, colleague, or supervisor. This aspect of communication and introduction needs to be learned. For those who have grown to adulthood in Asia, the process of learning was automatic; however, for westerners the process and act of bowing must be learned and practiced.

Finally, communication must be intentional to be effective. Communicating with clients, colleagues, staff, and others should be related to a specific purpose. That purpose may be to establish a working relationship, obtain information, create boundaries, persuade others to do something, facilitate decision making, or to exert power. Unintentional communication is something to be avoided, especially within the context of financial planning. The results of unintentional communication can be disastrous when attempting to build strong client – planner relationships. Unintentional dialog can cause client to lose focus and/or create conflicts.

In general, there are four general categories of communication:② (1) Intrapersonal, (2) Interpersonal, (3) Group, and (4) Mass. Intrapersonal communication refers to the internal

① Devito, J. A. (1986). *The communication handbook: A dictionary*. New York: Harper & Row.

② Dimbleby, R., &Burton, G. (1985). *More than words: An introduction to communication*. New York: Methuen.

dialog people have with themselves. Interpersonal communication, on the other hand, deals with communication between two people or sometimes within families or small groups. Group communication involves transmitting information within and to larger groups of people. Mass communication involves messaging to very large groups, typically through electronic channels. Financial planners who are interested in building a successful practice must develop an expertise in *interpersonal* communication strategies.

Robert Heath and Jennings Bryant① defined interpersonal communication as follow:

Interpersonal communication is dyadic interaction in which people negotiate relationships by using communication styles and strategies that become personally meaningful as the persons involved attempt to reduce uncertainty (about themselves, their partners, and their relationships), to be self – efficacious, and to maximize rewards through interactions.

This definition has important implications for financial planners. First, interpersonal communication is relationship driven. Second, communication goes beyond the content of a message. Those who are engaged in interpersonal communication nearly always interpret the content and context of what is heard and seen, as well as interpreting the effect of what is said. Third, clients tend to engage meaningfully with a planner only when they perceive the benefits of doing so outweigh the costs. Clients who trust their planner and those who make an emotional connection, through appropriate communication, tend to stay engaged in the planning process. When a client first meets a financial planner the only way to measure the potential cost of the relationship is by evaluating the planer's words and actions. That is, clients assess the worth of a financial planner primarily through what they learn via communicating with the planner. This helps explain why often financial planners and other advisers who have lower benchmarked rates of return or sub – optimal performance measures seldom lose clients. These advisers have learned that many clients view relationship benefits and costs as a key factor in determining whether to move forward with financial planning.

Relationship Benefits and Costs

The strength of any client – planner relationship is based on the quality of communication. As noted above, it is possible to quantify the value of a relationship. Clients make relationship

① Heath, R. L., & Bryant, J. (1992). *Human communication theory and research: Concepts, contexts, and challenges.* Hillsdale, NJ: Lawrence Erlbaum Associates.

decisions on the basis of costs versus benefits. This can be seen in the following formula that was originally developed by Dalmas Taylor and Irwin Altman: ①

Assessment of Relationship = Relationship Rewards - Relationship Costs

The assessment of the relationship results in one of the two following outcomes:

(1) Decision to Remain in Relationship = Relationship Rewards > Relationship Costs OR

(2) Decision to Terminate Relationship = Relationship Rewards < Relationship Costs

So, what are the benefits and costs inherent in a financial planning relationship? To find the answer it is first essential to understand a key assumption underlying these formulas: the growth of a relationship occurs with some hardship and struggle. It is precisely how a planner and client evaluate rewards that determine how a crisis will shape the relationship. Obvious rewards for a client include increased financial knowledge, confidence, and wealth. Costs include money, time, and effort. Financial planners also receive benefits from clients, including increased income, satisfaction, and prestige. Planner costs include time, effort, and lost opportunities.

Client - planner relationships can also be viewed as providing both costs and benefits. For example, a financial planner may enthusiastically look forward to meeting with a client, even though the client's financial situation itself is unrewarding. Clients may find that the planner - client relationship is too costly. It makes no difference if the planner sees things differently. Maybe the client finds the planner's personality to be abrasive. If, at some point, the client evaluates the interpersonal relationship to be more costly than the value of advice received, the client will likely terminate the relationship.

Clients, as well as financial planners, also engage in cost forecasting. They take what occurs in the relationship today to estimate what will happen in the future. Clients do this to estimate the long - term benefits and costs associated with the relationship. Consider a situation where a planner meets with a client multiple times. At each meeting, the planner emphasizes the importance of investing in equities for retirement. However, after each meeting stock prices fall. The client may conclude that the planner's advice is incorrect and costly. The client may then

① Taylor, D. A., & Altman, I. (1987). Communication in interpersonal relationships: Social penetration processes. In M. E. Roloff& G. R. Miller (Eds.), *Interpersonal processes: New directions in communication research* (pp. 257 - 277). Newbury Park, CA: Sage.

decide to terminate the relationship based on an internal forecast of future losses. Of course, this forecast is probably incorrect because it is based on an incorrect input; namely, linking market performance to a planner's advice. Over the long haul, the client might do better purchasing shares in down markets, but the mental cost of losing money may outweigh the long - term benefit of remaining in the client - planner relationship.

This last point is of particular importance to financial planners. It is imperative to remember that creating a trusting relationship—one based on disclosure andconfidence—can be costly. Moving from a discussion based on cursory dialog to one focused on in - depth analysis and review may require a financial planner to challenge, prompt, or confront a client. Doing so can cause the client to feel stress, which is almost always viewed at a high cost. Client responses can likewise cause financial planner stress. It is foolish to believe that clients will accept confrontation without pushing back or at times oppose a new viewpoint or suggestion.

Financial planners need to ask questions related to income, net worth, family life, goals, and desires. The issue is not whether these questions should be asked, but rather when and how these types of queries should be made. Ultimately, a client's choice to continue in a working relationship will be based on an evaluation of how satisfied they are with the outcomes associated with the interpersonal communication process. This evaluation is relatively subjective and undertaken by both planner and client. At the core of this assessment is how well the planner and client are communicating—sending, receiving, interpreting, and resending messages.

In order to move through the stages of a relationship—to penetrate interpersonal communication barriers—a financial planner must take control of, from the initial moment of orientation exchange, the communication process. This has less to do with manipulation or direct control over a client and much more to do with ensuring that each client perceives receiving more benefits than costs. Because planner communication, both verbal and non - verbal, is the primary way in which a client can evaluate benefits and costs, it is imperative that financial planners develop, practice, and continually update their interpersonal communication skills.

Relationship Management: Enhancing Client Trust and Commitment

There are numerous benefits associated with enhanced interpersonal communication skills. One of the most important outcomes for financial planners has to do with increased client trust and commitment. Communication, both verbal and non - verbal, can be the most important factor in shaping a client's perceptions of planner competency. While it is true the technical proficiency, physical appearance, and reputation all play an important role in shaping a client's perceptions, it is a financial planner's ability to communicate effectively that leads to long - lasting client - planner relationships. This insight has both positive and negative outcomes. On the positive side, financial planners who are skilled at listening, framing a client's goals and needs, interpreting client cues, and responding in ways that are supportive and directive have more opportunities to gain the trust of their clients. On the negative side, some financial planners may be tempted to use their communication skills and abilities in ways that create conflict. It is, for example, possible to gain a client's confidence so that the client can more easily be manipulated.

This chapter is *not* about client manipulation! This chapter is also *not* about how to be a better salesperson. While it is certainly true that great communicators also tend to be outstanding salespeople, the role of sales should always be secondary to providing outstanding client service. A key question that every financial planner needs to answer is this: what is the primary financial planning point of delivery? Client can be categorized into one of two delivery preferences. These categories can be framed along a reversing continuum. This can be seen in Figure 2. On the left side of the continuum are clients who view the financial planning process as purely a transactional commodity. These clients view financial planners similarly to real estate agents, tax preparers, plumbers, electricians, and auto mechanics. Clients who fall into this category are willing to work with any advisor who meets the client's current needs for a product or service. The value of advice and the importance of a long - lasting client - planner relationship are of little value to these clients. Some who fall into this category may hold less extreme attitudes, but it is true that they still view the financial planning process as a product delivery mechanism rather than a wealth maximizing process built on relationships. Financial planners who target clients in the transactional marketplace will have a radically different approach to client communication than planners who work with clients seeking relational partnerships.

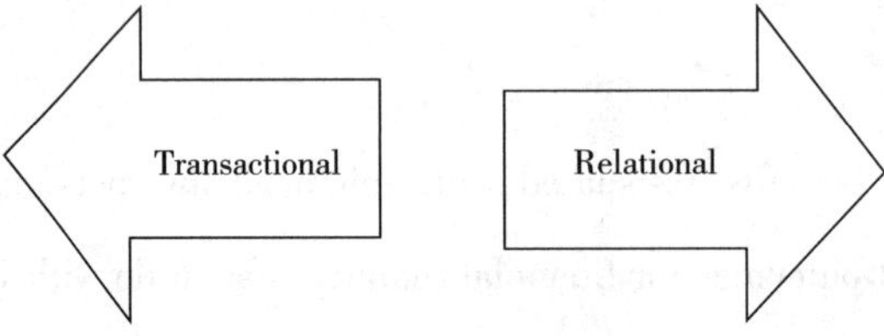

Figure 2 Financial Planning Process Continuum

On the other side of the continuum are clients who embrace the thought that financial planning is an interpersonal process designed to help a client reach financial goals. These clients are less interested in products and more interested in working with advisors they trust. For relational clients, the client - planner relationship itself, more so than products, services, or performance, determines whether or not they continue to work with a financial planner.

As was the case with transactional consumers, relational focused clients fall along a continuum. Some may see their advisor as a "therapist," "counselor," "coach," "mentor," or "life advisor." These clients will be wiling, and expect, to interact with their financial planner on an ongoing basis. They may intertwine their personal and professional lives with that of their financial planner. For example, the client may not make any significant life choices without consulting their planner. Other clients are less extreme in their reliance on a financial planner. These consumers have a desire to work with someone they can trust with their deepest financial secrets, but they may also be interested in balancing advice from other sources.

Sometime a financial planner is forced, by culture or employment contract, to focus their efforts on one market segment or the other. A financial planner will know that his or her focus is in the transactional marketplace if a high percent of current clients fall into the following categories:

✓ Seeking topic specific advice rather than comprehensive help

✓ Preferring short meetings

✓ Being happy meeting once per year

✓ Preferring small talk to discussions about goals and dreams

✓ Rarely talking about legacy issues

✓ Occasionally or frequently canceling meetings

✓ Conducting their own research and asking for information to support their findings

✓ Being reluctant to make referrals

✓ Being willing to purchase products but hesitant to engage in comprehensive financial planning

Opportunities exist for financial planners on both sides of the continuum. Saying this, however, it is important to note that the most successful financial planners—as measured by assets under management, practice size, reputation, and income—tend to be those who are relationship oriented. While it is true that possessing communication skills is important for all financial planners, the only way to build a successful relationship driven practice is to obtain, practice, and improve communication skills. The path to building a practice grounded on relationships, rather than transactions, is based on the foundation of communication skills.

The art of communication begins long before a client walks into the office environment. Aspects of marketing, such as an internet presence, brochures, sponsorships, and other written and broadcast media, all provide a frame of reference for clients. These marketing materials "speak" to clients in both objective and subjective ways. For example, one firm's marketing materials may conjure images of deep - rooted experience and prestige, while another firm's materials may indicate a more casual planning approach.

Financial planners who are interested in developing a practice based on relational elements must take steps to manage how clients experience and interpret the planning process. This begins, as the examples from above highlight, prior to a client entering the office environment. If clients are at ease, comfortable, and in a low stress state they will be more likely to engage in meaningful conversation, more prone to disclose personal, family, and financial information, and most importantly, more inclined to implement financial planning recommendations. ① As dialog continues over time, in a low stress environment, the client will increasingly look at their financial planner as a trusted advisor. This trust should be built on shared values, commitment,

---

① Stress creates a "fight or flight" response in most humans. As stress increases, a person's first and natural reaction is either to object, argue, or fight what is being presented or to flee or exit the source of the stress. If a financial planner's office environment acts as a stressor, this "fight or flight" response will be present from the outset of the initial discussion, thus creating an extra communication barrier the financial planner must overcome.

and trust.

Assessing Communication Style

People use verbal and nonverbal cues to communicate. Words come to mind as the primary form of verbal communication. How words are framed into sentences does pay a critical role in shaping the communication process. Nonverbal communication is also extremely important. Nonverbal communication includes using body language to provide others with subtle (and sometime not so subtle) messages about the manner in which verbal content is being communicated and received. Examples include facial expressions, gestures, body positioning, and special positioning. Imagine, for instance, that a client sits back in their chair with their legs crossed and their arms folded across their chest. The client, in this situation, is sending a clear message that she is currently not receptive to what is being said or what she feels might be spoken in the future. Crossing of legs and arms sends a nonverbal cue that the listener has "shut down" their responsiveness. Leaning back in the chair also sends a nonverbal hint that the listener is becoming disengaged in the conversation. On the other hand, moving forward as someone else speaks, smiling, and nodding one's head are usually perceived as positive nonverbal feedback.

It is important to note, however, that the use and interpretation of nonverbal communication techniques can be very confusing. Social and cultural norms almost always trump prescribed and otherwise useful communication strategies. For example, in the United States it is appropriate for someone to cross their legs. In some cultures, the crossing of legs, especially when the sole of the shoe faces another person, is considered rude. What one person does naturally can sometimes be perceived by another person as inconsiderate. As such, it is very important to understand the culture in which one works and to then adopt the norms present in that society.

Often, miscommunication can occur because the client and financial planner do not share the same experiential map. An experiential map refers to the way in which someone define reality and explains behavior. This is most apparent in terms of learning and communication style preferences. In general, people tend to prefer learning and communicating using one of the following dominant styles: (1) visual, (2) auditory, or (3) kinesthetic. This is not to say that people only use one of the styles when engaged in conversation; rather, this means that everyone has a preferred conversational approach.

Consider the typical visual learner. This person learns best when shown figures, graphs, charts, videos, and presentations. When given a financial plan, a visual communicator will usually flip through the plan looking for visual summaries of analyses and recommendations. Later, this client will read the plan in its entirety. When talking, a visual learner will say something like, "What you are saying really makes sense. I can see exactly what you mean."

An auditory learner relies on what they hear, rather than on what they see. These types of people enjoy attending lectures. They also like to talk more than others and engage in lively discussions. A clue that someone may be an auditory communicator is when someone says, "I hear what you are saying and it makes a lot of sense" or "Did you hear that housing prices dropped three percent last year?"

A kinesthetic communicator is one who prefers to be actively involved in the learning process. These learners like to touch, feel, and write notes. When presented with a financial plan, they may prefer to see the formulas used to arrive at output and then attempt to replicate the calculations on their own. Often, kinesthetic learners like to draw pictures. They also use mental imagery when discussing topics. A giveaway that someone prefers a kinesthetic approach to communication is if they say something like, "I cannot even imagine going into retirement with less than $ 3 million saved."

As a financial planner, it is first important to evaluate your own communication preference. It is then equally important to evaluate the communication and learning preferences of prospective and current clients. Although it seems somewhat simplistic, it is equally true that many client - planner working alliances have failed because the financial planner failed to acknowledge and use his or her client's preferred learning style when presenting a plan. A financial planner who is an auditory learner, for example, can seem totally disconnected from a client whose learning style is visual. It can "appear" to the client that the auditory planner is not listening or responding, when, in fact, the planner is doing everything possible to be clear.

It turns out that in the United States, the majority of Americas have a visual learning bias. A smaller number have an auditory preference. The least popular learning style is kinesthetic. As a rule, financial planners should adapt their communication style to meet the learning preference of their clientele. Table 3 provides assessment techniques that can be used by financial planners to place clients into one of the three primary communication style preference categories

Table 3 Ways to Assess Communication and Learning Style Preference

Personal Characteristic	Visual	Auditory	Kinesthetic
Likes to Listen		✓	
Makes Decisions Only After Listening to a Proposal		✓	
Learns by Watching Others	✓		
Likes to Read	✓		
Enjoys Taking Notes	✓		
Makes Decisions After Evaluating All Options and Doing Research	✓		
Learns by Doing Things			✓
Makes Decisions by Evaluating the Current Situation with Past Experience and Outcomes			✓

Questioning

For financial planners, the process of asking questions is different from the way some other professionals gather information. Consider the case of attorneys and physicians. Lawyers and doctors rarely ask questions as a means of discovery so that a quick diagnosis can be made. Financial planners are generally not as pressed for time, and as such, use questions to enhance the client – planner experience. Questioning methods that are designed to promote a strong working alliance are developed from an emotionally honest perspective rather than a purely discover perspective. Resolving to be better understand another person through questions and answers is a foundational element of financial planning. The remainder of this section explores some of the many ways questions are used in the planning process.

Open Questions

Questions can be categorized as either open or closed. A closed question can be answered with a simple "yes" or "no" response. Open ended questions begin with words like: "when," "why," "who," "how," "tell me," "where," or "what." The use of "why" questions should be minimized. Clients can perceive a question that starts with "why" as being a form of accusation. Why questions often result in defensive responses.

Closed Questions

A close ended question is one that provides the other person only a limited number of answers. Closed questions typically begin with one of the following terms: "Are you …," "Do you …," "is this . . ," or "is that …" Attorneys are notorious for asking close ended question. Financial planners should avoid the use of these questions and only use this approach to gather specific information needed during the financial planning process.

Choosing Between Open and Closed Questions

Closed questioning methods can be very effective whenever a financial planner needs to prompt action on the part of a client. Consider the following situation in which closed questioning methods might be effective:

Planner: "We have spent the past month working through retirement planning calculations. Do you have any additional questions at this point?"

Client: "No."

Planner: "Are you ready to move forward with implementing your retirement plan?"

Client: "Yes, I think we should move ahead."

Most of the time, however, the client – planner relationship is focused on learning more about a client's goals, dreams, and resources. Moving a client towards a choice decision is not as important. In these situations it is more appropriate to use open ended questioning as a way to promote discussion with few imposed controls.

Swing Questions

Therapists have been using swing questions for decades. A swing question is designed to elicit additional information from clients by disguising an open question as a closed inquiry. Questions that begin with words such as "will," "can," "could," or "would" allow someone to answer succinctly while offering an opportunity for the client to add much more to their answer. The following are examples of swing questions:

- "Will you give me an idea of how much is in the account?"
- "Could you call your attorney tomorrow and ask about what additional information is needed on the disclosure statement?"
- "Can you tell me a bit more about your employer – provided life insurance plan?"
- "Would you be willing to visit with our in – house accountant next Wednesday?"

Caution needs to dominate whenever swing questions are used. Swing questions should be minimized during prospective client meetings. New clients can interpret these questions as being manipulative. As such, swing questions should be asked only when the client and planner have developed a strong relationship.

Implied and Projective Questions

Financial planners often use implied and projective questions when working with clients. An implied question is usually formed as an indirect query. As was the case with swing questions, implied questioning should only be used when the client – planner relationship is already well established. By its very nature, an implied question solicits information indirectly using phrases like "I wonder" or "you must." For example, a financial planner might ask, "I wonder what your plans are when you retire." This is an indirect way of asking, "What do you plan to do when you retire."

Projective questions are used most often by therapists as a way to capture deeper emotional responses, unconscious thoughts, values, and feelings. Projective questions often begin with words such as "what if," "if you," or "what would." Here is an example: "If you had three wishes, what would you wish for?" Here is a planning example: "If you could go leave a legacy today what would you like to be remembered for among your friends, family, and colleagues?" Answers to these types of questions allow a client to visualize, and to some extent, articulate their life dreams.

Scaling Questions

Scaling questions can be used to effectively help clients communicate their ideas, perceptions, hopes, dreams, and fears in a way that relies on numbers rather than words. Scaling questions can also be used to help reinforce the positive aspects of the planning process. Generally, scaling questions should be used whenever a planner would like his or her client to indicate an impression, observation, prediction, or other response on a scale, which is typically from 0 to 10 or 1 to 10. Consider the following example:

Planner: "We have estimated your retirement savings need. It turns out that you will need to save about 10 percent more of your salary in order to reach your financial goal. How does that make you feel?"

Client: "I am not sure."

Planner: "Okay, let's look at the situation this way. On a scale of 1 to 10, with 1 being totally not confident and 10 being absolutely confident, how would you rate your confidence in being able to save more for retirement?"

Client: "When you put it that way, I would say about a 7."

Scaling questions offer a way to obtain needed information, especially validation, because these types of questions help clients articulate concerns, aspects of behavioral change, and willingness to engage in new planning activities in a non – threatening manner. Scaling questions can be used with almost every client or prospective client. Answers to scaling questions almost always provide a jumping off point to deeper conversations about goal formation, recommendation implementation, and other planning issues. If used throughout the planning process, scaling questions can also provide an assessment measure of planner effectiveness. Over time, for example, a planner would want to see their client "move up the ladder" in terms of scores on a scale.

Summary Questioning Rules

Often novice financial planners take the process of asking questions for granted. Rather than being something done on a spur of the moment basis, questioning should be well thought out and strategically applied. Among clients, questions generate answers and reactions among clients that move the planning process forward. Regardless of the type of question, financial planners should follow the following questioning guidelines, as outline by Sommers – Flanagan and Sommers – Flanagan(1993)[①] in their seminal text on therapeutic interviewing:

1. Be as explicit as possible by sharing information with clients and providing a consistent format for client – planner dialog.

2. Each client's responses should direct the flow of conversation. It is important to listen and respond appropriately.

3. Question should relate directly to each client's needs and circumstances.

4. Question should be used to both solicit information and to help a client stay focused on aspects of the financial planning process.

5. Financial planners should be careful when exploring sensitive areas with clients. What may not seem particularly sensitive or important to a financial planner may traumatic for a client. Questions related to socioeconomic status, gender preference, individual and family difficulties,

---

① Sommers – Flanagan, J., & Sommers – Flanagan, R. (1993). *Foundations of the rapeutic interviewing*. Needham Heights, MA: Allyn and Bacon.

and other similar topics should be presented with care and empathy.

Enhancing Professional Skills and Building a Successful Career

This book, and this chapter in particular, was written to help those who are new to the field of financial planning achieve career success. Financial planning, both as a process for helping others achieve financial goals and as a long – term career path, offers unlimited possibilities for those who have the talent and motivation to succeed. Success as a financial planner involves developing, grooming, and growing a diverse skill set. Unlike other professional endeavors where success is linked to just a few key skill sets, financial planning requires practitioners to be well versed in a wide variety of topics and skill attributes. Figure 3 illustrates some of the most important factors associated with building a successful financial planning career.

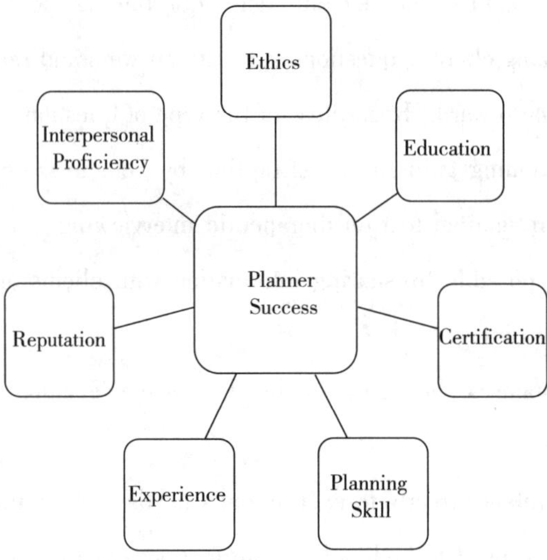

Figure 3 Characteristics of Financial Planner Success

Ethics

At the top of the list of factors leading to financial planning career success is ethics. As described in detail in this chapter, it is essential that a financial planner adopt a clear ethical foundation for their practice. At a minimum, it is important for financial planners to obtain appropriate local, state, and federal licenses when providing investment advice to clients.① Other factors related to the ethical practice of financial planning include adopting and following a clearly written code of ethics and practice standards. These standards should include provisions for what the FPSB calls working "in the interest of clients and to uphold and promote the interests of the financial planning profession for the benefit of society."②

Education

Twenty five years ago, the notion of obtaining an academic degree in financial planning was unheard of. The majority of financial planning practitioners either did not hold a college degree or their degree was focused on another field of practice. Beginning in the late 1980s, college and universities began offering degree tracks in financial planning. Today, in the United States, it is possible to study financial planning at some of the nation's oldest, largest, and most respected institutions. Increasingly, consumers have come to expect their financial planner to have both a college degree and a specialization in financial planning. Traditionally, planners have met this consumer demand by obtaining specialized training via a certification program. Most often, certification programs are offered on a non – credit basis and include a maximum of six or seven courses devoted to the financial practice areas. Certification training is appropriate for those with experience and a background in insurance, investments, or other specialized planning topics. However, for those who just entering the profession, obtaining a college degree in financial planning may be the single best way to maximize career success.

CFP Board provides a web link to find both certificate and college degree programs offered by U. S. institutions: http://www. cfp. net/become – a – cfp – professional/find – an – education – program. Those who are beginning their careers outside the United States often find that studying online or through partnership programs with U. S. colleges and universities provides excellent training in the fundamentals of financial planning. Obviously, those living outside the United States must finish their educational training by obtaining background in local tax and estate planning topics.

---

① In the United States, these licenses include Series 7 and 63 and Series 65 or 66 Registered Investment Adviser Law exams.

② Financial Planning Standards Board. 2011. *Financial planner competency profile*. Denver: FPSB.

Certification

Worldwide, more than 150,000 individuals hold the CFP mark. This makes the Certified Financial Planner certification the largest financial planning credential in the world. Just as consumers now assume that their financial planner have specific training in financial planning, consumers are increasingly demanding advanced certification training for their advisers. Certification is a key tool used by successful financial planners to differentiate themselves in the marketplace. The wealthiest and most savvy clients expect their advisory team to be certified. As such, it simply makes sense for a new financial planner to devote time, study, and money to obtain one or more certifications. Beyond the CFP mark, financial planners should obtain certification in specialized areas, such as investment management, retirement planning, tax planning, and estate planning. There are also a number of well - respected designations for those involved in providing insurance planning services.

Planning Skill

As documented throughout this chapter, financial planning entails much more than product knowledge. A competent financial planning—one who is building a successful career—must have the skill set to successful gather data, analyze the data, and synthesize the analysis into a financial plan. This ability is not something that everyone can develop. Only those who have a passion for skill development obtained through training, self - study, education, and certification and licensure are able to develop and maintain such skills.

Experience

Novice financial planners often question why experience is not higher on the list of key factors associated with financial planning career success. The reason is simple. Experience is often overrated, especially by those with a long history in the profession. While experience gained through practice is extremely important as a tool to increase planning efficiency, experience alone is not as important as proper training, education, and ongoing continuing education. Often, those who brand new to the profession bring knowledge of new planning tools and techniques that surpass what a more experienced planner can offer. Of course, the ultimate combination of career success depends on combining training, education, certification, continuing education, and experience; however, simply because someone has been in the business of providing financial advice for a long time does not guarantee that their services are the most effective in helping clients reach their financial goals.

Reputation

A new financial planner must ask two important questions about himself or herself:

1. Will people do business with them?
2. Would someone refer another person to do business with them?

Unless the novice planner can answer "yes" to both questions, the probability of long – term career success as a financial planner is very low. Basically, these two questions provide an insight into the degree of trust a financial planner has created among consumers. So, how does one go about creating an environment of trust so that people will gladly do business with a new financial planner?

The answer to this question often surprises new financial planners. As taught at colleges and universities, financial planning, as a process – oriented field of practice, may appear to be a very technical, precise, and time consuming strategic process. This perception, in fact, is not entirely correct. Financial planning is just as much a humanistic client – centered profession as it is a technical one. Years ago a large planning firm coined the phrase that to be a great financial planner a person must "have the heart of a therapist and the mind of capitalist." This simply means that the most successful financial planners build trust by engaging closely with their clients, while at the same time using their skills and abilities to build workable financial plans.

Trust is built on reputation. Clients who trust their financial planner will continue to do business with the adviser and refer their friends, colleagues, and neighbors to do the same thing. As such, it is imperative that a financial planner, especially those who are new to the profession, begin to build a reputation as both competent and personable as soon as possible. Oftentimes, reputation is built at the community level. Occasionally, a financial planner will build a reputation nationally. Typical methods used to develop a positive reputation include:

- Volunteering for community service

- Serving on local, regional, and national advisory boards
- Publishing papers and books
- Writing columns for respected papers and journals
- Publishing market commentaries online
- Posting blogs that provide market insights
- Mentoring students studying financial planning
- Volunteering to support local and regional financial planning associations
- Joining a national financial planning organization
- Obtaining a well – respected financial planning certification
- Creating a network of non – competing professionals, such as accountants, tax preparers, attorneys, and therapists
- Conducting seminars on topics of interest to the community

This list is limited to only those activities that are known to help create a positive image among consumers. Beyond doing these types of things, the most successful financial planners tend to link their practice approach with a personal or professional passion. Consider the case of a financial planner who was born and raised in Hong Kong but now lives in Atlanta. Rather than spend time, money, and effort broadly marketing her services to anyone within the Atlanta region, she would be better served using her cultural, linguistic, and professional skills to create a reputation among recent Chinese immigrants to the United States. This will require her to obtain special training in U. S. Visa and immigration law, cross – national taxation, and asset allocation methodologies. The payoff is likely large. Rather than competing against a large number of advisers in the broad planning market, this financial planner will likely become a trusted planner to those who need her specialized service. When viewed from this perspective, every financial planner has a unique skill set that can be maximized to create an outstanding reputation.

Interpersonal Proficiency

Consider again the list of activities from above that financial planners often use to build a positive reputation in their community. Doing just one or two of these things every week is time consuming. Engaging in three, four, or more activities can quickly engage the majority of a financial planner's time. This is, actually, expected. Generally, a novice financial planner should expect to spend 2 to 3 hours building a reputation, marketing services, and meeting with prospective clients for every 1 hour of actual planning conducted. The first three years of practice tends to be filled with long hours of networking and building client – planner relationships. It is during these early years where interpersonal proficiencies really help establish a planner's career path. Specific interpersonal proficiencies include:

- Seeking out engagements with consumers
- Approaching affiliated professionals with opportunities for networking
- Volunteering to serve of advisory boards
- Advertising services through media outlets
- Being accessible to those in the media for stories and quotes

Interpersonal proficiencies are based on two key factors. First, the most successful financial planners tend to have a passion for helping others. This passion is driven by the satisfaction of seeing recommendations implemented and tracking the positive impact recommendations have in shaping a client's life. Those who have reached the pinnacle of financial planning success often view their clients as family. Clients, likewise, more often than not adopt their financial planner as their most trusted adviser. As such, much of the planner's reward for service is through personal satisfaction of a job well done as much as it is financial. Second, interpersonal proficiency is driven by the communication skills of the planner. The importance of appropriate communication with clients cannot be overemphasized. The best financial planner is not always the brightest or the smartest. The best financial planner is the one that can most effectively gauge a client's desires and the collect, analyze, and synthesize data in such a way that the client's financial fears are reduced. This is a talent that is driven by communication skills. Of course, financial planners must have the technical competency to create a financial plan, but without interpersonal proficiency, it is unlikely that such a plan will ever be put into practice.

Building a career as a financial planner is not necessarily easy; however, there are few professional endeavors that are more rewarding than being a financial planner. The most successful financial planners often become a trusted colleague and friend to their clients. For those who can forge through the first three to four years of building a practice, opportunities for career advancement are almost unlimited. As shown throughout this book, the demand for financial planning services is increasing worldwide at fantastic rates. The ratio of planners to potential clients is quite small, which means that many opportunities for success await those who can combine an ethical foundation with education, certification, planning skills, experience, reputation, and interpersonal proficiency.

Appendix The Application of Financial Planning Tools

1 The application of financial calculator

1.1 Classification of financial calculators

Financial calculator is a professional calculator that performs financial functions commonly used in banking, securities, insurances, real estates, investments, business and commerce communities. It can easily integrate the standard financial functions and advanced financial functions, which makes financial calculation more convenient. This chapter will take BAII PLUS as an example to introduce the use of financial calculator.

1.2 Basic calculator settings

Indicator	Meaning
2nd	Press [2nd] to access the second function of the next key pressed.
COMPUTE	Press [CPT] to compute a value for the displayed variable.
ENTER	Press [ENTER] to assign the displayed value to the displayed variable.
SET	Press [2nd SET] to change the setting of the displayed variable.
BGN	Time Value of Money (TVM) calculations use beginning - of - period payments. When BGN is not displayed, TVM calculations use end - of - period payments (END).

1.3 Decimal point setting

The default display is two decimal places. Users can change the number of decimal places based on their own needs. Financial calculator displays up to 8 decimal places.

Example: changing the number of decimal places to 4

Press	Display
2nd [Format] 4 ENTER	DEC = 4.0000
2nd [QUIT]	0.0000

The setting of four decimal places will remain valid (even if power on and off) until the user changes it again.

1.4 Resetting and clearing calculator memories

Press CE/C to clear general numerical entries. In order to clear the prompted worksheet, press 2ND CPT to select its second function QUIT and 0.0000 appears, confirming that the calculator is clear. Time – Value – of – Money (TVM) variables include Number of periods (N), Interest rate per year (I/Y), Present value (PV), Payment (PMT), and Future value (FV). TVM variables will save the result from the last operation, which cannot be clear with either OFF or CE/C. The correct way to reset the TVM worksheet variables is to press 2ND QUIT and 2ND CLR TVM. [Note: for the simple expression, where direct writing the second function keys, that is, pressing 2ND and the corresponding key. For example, QUIT means press 2ND CPT.]

To clear all calculator memories, press MEM and CLR WORK. To reset the calculator, you can press RESET button in back of the calculator. This will restore all default settings.

1.5 Computing payment and compound interest

There are two payment types: the Beginning – of – period payments (BGN) and the End – of – period payments (END). The default setting is END.

To change the payments period to BGN:

Press	Display
2nd [BGN]	END
2nd [SET]	BGN
CE/C	0.0000

The BGN indicator appears in the upper right corner of the display, which represents the current payments period is BGN mode.

To change the payments period to END:

Press	Display
2nd [BGN]	BGN
2nd [SET]	END
CE/C	0.0000

Change the payments period (END/BGN) by pressing 2ND BGN and 2ND SET.

1.6 Using the TVM variables

N, I/Y, PV, PMT, and FV are five TVM variables. As long as you key in values for any of four variables, you can find the value for the fifth variable. To assign a value to a TVM variable, key in a number and press a TVM key (i. e. PV). To compute a value for an unknown variable, press the compute indicator CPT, and then press the key for the unknown variable (i. e. FV).

Enter negative values for cash outflows (i. e., investments, deposits, living expenses, loan payments) and positive values for cash inflows (i. e., incomes, sold investments, borrowed principals).

1.7 Computing TVM

Indicator	Meaning
N	Number of periods
I/Y	Interest rate per year
PV	Present value
PMT	Payment
FV	Future value

1.8 Clearing the TVM worksheet

Press	Display
CE/C	0.0000
2ndCLR TVM	0.0000

2. Using Excel to calculate the TVM variables

2.1 The calculation of future value (FV) and present value (PV)

The FV is the value of the current sum of money at a specified date in the future based on a specific rate of growth. The PV is the current worth of a future sum of money given a specified rate of return.

2.1.1 The simple interest: FV and PV

Simple interest is the interest calculated only on the principal. Interest generated in previous period is not added to principal in the following period.

2.1.1.1 Simple interest FV

Assumption: P is a current sum of money, is the simple interest, n is number of investment periods, Fs is the value of current sum of money at the end of year n. The value of Fs equals to the sum of principal and interests at the end of year n, therefore,

$$F_s = P + P * i_s * n = P * (1 + i_s * n)$$

The simple interest FV can be calculated in Excel by entering the calculation formula in the corresponding cell.

For example, a person deposits $1,000 into his bank account. The simple annual interest rate is 5%. After five years, the sum of principal and interests is $1,250. See below.

B4 | fx =B1*(1+B2*B3)

	A	B	C	D	E
1	PV	1000			
2	I/Y	5.00%			
3	N	5			
4	FV	$1,250			

2.1.1.2 Simple interest PV

Simple interest PV can be calculated with a given simple interest FV. This process is also known as discounting. The interest rate in this procedure is called discount rate. The formula is:

$$P = F_s/(1 + i_s * n)$$

The simple interest PV can be calculated in Excel by entering the calculation formula in the corresponding cell.

For example, a person plans to withdraw \$1,000 five years from today, the simple annual interest is 5%, the amount of money he needs to deposit today is \$800. See below.

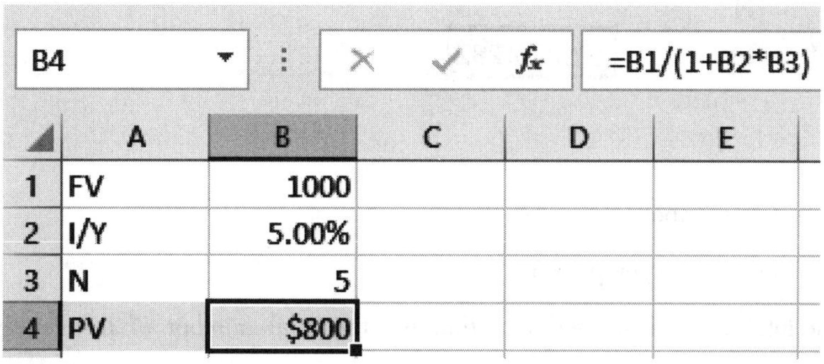

B4 =B1/(1+B2*B3)

	A	B	C	D	E
1	FV	1000			
2	I/Y	5.00%			
3	N	5			
4	PV	\$800			

2.1.2 The compound interest: FV and PV

Compound interest is interest calculated not only on the principal but also on the accumulated interest that generated by previous periods of a deposit.

2.1.2.1 Compound interest FV

Compound interest FV is the value of the current sum of money at a specified date in the future based on a compound interest rate.

Assumption: P is a current sum of money, iis compound interest, n is number of investment periods, F is the value of current sum of money at the end of year n. The formula is:

$$F = P(1 + i)^n$$

The compound interest FV can be calculated in Excel by entering the calculation formula in the corresponding cell.

For example, a person deposits \$1,000 into his bank account. The interest rate is 5% and compounded annually. After five years, the sum of principal and interests is \$1,276.282. See below.

Also, compound interest FV can also be calculated with FV function calculation.

FV function: calculates the future value of a current investment based on a constant interest rate.

B4 | × ✓ f_x | =B1*(1+B2)^B3

	A	B	C	D	E
1	PV	1000			
2	I/Y	5.00%			
3	N	5			
4	FV	$1,276.282			

Syntax: FV (rate, nper, pmt, pv, type)

Rate: the interest rate per period.

Nper: the total investment periods, that is, the total number of payment periods in the investment.

Pmt: the payment made in each period. It cannot change over the life of the annuity. Pmt contains principal and interest but no other fees or taxes. If pmt is omitted, pv must be included in the function.

Pv: the present value. Present value is the amount of money that exists from the beginning of an investment. It is also the lump – sum amount that a series of future payments is worth right now, which known as principal. If pv is omitted, it is assumed to be 0, but pmt must be included.

Type: the number 0 or 1. It indicates whether the payment is due at the beginning of each period (type = 1) or at the end of each period (type = 0). If type is omitted, it is assumed to be 0.

Note: make sure to confirm the consistency of rate and nper. For example, you have a four – year loan at annual interest 12%. If you make monthly payments, the rate should be 12%/12, nper should be 4 * 12. If you make annual payments, rate should be 12% and nper should be 4.

For all the arguments, cash outflows, such as bank deposit, should be entered as negative numbers; cash inflows, such as dividend, should be entered as positive numbers.

Use the compound interest example, see below for FV function calculation.

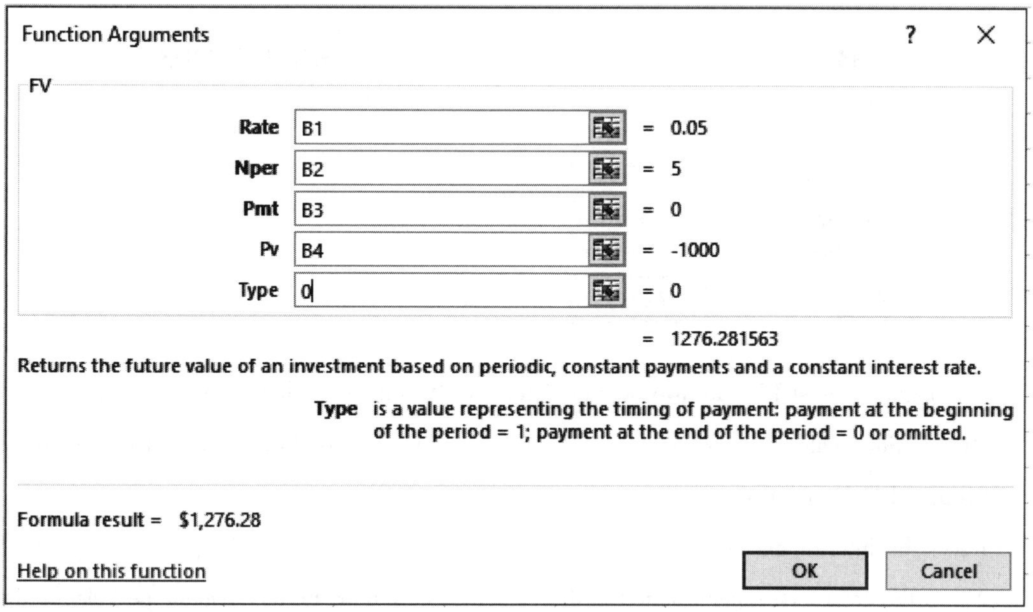

Function Arguments

FV

Rate B1 = 0.05

Nper B2 = 5

Pmt B3 = 0

Pv B4 = -1000

Type 0 = 0

= 1276.281563

Returns the future value of an investment based on periodic, constant payments and a constant interest rate.

Type is a value representing the timing of payment: payment at the beginning of the period = 1; payment at the end of the period = 0 or omitted.

Formula result = $1,276.28

Help on this function

OK Cancel

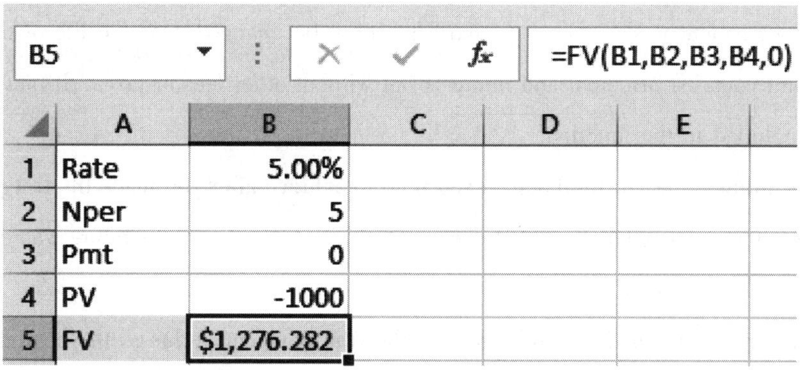

B5 =FV(B1,B2,B3,B4,0)

	A	B	C	D	E
1	Rate	5.00%			
2	Nper	5			
3	Pmt	0			
4	PV	-1000			
5	FV	$1,276.282			

2.1.2.2 Compound interest PV

Compound interest PV is the current worth of a future sum of money given a compound discount rate. Discounting is the reverse process of compounding. It can be calculated by given compound FV, discount rate, and discount period. The formula is:

$$P = F/(1+i)^n$$

The compound interest PV can be calculated in Excel by entering the calculation formula in the corresponding cell.

For example, a person plans to withdraw $1,000 after five years. If the compound annual interest rate is 5%, he needs to deposit $783.53 today. See below.

B4 | =B1/(1+B2)^B3

	A	B	C	D	E
1	FV	1000			
2	I/Y	5.00%			
3	N	5			
4	PV	$783.526			

Compound interest PV can also be calculated by PV function calculation.

PV function: calculates the present value of an investment based on a constant interest rate.

Syntax: PV (rate, nper, pmt, fv, type)

Rate: the interest rate per period.

Nper: the total investment periods, that is, the total number of payment periods in the investment.

Pmt: the payment made in each period. It cannot be changed over the life of the annuity. Typically, pmt contains principal and interests but without other fees or taxes. If pmt is omitted, fv must be included in the function.

Fv: the future value, or the balance you plan to achieve after you made the last payment. If fv is omitted, it is assumed to be 0 (for example, a loan with a zero future value). If fv is omitted, pmt must be included.

Type: the number 0 or 1. It indicates whether the payment is due at the beginning of each period (type = 1) or at the end of each period (type = 0). If type is omitted, it is assumed that the payment is made at the end of each period (0).

Note: make sure the units for rate and nper are consistent. For example, a four - year loan with 12% annual interest rate. If you make monthly payments, the rate should be 12%/12 and nper should be 4 * 12. If you make annual payments, it should be 12% and 4.

For all the arguments, cash outflows, such as bank deposit, should be entered as negative numbers; cash inflows, such as dividend, should be entered as positive numbers.

Use the above example, see below for PV function calculation.

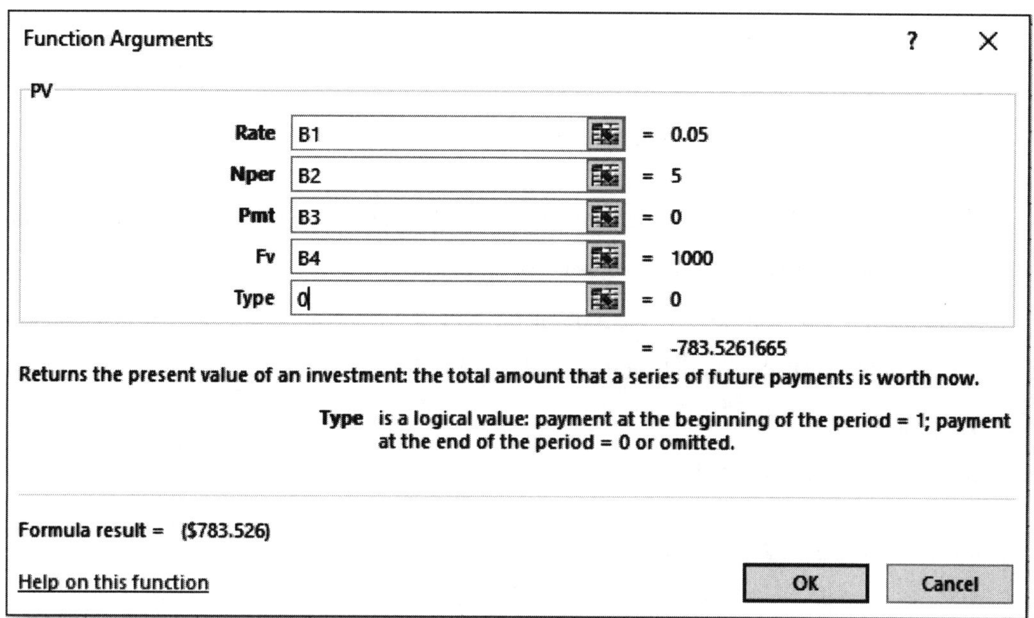

B5 =PV(B1,B2,B3,B4,0)

	A	B	C	D	E
1	Rate	5.00%			
2	Nper	5			
3	Pmt	0			
4	FV	1000			
5	PV	($783.526)			

2.2 Annuity: FV and PV

Annuity refers to a series fixed amount of payment that paid in a certain period of time. Based on the time of occurrence and the duration, annuity can be divided into four types.

(1) Ordinary annuity: a series equal payment made at the end of each period.

(2) Annuity due: a series equal payment made at the beginning of each period.

(3) Perpetual annuity: a type of ordinary annuity with an infinite time of occurrences.

(4) Deferred annuity: a type of ordinary annuity that occurs after a certain period of time.

2.2.1 Ordinary annuity FV and PV

2.2.1.1 Ordinary annuity FV

$$FV = PMT * \left(\frac{(1+r)^n - 1}{r}\right)$$

Ordinary annuity FV can be calculated by Excel FV function. FV function calculates the future value of an annuity based on a constant interest rate.

For example, a person invests \$2,000 at the end of each year into a savings account with annual compounding. If the annual interest rate is 3%, how much will he have in the account after five years?

Insert FV function, see below.

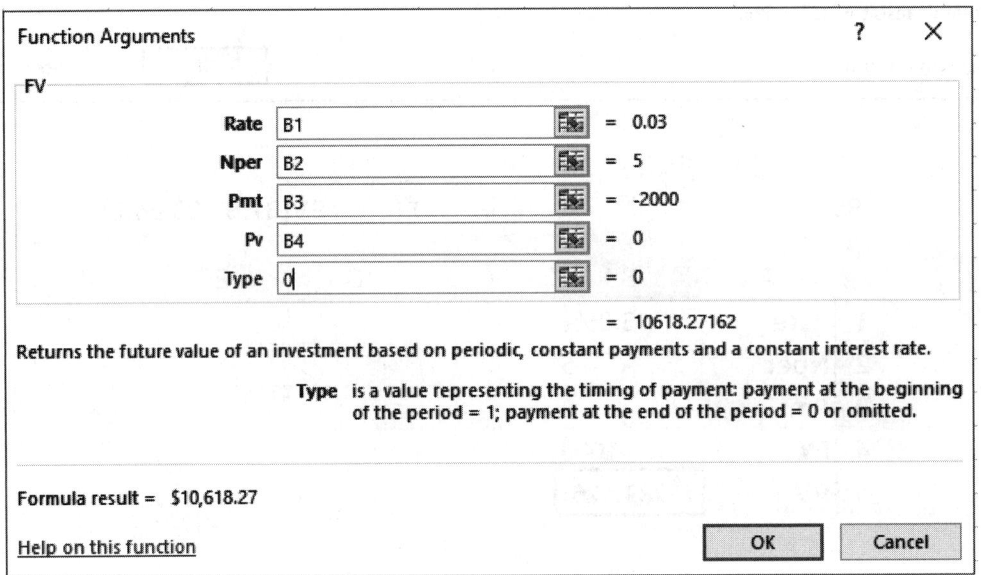
Function Arguments
FV
Rate B1 = 0.03
Nper B2 = 5
Pmt B3 = -2000
Pv B4 = 0
Type 0 = 0
= 10618.27162
Returns the future value of an investment based on periodic, constant payments and a constant interest rate.
Type is a value representing the timing of payment: payment at the beginning of the period = 1; payment at the end of the period = 0 or omitted.
Formula result = $10,618.27
Help on this function
OK
Cancel

B5 =FV(B1,B2,B3,B4,0)

	A	B	C	D	E
1	Rate	3.00%			
2	Nper	5			
3	Pmt	-2000			
4	PV	0			
5	FV	$10,618.27			

2.2.1.2 Ordinary annuity PV

$$PV = PMT * \left(\left(1 - \frac{1}{(1+r)^n}\right)/r\right)$$

Ordinary annuity PV can be calculated through Excel PV function. PV function calculates the present value of future annuities based on a constant interest rate.

For example, a person wants to withdraw \$2,000 from his savings account at the end of each year for the next four years. How much money must he deposit today into the savings account if he can earn 10% annual interest?

Insert PV function, see below.

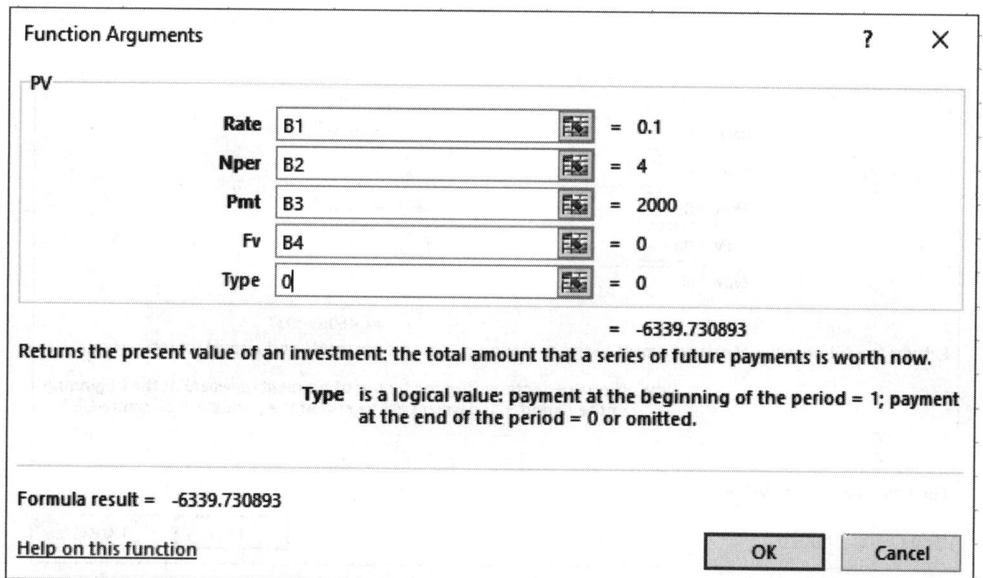
Function Arguments
?
PV
Rate B1 = 0.1
Nper B2 = 4
Pmt B3 = 2000
Fv B4 = 0
Type 0 = 0
= -6339.730893
Returns the present value of an investment: the total amount that a series of future payments is worth now.
Type is a logical value: payment at the beginning of the period = 1; payment at the end of the period = 0 or omitted.
Formula result = -6339.730893
Help on this function
OK
Cancel

B5 =PV(B1,B2,B3,B4,0)

	A	B	C	D	E	F
1	Rate	10.00%				
2	Nper	4				
3	Pmt	2000				
4	FV	0				
5	PV	(\$6,339.73)				

2.2.2 Annuity due FV and PV

2.2.2.1 Annuity due FV

Each payment occurs at the beginning of each period.

$$F = PMT(1+i) + PMT(1+i)^2 + \cdots + PMT(1+i)^{(n-1)} + PMT(1+i)^n$$

Annuity due FV can be calculated by Excel FV function.

For example, a person invests $8000 at the beginning of each year into a savings account with annual compounding. If the annual return of the account is 4%, how much money will he have in the account after five years?

Insert FV function, see below.

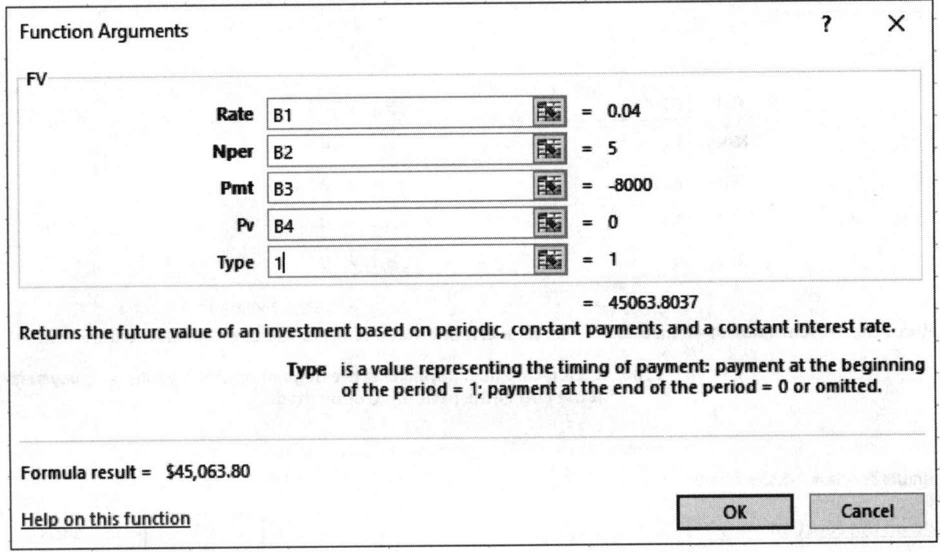
Function Arguments
?
FV
Rate B1 = 0.04
Nper B2 = 5
Pmt B3 = -8000
Pv B4 = 0
Type 1 = 1
= 45063.8037
Returns the future value of an investment based on periodic, constant payments and a constant interest rate.
Type is a value representing the timing of payment: payment at the beginning of the period = 1; payment at the end of the period = 0 or omitted.
Formula result = $45,063.80
Help on this function
OK
Cancel

Here, pv is omitted and type is 1 indicates annuity due.

B5 =FV(B1,B2,B3,B4,1)

	A	B	C	D	E
1	Rate	4.00%			
2	Nper	5			
3	Pmt	-8000			
4	PV	0			
5	FV	$45,063.80			

2.2.2.2 Annuity due PV

$$PV = PMT_1 + \frac{PMT_2}{(1+r)} + \frac{PMT_3}{(1+r)^2} + \cdots + \frac{PMT_n}{(1+r)^{(n-1)}}$$

Annuity due PV can be calculated by Excel PV function.

For example, a company wants to rent an equipment in the next three years. Based on the lease contract, the company agreed to pay \$6,000 rent fees at the beginning of each year. If the annual discount rate is 10%, what is the present value of the total rental costs?

Insert PV function, see below.

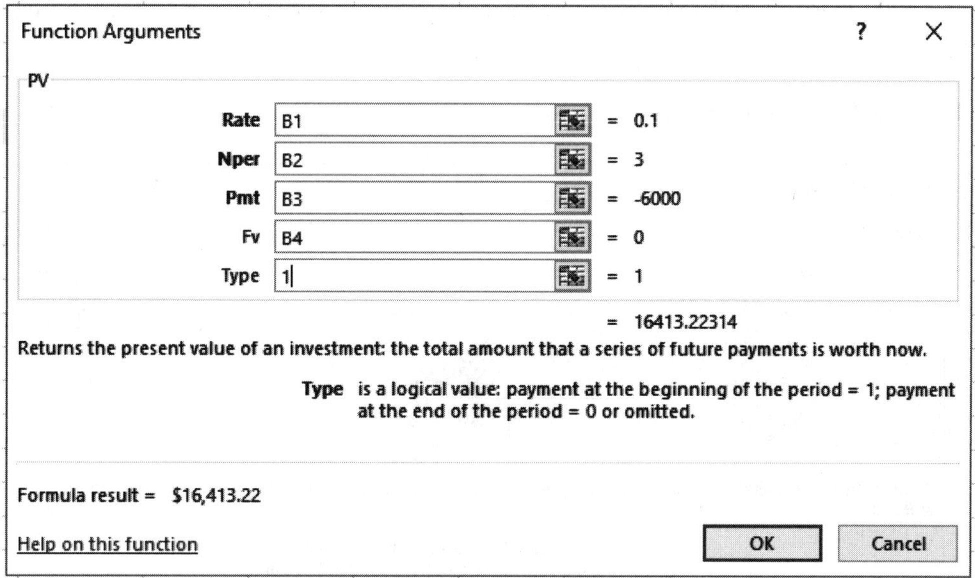
Function Arguments
?
PV
Rate B1 = 0.1
Nper B2 = 3
Pmt B3 = -6000
Fv B4 = 0
Type 1 = 1
= 16413.22314
Returns the present value of an investment: the total amount that a series of future payments is worth now.
Type is a logical value: payment at the beginning of the period = 1; payment at the end of the period = 0 or omitted.
Formula result = $16,413.22
Help on this function
OK
Cancel

B5 =PV(B1,B2,B3,B4,1)

	A	B	C	D	E
1	Rate	10.00%			
2	Nper	3			
3	Pmt	-6000			
4	FV	0			
5	PV	$16,413.22			

3. Practical examples

[Example One] Your friend opened a grocery store in Columbia. He invites you to invest in his business. He promises that if you lend him $20,000 now, he will pay you back $400 each month for the next five years. Assuming that you deposit the same amount of money into a savings account, if the annual interest rate of the account is 6%, will you lend him the money? why?

Use TVM to calculate the rate of return for investing in grocery store and compare it with the annual interest rate 6%. Choose the one with higher rate of return.

Excel method: use RATE function. Note: $n = 5 * 12 = 60$

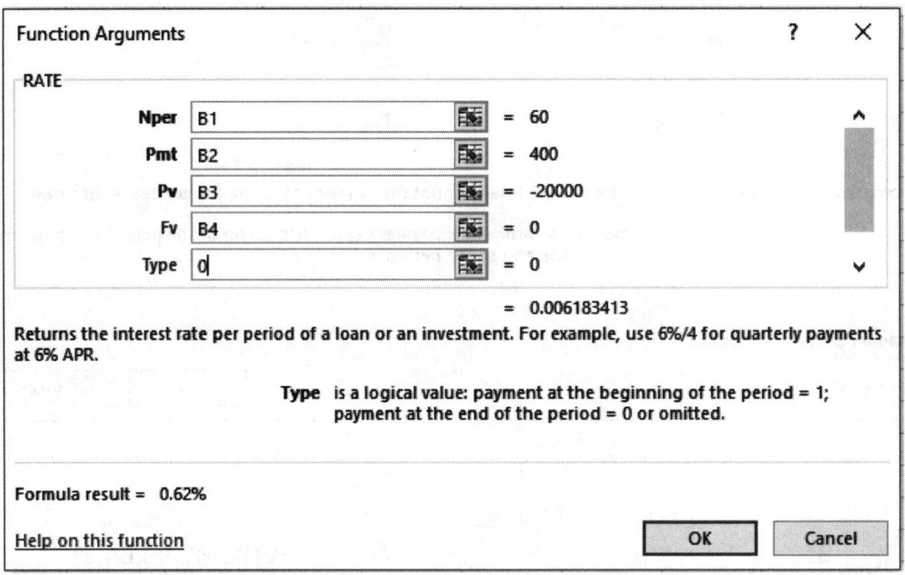
Function Arguments
RATE
Nper B1 = 60
Pmt B2 = 400
Pv B3 = -20000
Fv B4 = 0
Type 0 = 0
= 0.006183413
Returns the interest rate per period of a loan or an investment. For example, use 6%/4 for quarterly payments at 6% APR.
Type is a logical value: payment at the beginning of the period = 1; payment at the end of the period = 0 or omitted.
Formula result = 0.62%
Help on this function
OK
Cancel

B5 =RATE(B1,B2,B3,B4,0)

	A	B	C	D	E	F
1	Nper	60				
2	Pmt	400				
3	PV	-20000				
4	FV	0				
5	Rate	0.62%				

Use financial calculator:

Press	Display
2ndP/Y ↓1 ENTER	Set period per year to 1
2nd [QUIT]	0.0000
400 PMT	PMT = 400
0 FV	FV = 0
60 N	N = 60
20,000 +/- PV	PV = -20,000
CPTI/Y	Find i = 0.62%

The rate of return for investing in store is 0.062% * 12 = 7.42% , which is greater than the bank annual interest rate 6%. Therefore, lending money to your friend is a better choice.

[Example Two] In order to celebrate your fifth anniversary, you and your spouse plan to have a three - week vacation by taking the Mediterranean cruise. Your five years' anniversary has passed three and half years, and the current cost for this trip is $6,000 per person. You have already saved $2,000 in a savings account which yields a 6% annual rate. The cruise cost has a 7.5% increase rate. (1) How much money do you need to save monthly to afford this trip? (2) How much money do you need to save at the end of each year?

The first step for this question is to calculate FV of the total costs for this trip and your savings after 1.5 years. Then, find PMT.

(1) Excel method: use FV function. Note: PV = 6,000 * 2 = 12,000

Trip costs:

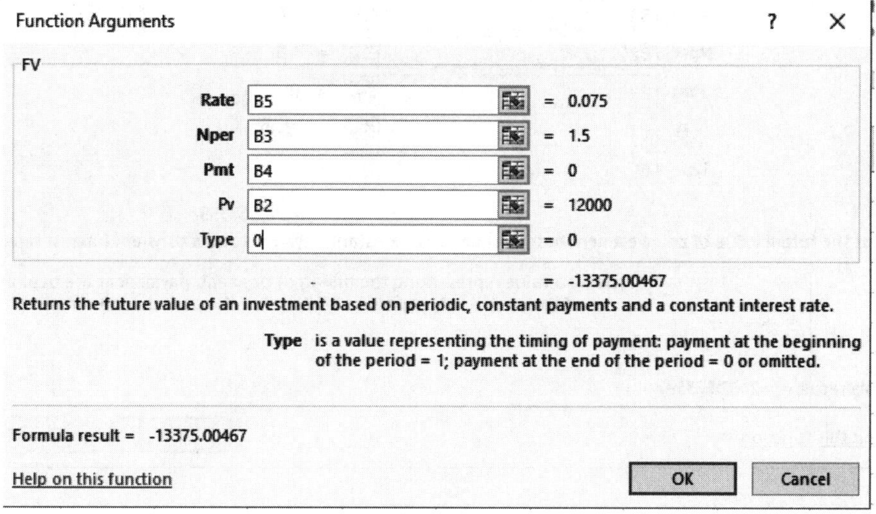
Function Arguments
FV
Rate B5 = 0.075
Nper B3 = 1.5
Pmt B4 = 0
Pv B2 = 12000
Type 0 = 0
= -13375.00467
Returns the future value of an investment based on periodic, constant payments and a constant interest rate.
Type is a value representing the timing of payment: payment at the beginning of the period = 1; payment at the end of the period = 0 or omitted.
Formula result = -13375.00467
Help on this function
OK
Cancel

B5 fx =FV(B4,B2,B3,B1,0)

	A	B	C	D	E
1	PV	12000			
2	Nper	1.5			
3	Pmt	0			
4	Rate	7.50%			
5	FV	($13,375.00)			

Use financial calculator:

Press	Display
2ndP/Y ↓1 ENTER	Set period per year to 1
2nd [QUIT]	0.0000
7.5 = I/Y	i = 7.5%
0 PMT	PMT = 0
1.5 N	N = 1.5
12,000 PV	PV = 12,000
CPTFV	Find FV = 13,375

Savings:

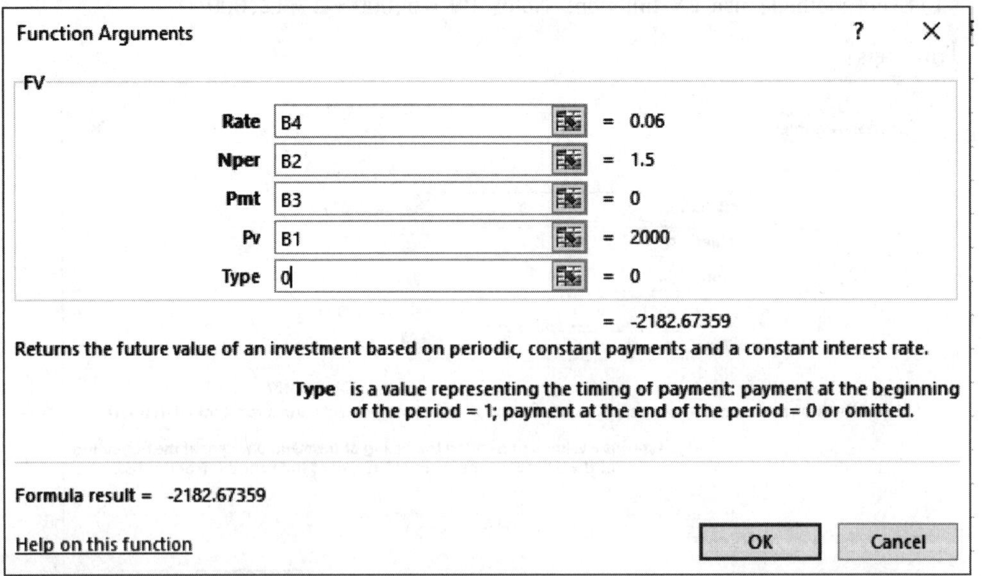
Function Arguments
FV
Rate B4 = 0.06
Nper B2 = 1.5
Pmt B3 = 0
Pv B1 = 2000
Type 0 = 0
= -2182.67359
Returns the future value of an investment based on periodic, constant payments and a constant interest rate.
Type is a value representing the timing of payment: payment at the beginning of the period = 1; payment at the end of the period = 0 or omitted.
Formula result = -2182.67359
Help on this function
OK
Cancel

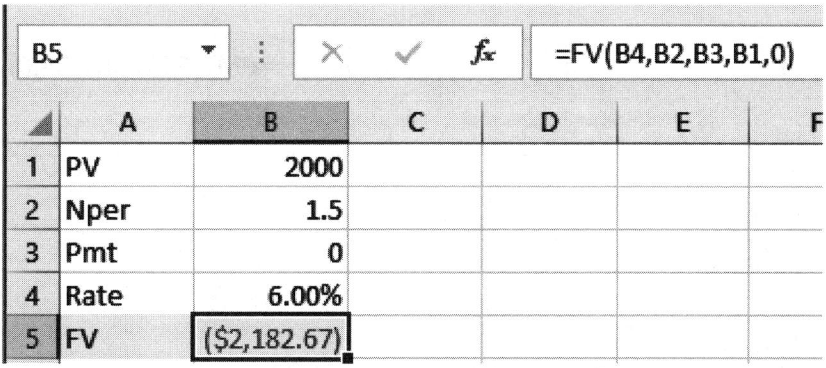

B5 =FV(B4,B2,B3,B1,0)

	A	B	C	D	E	F
1	PV	2000				
2	Nper	1.5				
3	Pmt	0				
4	Rate	6.00%				
5	FV	($2,182.67)				

Use financial calculator:

Press	Display
2ndP/Y ↓1 ENTER	Set period per year to 1
2nd [QUIT]	0.0000
6 I/Y	i = 6%
0 PMT	PMT = 0
1.5 N	N = 1.5
2,000 PV	PV = 2,000
CPTFV	Find FV = −2182.67

Find the difference between the trip costs and your savings. 13,375 − 2,182.67 = 11,192.33. This will be the FV for calculating monthly and annual Pmt. Rate should be real interest rate: i = ((1 + 0.075)/(1 + 0.06) − 1)/12.

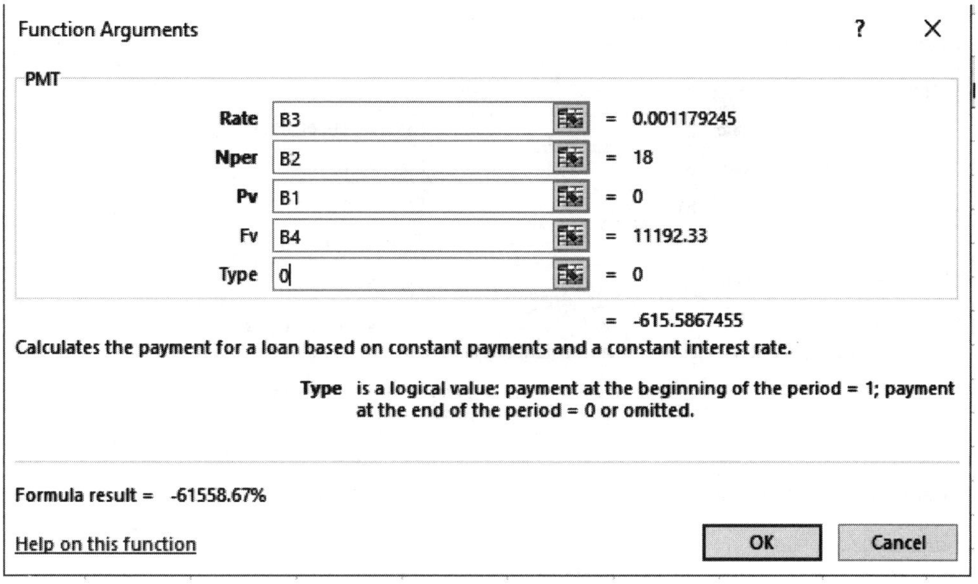

Function Arguments ? ×

PMT

Rate	B3	= 0.001179245
Nper	B2	= 18
Pv	B1	= 0
Fv	B4	= 11192.33
Type	0	= 0

= -615.5867455

Calculates the payment for a loan based on constant payments and a constant interest rate.

Type is a logical value: payment at the beginning of the period = 1; payment at the end of the period = 0 or omitted.

Formula result = -61558.67%

Help on this function

OK Cancel

B5 | =PMT(B3,B2,B1,B4,0)

	A	B	C	D	E
1	PV	0			
2	Nper	18			
3	Rate	0.12%			
4	FV	11192.33			
5	Pmt	($615.59)			

Use financial calculator:

Press	Display
[2ndP/Y] ↓1 [ENTER]	Set period per year to 1
[2nd] [QUIT]	0.0000
((1 +0.075)/(1 +0.06) -1)/12 = [I/Y]	i =0.12%
11,192.33 [FV]	FV = 11,192.33
1.5 * 12 [N]	N = 18
0 [PV]	PV = 0
[CPTPMT]	Find PMT = -615.59

(2) How much you need to save at the end of each year? Note: i = (1 + 0.075)/(1 + 0.06) - 1

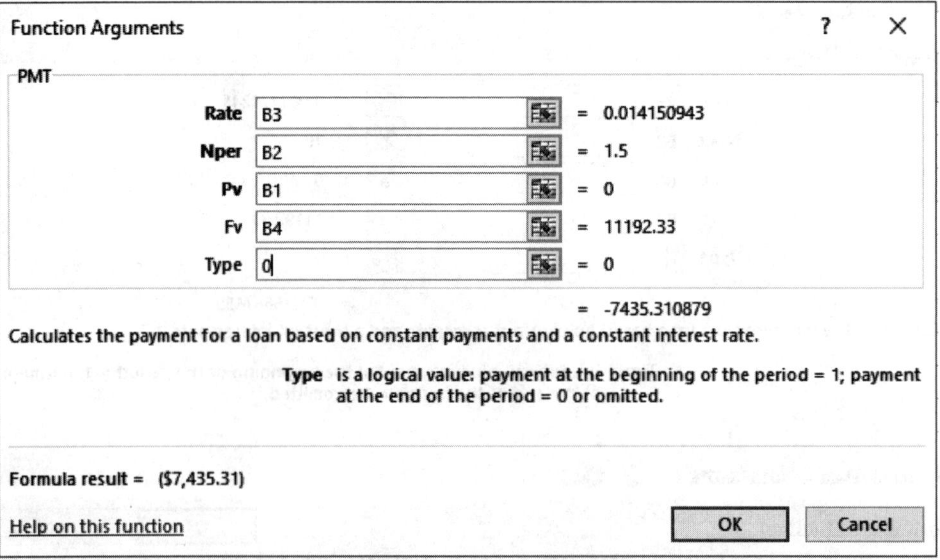
Function Arguments
PMT
Rate B3 = 0.014150943
Nper B2 = 1.5
Pv B1 = 0
Fv B4 = 11192.33
Type 0 = 0
= -7435.310879
Calculates the payment for a loan based on constant payments and a constant interest rate.
Type is a logical value: payment at the beginning of the period = 1; payment at the end of the period = 0 or omitted.
Formula result = ($7,435.31)
Help on this function
OK
Cancel

B5 =PMT(B3,B2,B1,B4,0)

	A	B	C	D	E
1	PV	0			
2	Nper	1.5			
3	Rate	1.42%			
4	FV	11192.33			
5	Pmt	($7,435.31)			

Use financial calculator:

Press	Display
2ndP/Y ↓1 ENTER	Set period per year to 1
2nd [QUIT]	0.0000
((1 +0.075)/(1 +0.06) -1) = I/Y	i = 1.42%
11,192.33 FV	FV = 11,192.33
1.5 N	N = 1.5
0 PV	PV = 0
CPTPMT	Find PMT = -7,435.31

[Example Three] Your uncle recently won a $350 million lottery. He has the option of receiving $257 million as a one-time lump sum today or 2.2 million at the end of each month for the next thirty years. If your uncle has a time value of money of 10% annually, which payment option is better?

Use TVM, convert the value of the second option to PV. Then, compare it with $257 million.

Excel method: use PV function. Note: i = 10%/12 = 0.83%; n = 30 * 12 = 360.

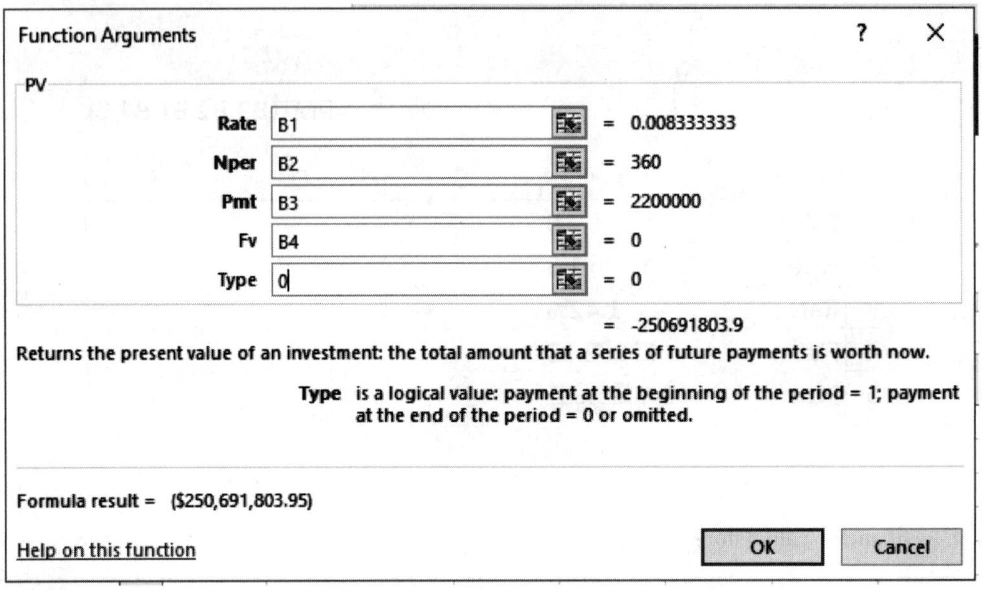

Function Arguments

PV

Rate	B1	=	0.008333333
Nper	B2	=	360
Pmt	B3	=	2200000
Fv	B4	=	0
Type	0	=	0

= -250691803.9

Returns the present value of an investment: the total amount that a series of future payments is worth now.

Type is a logical value: payment at the beginning of the period = 1; payment at the end of the period = 0 or omitted.

Formula result = ($250,691,803.95)

Help on this function

OK Cancel

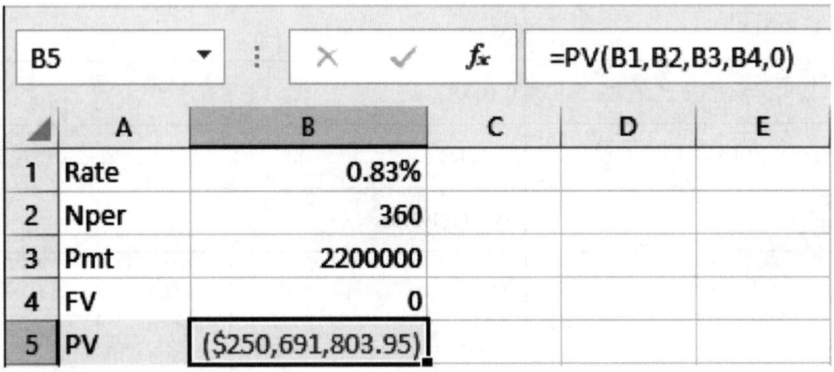

B5 =PV(B1,B2,B3,B4,0)

	A	B	C	D	E
1	Rate	0.83%			
2	Nper	360			
3	Pmt	2200000			
4	FV	0			
5	PV	($250,691,803.95)			

Use financial calculator:

Press	Display
2ndP/Y ↓1 ENTER	Set period per year to 1
2nd [QUIT]	0.0000
10/12 = I/Y	i = 10%/12
0 FV	FV = 0
360 N	N = 360
2,200,000 PMT	PMT = 2,200,000
CPTPV	Find PV = −250,691,803.9

250,691,803.9 < 257,000,000. Therefore, the first option is better.

[Example Four] Thomas bought a house for $500,000. He plans to move out and sell the house five years later. Assume that he has a 30 – year loan with 7.25% annual interest rate. (1) How much money he needs to pay back when he sells the house? (2) If the house appreciates 10% per year, how much will he gain after pay off the loan?

(1) How much money he needs to pay back when he sells the house?

Use TVM to calculate monthly payment. Then, find FV.

Step one: find PMT. Note: i = 7.25%/12 = 0.6%; n = 30 * 12 = 360.

Excel method: use PMT function.

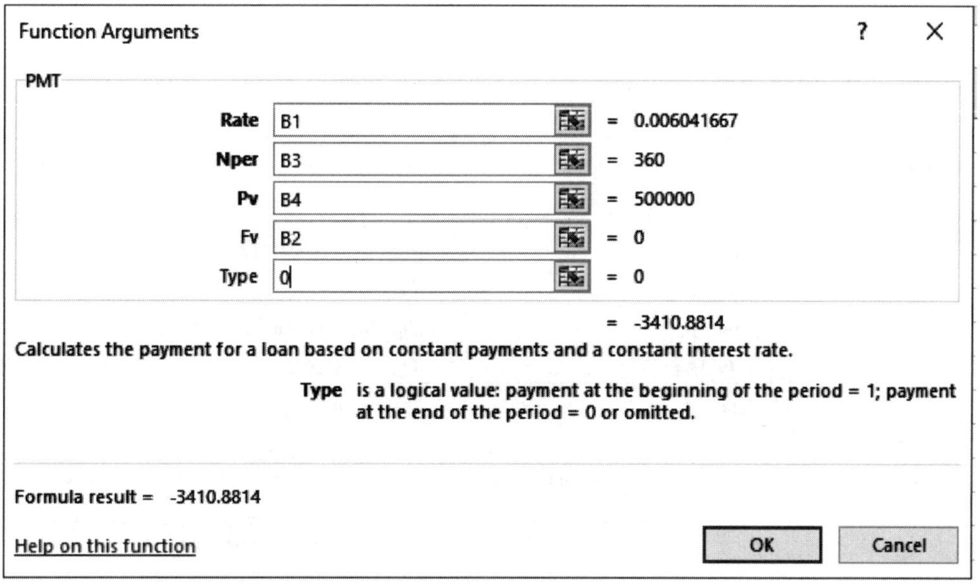

Function Arguments ? X

PMT

Rate	B1	=	0.006041667
Nper	B3	=	360
Pv	B4	=	500000
Fv	B2	=	0
Type	0	=	0

= -3410.8814

Calculates the payment for a loan based on constant payments and a constant interest rate.

Type is a logical value: payment at the beginning of the period = 1; payment at the end of the period = 0 or omitted.

Formula result = -3410.8814

Help on this function OK Cancel

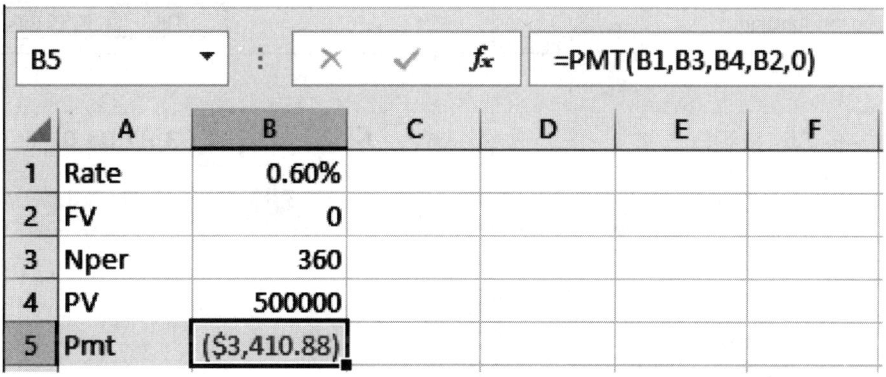

B5 =PMT(B1,B3,B4,B2,0)

	A	B	C	D	E	F
1	Rate	0.60%				
2	FV	0				
3	Nper	360				
4	PV	500000				
5	Pmt	($3,410.88)				

Use financial calculator:

Press	Display
2ndP/Y ↓1 ENTER	Set period per year to 1
2nd [QUIT]	0.0000
7.25/12 = I/Y	i = 7.25%/12
0 FV	FV = 0
360 N	N = 360
500,000 PV	PV = 500,000
CPTPMT	Find PMT = −3,410.88

Step two: find FV, the amount of money he needs to pay back after he sells the house. Note: $i = 7.25\%/12 = 0.6\%$; $n = 5 * 12 = 60$.

Excel method: use FV function.

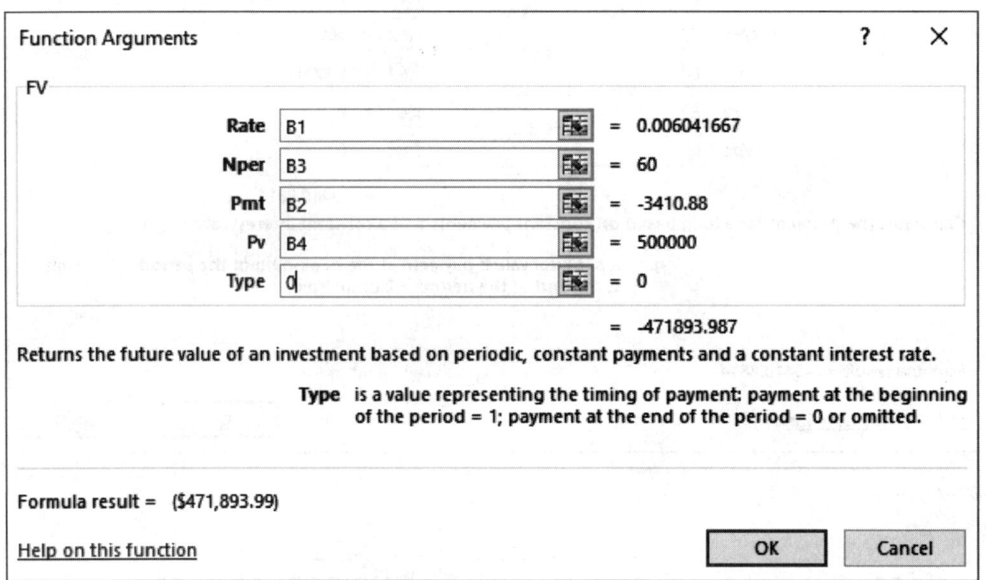
Function Arguments
FV
Rate B1 = 0.006041667
Nper B3 = 60
Pmt B2 = -3410.88
Pv B4 = 500000
Type 0 = 0
= -471893.987
Returns the future value of an investment based on periodic, constant payments and a constant interest rate.
Type is a value representing the timing of payment: payment at the beginning of the period = 1; payment at the end of the period = 0 or omitted.
Formula result = ($471,893.99)
Help on this function
OK
Cancel

B5 =FV(B1,B3,B2,B4,0)

	A	B	C	D	E
1	Rate	0.60%			
2	Pmt	-3410.88			
3	Nper	60			
4	PV	500000			
5	FV	($471,893.99)			

Use financial calculator:

Press	Display
2ndP/Y ↓1 ENTER	Set period per year to 1
2nd [QUIT]	0.0000
7.25/12 = I/Y	i = 7.25%/12
3,410.88 +/- PMT	PMT = -3,410.88
60 N	N = 60
500,000 PV	PV = 500,000
CPTFV	Find FV = 471,893.99

When he sells the house, he still needs to pay $471,893.99.

(2) If the house appreciates 10% per year, how much money will he gain after pay off the loan?

Excel method: use FV function.

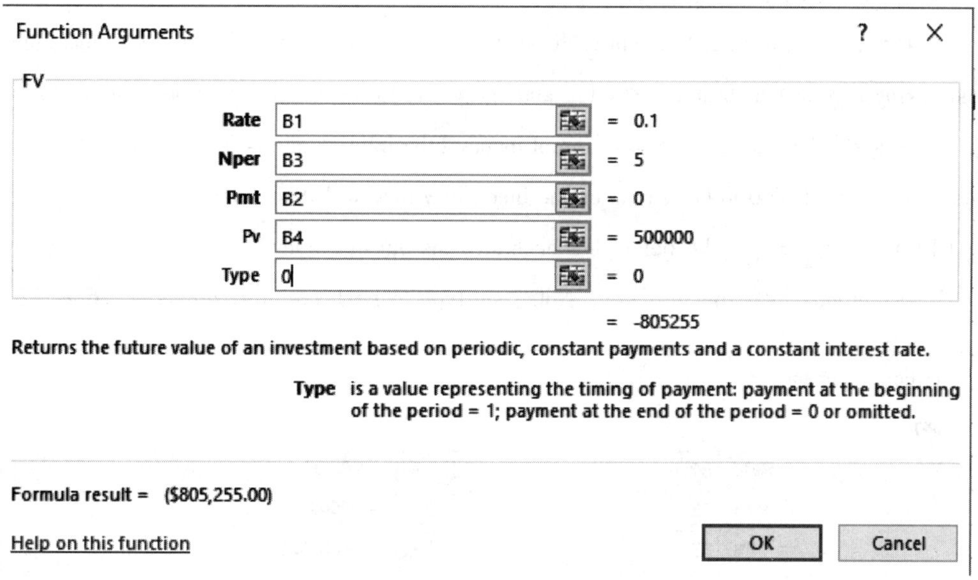

Function Arguments ? X

FV

Rate	B1	= 0.1
Nper	B3	= 5
Pmt	B2	= 0
Pv	B4	= 500000
Type	0	= 0

= -805255

Returns the future value of an investment based on periodic, constant payments and a constant interest rate.

Type is a value representing the timing of payment: payment at the beginning of the period = 1; payment at the end of the period = 0 or omitted.

Formula result = ($805,255.00)

Help on this function

OK Cancel

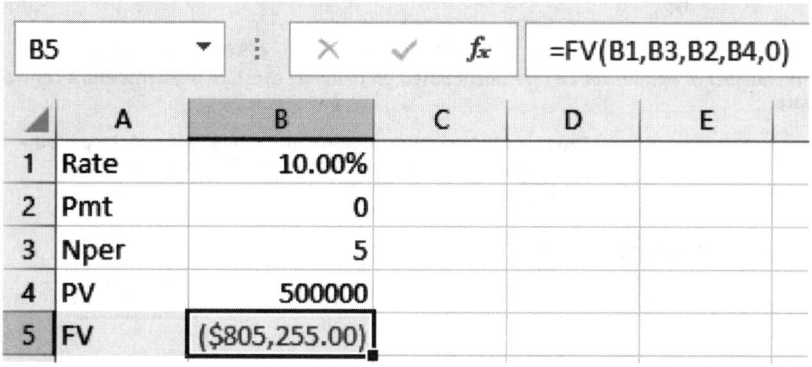

B5 =FV(B1,B3,B2,B4,0)

	A	B	C	D	E
1	Rate	10.00%			
2	Pmt	0			
3	Nper	5			
4	PV	500000			
5	FV	($805,255.00)			

Use financial calculator:

Press	Display
2ndP/Y ↓1 ENTER	Set period per year to 1
2nd [QUIT]	0.0000
10 I/Y	i = 10%
0 PMT	PMT = 0
5 N	N = 5
500,000 PV	PV = 500,000
CPTFV	Find FV = -805,255

Therefore, if the house appreciated 10% per year, when he sells the house he gains 805,255 - 3,410.88 * 5 * 12 - 471,893.99 = $128,708.2.

[Example Five] Jenny (age 60) talked with you about her retirement concerns. She wants to save $700,000 as an immediate annuity. If her living expenses is $60,000 per year (including the cost of taking care of her disability child), and she wants to receive $5,000 per month. (1) How long will it take before her account runs out of money (the interest rate is 6% annually)? (2) If she wants to leave $200,000 to her son after she died, how long will this annuity last?

(1) How long will it take before her account runs out of money?

Excel method: use Nper function. Note: set type to be 1 (annuity due). i = 6%/12

Function Arguments ? X

NPER

Rate B1 = 0.005

Pmt B2 = 5000

Pv B3 = -700000

Fv B4 = 0

Type 1 = 1

= 239.0819287

Returns the number of periods for an investment based on periodic, constant payments and a constant interest rate.

Type is a logical value: payment at the beginning of the period = 1; payment at the end of the period = 0 or omitted.

Formula result = 239.0819287

Help on this function OK Cancel

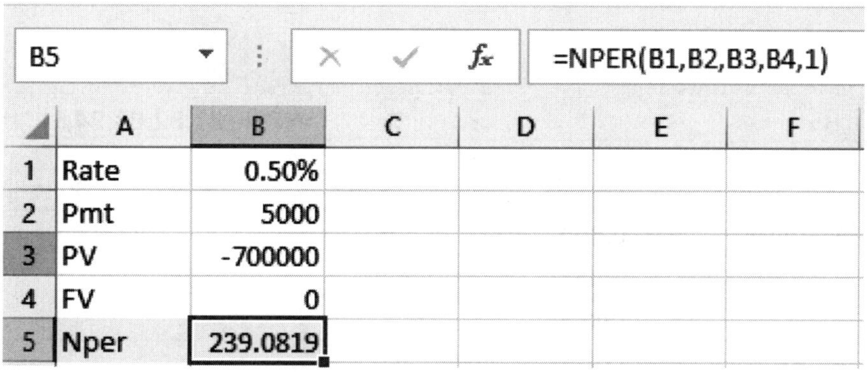

B5	=NPER(B1,B2,B3,B4,1)				
	A	B	C	D	E	F
1	Rate	0.50%				
2	Pmt	5000				
3	PV	-700000				
4	FV	0				
5	Nper	239.0819				

Use financial calculator:

Press	Display
2ndP/Y ↓1 ENTER	Set period per year to 1
2nd [QUIT]	0.0000
2nd [BGN] 2nd [SET] CE/C	Set to begin mode
6/12 = I/Y	i = 6%/12
5,000 PMT	PMT = 5,000
0 FV	FV = 0
700,000 +/- PV	PV = -700,000
CPTN	Find N = 239.08

Therefore, the annuity will last 239.08/12≈20 years.

(2) If she wants to leave $200,000 to her son after she died, how long will this annuity last?

Excel method: use Nper function. Note: set type to be 1 (annuity due). i = 6%/12

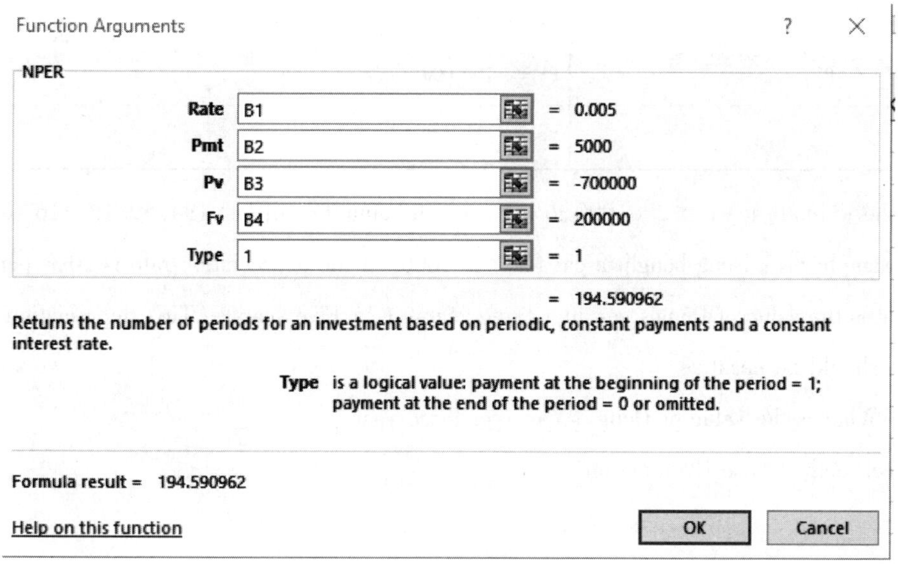

Function Arguments

NPER

Rate	B1	= 0.005
Pmt	B2	= 5000
Pv	B3	= -700000
Fv	B4	= 200000
Type	1	= 1

= 194.590962

Returns the number of periods for an investment based on periodic, constant payments and a constant interest rate.

Type is a logical value: payment at the beginning of the period = 1; payment at the end of the period = 0 or omitted.

Formula result = 194.590962

Help on this function

OK Cancel

B5 | fx =NPER(B1,B2,B3,B4,1)

	A	B	C	D	E	F
1	Rate	0.50%				
2	Pmt	5000				
3	PV	-700000				
4	FV	200000				
5	Nper	194.591				

Use financial calculator:

Press	Display
[2ndP/Y] ↓1 [ENTER]	Set period per year to 1
[2nd] [QUIT]	0.0000
[2nd] [BGN] [2nd] [SET] [CE/C]	Set to begin mode
6/12 = [I/Y]	i = 6%/12
5,000 [PMT]	PMT = 5,000
200,000 [FV]	FV = 200,000
700,000 [+/- PV]	PV = -700,000
[CPTN]	Find N = 194.59

If she wants to leave \$200,000 to her son, the annuity will last 194.59/12≈16 years.

[Example Six] Doug bought a car for \$30,000. If the depreciation rate is 20% per year, (1) what is the value of Doug's car after three years? (2) Five years? (Tip: depreciation means the Rate should be negative).

(1) What is the value of Doug's car after three years?

Excel method: use FV function

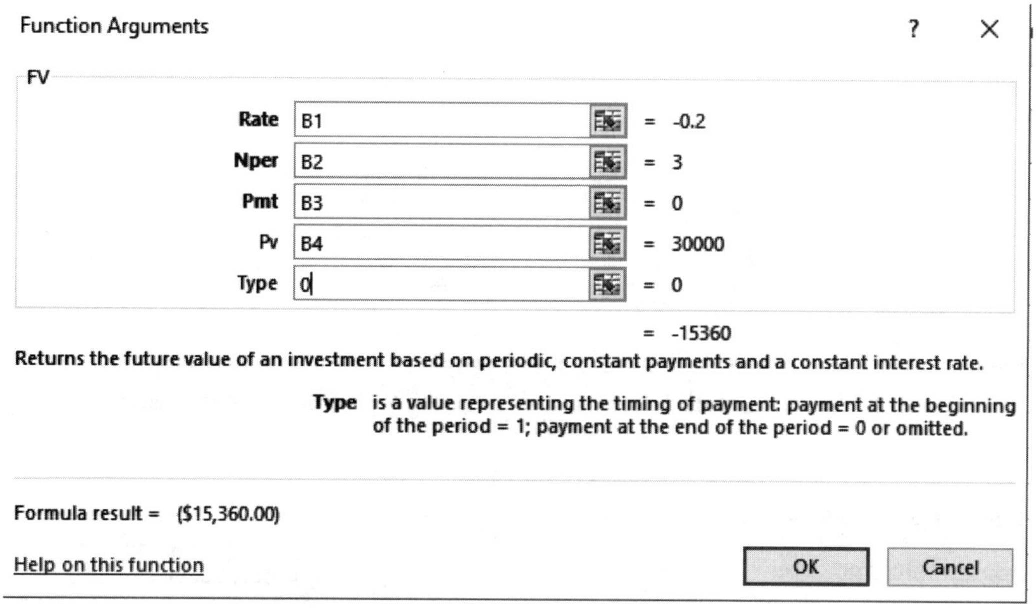

Function Arguments ? ×

FV

Rate	B1	=	-0.2
Nper	B2	=	3
Pmt	B3	=	0
Pv	B4	=	30000
Type	0	=	0

= -15360

Returns the future value of an investment based on periodic, constant payments and a constant interest rate.

Type is a value representing the timing of payment: payment at the beginning of the period = 1; payment at the end of the period = 0 or omitted.

Formula result = ($15,360.00)

Help on this function

OK Cancel

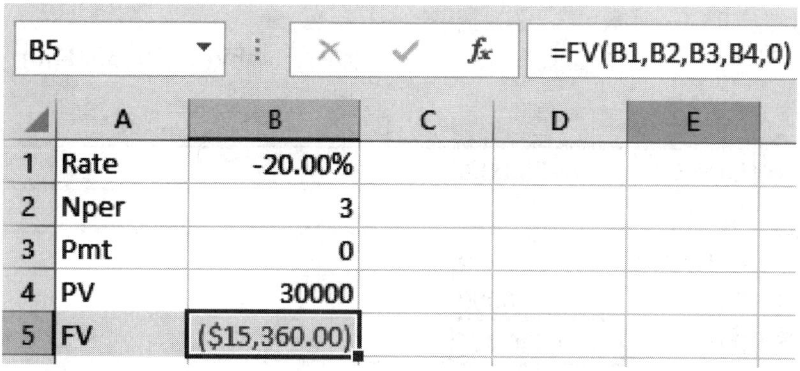

B5 × ✓ fx =FV(B1,B2,B3,B4,0)

	A	B	C	D	E
1	Rate	-20.00%			
2	Nper	3			
3	Pmt	0			
4	PV	30000			
5	FV	($15,360.00)			

Use financial calculator:

Press	Display
2ndP/Y ↓1 ENTER	Set period per year to 1
2nd [QUIT]	0.0000
20 +/- I/Y	i = -20%
0 PMT	PMT = 0
3 N	N = 3
30,000 PV	PV = 30,000
CPTFV	Find FV = -15,360

(2) What is the value of Doug's car after 5 years?

Function Arguments ? ×

FV

Rate	B1	=	-0.2
Nper	B2	=	5
Pmt	B3	=	0
Pv	B4	=	30000
Type	0	=	0

= -9830.4

Returns the future value of an investment based on periodic, constant payments and a constant interest rate.

Rate is the interest rate per period. For example, use 6%/4 for quarterly payments at 6% APR.

Formula result = ($9,830.40)

Help on this function

OK Cancel

B5 =FV(B1,B2,B3,B4,0)

	A	B	C	D	E
1	Rate	-20.00%			
2	Nper	5			
3	Pmt	0			
4	PV	30000			
5	FV	($9,830.40)			

Use financial calculator:

Press	Display
2ndP/Y ↓1 ENTER	Set period per year to 1
2nd [QUIT]	0.0000
20 +/- I/Y	i = -20%
0 PMT	PMT = 0
5 N	N = 5
30,000 PV	PV = 30,000
CPTFV	Find FV = -9830.40